The Wild East

About the Author

A print journalist since 1969 and a lobby correspondent in the Commons since 1978, Ian Hernon covered the Troubles in Northern Ireland and more mayhem in the Middle East. He ran the oldest Parliamentary news agency for fifteen years. For five years until 2018 he was deputy editor of *Tribune*. He is the author of a dozen books including the bestselling *Britain's Forgotten Wars*.

The Wild East

Gunfights, Massacres and Race Riots
Far from the American Frontier

Ian Hernon

AMBERLEY

For Reuben, Freya and Theo, my grandchildren.

This edition published 2022

Amberley Publishing
The Hill, Stroud
Gloucestershire, GL5 4EP

www.amberley-books.com

British Library Cataloguing in Publication Data.
A catalogue record for this book is available from the British Library.

ISBN 978 1 3981 0910 0 (paperback)
ISBN 978 1 4456 8928 9 (ebook)

Origination by Amberley Publishing.
Printed in the UK.

Acknowledgements

I love America. I love the sweep of its history and the speed of change. But all great nations are built of myths. As a child of the 1950s, my early years were spent in front of a black and white TV watching *Rawhide*, *The Rifleman*, *Wells Fargo*, *Bonanza*, *The Big Valley*, *Wagon Train* and many, many more. Even at a tender age I knew that the reality wasn't so black and white. The essential truth is that often terrible things were done for understandable reasons and good things emerged from evil acts. But expanding literacy, the movies and TV skewed the stories towards the Western frontier of romance, leaving behind the tales of the even more violent East during the same period. Or at least, that is what I argue in this book.

I should also point out that in no way am I denigrating the cowboy ethos of self-sufficiency and rugged individuality. On road trips through hardscrabble areas of Montana, Wyoming, South Dakota and Idaho I was treated everywhere with old-fashioned courtesy and friendly hospitality. My sincerest thanks go to those cowboys, wranglers, barkeepers, mechanics, tour guides, academics and others I met there.

My thanks, too, go to those hombres at Amberley Publishing, commissioning editor Shaun Barrington and book editor Alex Bennett.

And, as always, my family.

Contents

The past is never dead. It's not even past.

William Faulkner

Introduction

'the most perfect order and decorum'

The scene was set for a classic Western showdown. On a dusty main street, a sheriff backed by townspeople faced down a gang of heavily armed hired gunslingers. Tensions rose, hard words were exchanged, and someone drew. A few minutes later ten men were dead or dying, and several more suffered gunshot wounds. The hired guns – those who remained on their feet that is – fled. But this was not a shootout in the Wild West of Wyoming or Montana or South Dakota in the 1880s, or a Hollywood re-imagining of such an event. This was not Dodge City or Abilene. This was the West Virginia mining town of Matewan on 19 May 1920. By contrast, the more celebrated gunfight at the OK Corral in Tombstone lasted thirty seconds and left three dead. And Matewan was not an aberration.

The growing accessibility of the printed word, from cheap dime novels to 'respectable' journals, propagated the myth of the Wild West, along with burgeoning panoramic Western art as spectacular new vistas opened up, and the process was accelerated by the emerging movie industry. But from the end of the Civil War to well into the twentieth century, the East was a far more dangerous place to be, for all save Native Americans. The clashes were inevitable given waves of immigration from the Old World – bringing ancient enmities – and given the rise of an industrial capitalism in which robber barons prospered, and whose viciousness was demonstrated on a far greater scale than anything seen in the West of legend. The exceptions, of course, were the genocidal Indian Wars as the frontier was pushed westwards. But while the slaughter of ill-armed 'savages' on the frontier was romanticised, and sordid outlaws lionised, battles against slum landlords and unscrupulous bosses in the cities were seen as more of a stain on the ethos and character of a new nation striving for acceptance and, finally, for dominance on the world stage.

The early part of the nineteenth century saw the beginnings of the Western myth with James Fenimore Cooper's 1826 novel *The Last of the Mohicans* and Francis Parkman's *The Oregon Trail* (1849). Such early sagas had claim to authenticity, as did Mark Twain's later *Roughing It* (1872) and Owen Wister's *The Virginian*, published in 1902. But by the time of the latter, dime novelists, dramatists, showmen, glory claimers and some frauds had turned the frontier into fantasy. The reasons, although complex, are obvious. As the nation expanded from its original thirteen colonies on the eastern seaboard, the public perception of the West was clear. Jeff Guinn wrote: 'People of limited means yearned to own land, the West was where they could, and that was all there was to it. Most Americans were farmers, or wanted to be if they could acquire sufficient property.'[1]

The subsequent wagon trains rolling west acquired their own mythology. While there were obvious dangers, and families on the trail displayed grit and determination, the risk of Red Indian attack was perhaps the least of them. Between 1842 and 1859, around 30,000 white emigrants died *en route* to their promised land; less than 400 were killed by the threatened tribes. Some 90 per cent died from disease, particularly cholera, which in turn wiped out considerably more than 100 times as many natives as did the US cavalry of compulsive legend. Even including the high incidence of such diseases, the 3 per cent death rate on the westward wagon trains was only marginally higher than the national average.[2]

Despite such renowned battles and massacres as Little Big Horn, the Rosebud, Fetterman and Washita, many US soldiers on the frontier barely glimpsed a hostile 'Injun'. Their main enemies were hunger, exhaustion, low pay, disease, lack of essential supplies and a grinding boredom which led to alcohol overdoses, brawls and desertion. Army medical records for the time show a higher chance of becoming a casualty through illness rather than in action: eight men per thousand died of disease, compared to five per thousand dying of battle wounds, domestic injuries and accidents.

The West provided the growing nation with its entertaining and diverse folklore. The depiction of such semi-fictional heroes as 'Buffalo

Bill' Cody on eastern stages did, however, echo wider social unrest. Louis S. Warren argued convincingly that the lower-class audiences who flocked to William Cody's early stage shows 'saw Buffalo Bill as their hero in their struggle against the privileged classes and foreign immigrants'. The Panic of 1873 and the Great Strike of 1877 'set labour and capital at each other's throats, and often pitted labouring American natives against immigrant "scabs".' In the economic downturn that followed 1873, renters in the New York region rose up against the 'impositions of landlords'. The Tenants Mutual Society 'countenanced the burning and destruction of the property of exacting landlords'. Property was indeed burned in Montgomery County, while second- and third-generation American gangs battled with Irish and German rivals for control over city slums. Warren wrote: 'The fact that native-born city toughs and rebellious workingmen (often) appropriated the name Buffalo Bill suggests how much they claimed him as their own in their battles against the impositions of landlords, employers and immigrant rivals.'[3]

There was an undercurrent of unapologetic racism in the way riot-torn eastern urban areas embraced the myths of Buffalo Bill, Wild Bill Hickok, George Armstrong Custer and other fables based on real people. Warren wrote that 'artists and writers increasingly – and paradoxically – presented white virtues as products of frontier struggle and the westward movement of Anglo-Saxondom ... now, at least in the minds of many thinkers, the relatively empty spaces of the trans-Missouri West became a final, fading crucible of whiteness which stood in gleaming contrast to the mongrel city.' Warren used as an example the attitude of William Remington, later to be acknowledged as one of the greatest frontier artists. Remington was a New York-born Yale dropout who in 1881 took a temporary job on a Montana ranch. He wrote that America was becoming degenerate, overrun by 'Jews, Injuns, Chinamen, Italians, Huns – the rubbish of the earth I hate'. He went on: 'I've got some Winchesters and when the massacring begins, I can get my share of 'em, and what's more, I will... Our race is full of sentiment.'[4]

Remington's racism, however, was endemic in the East rather than the West, and his bloodthirsty attitude was not widely shared on the actual frontier. Neither was the capacity for violence, casual, racial or otherwise. The 1969 National Commission on the Causes and Prevention of Violence showed that American violence has traditionally been an urban rather than frontier problem. The myth of the West 'boasts' that in some cattle towns killings averaged one or two a night. Yet Robert K. Dykstra's 1967 analysis of the five most important, and infamous, Kansas cattle towns – Abilene, Dodge City, Wichita, Ellsworth and Caldwell – from 1870 to 1885 showed that during those fifteen years there were forty-five homicides, an average of 1.5 per cattle season. He found no reports of a formal shootout beloved of later film-makers, just the occasional sordid murder. The number of killings never exceeded five in any one year. Only Ellsworth (1873) and Dodge City (1878) reached that total. In 1871 in Abilene, Wild Bill Hickok killed two men, one of them accidentally – his deputy.

Hickok was a Civil War veteran, a former spy for the Union side, a buffalo hunter, a lawman and a genuine killer, but he was not averse to exaggeration. While working as a scout at Fort Harker, Kansas, in May 1867, he was attacked by a large group of Indians, who fled after he shot and killed two. In July, Hickok told a newspaper reporter that he had led several soldiers in pursuit of Indians who had killed four men near the fort on 2 July. He reported returning with five prisoners after killing ten. Witnesses confirm that the story was true in part: the party did set out to find those who had killed the four men, but the group returned to the fort 'without nary a dead Indian, [never] even seeing a live one'.[5] An Easterner made Hickok famous. That same year Colonel George Ward Nichols wrote a lurid account for *Harper's* headlined 'Wild Bill, the Scout of the Plains' which mixed fact and fiction and became a template for the creation of colourful heroes for the Eastern market. Other publications swiftly followed. In Central City, Colorado, it was reported that Hickok had rescued a party of ranchers from attacking natives by 'riding the gauntlet through the enemy's line, receiving only a slight wound in the foot'. From then on even the slightest disturbance involving Hickok merited newspaper headlines.[6] Scores of shoot-outs were attributed to him, but Hickok's tally was more modest than the legend – he fatally shot six men, and possibly a seventh; enough, perhaps.

In 1876 Hickok was himself shot dead while playing cards in Deadwood, South Dakota, but there were only three other slayings in Deadwood that year despite the mining town's reputation for murderous mayhem, and 1876 remains the town's most violent year. The speed with which order was established afterwards was astonishing, partly due to the arrival, the day before Hickok's murder, of former Montana lawman Seth Bullock. He unofficially took on the sheriff's duties with the sanction of the Board of Health and Street Commissioners, a body set up by a citizenry more afraid of smallpox and other health hazards than of drunken gunfighters or marauding Indians. The Board established a pest house for the quarantine of smallpox victims, a cemetery, a police service and a fire department, and a town planning grid. They also created ordinances which levied taxes and licences for gambling and prostitution. Bullock enforced the law without killing anyone. On one occasion he dispersed a crowd of striking miners occupying the Keets mine in Hidden Treasure Gulch by dropping sulphur bought in Chinatown down an air vent, thereby avoiding a potentially lethal confrontation.[7]

As the economy changed from gold panning to deep mining, Deadwood lost its rough and rowdy character and developed into a prosperous town. In September 1879, a fire devastated it, destroying more than 300 buildings and consuming the belongings of many inhabitants. Many of the newly impoverished left town to start again. But that year Thomas Edison demonstrated the incandescent lamp in New Jersey and Judge Squire P. Romans founded the 'Pilcher Electric Light Company of Deadwood' in September 1883. He ordered an Edison dynamo, wiring and fifteen globe lights. Deadwood had electricity less than four years after its invention, and less than a year after commercial service was started. The town declined again until Hollywood and stage musicals put it back on the tourist trail.

The Black Hills of Dakota, including Deadwood and the neighbouring mining town of Lead, saw tens of thousands of incomers in America's last great gold rush. The *County Undertaker* in 1878 recorded sixteen murders across the whole area, the equivalent of a few nights' mayhem in contemporary Chicago or New York. Smith declared that all the statistics and comparisons with other cities proved 'our Black Hills as healthy as any other locality in the world'.[8]

Virginia City, a mining boom town in Nevada, was, in 1876, like Deadwood, a collection of faro joints, saloons and brothels, but a foreign visitor that year complained that instead of witnessing murder before breakfast he had seen nothing but 'the most perfect order and decorum'.[9] In Colorado City it was claimed that there was not one lock on any store or office: 'In warm weather the merchant did not even close the front door of his store before going home at night. The next morning when he came to work, as apt as not, he would find a group of freighters or cowboys who had arrived in town during the night asleep on the counters or floor, or perhaps someone passing through during the night had helped himself to a pair of California pants or a plug of chewing tobacco, but if he did he left the price of the item where the merchant could find it.'[10]

Tombstone saw just five homicides in 1881, and three of those were the work of the Earp brothers and Doc Holliday at the O.K. Corral. Ore was close to the surface in the Arizona town's mines and many residents became rich and spent lavishly on Eastern comforts. The silver industry and attendant wealth attracted many professionals and merchants who brought their wives and families, and with them swiftly came churches and ministers. They also brought a Victorian sensitivity and moral rectitude dressed in the most up-to-date fashions.[11] The town was the epitome of modernism, with well-advanced plans to create a sewer system and telephones linking the mines to the Mining Exchange and the glitziest, most lavish hotels. Visitors expressed their amazement at the quality and diversity of products that were readily available in the area.

The men who worked the mines were largely European immigrants, while the Chinese did the town's laundry and provided other services. Thanks to prosperity and an ordinance banning the carrying of firearms, Tombstone was a safe place to do business. Most citizens during the boom time had never witnessed, let alone participated in, a gunfight. But by the end of 1883 the town's silver boom was over and the respectable townsfolk and the workforce drifted away. Those who were left cashed in on the tourist trade by fostering the myth that it was a town too tough to die. The infamous O.K. Corral gunfight was little known outside the area until it was reinvented as a parable of good *versus* evil, rather than a squalid spat between two rival criminal factions and a political contest over who controlled the gaming tables. Hollywood later completed the task. Jeff Guinn wrote that the gunfight 'became a pivotal moment in American annals because misunderstandings, exaggerations, and downright lies about it provided impetus for future generations to form a skewed, one-dimensional view of frontier history. In fact, it represented an unintentional, if inevitable clash between evolving social, political forces.'[12]

In an analysis of crime in the frontier mining towns of Aurora, Nevada, and Bodie, California, Roger McGrath concluded: 'Popular wisdom says that generations of living on and conquering frontiers have made Americans a violent and lawless people. Popular wisdom is wrong. So is much scholarly literature that has drawn conclusions about violence and lawlessness from anecdotal evidence and specious assumptions. The kind of crime that pervades American society today has little or no relation to the kind of lawlessness that occurred on the frontier if Aurora and Bodie are at all representative of western communities. Robbery of individuals, burglary, and theft occurred only infrequently, and rape seems not to have occurred at all. Racial violence and serious juvenile crime were absent also. The homicides that occurred almost invariably resulted from gunfights between willing combatants. The old, the weak, the innocent, the young, and the female were not the targets of violent men. In fact, all people in those categories would have been far safer in Aurora or Bodie than they are today in any major US city. Even most smaller cities and towns are far more crime ridden and dangerous than were Aurora and Bodie. There simply is no justification for blaming contemporary American violence and lawlessness on a frontier heritage. The time is long past for Americans to stop excusing the violence in society by trotting out that old whipping boy, the frontier. On the contrary, it would seem that the frontier, instead of representing America at its worst may have, in many respects, represented the nation at its best.'[13] But at the time, the frontier was the stuff of instant legend.

Historian W. Eugene Hollon wrote: 'To millions of people throughout the western world, the American frontier represented a combination of El Dorado, Zion and Shangri-la. It offered adventure, excitement and opportunity for wealth. The openness of the country, fertility of the soil, abundance of game, and lack of restrictions constituted the stuff that dreams are made of. Yet the frontier never lived up to this ideal, and many of those who went there found it better to keep the dream alive for others than admit the truth. Perhaps this accounts for the tendency of some to exaggerate and to depict the good characteristics of the frontier as very good, and the bad as very bad.' Hollon interviewed dozens of elderly people who had participated in the 1880s settlement of Oklahoma Territory. 'When I asked them about the recent frontier,' he wrote, 'the answer that a great majority gave was the wretched loneliness and almost total lack of excitement.'[14]

Walter Preston Webb wrote of contemporary Western mythology: 'They write of cowboys as if they were noble knights, and cowmen kings. They do biographies of bad men, Billy the Kid, the Plummer Gang, Wyatt Earp and Wild Bill Hickok ... They blow up the abandoned saloon into an art museum, the Boot Hill into a shrine for pilgrims. In Montana Charles Russell is better than Titian, and in the

Black Hills Frederick Remington is greater than Michelangelo. Custer, who blundered to his death, taking better men with him, found a place in every saloon not already pre-empted to that travesty of justice, Judge Roy Bean.'[15]

The famed lawman and gunslinger Bat Masterson was reputed to have shot dead between twenty and thirty bad men, although his actual tally was three. He was largely the author of his own myth. Pestered by souvenir hunters to sell his deadly firearm, he bought a battered old Colt .45 at a New York pawn shop and cut twenty-two notches in the handle and sold it to a gullible collector for a handsome profit. When asked about the veracity of the notches, he later said: 'I didn't tell him yes, and I didn't tell him no, and I didn't exactly lie to him. I simply said I hadn't counted Mexicans and Indians, and he went away tickled to death.'[16] Billy the Kid was said to have killed a man for each of his twenty-one years; although he was undoubtedly a murderous psychopath, only three deaths are authenticated, and the total may be just double that number.

Frontier settlements such as Deadwood may well have been dangerous during their first months as shanty towns when everyone carried firearms and the principal businesses were saloons, brothels and gambling houses, but within a year or two schools and churches also sprang up and dens of iniquity were either shut down or regulated. Exceptions were such mobile, temporary settlements as the various 'Hells on Wheels' that shadowed the building of the trans-continental and other railway lines and which provided a moveable feast for thirsty and randy construction workers.

As Hollon and many others have pointed out, Westerners themselves must share much of the blame for the frontier image, having emphasised the more bizarre events and developed a talent for taking something small and blowing it up to giant size. Hollon wrote: 'If one judged from the historical markers along the highways of central Wyoming, for example, it would appear that the most important event of the region's entire history was the hanging of "Cattle Kate" Watson and James Averell on the Sweetwater in 1889. The invasion of Johnson County, further north, two years later by Wyoming cattle ranchers is made to appear more extensive than the sacking of Rome by the Huns and Vandals. The plain truth is that Westerners have had to make do with what little historical material they have had to work with.'[17]

The catalyst, in the late nineteenth century, was the dime novel. Cheaply and accessibly, it fed into the psyche of a new nation whose borders were rapidly expanding. The pioneer of dime novel fantasies, boosted by growing literacy and cheap printing techniques, was Ned Buntline. Aptly, Buntline was a character of his own invention. He was born Edward Zane Carroll Judson in Harpersfield, New York, the son of a lawyer who wanted him to be a clergyman. As a young teenager he ran away to sea as a cabin boy and was later commissioned a midshipman in the Navy. As a seaman, he served in the Seminole Wars but saw little combat. After four years at sea, he resigned. During the Civil War, he enlisted in the 1st New York Mounted Rifles and was made sergeant before being dishonourably discharged for drunkenness.[18] He spent several years in and around New York setting up newspapers which generally failed and campaigning against immigrants and for temperance. In 1844, he adopted the pen name 'Ned Buntline' from the nautical term for a rope at the bottom of a square sail. Facing bankruptcy, he fled from Ohio to Kentucky.

In 1847, the Boston publisher and author Maturin Murray Ballou paid Buntline $100 to write *The Black Avenger of the Spanish Main: or, The Fiend of Blood*, a melodramatic pirate novel. Back in New York, Buntline was one of the instigators of the Astor Place Riot (*see Chapter 1*) which left twenty-three people dead. He was fined $250 and sentenced to a year's imprisonment in September 1849. After his release, he wrote sensational stories for weekly newspapers, and his income was estimated at an extraordinary $20,000 a year. Although a heavy drinker, he criss-crossed the country giving lectures about temperance. Buntline approached Wild Bill Hickok in Nebraska with a view to writing a dime novel about him, but Hickok ordered him out of town. He meekly complied.[19] It was also in Nebraska in 1869, on one of his temperance lecture tours, that he met William F. Cody. They became friends and he later claimed that he created the nickname 'Buffalo Bill' for the hero of his serial novel *Buffalo Bill, the King of the Border Men*, published in the *New York Weekly*. Buntline also wrote a Buffalo Bill play, *Scouts of the Prairie*, which was performed by Cody himself and which opened in Chicago in December 1872. It was panned by critics but was performed to packed theatres across the country for years.

Later in life, Buntline embellished his military career, claiming to have been chief of scouts in the Indian Wars, with the rank of colonel, and to have received twenty wounds in battle. He died at home in Stamford, New York, in 1886. He was once one of the wealthiest authors in America, but his wife had to sell their beloved home,

'The Eagle's Nest', to pay his debts. Buntline's novels may have had unintended consequences. Some avid readers became thrilled with the exploits of Western outlaws. The female bandits Little Britches and Cattle Annie, for instance, read dime novels which allegedly aroused their interest in the Doolin gang and may have propelled them into a youthful life of crime.[20] But Buntline's greatest legacy lay in the myths he wove. An Eastern charlatan was the foremost chronicler of the West.

And it was the East, with its bustling cities and voracious appetite for sensation, which provided the mass audience fought over by press barons, dime novel publishers and theatre impresarios. The last decades of the nineteenth century formed a 'Gilded Age' in which sensation could only be delivered through the prism of violence, real or imagined. Gary L. Roberts argued that the admiration for semi-fictional outlaws and lawbreakers went hand in hand with envy for 'rugged' capitalists. That, together with the disillusionment that ensued after the Civil War, the rise of materialism and labour unions, the lack of concern for the poor and the extermination of Native Americans, resulted in the absence of a widespread social conscience. Roberts went on: 'Moreover, the rhetoric of the war, with its praise for physical courage and boldness romanticized violence and produced a high respect for those virtues, even among criminals.'[21] The irony, one of many, is that violence in the West could not hold a candle to that in the East.

Buffalo Bill, however, was not entirely a creation of Buntline or, completely, of himself. His boasts of riding for the Pony Express as a young teenager are, at best, questionable, but he served honourably in the Civil War on the Union side and did scout for the US Army during the Indian Wars. According to Cody's account in *Buffalo Bill's Own Story*, the Utah War was where he began his career as an 'Indian fighter'. He wrote:

> Presently the moon rose, dead ahead of me; and painted boldly across its face was the figure of an Indian. He wore this war-bonnet of the Sioux, at his shoulder was a rifle pointed at someone in the river-bottom 30 feet below; in another second he would drop one of my friends. I raised my old muzzle-loader and fired. The figure collapsed, tumbled down the bank and landed with a splash in the water. 'What is it?' called McCarthy, as he hurried back. 'It's over there in the water.' 'Hi!' he cried. 'Little Billy's killed an Indian all by himself!' So began my career as an Indian fighter.

After his meeting with Buntline, Cody became world famous for *Buffalo Bill's Wild West*, a touring show, which travelled around the United States, Great Britain and Europe. Audiences were enthusiastic about his version of the American West. In 1893, Cody changed the title to *Buffalo Bill's Wild West and Congress of Rough Riders of the World*. The show began with a parade on horseback, with participants from horse-culture groups that included US and other military, cowboys, gauchos, Arabs, Mongols and Native Americans. Sitting Bull appeared with a band of twenty of his braves. The world was hungry for sensation with a veneer of educational benefit. Queen Victoria ordered a private showing, as did much of European royalty along with Pope Leo XIII. Back in America, audiences lapped it up for decades. Later in life, Cody supported conservation and the rights of both women and Native Americans. In his shows, the Indians were usually depicted attacking stagecoaches and were driven off by cowboys and soldiers. Many family members travelled with the men, and Cody encouraged the wives and children of his Native American performers to set up camp – as they would in their homelands – as part of the show. He wanted the paying public to see the human side of the 'fierce warriors' and see that they had families like any others and had their own distinct cultures.

But by then so many myths had been sown which proved impossible to unravel. For example, during the three-year lifetime of the transcontinental Butterfield stage line, it was never stopped by outlaws, and only once by Native Americans.[22] The stagecoach chase enshrined in John Ford movies rarely happened, but as a character in John Ford's *The Man Who Shot Liberty Valence* said: 'When in doubt, print the legend.'

Warren wrote: 'Cody's experience on the Great Plains was seminal to his realisation than even his young life could be a story, lived for the amusement of the public. Incongruous as it might seem, scouting and hunting were paths to show business, and Cody's development of a show persona reflected many of the lessons he learned in the Indian Wars and on the buffalo range ... he was also an intuitive performance genius who borrowed readily from a popular theory of history, "the progress of civilization", to turn himself into the "representative man" who had "passed through every stage" of frontier development.'[23]

Mythologising continued well into the second half of the twentieth century. Across the Great Plains and the Rockies, in Montana, Idaho and Wyoming, the earlier tall tales of Mountain Men were swallowed as fact. One of the most boastful, John Johnson, boasted of killing hundreds of Crow Indians and other tribespeople, either side of the Civil War, in revenge for the murder of his family. His boasts were passed down to the children and grandchildren of his compatriots. In 1958 the author Raymond Thorp pulled the stories into one volume, *Crow Killer*, one of the sources for the superb film *Jeremiah Johnson*, starring Robert Redford as the eponymous hero, and directed by Sydney Pollack. It may have been a decent representation of early frontier life, but the story was based on lies given veracity by the racism of the time. In his 2015 introduction to *Crow Killer*, the independent scholar Nathan E. Bender wrote: 'Examination of Raymond Thorp's oral sources for his book finds his two main informants being the Wild West showman Doc Carver and White-Eye Anderson, one of Johnson's former trapping partners. Chief Joseph Medicine Crow, historian of the Crow Nation, maintains that the central story is fictitious, not supported by Crow oral history, and that Johnson had actually been a close friend of theirs with whom they often ate raw deer livers.'[24]

It was little wonder that when cinema grew from flickering lanterns in converted storefronts to a global industry, Buffalo Bill became the most fictionally filmed frontier hero, followed in order by Billy the Kid, Jesse James, Wild Bill Hickok, Custer and Wyatt Earp. It is little wonder, also, that the Western movie dominated during the first seventy-five years of the twentieth century. Early Western movie writers and directors were influenced by the romantic folk tales of the frontier with their simplistic plotting and immutable moral values of good *versus* evil, themes that were easy to write and to translate to the screen. The landscapes of Monument Valley, Utah, the Wind River Reservation, Wyoming, and Lame Deer, Montana, made perfect movie backdrops as the technology developed. The physical requirements of the genre were the main reason for the fledgling industry's migration from the eastern seaboard to Hollywood. The stories told, while often nuanced, well-written and containing complex character studies, nevertheless generally reinforced the American self-image of resilience, self-reliance, stubborn courage and moral rectitude, attributes which may well have inhabited the first frontier folk, but not all that followed them. Many producers, directors and stars made their best movies within the genre, notably John Ford, Budd Boetticher, Anthony Mann, John Wayne, James Stewart and, from the 1960s, Sam Peckinpah and Clint Eastwood. Numerous TV series completed the job even as 1950s optimism gave way to disillusioned cynicism.

There were no theatrical and cinematic geniuses, and few reliable contemporary writers, to chronicle the explosive and deadly history of the industrial and urban East. But while the Western myths were being created in the post-Civil War and early twentieth-century era, racial violence against blacks, Hispanics and Chinese matched, or possibly even surpassed, such ethnic slaughter as Wounded Knee and Sand Creek, and certainly surpassed in shame the celebrated Battle of the Little Bighorn. Riots, organised crime, political corruption, racism, vested interests and the growth of mass media all colluded to create a cauldron in the East rather than West. The clashes between the burgeoning labour movements and unscrupulous capital, often intertwined with racial bigotry, made the Johnson County War and other celebrated Western tales, in comparison, look like a drop in a saloon spittoon.

This book, hopefully, might help redress the balance.

1

New York: From the Macbeth Riots to the King of Bank Robbers

'Down with the codfish aristocracy!'

The 1840s saw the rise of the Nativist movement which pitted second- and third-generation Americans against waves of incomers from the downtrodden of Europe. Such competition inevitably meant violent confrontation, and one of the earliest and most bloody manifestations of that was centred around the hot issue of who was the best Shakespearean actor – a Yankee or a Brit – in the still-young nation. Only in America.

The triggers were provided by the various stages of immigration that built America. First came the 'old immigrants', from Britain, Germany and Scandinavia following independence. Then came the Poles, Italians, Irish and Jews, arriving from around 1820. Both groups largely consisted of low-skilled, low-wage laborers. The inscription on the Statue of Liberty reads: 'Give me your tired, your poor, Your huddled masses, yearning to breathe free, The wretched refuse of your teeming shore, Send these, the homeless, tempest-tost to me, I lift my lamp beside the golden door.' But rarely did that welcome match the reality. The immigrants had, in most cases, survived up to forty days at sea, in cramped, insanitary conditions, on leaky ships swept by sicknesses of both the body and the soul. Many arrived with just a few dollars, a determination to make good in the new promised land, and no English. The second wave overwhelmed the housing capacity of the young cities, contributing to the creation of slums and a surge in crime. The photographer Jacob Riis wrote: 'The slum is as old as civilization. Civilization implies a race [among social strata] to get

22

ahead ... They drag one another farther down. The bad environment becomes the heredity of the next generation. Then, given the crowd, you have a slum ready-made.'[1]

The term 'nativism' was first used by 1844, but the seeds were sown in 1798 legislation which lengthened the citizenship process to fourteen years to weaken the political role of radical immigrants from France and Ireland. The legislation was largely repealed, but the underlying sentiments – and bigotry – refused to go away as a new ethnic group who regarded themselves as 'pure' Americans had evolved on both sides of the War of Independence from the British.[2] The Nativists objected primarily to Irish Roman Catholics. As ever, economic factors came into play as impoverished immigrants undercut and took jobs previously held by 'Americans'. Such sentiments were widespread, disregarding the notion that Nativists had supplanted Native Americans.

In 1836, Samuel Morse ran unsuccessfully as New York City mayor on a Nativist ticket and Nativist fraternities were formed. Charles B. Allen founded the Order of the Star-Spangled Banner; to join, a man had to be twenty-one, a Protestant, a believer in God, and willing to obey without question the dictates of the order. They were known as the 'Know Nothings' because if asked, they said they 'know nothing about' the secret society. In Charlestown, Massachusetts, a Nativist mob burned down a Catholic convent in 1834, and in the 1840s, small-scale riots between Catholics and Nativists took place in several American cities. In Philadelphia in 1844, for example, a series of Nativist assaults on Catholic churches and community centres resulted in the professionalisation of the police force.

In the first half of the nineteenth century, theatres were the main gathering places in most towns and cities. Star actors drew an immensely loyal following among audiences who had always treated theatres as places to express strong feelings, not just towards the actors, but towards their audience fellows, particularly if they were of different classes or political beliefs. Theatre riots were common.[3] The American theatre was then dominated by British actors and managers and for decades that had created animosity – the Stamp Act riots of 1765 saw a theatre torn apart while British actors were performing on stage.[4] New York's infamous Nativist and anti-Catholic gang known as the Bowery Boys were keen theatre-goers. Historian Richard Butsch wrote that 'they brought the street into the theater, rather than shaping the theater into an arena of the public sphere'.[5] The Bowery Theatre, built in 1826, became a magnet for the working man and for the gangs. Walt Whitman described it 'packed from ceiling to pit with its audience, mainly of alert, well-dressed, full-blooded young and middle-aged men, the best average of American-born mechanics'.[6] Shakespeare's plays went down equally well with the educated elite and street gangs. His prose was well known throughout every stratum of society.[7] In an America that had yet to establish its own theatrical traditions, the way to prove its cultural prowess was to do Shakespeare as well as the British.[8]

Edwin Forrest was the first truly American stage star. Born in Philadelphia, the son of a Scottish merchandise peddler, the eleven-year-old Forrest made his first appearance on the legitimate stage playing the female lead in the melodrama *Rudolph: or, The Robbers of Calabria*. When attending a lecture in early 1820, he volunteered for an experiment on the effects of nitrous oxide and while under the influence, he broke into a soliloquy from Shakespeare's *Richard III* that impressed eminent Philadelphia lawyer John Swift so much that he arranged a professional stage audition. Forrest soon gained fame for portraying blackface caricatures of African Americans.[9] In 1826 he had a great success at the Bowery as Othello and that success was repeated in every city he visited on both sides of the Atlantic.

Forrest visited London for a second time in 1845 and was embraced by cultured English and Scottish society. But when he attempted to play Macbeth in a brash, American style, the performance was hissed by the audience. Forrest wrongly attributed that to the professional jealousy of the English stage star William Charles Macready, even though Macready had been both friendly and helpful to him when he first came before London audiences. A few weeks later, when Macready was playing Hamlet in Edinburgh, Forrest stood up in a private box and hissed the English actor.

A more violent clash was inevitable. The question of who was the greater actor was a headline-grabber in the American media, filling columns with partisan criticism. There was also a growing sense of cultural alienation from Britain among mainly working-class Americans, along with Irish immigrants; though Nativist Americans were hostile to the latter, both found a common cause against the British. A class struggle was waged between Forrest's homespun supporters and the largely Anglophile upper classes, who supported Macready. The two actors came to represent two opposing views about the future of both American culture and class structures. Forrest's muscular frame and impassioned delivery were seen as admirably 'American' by his working-class fans, especially compared to Macready's more genteel style. Wealthier theatregoers, to avoid mingling with the immigrants and the gangs of the Five Points neighbourhood, built the Astor Place Opera House near Broadway, between the most affluent and the most crowd-pleasingly vulgar entertainment venues. Its dress code included kid gloves and white vests, and the very existence of the Astor Opera House was taken as a provocation by populist Americans.

On Macready's second visit to America, Forrest pursued him around the country, often appearing in the same plays at the same time. On Macready's third and final trip to America, half the carcass of a dead sheep was thrown at him on the stage.[10] Forrest instigated divorce proceedings against his English wife for immoral conduct, and the verdict came down against Forrest on the day that Macready arrived in New York for his farewell tour, intensifying his sense of outrage. Macready was scheduled to appear in *Macbeth* at the Opera House, while an enraged Forrest was scheduled to perform as Macbeth on the same night, only a few blocks away at the huge Broadway Theater.[11] On 7 May 1849, Forrest's supporters bought hundreds of tickets to the top level of the Opera House, and halted Macready's performance by pelting the stage with rotten eggs, lemons, bottles and ripped-up seats. The crowd shouted 'Down with the codfish aristocracy!', and the cast were forced to perform in mute pantomime, as they could not make themselves heard. Meanwhile, at Forrest's own performance that night, the audience rose and cheered when Forrest spoke Macbeth's line 'What rhubarb, senna or what purgative drug will scour these English hence?'

After his disrupted performance, Macready announced he was going back to England on the next boat, but he was persuaded to stay and perform again by a petition signed by forty-seven wealthy and renowned New Yorkers – including authors Herman Melville and Washington Irving – who told him that 'the good sense and respect for order prevailing in this community will sustain you on the subsequent nights of your performance'. On 10 May, Macready once again took the stage as Macbeth.

Police chief George Washington Matsell told new mayor Caleb Woodhull that he had insufficient manpower to quell a serious riot, and Woodhull called out the militia. General Charles Sandford assembled the state's Seventh Regiment in Washington Square Park, along with mounted troops, light artillery and hussars, a total of 350 men who would be added to the 100 policemen outside the theatre in support of the 150 inside. More policemen were assigned to protect the homes of the city's wealthy families. Captain Isaiah Rynders, a Tammanay Hall backer of Forrest, had been one of those behind the mobilisation against Macready on 7 May. He had distributed handbills and posters in saloons and restaurants across the city, inviting working men and patriots to show their feelings about the British, asking 'SHALL AMERICANS OR ENGLISH RULE THIS CITY?' Free tickets were handed out to Macready's show, as well as plans for where the mob should deploy.[12]

By the time the play opened at 7.30 p.m., up to 10,000 people filled the streets around the theatre. One of the most prominent among those who supported Forrest's cause was Ned Buntline, the dime novelist who was Rynders' chief assistant (*see Introduction*). Buntline and his followers set up relays to bombard the theatre with stones and fought running battles with the police. They and others inside tried but failed to set fire to the building. The audience was under siege; nonetheless, Macready finished the play, and slipped out in disguise. A local journalist reported: 'As one window after another cracked, the pieces of bricks and paving stones rattled in on the terraces and lobbies, the confusion increased, till the Opera House resembled a fortress besieged by an invading army rather than a place meant for the peaceful amusement of civilized community.'[13] Sidney H. Stewart, the Clerk of Police, was inside the theatre and reported:

The first breach of peace on the house was a large paving stone which came through the window into the house; the house continued to be assailed from those without; an alarm was given that a fire was below under the dress circle; it was soon extinguished; large stones were thrown at the doors on Eighth street, smashing in the panels, and doing other damage; the police were ordered into Eighth street, say fifteen men; on my going into the street, I saw a large concourse of people, but those near the door of the theatre were mostly boys, who were apparently throwing stones; several of them were arrested by the police and brought in ... the majority of those throwing stones were boys from the ages of 12 to 18 years; several of the policemen at this time complained of being struck with stones and badly hurt; the policemen kept making arrests, and bringing them in; I cannot say how many; the crowd appeared to be increasing and more dense; the mob appeared to be determined to accomplish some particular act; there seemed to be a strong determination, although they only threw stones; the military then came.[14]

The troops, who arrived at 9.15 p.m., were attacked, with several injured. Finally, the soldiers lined up and, allegedly after unheard warnings, opened fire, first into the air and then several times at point-blank range into the crowd. Many of those killed were innocent bystanders, and seven of the dead were Irish immigrants. Dozens of injured and dead were laid out in nearby saloons and shops, and the next morning mothers and wives combed the streets and morgues for their loved ones.

The next night a meeting in City Hall Park attracted thousands to hear speakers crying out for revenge against the authorities whose actions they held responsible for the fatalities. During the melee, a young boy was killed. An angry crowd headed up Broadway toward Astor Place and fought running battles with mounted troops from behind improvised barricades, but this time the authorities quickly got the upper hand.[15]

Altogether, up to thirty-one rioters were killed and forty-eight were wounded, and fifty to seventy policemen were injured.[16] The militia suffered 141 injured by various missiles. The city's elite were unanimous in their praise of the authorities for taking a hard line against the rioters. Publisher James Watson Webb wrote: 'The promptness of the authorities in calling out the armed forces and the unwavering steadiness with which the citizens obeyed the order to fire on the assembled mob, was an excellent advertisement to the Capitalists of the old world, that they might send their property to New York and rely upon the certainty that it would be safe from the clutches of red republicanism, or chartists, or communionists [sic] of any description.'[17]

The Astor did not survive its reputation as the 'Massacre Opera House' at 'DisAster Place,' as burlesque shows branded it. It began another season, but soon gave up, the building eventually becoming part of the New York Mercantile Library.[18] The riot marked the first time a state militia had been called out and had shot into a crowd of citizens, and it led to the creation of the first police force armed with deadly weapons.[19]

The Nativists went public in 1854 when they formed the 'American Party'. Former president Millard Fillmore ran on that ticket for the presidency in 1856. In Louisville, Kentucky, election-day rioters killed at least twenty-two people in attacks on German and Irish Catholics on 6 August 1855, in what became known as 'Bloody Monday'.[20]

Such violence, intermingled with disease and poverty, was a major factor in the drive westward before and, to a greater degree after, the Civil War.

* * *

New York City's Ellis Island was the major port of entry to the United States, and 'has throughout the country's history been the cauldron into which highly diverse immigrant groups have been poured'.[21] Their collective arrival spurred gang development in the squalor and overcrowding of the Lower East Side. That area of the city – particularly around the Five Points – fell victim to political, economic and social disorganisation.

The earliest gangs of New York were not necessarily criminal. Many street gang members were employed, mostly as common laborers, but also as bouncers in saloons and dance halls, and as longshoremen. A few were apprentice butchers, carpenters, sailmakers and shipbuilders. 'They engaged in violence, but violence was a normal part of their always-contested environment; turf warfare was a condition of the neighbourhood.' Gangs formed the 'basic unit of social life among the young males in New York in the nineteenth century'.[22] The more dangerous street gangs became engaged in brutal territorial disputes, and 'the more sophisticated they became, the more violent they became. 'From its earliest days when the Dutch and English struggled for political and economic control, through the nineteenth century when new groups such as Germans and the Irish settled in great numbers, and up through the early twentieth century with the arrival of southern and eastern Europeans, the city has always been an ever-evolving mix of ethnic groups.'[23]

The Forty Thieves was made up almost exclusively of Irish immigrants to the Five Points district. It was formed in 1825 by Edward Coleman to kick against social discrimination evident in the district's slums and others nearby in Canal Street, the Bowery, Broadway and Mulberry Street, but it quickly turned to crime. Coleman controlled the Five Points with an iron fist, but his private life led to his downfall. He married a 'Hot Corn Girl' named Ann in 1838; as her husband Coleman was entitled to her earnings, but when she did not earn as much as he expected, Coleman beat her so severely she later died. Coleman was quickly convicted of her murder and on 12 January 1839, he became the first man to be hanged at the newly built Tombs Prison.

Before and after Coleman's demise, the Forty Thieves met at a Centre Street grocery store owned by a notorious handler of stolen goods, Rosanna Peers, who also ran an underground speakeasy. As a social unit, the gang intermingled with the local fire company, the fraternal orders and the political clubs.[24]. Barroom brawling was a common feature. Gang members would be given assignments and issued strict quotas on the gang's share of illegal activities. They established relations with the corrupt Tammany Hall political administration which provided community services in exchange for money and electoral support.[25]

That relationship sparked intense rivalry as the Forty Thieves were gradually supplanted by a new generation of violent hooligans generally known as the Dead Rabbits. They emerged, in part at least, from the Roach Guards, a 100-strong gang, and all were Irish in both background and popular prejudice. The name, reportedly from their practice of going into battle with a rabbit on a pike, captured the public imagination. Historian Tyler Anbinder wrote that 'for more than a decade, "Dead Rabbit" became the standard phrase by which city residents described any scandalously riotous individual or group'.[26] One of the most feared Dead Rabbits was Hell-Cat Maggie, a woman who filed her teeth to jagged points and wore brass fingernails into battle. Their street army often included elements of the Plug Uglies, a loose gang which had originated in Baltimore, named after the plug hats they stuffed with wool and leather to be used as primitive helmets. The name also became a generic byword for a ferocious fighter with feet, fists, clubs and knives.

The Dead Rabbits repeatedly clashed with Nativist political groups seeking to drive out Irish Catholics.[27] Their chief rivals were the Bowery Boys, native-born New Yorkers who supported the Know Nothing anti-immigrant political party. One of the most prominent Dead Rabbits was John Morrissey, a former champion boxer and Irish-born criminal linked to the Tammany Hall Democrats, who led the fight against the Nativist 'Bill the Butcher' Poole and his Bowery Boys. Poole was shot dead, possibly in the back, on 25 February 1855 by Lew Baker and Jim Turner, friends of Morrissey, at Stanwix Hall, a bar on Broadway. Morrisey later became a Democratic state senator and member of the US House of Representatives and vigorously represented Irish American Catholics for years.

Despite their fearsome reputation, the majority of the Bowery Boys led law-abiding lifestyles for most of the week. The gang was made up of volunteer firemen – a profession which provided rich pickings through theft, looting and extortion and which often led to pitched battles with rival fire companies – who also worked as tradesmen, mechanics and butchers. They wore stovepipe hats, red shirts and dark trousers tucked into boots. According to one historian, 'it would be a mistake to identify the Bowery Boys as a specific group at a specific time ... there were several gangs who referred to themselves as the Bowery Boys at various times under different leaders during the antebellum years'.[28]

Mike Walsh was the leader of the one of the gang's first incarnations. He became an elected official and reached the peak of his popularity in 1843, when he created the political clubhouse he called the 'Spartan Association'. Walsh was sentenced to jail twice, but the Bowery Boys became so powerful that they were able to bail him out. The front page of *The Subterranean* editorialised: 'We consider the present infamous persecution of Mike Walsh a blow aimed at the honest laboring portion of this community.' Due to the threat of violence in the streets, Walsh was let out midway through his sentence as he was considered by many to be the 'champion of the poor man's rights'. Walsh was eventually taken to Tammany Hall to be nominated for a seat in the state legislature. Walsh died in 1859 and his obituary read that the leader of the Bowery Boys was an 'original talent, rough, full of passionate impulses ... but he lacked balance, caution – the ship often seemed devoid of both ballast and rudder'. The obituary was thought to be written by the poet Walt Whitman.[29]

The two rival gangs fought more than 200 gang battles over a decade, and they often outmanned the police force and state militias. Under the leadership of Isaiah Rynders, the Boys acted as enforcers to 'persuade' voters during elections to vote for their favoured candidates. New York's Democrats were divided into two camps: those who supported Mayor Fernando Wood and those who opposed him. The Bowery gangs were among the latter, while the Dead Rabbits were supporters of Wood. The Bowery Boys threw their support in league with state Republicans who proposed legislation that would disband the Municipal Police Department, in which Wood's supporters had a controlling interest, and replace it with a state-run Metropolitan

Police Department. Wood refused to comply, and for the first half of 1857, the two rival departments battled it out on the streets of the city until the courts ordered the Municipals to disband that July.

On 4 July, while the rest of New York City was celebrating Independence Day, a bloody fight occurred with the Metropolitan Police and the Bowery gangs against the Municipal Police, Mulberry Street Boys, the remnants of the Roach Guards, and Dead Rabbits in Bayard Street, with up to 1,000 gang members taking part over two days, and hundreds more taking advantage by looting.[30] The riot kicked off when the Dead Rabbits raided a Bowery Boys clubhouse. They were confronted outside the building by their rivals and were driven back after vicious street fighting, the Five Pointers retreating to Paradise Square. The following morning, the Five Pointers returned to the Bowery with the Roach Guards and attacked the *Green Dragon*, a popular Broome Street venue for the Bowery Boys and other local criminals. Armed with iron bars and large paving blocks, they wrecked the barroom, ripped up the dancefloor and drank every drop of alcohol. News of the incident quickly reached the Bowery Boys, who then called upon other gangs of the Bowery to join them and confronted the Five Pointers at Bayard Street.[31]

At around 10 a.m., amid savage fighting, a lone patrolman used his club to move through the gangsters in an attempt to take the ring leaders into custody. He was knocked down and attacked by the crowd, stripped of his uniform, and beaten with his own nightstick. He crawled back to the sidewalk and, wearing only his cotton drawers, ran towards the Metropolitan headquarters on White Street to report the fighting before he collapsed. A small police squad was sent but, on reaching Centre Street, they were forced to retreat after several officers were injured. They made a second attempt, this time fighting their way into the mob, and arrested two men believed to be the leaders. The gangsters responded by storming into the houses lining The Bowery and Baynard Street, forcing residents out, and climbed to the rooftops from where they showered the Metropolitan officers with stones and brickbats until they fled. The *New York Times* reported:

> Brick-bats, stones and clubs were flying thickly round, and from the windows in all directions, and the men ran wildly about brandishing firearms. Wounded men lay on the sidewalks and were trampled upon. Now the Rabbits would make a concerted rush and force their antagonists up Baynard Street to the Bowery. Then the fugitives, being reinforced, would turn on their pursuers...[32]

When the police left without their prisoners, there was a brief truce which was broken by taunts from women from the Five Points. The result was further bloody mayhem. Residents and store owners all along the Bowery, as well as on Baxter, Bayard, Elizabeth and Mulberry streets, were forced to barricade their buildings and protect themselves with pistols and muskets as looters tried to force entry.[33]

Fighting continued until early afternoon when a larger police force arrived, sent by Police Commissioner Simeon Draper, and marched in close formation towards the mob. After hard fighting, they cleared the streets forcing both the Dead Rabbits and the Bowery Boys into the buildings and to the rooftops once again.[34] The police followed, striking out with their clubs. Pockets of gangsters refused to surrender and one man, while fighting police, fell off the roof of a Baxter Street tenement, fracturing his skull. He was promptly surrounded by Bowery Boys who stomped him to death.[35] Two leaders of the Dead Rabbits were finally arrested by police despite heavy resistance and were hauled off to a nearby police precinct.

Fighting resumed as soon as the police left. Barricades were set up with pushcarts and stones from which gangsters shot muskets, hurled bricks and used clubs in brutal fashion. A Dead Rabbit who stepped in front of his barricade shot dead two Bowery Boys and wounded two others despite coming under heavy fire himself. He was finally knocked unconscious, reportedly by a small boy whose brother was a Bowery Boy, and who had crawled along the barricade and hit him with a brickbat from behind.[36] The police returned to the area but were unable to re-enter the fray, and that evening they called upon Captain Isaiah Rynders to use his influence to stop the battle. Rynders, then the political boss of the Sixth Ward, agreed and upon his early evening arrival he addressed the rival mobs from the barricades. They refused to listen, and Rynders was pelted with rocks. Badly shaken, he advised Draper to call in the military.[37] At around 9 p.m., the Eighth and the Seventy-First Regiments of the New York State Militia under Major-General Charles W. Sandford marched down White and Worth streets with fixed bayonets. Accompanied by two police detachments of seventy-five men each, they moved ahead of the guardsmen clubbing gangsters and rioters. The show of force was enough to panic the gangsters who promptly fled back to their hideouts. Around 500 troops remained at the City Arsenal until 4 a.m., although police and national guardsmen continued to patrol the district for the rest of the night and into the next day.

During the two days, eight men were killed and between thirty and one hundred others injured, roughly half requiring hospitalisation. It was believed that many more gang members were carried off by their friends and that over the next few days those who succumbed to their wounds were buried in cellars, hidden passageways and other locations in the Five Points and Paradise Square. According to underworld legend, these sites would be used for secret burials by street gangs for several decades.[38]

Afterwards, occasional violence against Bowery Boys who ventured into the Five Points was reported. The most serious incident occurred the next day, when a group of Bowery Boys fought members of the Kerryonians in Centre Street, but they were chased back to the Bowery by the time police arrived. Sporadic fighting continued for another week, most being confined to German American neighbourhoods in the East Side, with younger criminals emulating the Irish gangs.[39] And then the gangs went back to normal business.

The poorer bars that gang members frequented often had a sole piano player, invariably known as 'The Professor', and resembled the archetypal Hollywood Western saloon. But from 1860 a new type of dive spread across the city, the concert saloon, providing liquor, dancing and lewd theatrical entertainment. Inevitably, they lured the rougher elements and gangsters, and were often used as a front for criminal enterprises. There was Harry Hill's place in West Houston Street, which later hosted John L. Sullivan's first boxing bout in New York, when he beat Steve Taylor in under three minutes. *The Black and Tan*; in a basement on Bleeker Street, it was run by Frank Stephenson, whose thin face was so bloodless he resembled a corpse; it was frequented mainly by blacks and white women – a volatile combination in that era and for more than a century afterwards. Billy McGlory's *Armory Hall* on Hester Street, meanwhile, was notorious for the shake-downs and beatings inflicted on customers by the bar's bouncers, and for the wantonness of its prostitutes. Close to the Mulberry Street police headquarters was a gambling den which catered only to police officers, and a little way away was the joint run by Mike Kerrigan, better known as Johnny Dobbs, a former river pirate who had side lines in bank robberies and fencing stolen goods.[40]

Sections of New York city were as lawless as any fantasy dreamt up by Western dime novelists. And then the Civil War came.

***

Major-General Charles Sandford reported to his superiors that one of his staff officers was seriously wounded while gallantly leading a charge down 42nd Street, and others under his command were killed while storming barricades. The enemy was 'in every instance defeated or dispersed' because no blank cartridges were issued. Fires raged, riot and gun battles were the order of the day, and black men were lynched, their bodies torched.

Such laconic dispatches cannot hide the ferocity, at the height of the Civil War, of actions not on the battlefield but on the streets of New York – Sandford was commander of the first division of the city's National Guard. The *Washington Times* editorialised: 'The nation is at this time in a state of Revolution, North, South, East, and West.' The reason for the violent uproar was Abraham Lincoln's issuing on 3 March 1863 of the Enrollment Act of Conscription. Although draft riots took place in many Northern cities, those that broke out in New York during a scorching-hot week were both the most violent and the most publicised. Henry Raymond wrote in the *New York Times*: 'This mob is not the people, nor does it belong to the people. It is for the most part made up of the vilest elements in the city.' Herbert Asbury wrote that the riots were 'an insurrection of the criminal element against the established order. The disturbances were the natural end of the ruinous road along which the city had travelled during the preceding fifteen years, and the logical result of the governmental corruption which had permitted Manhattan Island to become the Mecca of criminals from all parts of the United States and the slums of Europe.'[41]

The state's popular governor, Democrat Horatio Seymour, made no secret of his contempt for Lincoln, a sentiment which struck a chord with many New Yorkers tired and disillusioned by the apparent military stalemate after two years of bloody warfare with their Southern neighbours. New York's economy had long been linked to the South; more than half its exports were of plantation cotton, and upstate mills processed cotton for manufacturing. In January 1861 New York's mayor, Democrat Fernando Wood, urged the Board of Aldermen to 'declare the city's independence from Albany and from Washington'. He said it 'would have the whole and united support of the Southern States'.[42] Although the concept of secession in the heart of the North may have been fanciful, it had some support as the city was teeming with Irish and German immigrants resentful of blacks, and Tammany Hall stirred up more racial tensions. New York political offices were historically held by Democrats before the war, but the presidential election of Lincoln saw a major shift. A Republican, George Opdyke, was elected mayor, but was then implicated in profiteering scandals. Lincoln's Emancipation Proclamation in January 1863 alarmed much of the working class in New York, who feared that freed slaves would migrate to the city and take jobs for low pay. In March white longshoremen refused to work with blacks and rioted, attacking 200 black men.[43]

By the time the names of the first draftees were drawn in New York City on 11 July, reports about the carnage of Gettysburg had been published. Lincoln's call for 300,000 more young men to fight a seemingly endless war frightened even those who supported the Union cause. New citizens learned they were expected to register for the draft to fight for their new country. Moreover, the Enrollment Act contained several exemptions, including the payment of a 'commutation fee' that allowed wealthier and more influential citizens to buy their way out of service. Black men were excluded from the draft as they were largely not considered citizens. Most resentful of all were Irish immigrants, who strongly objected to fighting on behalf of their black rivals at the bottom of the social pile.

On Sunday 12 July, the names of the draftees drawn the day before by the provost marshal were published in newspapers. Within hours, groups of irate citizens, most from the working classes, banded together across the city. A furious crowd of around 500, led by the volunteer firemen of Engine Company 33, popularly known as the Black Joke, attacked the Ninth District draft office.[44] Their leader had been drawn in the draft and they had previously announced their intention to smash the drafting wheel and destroy all records. A single shot signalled a rush to the door. Police stationed outside were overwhelmed and retreated inside, followed by the enraged crowd which threw large paving stones through windows, burst through the doors, and set the building ablaze. When another fire department responded, rioters broke up their vehicles. Others killed horses that were pulling streetcars, smashed the cars and cut telegraph lines.

Martha Derby Perry, the wife of assistant surgeon John Perry of the 20th Massachusetts Volunteers, provided a vivid eyewitness account of the rioting. She had been sitting at the bedside of her husband, who was recovering from a severe leg fracture after falling from a horse.

On the first day of the riot, in the early morning, I heard loud and continued cheers at the head of the street and supposed it must be news of some great victory. In considerable excitement I hurried downstairs to hear particulars, but soon found that the shouts came from the rioters who were on their way to work. About noon that same day we became aware of a confused roar; as it increased, I flew to my window, and saw rushing up Lexington Avenue, within a few paces of our house, a great mob of men, women and children; the men, in red working shirts, looking fairly fiendish as they brandished clubs, threw stones, and fired pistols. Many of the women had babies in their arms, and all of them were completely lawless as they swept on ... John, his injured leg in a plaster cast, threw his military coat over his shoulders, utterly unconscious of the fact that if the shoulder straps had been noticed by the rioters they would have shot him, so blind was their fury against the army. The mass of humanity soon passed, setting fire to several houses quite near us, for no other reason, we heard afterward, than that a policeman, whom they suddenly saw and chased, ran inside one of the gates, hoping to find refuge. The poor man was almost beaten to death, and the house, with those adjoining, burned. At all points fires burst forth, and that night the city was illuminated by them. I counted from the roof of our house five fires just about us.[45]

Police Superintendent John A. Kennedy left police HQ in plain clothes to judge the scale of the disturbance, but he was recognised, clubbed to the ground and stomped.[46] He managed to get back on his feet but was chased and thrown from a railway embankment onto rocks below. Incredibly, he again staggered further on where he faced another gang who knocked him into a mudhole. He was only saved when a prominent citizen persuaded the mob that the policeman was dead.

Meanwhile, Sergeant 'Fighting Mac' McCredie took command of operations as street battles broke out around Third Avenue and 45th Street. With forty-four men, he charged the mob and briefly forced it to retreat, but with thousands now pouring into the fray they were quickly swamped. Every policeman was injured or disabled. McCredie was struck with such force that he shattered the door panels of a house. Badly dazed, he ran up the steps to the second floor. There he was hidden between two mattresses by a young

German woman who convinced the pursuing mob that he had jumped through her window to escape. Her home was torched, but after the attackers had left the woman hoisted McCredie on her back and carried him to Lexington Avenue, from where a carriage took him to the police station.[47]

Of that day of turmoil and running battles, Asbury wrote:

> By one o'clock the mob had swept southward to Thirty-Fifth Street, where Captain Streets and a strong force of patrolmen made a desperate stand but were finally overwhelmed and fled in disorder. Meanwhile, a detachment of the Invalid Corps, numbering fifty men armed with sabre and musket, marched up Third avenue, and were greeted by a shower of paving stones and brickbats, which killed one of the soldiers and wounded half a dozen others. Bewildered by the unexpected attack, the commander ordered the first rank to fire with blanks, but the volley had no other effect than to further inflame the mob and leave half the troops defenceless. With a roar the great throng charged, and the second rank of the Invalids fired with ball cartridges, killing and wounding six men and one woman. For an instant the mob was checked, and then the rioters attacked with greater ferocity than before. Before the troops could reload, their guns had been wrested from their hands and they were being clubbed and shot with their own weapons. Hopelessly outnumbered, the soldiers turned and fled pell-mell down the street, leaving a score of dead and wounded. The mob proceeded to torture and mutilate them.[48]

Sections of the mob headed for the State Armory on Second Avenue and the nearby Union Steam Works which had been converted into an arms factory, both of which contained stacks of carbines and ammunition, where they were met by strong and well-armed police detachments. At around 4 p.m. the rioters attacked. The first into the Armory was shot in the head, but others battered their way in and the police under a Sergeant Burdick managed to crawl out through a small hole in a rear wall. The rioters ransacked the ground floor, but the armaments were stored on the third floor. By the time the vanguard had reached that level, several fires had been started below them. Outside another strong police force gathered. Those rioters who ran out unarmed were let through, but those carrying guns and ammunition were clubbed without mercy. As the flames took hold some rioters jumped from the third floor and either died or were severely injured. The number who died within the Armory was never confirmed, but later workmen clearing the rubble carried out more than fifty buckets of charred human bones.

In the first day of rioting, before the proper military could be deployed, the mainly ethnic Irish mobs ransacked or destroyed numerous public buildings, two Protestant churches, the homes of various abolitionists or sympathisers, many black homes, and the Colored Orphan Asylum. The four-storey orphanage at 43rd Street and Fifth Avenue was a 'symbol of white charity to blacks and of black upward mobility' that then provided shelter for 233 children under twelve years. A mob of several thousand, including many women and children, looted the building of its food and supplies. Luckily, local police secured sufficient time for the children to be led to safety by the home's superintendent before the building burned down. One little black girl who had been overlooked in the rushed exodus was found hiding under a bed and killed by the mob. The other children were driven in stages to a police station and later removed under escort to Blackwell's Island in the East River.

The Bull's Head hotel on 44th Street, which refused to provide alcohol to the mob, was torched. The mayor's residence on Fifth Avenue, the Eighth and Fifth District police stations, and other buildings were attacked and set on fire. Other targets included the office of the *New York Times*, where the mob was turned back by staff manning Gatling guns under the command of the newspaper's founder, Henry Jarvis Raymond.[49] Several fire companies responded, but some firefighters were sympathetic to the rioters, as they had also been drafted. Later in the afternoon, authorities shot and killed a man as a crowd attacked the Second Avenue Armory, breaking all the windows with paving stones.[50]

As with the orphanage, rioters vented their greatest fury on black people. The mob beat, tortured and killed blacks picked at random, including one man who was attacked by a crowd of 400 with clubs and paving stones, then hanged from a tree and set alight.[51] He was far from alone, as police regularly found more charred skeletons hanging from trees or lamp posts. Most had been beaten to a pulp before being strung up. It was claimed that women who followed the rioters cut the lynched men with knives, poured oil into the wounds, lit them up and danced under the human torches. Mobs killed at least twenty black people, not all by lynching, and destroyed their known homes and businesses, such as James McCune Smith's pharmacy at 93 West Broadway, believed to be the first owned by a black man in the United States.[52] Twenty black families were burned out of their homes on Leonard and Baxter streets alone, while Crook's restaurant was sacked and its black waiters attacked.

Near the midtown docks, tensions brewing since the mid-1850s boiled over. Rioters went in search of 'all the negro porters, cart-men and laborers'. White dockworkers destroyed brothels, dance halls, boarding houses and tenements that catered to blacks. Big Sue's bar was demolished after a gang of Irish women beat her severely, and the liquor supplies were passed out to the howling, and increasingly drunk, mob. A brothel in Water Street was burned and the occupants tortured because they refused to surrender a black servant. In New Bowery, three black men took refuge on a roof and the mob set fire to the building. The terrified men clung by their fingertips to the coping of the gable wall while the rioters screamed abuse from below. Finally, as the fire scorched their hands, they dropped and were stamped to death.[53]

Leslie Harris wrote: 'Ironically, the most well-known center of black and interracial social life, the Five Points, was relatively quiet during the riots. Mobs neither attacked the brothels there nor killed black people within its borders. There were also instances of interracial cooperation. When a mob threatened black store owner Philip White in his store at the corner of Gold and Frankfurt Street, his Irish neighbors drove the mob away, for he had often extended them credit. And when rioters invaded Hart's Alley and became trapped at its dead end, the black and white residents of the alley together leaned out of their windows and poured hot starch on them, driving them from the neighborhood. But such incidents were few compared to the widespread hatred of blacks expressed during and after the riots.'

Throughout the evening another portion of the crowd assembled in Printing House Square and stormed the *Tribune* offices. Police Sergeant Devoursey killed and maimed several as he defended the main door, but the mob finally trampled over him and set the building alight. The editorial and printing staff escaped down a back stairway, but proprietor Horace Greeley was chased into a Park Row restaurant. A quick-thinking waiter hid him under a cloth-covered table. Later during the riots Greeley secured arms from the Brooklyn Navy Yard and, with 150 soldiers, kept the *Tribune* building secure. Gatling guns were positioned at the windows and a howitzer's muzzle protruded from the main entrance.

Overall, the police were badly outnumbered and unable to quell the riots, but they kept the rioting out of Lower Manhattan. When the violence erupted there were just 800 policemen on duty, but by nightfall, as off-duty officers flocked to help, there were around 1,500 in the field.[54]

On Monday night heavy rain extinguished fires and sent rioters scurrying home for shelter, but the mob returned just before dawn the next day. Rioters burned down the home of prison reformer Abby Gibbons, the daughter of prominent abolitionist Isaac Hopper. They also attacked several 'amalgamationists', white women who were married to black men, and Mary Burke, a white prostitute who catered to black men. The women escaped.[55] More than a thousand men and women, many still drunk from the night before, surged into Clarkson Street and hanged a black man, William Jones, from a tree after he tried to defend his family and prevent the burning of their rickety home. Another black man called Williams was attacked at Washington and Leroy and the mob leader stove in his skull with a large stone. The crowd was dispersed by police before his body could be set alight.[56]

Martha Derby Perry described the 'fearful' second day from her perspective:

Men, both colored and white, were murdered within two blocks of us, some being hung to the nearest lamppost, and others shot. An army officer was walking in the street near our house, when a rioter was seen to kneel on the sidewalk, take aim, fire and kill him, then coolly start on his way unmolested. I saw the Third Avenue street car rails torn up by the mob. Throughout the day there were frequent conflicts between the military and the rioters, in which the latter were often victorious, being partially organized, and well-armed with various weapons taken from the stores they had plundered. I passed the hours of that dreadful night listening to the bedlam about us; to the drunken yells and coarse laughter of the rioters wandering aimlessly through the streets, and to the shouts of a mob plundering houses a block away.[57]

On Ninth and First Avenues the throng hacked down telegraph poles and lamp posts to add to barricades of carts, barrels and looted furniture. Inspector Daniel Carpenter mustered 200 policemen and marched to the Union Steam Works which still contained numerous firearms and stores of ammunition. They were confronted by a mob armed with muskets, swords and pistols. Others manned the rooftops, armed with piles of bricks. The two lines of policemen marched slowly northward until, at 32nd Street, they were bombarded from the rooftops and attacked front and rear by the mob. Carpenter's men used their clubs with savage force and within fifteen minutes the crowd had broken up into sullen, bleeding groups. Fifty policemen charged up the stairs of the surrounding houses and attacked those who had been hurling missiles. Several jumped to their deaths to avoid the swinging batons. About fifty rioters occupied a saloon and fired muskets and pistols out of the windows. The police cleared them out without loss. A bullet passed harmlessly through the cap of one officer who then grabbed the gunman and bodily threw him from a window; the mobster's brains splattered across the pavement.[58]

Governor Horatio Seymour arrived at City Hall and attempted to calm the crowd by saying that the Enrollment Act was unconstitutional. He told an unruly audience of around 800:

> I beg you to listen to me as a friend ... I implore you to take care that no man's property or person is injured; for you owe it to yourselves and to the government under which you live to assist with your strong arms in preserving peace and order ... and if you do this, and refrain from further riotous acts, I will see to it that all your rights shall be protected ... On Saturday last I sent the adjutant-general of the state to Washington, urging the draft's postponement. The question of the legality of the Conscription Act will go to the courts ... If the conscription shall be declared to be legal, then I pledge myself to use every influence with the state and city authorities to see that there shall be no inequality between the rich and the poor ... There is no occasion for resisting the draft, for it has not yet been enforced. And now ... I beg you to disperse, leave your interests in my hands, and I will take care that justice is done to you, and that your families shall be fully protected.

The *New York Times* criticised Governor Seymour's speech, editorialising: 'No civilized government could in decency maintain relations of amity with a community of cowards, bullied by cut-throats and governed in their greatest straits by hordes of thieves.'[59] In any case, the mob was in no mood to listen.

General John E. Wool, commander of the Eastern District, brought approximately 800 soldiers and Marines from forts in New York Harbour, West Point and Brooklyn Navy Yard. He ordered the militias, who had been deployed in Pennsylvania to help regulars repel a confederate incursion, to return to New York.[60]

The *New York Times* reported that Plug Uglies and Blood Tubs gang members from Baltimore, as well as 'Scuykill Rangers [*sic*] and other rowdies of Philadelphia', had come to New York during the unrest to participate in the riots alongside the Dead Rabbits. The newspaper editorialised that 'the scoundrels cannot afford to miss this golden opportunity of indulging their brutal natures, and at the same time serving their colleagues the Copperheads and secesh [secessionist] sympathizers'.[61] Business in the city had been virtually suspended, with factories closed and stores boarded up. The streetcars and omnibuses ceased to rumble through the city, as did the drays and carts which normally filled the streets. Only the liquor stores remained open. Law-abiding citizens attempting to escape with their families crowded the railway stations and the piers, fighting for seats on trains and boats. The roads of Westchester county were jammed with refugees.

Late on the Tuesday night Governor Seymour issued a proclamation that the city was in a state of insurrection, and at midnight word came from Secretary of War Edwin M. Stanton that five regiments were being rushed to the metropolis. The situation marginally improved on Wednesday, the hottest day of the year, when assistant provost marshal Robert Nugent was told by his superior officer, Colonel James Barnet Fry, to postpone the draft. As a result, some rioters stayed home. But when militias returned they used harsh measures against the remaining mobs and mass violence again flared. A battery of four howitzers, belonging to the Eighth New York National Guard, was attached to the force which reported to General Wool on the dock. A large mob gathered and tried to snatch two black cooks serving the artillery company. The two targets were protected by the company.

Mrs Perry described the third day of mayhem:

Hurrying to the kitchen, I found our colored servants ghastly with terror, and cautioned them to keep closely within doors. One of them told me that she had ventured out early that morning to clean the front door, and that the passing Irish, both men and women, had sworn at her so violently, saying that she and her like had caused all the trouble, that she finally rushed into the house for shelter. Now that I began to realize our danger, I tried with all my power to keep John in ignorance of it, for in his absolutely disabled condition the situation was most distressing. The heat was intense: and during the morning I sat in his room behind closed window shutters, continually on the alert to catch every outside noise, while watching the hot street below in the glare of sunlight.

Men and women passed with all sorts of valuables taken from plundered houses ... Later in the day a crowd of boys arrived with stout sticks, threw stones at our house ... and then rushed on. This added to my alarm, I having heard that a rush of street arabs always preceded an attack by the mob. Parties of Irishmen passed and pointed to our house, and a boy ran by shouting, 'We'll have fun up here tonight.' My heart felt overloaded as I looked at John in his helpless condition. What were we to do? Even if he were able to be moved, there was no way of accomplishing it.

When one of my brothers returned to lunch and reported the increasing strength of the mob, I told him of all I had seen and heard during the morning, and we considered the question of barricading the street doors and windows, but soon decided that it was useless. He then went to the police station to ask for information and help, but before leaving placed a ladder against the back wall of our back yard, so that in case of attack the servants might, by this means, escape to the adjoining premises, and from there to the next street...

The police had been already plundered of most of their firearms, and needed all their force to defend themselves. They could do literally nothing for us, but recommended barricading the front entrances to the house as well as we could. The city became frightfully still, and this silence was broken only by occasional screams and sharp reports of musketry. My brothers were calling at every house in the ward to induce the occupants to meet at the police station, armed with whatever weapon each could find, in order to organize and patrol the streets through the night. Meantime our servants were instructed to remain downstairs, and not to run until the house was actually attacked, then to rush to the ladder in the back yard; and I was to cover their retreat by hiding the ladder. At ten o'clock that evening we were left alone in absolute darkness, as the police sent word that light would increase our danger. John lay quietly on his cot, while I again sat by the window to catch the slightest sound...

During the night my brothers returned, and told us that just as the officers at the police station had agreed to combine with the citizens and patrol that vicinity, a man rushed in crying that the mob was murdering someone in our street. The whole force formed and charged up the avenue, but met only scattered bands of rioters, and these slunk away as the files of organized men appeared, stretching in solid lines from sidewalk to sidewalk, as the rioters supposed, fully armed. We heard afterward that this steadfast army, looking so formidable, while so feeble in reality, was all that saved us; that our house and the one opposite, as well as the police station, were distinctly marked by the mob for that night's work.[62]

The Perry family survived the riots.

Colonel H. J. O'Brien of the 11th Volunteers, with 150 assorted men, went to the aid of police on Second Avenue who were under fire. The troops were wheeled around and fired several volleys. When that failed, six-pounders were used to fire grapeshot and canister, which caused panic and carnage. One of the fatalities was a woman holding a baby, which miraculously survived. O'Brien marched his troops back to the Arsenal. Three hours later he returned to the vicinity to ensure the safety of his family who lived nearby. They had fled to Brooklyn before the fighting began to stay with relatives. He was recognised, however, and attacked by a crowd of both men and women. He was kicked and beaten and dragged along the cobblestones after a rope was twisted around his ankles. A Catholic priest administered the last rites. O'Brien was further tortured until he succumbed to repeated stabbings and heavy stones dropped on his head.[63]

The troops then aimed to restore order around Union Square, and to protect the Hotchkiss shell factory on 24th Street. The crowd shouted abuse but offered no violence. That changed when the contingent reached 22nd Street and came under ragged fire. The militia fired back and the crowd ran away. But a block further, more shots were fired. Colonel William Berens reported:

I returned the fire, and kept up the street, firing, until I arrived a Twenty-eighth street. Finding my small company of only 28 men, besides the men serving the howitzer, too small to disperse so large a mob as had collected, I dispatched Quartermaster Flack to headquarters, on Mulberry street, for re-enforcements. The mob seemed to be very generally armed. I then fought my way through the mob to the factory. One of my men was wounded, and several of the crowd were killed and wounded by our fire. On arriving at the factory, we found the door closed. I forced the door, and took possession. The mob gathered heavily around the factory and fired upon us. We returned their fire, and afterward sallied out upon them and drove them up Twenty-eighth street, as far as the corner of First avenue, and dispersed them.

At 2 p.m. Quartermaster Flack arrived with Companies A and D. Berens wrote:

At about 5 p.m. a priest came to me as a commissioner from the riotous populace, and urged me to quit the factory and return, stating the people agreed that if I did so the factory should not be injured. He stated further that the crowd threatened that if we did not leave they would burn us out. He implored me to accept the proposal, saying that he feared the worst consequences; that the mob was about 4,000 strong – altogether too large for my weak force to resist – and that he could not control or restrain them. I reported the offer made to me by the priest to General Brown. His answer was, to hold the place at all events, and to disperse the assemblage about me at the point of the bayonet, if necessary. Previous to the receipt of this response from General Brown, however, having refused the offered compromise, and the priest having retired beyond the reach of harm, and the crowd gathering heavily around the building we occupied, I found it necessary to open fire upon them, which was kept up until our assailants were driven back behind the corners of the neighboring streets.[64]

A detachment of infantry under General Dodge, supported by a troop of cavalry and a battery of howitzers under the regular army's Colonel Mott, marched to disperse a mob reported to be hanging blacks on Eighth Avenue. They found three victims dangling from lamp posts and a cheering crowd of up to 5,000. Mott rode into the crowd and succeeded in cutting down one of the bodies before skewering with his sword a rioter who tried to drag him off his horse. He returned to his men, who by now were under heavy attack. He ordered two howitzers to be loaded with grapeshot. The crowd ignored the threat and it took six rounds to finally disperse them. Such bloody incidents were repeated across the battle zone, notably when rioters attacked Jackson's foundry on 28th Street.

At around 6 p.m., 200 volunteers and fifty Duryea Zouaves (5th New York Volunteer Infantrymen), with two howitzers under Colonel E. E. Jardine, came under attack on First Avenue. When the artillery was deployed, the mob simply vanished into the flanking houses and poured down a ferocious fire onto the troops. According to some reports, up to twenty were killed and half the remaining were wounded. Jardine was shot in the thigh. The soldiers failed to pick off the sharpshooters and were ordered to fall back. Their retreat turned into a rout when the mob surged out of the surrounding properties.

The two howitzers were captured when the artillerymen were clubbed to the ground, but they were of no use to rioters because they lacked the necessary ammunition. Jardine crawled, with two other injured Zouaves, into a basement and were hidden by two women who covered them under a pile of kindling wood. They were found when the mob broke into the house and Jardine's two companions were immediately clubbed to death. But the mob leaders recognised Jardine as a friendly acquaintance and spared his life. The women, once the streets had quietened, took Jardine to a surgeon, and he survived.[65]

The incident proved to be the mob's last important success. Major-General Charles Sandford reported:

The north and west sides of the city were effectually cleared of rioters by detachments sent by me from the arsenal. In Broadway, Forty-second, Twenty-seventh, Twenty-eighth, Twenty-ninth, Thirtieth, Thirty-first, and Thirty-second streets, Seventh, Eighth, Ninth, and Tenth avenues, mobs were attacked, and in every instance defeated or dispersed. No blank cartridges were issued to or used by any of the troops under my orders. The gas-works, in Eighteenth and Nineteenth streets, and also upon the East River, Webb's shipyards, and the various manufactories threatened by the rioters, were fully protected, and numerous fires in buildings occupied by colored people and others obnoxious to the mob, were extinguished by the firemen after the rioters were dispersed. In these encounters, I regret to report that Major [Henry S.] Fearing, of my staff, was very seriously wounded while gallantly leading a charge upon the mob in

Forty-second street, and 1 private soldier was killed, and 22 officers and men dangerously, and 53 slightly, wounded, at the storming of the barricades erected by the rioters in Twenty-ninth street, and in other conflicts which followed.[66]

The final confrontation occurred on Thursday evening near Gramercy Park. At least twelve people died in skirmishes between rioters, the police and the Army, including one African American, two soldiers, a bystander, and two women. Rioters who took refuge were driven back onto the street by police armed with clubs and nightsticks. Once outside they were mown down by soldiers.

Major-General John Wool reported to his superiors:

For the last few days I have been engaged day and night in putting down a most serious and dangerous insurrection. We have done much to stay the infamous schemes of the rioters. Cannon and muskets have been used by us, and some 60 persons among the rioters have been (as reported) killed and wounded. With the very small force I had in the forts, and with the help of such citizens as were willing to enrol themselves, we have accomplished much, and, I think, have made an impression on the rioters which I hope will stay their purposes; but they make great threats if the draft is not abandoned.[67]

Wool added the following day:

We have been engaged night and day in suppressing the insurrection in New York. Some 50 or 60 rioters have been killed and wounded. I think we shall put it down to-morrow, if it is not at the present time. A fire is now raging in Brooklyn. The storehouses are on fire, and the shipping is in danger. Martial law ought to be proclaimed, but I have not a sufficient force to enforce it. A large number of houses have been plundered and many burned.[68]

While searching homes, Wool's forces found seventy carbines and revolvers, and barrels of paving stones. Late on 17 July, Wool reported: 'All quiet in this city up to this hour, and, from all appearances, we do not apprehend any trouble to-morrow. We have, however, many applications for military forces to protect the people in adjoining counties from dangers apprehended from those opposed to the draft.' The following day Wool wired Secretary of War E. M. Stanton:

> The rioters, it would appear, have generally returned to their ordinary occupations, and it is thought by those who seem to be best acquainted with the temper and feelings of the rioters, that they will not again disturb the peace and quiet of the city, unless the enforcement of the draft – temporarily suspended – should cause another effort to resist its execution, followed by burning and otherwise destroying the property of the city, and this example would, no doubt, be followed in the adjoining counties of the State. This gratifying result has been attained by unceasing efforts, night and day, with the very moderate force at command, when the emergency arose. I have received this morning from the War Department the order relieving me from the command of this department, and shall have great pleasure in turning over the command to Major-General Dix, with peace and order restored in this city.

On the Friday, Archbishop Hughes addressed a crowd and appealed to their religious duty, saying: 'Every man has a right to defend his home or his shanty at the risk of life. The cause, however, must be just ... I have been hurt by reports that you were rioters. You cannot imagine that I could hear those things without being pained. Is there not some way by which you can stop these proceedings and support the laws, none of which have been enacted against you as Irishmen and Catholics? You have suffered already. No government can save itself unless it protects its citizens.' He urged them to retire peacefully to their homes. The archbishop's appeal may have been well meant, or it could have been a cynical attempt to forestall criticism of the Church's failure to stop four days of appalling violence by its flock. Either way, it was too little, too late.

The exact death toll during the riots is unclear but respectable sources suggest that 119 or 120 people were officially reported killed, including eleven black men lynched over five days.[69] However, given the general confusion, plus the numbers incinerated in fires and reports that at least seventy blacks were missing, it is likely that the true figure could have been double that, at least, or even more. Herbert Asbury's claim that 2,000 were killed and 8,000 wounded[70] is regarded as a wild exaggeration. The most reliable estimates indicate at least 2,000 people were injured. Total property damage was somewhere between $1 million and $5 million ($19.5 million – $97.3 million in 2018, adjusted for inflation).

No one was prosecuted, let alone convicted, of inciting riot, insurrection, intimidation, looting, wounding, lynching or murder – the Tammany Hall politicians knew the culprits, but there were elections to come. And an uncivil war to win.

Historian Samuel Eliot Morison wrote that the riots were 'equivalent to a Confederate victory'.[71] Landlords, fearing that the mob would destroy their buildings, had driven blacks from their residences. Hundreds left New York in fear for their lives, including James McCune Smith. The city's white elite belatedly mobilised to provide relief to black riot victims, helping them find new work and homes. The Committee of Merchants for the Relief of Colored People provided nearly $40,000 to 2,500 victims of the riots. By 1865 the black population had dropped to under 10,000, the lowest since 1820. The white working-class riots had changed the demographics of the city, and whites exerted their control in the workplace; they became 'unequivocally divided' from blacks.[72]

On 19 August, the government resumed the draft in New York, and it was completed within ten days without further incident. Fewer men were drafted than had been feared: of the 750,000 selected nationwide for conscription, only about 45,000 were sent into active duty. While the rioting mainly involved the working class, middle- and upper-class New Yorkers had mixed feelings about the draft and the use of lethal federal power to enforce it.[73] In December 1863, the Union League Club recruited more than 2,000 black soldiers, outfitted and trained them, sending them off with a parade through the city to the Hudson River docks in March 1864. A crowd of 100,000 watched the procession, which was led by police.

New York's support for the Union cause continued, however grudgingly, and gradually Southern sympathies declined in the city. New York banks financed the North's war effort, and the state's industries were more productive than those of the entire Confederacy. By the end of the war, more than 450,000 soldiers, sailors, and militia had enlisted from New York State. Over 46,000 of them died during the war, more from disease than wounds.[74]

Civilians carried their own scars from the draft riots, many of them mental. Martha Derby Perry recalled: 'As we heard the heavy reports and responding yells, it seemed to me that I knew something of the horrors of war.'

***

After the Draft Riots, the power and influence of both the Dead Rabbits and the Bowery Boys declined and they were absorbed into new Irish criminal gangs rising up to take their place. The arrival of the Poles, Italians and Jews in New York City between 1880 and 1920 ushered in a second distinct period of gang activity in the city's slums. Members of a select committee[75] of the state legislature came to the city and saw how crime came to be the natural crop of people housed in crowded, filthy tenements with 'dark, damp basements, leaking garrets, shops, outhouses, and stables converted into dwellings'. A new generation of gangs emerged from the filth.

The Whyos Gang (named for a bird-like call the members used to alert one another) is said to have been 'the most powerful downtown gang between the Civil War and the 1890s'.[76] The gang had a take-out menu of its services, including punching ($2), nose and jaw bone broken ($10), leg or arm broken ($19), shot in the leg ($25), and 'doing the big job' ($100 and up). From small units narrowly identified with particular neighbourhoods, gangs branched out, diversified and merged.

The Whyos were at their peak by the late 1870s and early 1880s and were led by Mike McGloin, who began moving the gang into extortion, prostitution and murder for hire. McGloin insisted that prospective members must commit at least one murder, stating in 1883: 'A guy ain't tough until he has knocked his man out!' In 1884, McGloin was arrested for the murder of saloon owner Louis Hanier and hanged at Tombs Prison.

The gang's shifting headquarters included the notorious Bowery dive known as *The Morgue*. The tavern was the scene of at least 100 violent murders with frequent gunfights between drunken gang members. Josh Hines, often seen wearing a pair of pistols, would regularly arrive at illegal gambling dens and faro games demanding a percentage of the night's profits from the owners. While being questioned by a police detective regarding the extortion activities, possibly when several owners complained, Hines was said to have replied, 'Those guys must be nuts! Don't I always leave 'em somethin'? All I want is me fair share.'[77]

Another prominent member was 'Dandy' Johnny Dolan, an impeccably dressed thug who carried a copper eye gouger on his thumb. In 1875, as he attempted to rob a local jewellery store, owner James H. Noe intercepted him. Dolan hit him over the head with an iron bar, then proceeded to use the eye gouger on the prostrate man, taking the eyes with him to show to friends as a trophy. They were found in Dolan's possession while he was being interrogated by Police Detective Joseph M. Dorsey. He was eventually convicted of murder and hanged at Tombs Prison in April 1876.

The most notorious leaders of the Whyos were Danny Driscoll and Danny Lyons. In 1887 Driscoll and a man called John Garrity fought over a Five Points girl called Beezy Garrity. They engaged in a furious gunfight in which the object of their affections was killed by a stray bullet. Driscoll was convicted and hanged on 23 January 1888. Within eight months his gangster partner, Lyons, followed him to the scaffold. Lyons was a savage streetfighter and extortionist who added pimping to his crimes. He ran three girls who gave him a share of their earnings and, perhaps more valuable, information gathered in their streetwalking. He decided to add a fourth to his stable, a girl known as Pretty Kitty McGown. He kicked out her lover, Joseph Quinn, who vowed revenge. After drinking heavily during Fourth of July celebrations, they met the following morning in Paradise Square. They fuzzily blazed away at each other and Quinn was killed by a bullet to the heart. Lyons went into hiding but was tracked down and hanged on 21 August.[78]

The Whyos, their numbers decimated by incarceration and death, dissolved in the early 1890s, and a small number of very large gangs were organised as umbrella formations. Four such alliances were among the longest-lived gangs on the Lower East Side of Manhattan for nearly two decades straddling the turn of the twentieth century: the new Five Pointers, the Monk Eastmans, the Gophers and the Hudson Dusters.[79] The Gophers, named for their fondness for striking the unwary from cellars, ran Hell's Kitchen and boasted numerous 'colourful' characters. One Lung Curran started a craze for ambushing police officers and stealing their overcoats. Happy Jack Mulraney was so called because he always appeared to be laughing due to a partial facial rictus; when an old friend, Paddy the Priest, teased him about the disfigurement he shot the saloon keeper and robbed his till.[80]

Territorial disputes and reorganisations were commonplace, but the Jewish Monk Eastman Gang was particularly notable for having 'terrorized New York City streets'.[81]

* * *

During the turmoil after the Civil War, the likes of Jesse James and the Younger brothers gained lasting fame as outlaws who robbed banks and trains. But operating along the eastern seaboard was a far more successful bank robber responsible for what was dubbed the 'crime of the century'.

George Leonidas Leslie was born in 1842, two years after his parents arrived in America from England. His father started his own brewery in Cincinnati and the family prospered. When he reached the necessary age to be drafted into the Civil War, his father paid $300 to exempt him and he duly achieved a degree in architecture, graduating top of his class at the University of Cincinnati. He ran his own architectural firm in the city but when both his parents died in 1867 he sold the family home and brewery and his architectural firm, and went to New York. There he fell into the criminal lifestyle of the gangs.[82]

Leslie formed his own gang of skilled bank robbers, using his architecture skills. Before every robbery, he would seek out the building's blueprints from local planners and build scale models of his intended targets. Leslie would find out what type of vault or safe his target used and would spend months working out how to open it without the combination. Leslie used a device called the 'little joker,' a wire device inserted into a bank safe's lock in advance. Over time and extended use, the lock's tumblers left dents or marks on the wire that indicated the numbers of the combination. He would rent a safe-deposit box or open an account at a bank, allowing him to visit regularly and study its layout, work-shift patterns and personnel. He or an accomplice would first place, then remove, the little joker. Only when he was certain the heist was feasible, with a low chance of arrest, would he commit himself to the operation. Leslie would then select his accomplices and spell out in detail each man's role. He also developed connections with police and politicians who could be bought with the proceeds of crime.

Leslie was the mastermind, and his criminal associates would carry out the actual heists. They included Tom 'Shang' Draper, Jimmy Hope, 'Banjo' Pete Emerson, Jimmy Brady, Abe Coakley, John 'Red' Leary and 'Worchester' Sam Parris. His gang robbed many banks throughout the years. From the time Leslie arrived in the east in the late 1860s to 1878, it was estimated that they were responsible for 80 per cent of bank robberies in America. He constantly eluded the police and was dubbed 'The King of Bank Robbers'.

Most of the banks were not big scores; robberies such as those of the Wellsboro Bank of Philadelphia, Saratoga County Bank of Waterford, N.Y., South Kensington National Bank of Philadelphia and the Third National Bank of Baltimore netted relatively little in relation to the time and effort required to carry them out. They scored big, however, with the robbery of the Ocean National Bank in 1869 where they got away with $768,879 but left approximately $2 million on the floor of the bank. All this was preparation for the big one.

Leslie's big target was the Manhattan Savings Institution, which was known to contain millions of dollars at any one time. He planned the raid meticulously over three years, but his gang was getting disgruntled. Apart from the usual gripes over the division of spoils, the gang believed that he was spending too much time being a consultant for other bank robbers, taking fees without benefit to his associates. They also felt his lavish, hide-in-plain-sight lifestyle was a threat to their own activities. Herbert Asbury wrote: 'He posed as a man of independent means, and because of his education and family connections was accepted in good society in New York; he belonged to several excellent clubs and was known as a *bon vivant* and a man about town. He was a familiar figure at theatre openings and art exhibitions, and acquired a considerable reputation as an amateur bibliophile...'[83] He rarely associated with fellow criminals, was always dressed in the latest and most expensive fashions, and, although married, developed a reputation as a ladies' man. One of his conquests was Babe Irving, sister of Johnny Irving, who had been killed in a saloon brawl by Johnny the Mick. There were also rumours that he was being unfaithful with many women, including his associate Tom Draper's wife. These were dangerous men to cross, and in May 1878 Leslie disappeared. His body was found lying in a bush at Tramp's Rock in Yonkers on 4 June 1878. There were three bullet holes in the back of his head; beside his body was a silver-mounted revolver. There was no blood at the scene. No one could pass this off as suicide, and possibly this was intended.[84] Leslie's murder was never solved, but many believed that Tom Draper had pulled the trigger.

Leslie's gang carried on with the big robbery, using Leslie's plan, and got away with about $2.5 million. However, only $12,000 was cash; the rest was in bonds, which were difficult to convert into cash without using financial fences who were both unreliable and greedy. Leslie's gang slowly fell apart, and one by one most were arrested.

During the same period, the biggest haul of the James–Younger gang was $3,000 taken after derailing the Rock Island train in Iowa. They netted nothing from the disastrous Northfield, Minnesota, raid which split those gang members who survived. And Jesse James's last known robbery, of a store in Fayette, Mississippi, brought his by-then ragtag band $2,000. The Leslie gang is estimated to have stolen around $7 million in total. But then they never pretended to be Robin Hoods, and maybe the relative lack of bloodshed involved ensured they remain less glamorous and infinitely more obscure.

2

The Molly Maguires

'The state provided only the courtroom and the gallows.'

In the coalfields of Pennsylvania in the 1870s, several Irish immigrants came to prominence in the embryonic union created to counter the excessive greed of the mine owners. Some of them had seen their friends hanged for the wearing of the green in Ireland, and 'all of them from the first had known that their venture in union-building might lead to as desperate an end'.[1] There was the flamboyantly moustachioed Tom Munley, who had fled Ireland in 1864, and who had a wife and four children. There was Mike Doyle, a 'strongly built man' of thirty who had 'the dogged, defiant expression of a prize fighter'. There was the smooth-shaven Ed Kelly, who urged that the union put up candidates in the county elections. They were proving the backbone of the union and all were members of the Irish fraternal order the Ancient Order of Hibernians. All would take walks to the scaffold with many others because of their alleged connections to a semi-mythical organisation, the Molly Maguires. In almost all cases, their arrests, trials and executions were put-up jobs orchestrated by the bosses and the regional Establishment. Their fate was also largely due to the testimony of a single private detective.

* * *

The Molly Maguires were originally an Irish secret society which operated through the late eighteenth century and most of the nineteenth. They were heavily involved in agrarian resistance against often absentee

English landlords; they tore down fences and boundary walls, drove off livestock and ploughed fields converted to pasture. The Mollies claimed to be carrying out 'a just law of their own in opposition to the inequities of landlord law, the police and court system, and the transgressions of land-grabbers'. The Catholic Mollies felt victimised – usually with good reason – by Protestant landlords and their agents. Molly Maguires leaders were reported to have sometimes dressed as women, occasionally as mothers begging for food for their children.[2] The practice of men donning dresses and taking a female name was both a disguise and a form of social transgression. They blackened their faces with burnt cork.

The Mollies were also active in Liverpool, a city through which many Irish people passed on their way to a new life in America and Canada, fleeing the great potato famine. The Mollies are believed to have been present in the anthracite coalfields of Pennsylvania from at least the early 1870s. A legal self-help organisation for Irish immigrants existed in the form of the Ancient Order of Hibernians (AOH), but it is claimed that the Mollies existed as a secret organisation in Pennsylvania and used the AOH as a front. Many contemporaries, and historians, have doubted that the Mollies existed as any sort of organisation, rather being an underground movement motivated by personal grievances and not part of the struggle between organised labour and powerful industrial forces. Historians James Horan and Howard Swiggett were sceptical, but conceded: 'The difficulty of achieving strict and fair accuracy in relation to the Mollie Maguires is very great. Sensible men have held there never even was such an organization ... We do believe, however, that members of a secret organization, bound to each other by oath, used the facilities and personnel of the organization to carry out personal vendettas ...'[3]

The authorities and the bosses had few doubts, or scruples, however. Information passed from the Pinkerton detectives, intended only for the detective agency and their industrialist clients, was apparently also provided to vigilantes who ambushed and murdered miners suspected of being members, as well as their families.[4]

Coal mining had by the 1870s come to dominate north-eastern Pennsylvania, feeding America's insatiable appetite for energy, and powerful financial syndicates controlled the railroads and the coalfields. Coal companies had begun to recruit immigrants from overseas willing to work for less than the prevailing local wages. American-born workers, according to labour historian George Korson, 'were compelled to give way in one coal field after another, either abandoning the industry altogether for other occupations or else retreating, like the vanishing American Indian, westward'.

About 22,000 coalminers worked in Schuylkill County, Pennsylvania. Around 5,500 were children between the ages of seven and sixteen, who earned up to three dollars a week separating slate from the coal. Injured miners, or those too old to work at the face, were assigned to picking slate at the 'breakers', where the coal was crushed into a manageable size. Wages were low, working conditions were atrocious, and deaths and serious injuries numbered in the hundreds each year.

On 6 September 1869, a fire at the Avondale mine in Luzerne County killed 110 coal miners, the greatest mine disaster to that point in American history.[5] The families blamed the coal company for failing to finance a secondary exit for the mine: ' ... the mine owners without one single exception had refused over the years to install emergency exits, ventilating and pumping systems, or to make provision for sound scaffolding. In Schuylkill County alone 566 miners had been killed and 1,655 had been seriously injured over a seven-year period ...'[6] One of the first global relief efforts occurred after the Avondale disaster, with donations for the families of victims arriving from all over the world. Another result of the fire was the enacting of legislation establishing safety regulations for the coal-mining industry.

The disaster also caused thousands of miners to join the Workingmen's Benevolent Association (WBA), one of the first unions to represent coalminers in the US. The position of the union was made dramatically clear by representative Henry Evans during the subsequent inquiry: 'We intend to prove that it is wrong – WRONG – to send men to work in such mines, and that we have known it for long years; but we must work or starve; that is where the miners stand on this question, and we mean to use this occasion to prove it.' A reporter noted: 'A miner tells me that he often brought his food uneaten out of the mine from want of time; for he must have his car loaded when the driver comes for it, or lose one of the seven car-loads which form his daily work.'[7] As the bodies of the miners were brought up from the Avondale pit, WBA head John Siney climbed onto a wagon to speak to the thousands of miners who had arrived from surrounding communities: 'Men, if you must die with your boots on, die for your families, your homes, your country, but do not longer consent to die, like rats in a trap, for those who have no more interest in you than in the pick you dig with.'

The Panic of 1873 resulted in one of the worst depressions in the nation's history, caused by economic overexpansion, a stock crash and a decrease in the money supply; it went on for four years. By 1877 an estimated one-fifth of the nation's workingmen were completely unemployed, two-fifths worked no more than six or seven months a year, and only one-fifth had full-time jobs. The labour movement became militant and the Mollies were regarded as being in the forefront of unrest.

Franklin B. Gowen, the president of the Philadelphia and Reading Coal and Iron Company, which operated two-thirds of the mines in the region, as well as extensive railway interests, regarded as the wealthiest anthracite coal mine owner in the world, hired Allan Pinkerton's services to deal with the Mollies. Gowen radiated animal charm and he had been able to wheedle several millions out of English investors for his Philadelphia and Reading Railroad. A risk-taker, ever trying to expand, his ambition was boundless and many of his stockholders eyed him with distrust. British in his affectations, he had participated in the first game of cricket ever played at Pottsville, capital of anthracite, where he had been the district attorney as a young man after buying a substitute to serve in his place in the Union Army during the Civil War. His father, an emigrant from Northern Ireland, had been a sympathiser with the South and slavery, sending his son to a private school attended by the sons of plantation owners and the ironmasters of Schuylkill County. There is ample evidence that he saw himself as a hero who was to ride to national fame by his demonstration to the country's employers of the proper way of handling the growing labour problem.[8]

Gowen was hit hard by the depression and needed to rebuild his sagging prestige. He had borrowed millions of dollars to make the Reading Railroad one of the largest corporations the world had ever known, and he was horribly overextended. To regain the trust of his shareholders, he had to deal a deathblow to organised labour. In addition, an anti-monopoly league was being formed in which dealers were charging him with selling coal short-weight, withholding freight cars from rivals, delaying their shipments and conspiring to control production. He brooded that the primary source of his difficulties was the miners' union. Only by greatly reducing wages could he buttress his shaky financial position. But more than the miners' union, it was that group of young Irish miners in the Ancient Order of Hibernians who were standing in his way. It was they who opposed Siney when he talked of a reasonable attitude and arbitration instead of strikes and it was they who advocated strike rather than suffer a cut below the contract's minimum wage. If Gowen could get rid of the likes of Munley, Doyle, Kelly and the progressives they led in the miners' union, he would, he believed, be in the clear. At first he thought he would charge them with being Communists, and as late as 1875 he testified before a committee of the Pennsylvania legislature that the group was composed of foreign agents, 'advocates of the Commune and emissaries of the International'.[9]

He told Allan Pinkerton that the supposed Irish terroristic society not only dominated the region but most of the country. 'Wherever in the United States iron is wrought,' he said, according to the detective, 'from Maine to Georgia, from ocean to ocean – wherever hard coal is used as fuel, there the Molly Maguire leaves his slimy trail and wields with deadly effect his two powerful levers, secrecy and combination.' Pinkerton, duly convinced, demanded a $100,000 retainer and, once the money had been banked, told Gowen that the operative whom he would send into the coal fields must be a man who would have no more doubts than Gowen. For an ordinary operative might think that Gowen was engaged in 'persecution for opinion's sake' or that his plan of breaking the miners' union was only 'a conflict between capital on one side and labor on the other.'[10]

Pinkerton selected James McParland (sometimes called McParlan), a twenty-nine-year-old born in County Armagh, to go undercover against the Mollies. McParland arrived in New York in 1867 and had worked as a labourer and policeman, and then in Chicago as a liquor store owner until the 1871 Great Chicago Fire destroyed his business. It was only then that he became a private detective. The cold-eyed McParland, always ready for a party or a fight, had red hair, a sweet tenor voice, a large capacity for whiskey, and a past said to include a murder in Buffalo. His assignment was to join the Ancient Order of Hibernians and either get or manufacture evidence upon which militant union members could be identified and duly hanged. Since Gowen believed that the union miners were criminal conspirators, that trade unions themselves were criminal conspiracies, the Pinkerton operative was not to be particular as to how he settled with men believed to be beyond the law.

He was paid $12 a week plus generous expenses for the time. Using the alias 'James McKenna', he made Shenandoah his headquarters and soon claimed to have become a trusted member of the organisation.

McParland's assignment was to collect evidence of murder plots and intrigue, passing this information along to his Pinkerton manager. He also began working secretly with a Pinkerton agent assigned to the Coal and Iron Police. Although there had been fifty 'inexplicable murders' between 1863 and 1867 in Schuylkill County,[11] progress in the investigations was slow. There was 'a lull in the entire area, broken only by minor shootings'. For two years McParland travelled the coal fields but was unable to obtain any evidence of crime committed by the miners. He spent most of his time in saloons, occasionally joining in a brawl, always suggesting violence as the only course against the mine owners, and raising his voice in song. To his bosses, however, McParland wrote: 'I am sick and tired of this thing. I seem to make no progress.'[12]

McParland estimated that there were about 450 members of the AOH in Schuylkill County. McParland's biographer J. Anthony Lukas wrote: 'The WBA was run by Lancashire men adamantly opposed to violence. But [Gowen] saw an opportunity to paint the union with the Molly brush, which he did in testimony before a state investigating committee ... "I do not charge this Workingmen's Benevolent Association with it, but I say there is an association which votes in secret, at night, that men's lives shall be taken ... I do not blame this association, but I blame another association for doing it; and it happens that the only men who are shot are the men who dare disobey the mandates of the Workingmen's Benevolent Association."'

However, Molly Maguireism and full-fledged trade unionism represented fundamentally different modes of organisation and protest, and official statistics suggest that in the five-year existence of the WBA, the relations existing between employers and employees had greatly improved. The union had brought an end to the 'carnival of crime', and the leaders of the WBA were 'always unequivocally opposed' to the Molly Maguires.[13]

The union had attracted 30,000 members – 85 per cent of Pennsylvania's anthracite miners – but Gowen had built a combination of his own, bringing all of the mine operators into an employers' association known as the Anthracite Board of Trade. Gowen decided to force a strike and a showdown. F. P. Dewees, a contemporary and a confidant of Gowen, wrote that by 1873 'Mr. Gowen was fully impressed with the necessity of lessening the overgrown power of the "Labor Union" and exterminating if possible the Molly Maguires.' In December 1874, Gowen led the other coal operators to announce a 20 per cent pay cut.[14]

The miners went out on strike on 1 January 1875. From the first it was war, with Gowen bent on the absolute extermination of the unions. He and other operators unleashed a reign of terror, hiring and arming a band of mainly Welsh vigilantes called the 'Modocs' who joined the corporation-owned Coal and Iron Police in waylaying, ambushing and killing militant miners. Edward Coyle, a leader of the union and the Ancient Order of Hibernians, was murdered in March. Another member of the AOH was shot and killed by Modocs led by a mine superintendent. Patrick Vary, a mine boss, fired into a group of miners and, according to a later boast by Gowen, as the miners 'fled they left a long trail of blood behind them'. At Tuscarora, a meeting of miners was attacked; one miner was killed and several others wounded.

Another Pinkerton agent, Robert J. Linden, was brought in to support McParland while serving with the Coal and Iron Police. On 29 August 1875, Allan Pinkerton wrote a letter to George Bangs, Pinkerton's general superintendent, recommending vigilante actions against the Molly Maguires: 'The M.M.'s are a species of Thugs ... Let Linden get up a vigilance committee. It will not do to get many men, but let him get those who are prepared to take fearful revenge on the M.M.'s. I think it would open the eyes of all the people and then the M.M.'s would meet with their just deserts.'

On 10 December 1875, three men and two women were attacked in their home by masked men. The attack reflected the strategy outlined in Pinkerton's memo,[15] and the victims had been secretly identified by McParland as Mollies. One of the men was killed in the house, and the other two supposed Mollies were wounded but able to escape. A woman, the wife of one of the reputed Mollies, was shot dead.[16] McParland was outraged that the information he had been providing had found its way into the hands of indiscriminate killers. He protested in a letter to his Pinkerton supervisor that he did not object that Mollies might be assassinated as a result of his labour spying but he felt he should resign when it became apparent the vigilantes were willing to commit the 'murder of women and children', whom he deemed innocent victims. His letter stated:

> Friday: This morning at 8 A.M. I heard that a crowd of masked men had entered Mrs. O'Donnell's house ... and had killed James O'Donnell alias Friday, Charles O'Donnell and James McAllister, also Mrs. McAllister whom they took out of the house and shot

... Now as for the O'Donnells I am satisfied they got their just deserving. I reported what those men were. I give all information about them so clear that the courts could have taken hold of their case at any time but the witnesses were too cowardly to do it. I have also in the interests of God and humanity notified you months before some of those outrages were committed still the authorities took no hold of the matter. Now I wake up this morning to find that I am the murderer of Mrs. McAllister. What had a woman to do with the case—did the [Molly Maguires] in their worst time shoot down women. If I was not here the Vigilante Committee would not know who was guilty and when I find them shooting women in their thirst for blood I hereby tender my resignation to take effect as soon as this message is received. It is not cowardice that makes me resign but just let them have it now I will no longer interfere as I see that one is the same as the other and I am not going to be an accessory to the murder of women and children. I am sure the [Molly Maguires] will not spare the women so long as the Vigilante has shown an example.[17]

It was now clear that detectives' daily reports were routinely made available to Pinkerton clients in typed reports. Detective reports reveal that Pinkerton had been spying on miners for the mine owners in Scranton, where two WBA miners were killed by W. W. Scranton's men during the 1871 strike.[18] However, Benjamin Franklin, McParland's Pinkerton supervisor, persuaded him that the agency was innocent of such collusion. McParland retracted his resignation.

Frank Wenrich, a first lieutenant with the Pennsylvania National Guard, was arrested as the leader of the vigilante[19] attackers but released on bail. Another miner, Hugh McGeehan, a twenty-one-year-old who had been secretly identified as a killer by McParland, was fired upon and wounded by unknown assailants. Later, the McGeehan family house was attacked by gunfire.[20]

The miners, under the leadership of the AOH, began to fight back. Soon the state militia patrolled the coal patches, augmenting the Coal and Iron Police who were responsible to none but the corporations which paid them. The courts jailed mine leaders and on 12 May John Siney, who had favoured arbitration and had been against calling the strike, was arrested at a mass meeting of strikers in Clearfield County. An organiser for the miners' national association, Xingo Parkes, was also arrested, along with twenty-six other union officials, all on conspiracy charges. Judge John H. Owes instructed the jury that 'any agreement, combination or confederation to increase or depress the price of any vendible commodity, whether labor, merchandise, or anything else, is indictable as a conspiracy under the laws of Pennsylvania'. He sentenced them to up to one year's imprisonment.[21]

The union was nearly broken by the imprisonment of its leadership and by attacks conducted by vigilantes against the strikers. Gowen 'deluged the newspapers with stories of murder and arson' committed by the Molly Maguires. The press produced stories of strikes in Illinois, in Jersey City, and in the Ohio mine fields, all inspired by the Mollies. The stories were widely believed. In Schuylkill County the striking miners and their families were starving to death. A striker wrote to a friend: 'Since I last saw you, I have buried my youngest child, and on the day before its death there was not one bit of victuals in the house with six children.' Day after day, men, women and children went to the adjoining woods to dig roots and pick up herbs to keep body and soul together.

After six months, the strike was defeated, and the miners returned to work, accepting the 20 per cent cut in pay. 'We are beaten,' admitted John Walsh, a Civil War veteran and one of the union leaders who was exiled from the coal country, 'forced by the unremitting necessity of wives and little ones to accept terms which we have already told the Coal Exchange and the public, we would never under any other circumstances have been forced to accept.' And Joseph F. Patterson, another strike leader, later said, 'The organization was broken. The heart was knocked out of the brave fellows who built it up and sustained it.'

But those miners belonging to the Ancient Order of Hibernians continued the fight.[22] McParland acknowledged increasing support for the Mollies in his reports: 'Men, who last winter would not notice a Molly Maguire, are now glad to take them by the hand and make much of them. If the bosses exercise tyranny over the men they appear to look to the association for help. The defeat was humiliating, and much of the subsequent violence can be traced to the bitterness felt in the aftermath of a failed strike.'

McParland continued working undercover, and after months of little progress he reported plans by the 'inner circle' to assassinate a Welshman, Gomer James, who had shot and wounded one of the Mollies. Lukas wrote, 'November was a bloody month ... In the three days around 18 November, a Mollie was found dead in the streets of Carbondale, north of Scranton, a man had his throat cut, an unidentified man was crucified in the woods, a mining boss mauled, a man murdered in Scranton, and three men of [another Molly Maguires group] were guilty of a horror against an old woman, and an attempt to assassinate a Mollie by the name of Dougherty, followed and [Dougherty] at once demanded the murder of W. M. Thomas, whom he blamed for the attempt'.[23] On the last day of the month, with Gowen's strike breakers pouring in, the Summit telegraph office was burned and a train derailed. McParland advised his Pinkerton supervisor to send in uniformed police to preserve order.[24]

It was then that Gowen apparently decided that any measure was justified in dealing with those whom the courts had found were criminal conspirators in that they were trade unionists. Many operators furnished arms to their foremen. Militant miners often disappeared, their bodies sometimes being found later in deserted mineshafts. Gowen summoned McParland and told him that public sentiment was such that 'it was sufficient to hang a man to declare him a Molly Maguire'. McParland agreed to testify that all those whom Gowen wanted removed had freely and voluntarily confessed to him that they had committed various murders. His word was to be corroborated by various prisoners at various of the county's jails in return for their freedom.

By any moral standards it was a vile conspiracy, but the holdouts among the strikers were indeed activists. A plan to destroy a railroad bridge was abandoned due to the presence of outsiders. The Irish miners had been forbidden to set foot in the public square in Mahanoy City, and a plan to occupy it by force of arms was considered and abandoned. In the meantime, a messenger reported that W. M. 'Bully Boy' Thomas, the would-be killer of one of the Mollies, had been killed in the stable where he worked. McParland himself had been asked to supply the hidden killers with food and whiskey, according to the detective. His attackers, leaving him for dead on the stable floor, were not aware until two days later that he had survived.[25]

The Mollies allegedly planned to murder two nightwatchmen, Pat McCarron and Benjamin K. Yost, a Tamaqua Borough patrolman.[26] Jimmy Kerrigan and Thomas Duffy were said to despise Yost, who had arrested them on numerous occasions. Yost was shot as he put out a streetlight, which at that time necessitated climbing the lamp pole. Before he died, he reported that his killers were Irish, but were not Kerrigan or Duffy. McParland recorded that a Mollie named

William Love had killed a Justice of the Peace named Gwyther, in Giradville. Unknown Mollies were accused of killing saloon owner H. Gomer James while he was tending his Shenandoah bar. Then, McParland recorded, a group of Mollies reported to him that they had killed a mine boss named Sanger, and another man who was with him. Forewarned of the attempt, McParland had sought to arrange protection for the mine boss, but was unsuccessful, and McParland's true identity was subsequently uncovered.

When Gowen first hired the Pinkerton agency, he had claimed the Molly Maguires were so powerful they had made capital and labour 'their puppets'. When the trials of the alleged puppet masters opened, Gowen had himself appointed as special prosecutor.[27] The first trials were for the killing of John P. Jones. The three defendants, Michael J. Doyle, Jimmy Kerrigan and Edward Kelly, had elected to receive separate trials. Doyle went first, beginning 18 January 1876, and a conviction for first-degree murder was returned on 1 February. Kelly's trial began on 27 March and ended in conviction on 6 April 1876.[28]

The first trial of defendants McGeehan, Carroll, Duffy, James Boyle and James Roarity for the killing of Yost began in May 1876. Although Kerrigan had, along with Duffy, hated the nightwatchman enough to plot his murder, he nonetheless turned state's witness and testified against the union leaders and other miners. However, Kerrigan's wife testified in the courtroom that her husband had committed the murder. She said that she refused to provide him with clothing while he was in prison, because he had 'picked innocent men to suffer for his crime'. Gowen cross-examined her but could not shake her testimony. Others supported her amid speculation that Kerrigan was receiving special treatment due to the fact that McParland was engaged to his sister-in-law, Mary Ann Higgins.[29] A mistrial was declared due to the death of one of the jurors. A new trial was granted two months later, a trial in which Fanny Kerrigan did not testify. The five defendants were sentenced to death. Kerrigan went free.

The trial of Tom Munley for the murders of the mine foreman Thomas Sanger and William Uren swung entirely on the testimony of McParland despite the existence of an eyewitness account. The witness stated under oath that he had seen the murderer clearly, and that Munley was not the murderer. Yet the jury accepted McParland's testimony that Munley had privately confessed to the murder. As Gowen advanced to the jury rail to make his final plea in Munley's case, he must have known that he had to rise to real heights since there was scarcely any evidence against the defendant. He delivered a thunderous speech, quoted poetry and plays, and defied the Molly Maguires to kill him then and there if they dared. He told the jury:

> I feel, indeed, that if I failed in my duty, if I should shrink from the task that was before me, that if I failed to speak, the very stones would cry out. Standing before you now with the bright beams of victory streaming over our banners, how well I can recall the feeling with which I entered upon the contest, which is now so near the end. Do not think it egotism if I say with the hero of romance, 'When first I took this venturous quest I swore upon the rood, neither to turn to right nor left. For evil or for good ... Forward lies faith and knightly fame Behind are perjury and shame; In life or death I keep my word.'

It was magnificent, or so the jury apparently thought, and nothing could stand against it. Certainly not the life of an Irish miner. Munley was sentenced to death. Another four miners were put on trial and were found guilty on a charge of murder. McParland had no direct evidence but had recorded that the four admitted their guilt to him. Kelly was being held in a cell for murder, and he was reputedly quoted as saying, 'I would squeal on Jesus Christ to get out of here.' In return for his testimony, the murder charge against him was dismissed.[30]

On 21 June 1877, six men were hanged in the prison at Pottsvill, and four more at Mauch Chunk, Carbon County. State militia with fixed bayonets surrounded the prisons and the scaffolds. Miners arrived with their wives and children from the surrounding areas, walking through the night to honour the accused, and by 9 a.m. 'the crowd in Pottsville stretched as far as one could see'. The families were silent, which was their way of paying tribute to those about to die. The aged and impoverished father of Munley, who had walked 13 miles from Gilbertson, told his son that he knew he was innocent. Munley, soon to die with an air that reporters described as 'nonchalant and easy', asked after his wife. She was outside, weeping hysterically and shaking the locked prison gates, demanding admission. It was refused. She had arrived after six, it was said, the last moment for the admission of relatives. She seemed to go mad with grief, shrieking and flinging herself against the gate until she collapsed, crumpling to the ground outside the prison wall. Inside her husband had regained his composure and the chaplain later recalled that he 'had been a fine-looking man and that he showed no fear'.

All the condemned were handsome and young, freshly shaved, dressed in their best, and a prison guard told reporters: 'They looked like they were going to a wedding.' Each had in his lap a red rose. At 10.55 a.m., a creaking of the iron gates at the opposite end of the yard, reported the *Tribune*, 'caused all eyes to be turned there. Two minutes later two of the condemned men were brought out, McGeehan and Doyle. Their demeanour was one of entire self-possession. The degree of nerve of both men was extraordinary.' As they mounted the scaffold together they joined hands and a moment before the trap was sprung Doyle said to McGeehan, 'Hughie, let's die like men.' And so they all died.

The four hanged in Carbon were Alexander Campbell, John 'Yellow Jack' Donahue, Michael J. Doyle and Edward J. Kelly. They were executed for the murders of John P. Jones and Morgan Powell, both mine bosses, following a trial later described by local judge John P. Lavelle as a 'a surrender of state sovereignty. A private corporation initiated the investigation through a private detective agency. A private police force arrested the alleged defenders, and private attorneys for the coal companies prosecuted them. The state provided only the courtroom and the gallows.'

Campbell, just before his execution, allegedly slapped a muddy handprint on his cell wall, writing, 'There is proof of my words. That mark of mine will never be wiped out. It will remain forever to shame the county for hanging an innocent man.' Legend has it that despite many attempts to remove it, including building a new wall, the mark still remains today.[31]

In November, McAllister was also convicted. McParland's testimony in the Molly Maguires trials helped to send ten men to the gallows. The defence attorneys repeatedly sought to portray McParland as an *agent provocateur* who was responsible for not warning people of their imminent deaths. For his part, McParland testified that the AOH and the Mollies were one and the same, and the defendants guilty of the murders.[32] In 1905, McParland admitted that 'Kelly the Bum' hadn't just won his freedom for testifying against union leaders; he had been given $1,000 to 'subsidize a new life abroad' as well.

Ten more condemned, Thomas Fisher, John 'Black Jack' Kehoe, Patrick Hester, Peter McHugh, Patrick Tully, Peter McManus, Dennis Donnelly, Martin Bergan, James McDonnell and Charles Sharpe, were hanged at Mauch Chunk, Pottsville, Bloomsburg and Sunbury over the next two years. The last two of them, Charles Sharpe and

James McDonald, were hanged on 9 January 1879. The condemned men knew that it was probable that they had been pardoned by the governor and that it was likely that a messenger with a reprieve was on the way. But there was no delay in the executions; they were on a precise schedule. The condemned men neither begged nor flinched. The *New York World* reporter wrote: 'The demeanour of the men on the scaffold, their resolute and yet quiet protestations of innocence ... were things to stagger one's belief in their guilt. ... They were arrested and arraigned at a time of great public excitement, and they were condemned and hanged on "general principles".' He concluded his report by telling how a few minutes after the dead men had been cut from the dangling nooses, the governor's reprieve had arrived granting them life.[33]

Peter McManus was the last to be tried and convicted for murder at the Northumberland County Courthouse in 1878. This wave of judicial lynchings was greater than anything seen in the West. Hanging judge Roy Bean, the self-proclaimed 'Law West of the Pecos', sentenced just two men to death – and one of those escaped.

Joseph G. Rayback observed:

The charge has been made that the Molly Maguires episode was deliberately manufactured by the coal operators with the express purpose of destroying all vestiges of unionism in the area ... There is some evidence to support the charge ... the 'crime wave' that appeared in the anthracite fields came after the appearance of the Pinkertons, and ... many of the victims of the crimes were union leaders and ordinary miners. The evidence brought against [the defendants], supplied by James McParland, a Pinkerton, and corroborated by men who were granted immunity for their own crimes, was tortuous and contradictory, but the net effect was damning ... The trial temporarily destroyed the last vestiges of labor unionism in the anthracite area. More important, it gave the public the impression ... that miners were by nature criminal in character ...[34]

In 1979, Pennsylvania Governor Milton Shapp granted a posthumous pardon to John 'Black Jack' Kehoe after an investigation by the Pennsylvania Board of Pardons. The request for a pardon was made by one of Kehoe's descendants. John Kehoe had proclaimed his innocence until his death. The Board recommended the pardon after investigating Kehoe's trial and the circumstances surrounding it. Shapp praised Kehoe and the men called 'Molly Maguires' as 'martyrs to labor' and heroes in the struggle to establish a union and fair treatment for workers.[35]

Mine owners continued to use vigilantism, wage suppression, rigged courts, spying and propaganda to break unions and self-help groups like the AOH. In Scranton during the 1870s, five striking miners were killed, and an unknown number injured by militia and vigilantes.[36] In the 'Lattimer massacre', nineteen striking miners were shot dead and as many as fifty injured.

Richard Boyer and Herbert Morais wrote: 'When Franklin B. Gowen, once known as the King of the Reading Valley in Southeastern Pennsylvania, committed suicide in a lonely Washington hotel room in 1889 it was suggested by some that perhaps his brilliance had verged on insanity throughout his dramatic career. Others said he had taken his life when he felt his powerful but erratic brain losing its grip on reality. It was hinted then, as men discussed his solitary ending, that he had been near insanity even as his fevered eloquence sent nineteen Pennsylvania union miners to their deaths.'[37]

McParland, as we shall see, had a long and distinguished career.

3

The Great Upheaval

'we shall conquer, or we shall die.'

It was a classic exchange of fire alongside a railway track in 1877, but this was no Wild West shootout. A striking railwayman, William Vandergriff, seized a switch-ball to run a train full of troops onto a side track and stood guard as the train came to a stop. Militia man John Poisal jumped from the engine plate and tried to reverse the switch. The striker fired two shots at Poisal, one causing a slight flesh wound in the side of the head. The part-time soldier returned fire, shooting Vandergriff through the hip. Several other shots were fired at Vandergriff, striking him in the hand and arm. The arm would be amputated later that day, but to no avail – Vandergriff later succumbed to his wound.[1]

They were the first shots in what became known as the Great Upheaval, a showdown that has claim to have been America's first national strike as at its height it was supported by about 100,000 workers, shutting down nearly half of the US railway system. Over 100 people were killed in a few weeks and a thousand more were imprisoned. Millions of dollars' worth of damage was caused on the railways alone. The rich and the powerful genuinely feared that workers were rising in a revolution comparable to the Paris Commune just six years before. It was a time, wrote Irving Bernstein, of 'strikes and social upheavals of extraordinary importance, drama and violence which ripped the cloak of civilised decorum from society, leaving exposed naked class conflict'.[2]

A legacy exists today in the heavily fortified National Guard armouries constructed from the following year, urban fortresses

70

complete with gun loopholes, scattered across major towns and cities. They were built not to protect the people from foreign invaders, but to protect vested interests from popular revolt at home.

* * *

When the American Civil War ended, there was a boom in industrial construction, especially on the railroads, with roughly 35,000 miles of new track being laid from coast to coast between 1866 and 1873. Rail barons bribed congressmen for massive land grants, ruthlessly killed Native Americans and white homesteaders who stood in the way of national progress which they equated with their own profits, and demanded large amounts of capital investment. Speculators fed millions of dollars into the industry, causing abnormal growth and overexpansion. The surveying of the rail baron Jay Cooke's Northern Pacific Railway through Montana Territory was abandoned when army units led by drunken officers and the impetuous George Armstrong Custer failed to stop attacks by Sitting Bull's warriors.[3] Jay Cooke's bank, like many others, invested a disproportionate share of depositors' funds in the railroads, and became a federal agent in the government's direct financing of railroad construction. The impact on the nation's finances when the bank collapsed in September 1873 was huge, sparking a domino effect among other banks, temporarily shutting the New York Stock Exchange, and forcing over 5,000 businesses to close.[4]

The subsequent Long Depression, beginning in the US with the Panic of 1873 and lasting for over five years, was the longest in American history. Unemployment rose dramatically, reaching 14 per cent by 1876, including an estimated 1 million industrial workers. Wages overall dropped to 45 per cent of their previous level. Jeremy Brecher wrote: 'The wealthier classes observed these conditions and trembled ... Perhaps even more terrifying were the sullen, sallow faces of men, women and children, walking the streets with little in their stomachs and hardly a place to lay their heads.'[5] A bitter antagonism between workers and the industrial bosses escalated the tensions. Immigration from Europe was by now well underway, as was migration of rural workers into the cities, increasing competition for jobs and enabling companies to drive down wages and lay off workers. The precedent of the Paris Commune was constantly invoked, and a Workingman's Party was formed to, as it was widely promulgated, crush capitalism. The British traveller Goldwin Smith said that wealthy Americans were 'pervaded by an uneasy feeling that they were living over a mine of social and industrial discontent with which the power of the government, under American institutions, was wholly inadequate to deal; and that some day this mine would explode and blow society into the air'.[6]

The downturn had a devastating effect on the rail companies, shutting more than a hundred railroads in the first year and cutting construction of new rail lines from 7,500 miles of track in 1872 to 1,600 miles in 1875. Approximately 18,000 businesses failed between 1873 and 1875, in which year production in iron and steel alone dropped by 45 per cent. In 1876 alone, seventy-six railroad companies went bankrupt or entered receivership.[7]

The spark of revolution was provided on the railways with a 10 per cent pay cut, the second reduction in less than eight months, ordered by the boards of the Baltimore and Ohio Railroad Company (B&O). Railroad workers in the small railroad town of Martinsburg, West Virginia, had had enough. On 16 July 1877, workers in that town drove all the engines into the roundhouse and declared that no train would leave until the owners restored their pay. The local townspeople gathered at the railyard to show their support for the strikers. The local mayor tried to soothe the crowd but was shouted down, and when he ordered the arrest of strike leaders they simply laughed in his face. The police were powerless. No blacklegs could be found to drive the trains, and the police withdrew. The railyard was occupied by strikers to enforce the blockade.[8]

Trade unions were barely a factor in the dispute. Many of the new immigrant workers were Catholics, and their church had forbidden participation in secret societies since 1743, partially as a reaction against the anti-Catholicism of Freemasonry. An earlier attempt to call a strike against pay cuts on the Pennsylvania Railroad had collapsed because its embryonic union had been riddled with company spies, intimidated by the sacking of union and brotherhood members, and dogged by confusion and internal divisions. The B&O workforce realised they had no alternative but to act on their own, so the Martinsburg strike was impromptu with little organisation behind it.

Governor Henry M. Matthews sent in state militia units, the Berkeley Light Guards, to preserve the peace and restore train services. They boarded a cattle train which had previously been halted, their rifles loaded with ball cartridges. It was at this point that the incident occurred which took Vandergriff's life. The train's engineer and fireman disappeared, and many of the militia who were themselves railroad workers were reluctant to proceed. Calls for strike-breakers to drive the train were in vain. The officer in command telegraphed the governor to say he was helpless to control the situation, and the operation was abandoned.

The governor, determined to break the strike, ordered sixty Light Guards from the town of Wheeling. That proved to be another mistake. That town's box and can makers were already on strike and the townspeople fully supported the railwaymen. There was widespread talk of a general strike. When the Guards' train reached Martinsburg, it was met by a large but orderly crowd. The militia commander dared not use his men against the throng but marched them to the courthouse.

The B&O again pressed the governor for regular army troops. That was supported by the militia commander who wired from Martinsburg: 'The feeling here is most intense, and the rioters are largely cooperated with by civilians...' He added that any repetition of the day's events 'would precipitate a bloody conflict, with the odds largely against our small force'.[9] The Secretary of War referred to events in Martinsburg as 'an insurrection'. President Hayes duly sent 300 federal troops to the scene. They were bivouacked in the railway roundhouse and joined by the remaining militia. When 100 strikers stopped a train, their leader was arrested. Strike-breakers from Baltimore, backed by the military, were able to run some freight trains through the blockade. The strike seemed broken.

But workers in the surrounding area rallied behind the railwaymen. Striking boatmen on the Chesapeake and Ohio Canal, together with unemployed men, ambushed a freight train that had broken the Martinsburg blockade, forcing it to stop. The strike movement spread into Maryland and at Cumberland boatmen and rail men stopped another train and uncoupled the carriages. The train managed to steam away but at Keyser, West Virginia, a crowd took the crew off by force while soldiers looked on helplessly. Four miles away at Piedmont miners volunteered to stop further trains. They halted a train guarded by fifty regular troops.[10] A handbill was printed warning the B&O that 15,000 miners, local citizens, and 'the working classes of every state in the Union' would support the strikers, adding: 'Therefore let the clashing of arms be heard ... in view of the rights and in the defense of our families we shall conquer, or we shall die.'[11] As a result of such fraternal action, few trains sent from Martinsburg got as far as Keyser. At Cumberland one train was stopped by a crowd of migrant workers, boatmen and youths. When two of their leaders were arrested, they surrounded the mayor's house and carried off the prisoners shoulder-high.

Along the railroad negotiations between strikers and the B&O were unsuccessful, and Martinsburg set a pattern across various states – a strike in response to a pay cut, followed by failed attempts to break the blockade with military backup, with the wider population actively supporting the strikers. The strike spread to all divisions of the B&O and the firemen who had launched strike action were swiftly joined by engineers, brakemen and conductors. However, in some places the company found enough workers to reopen the lines, under the protection of the military and police. About forty men gathered at Camden Junction, 3 miles from Baltimore, and on the afternoon of 17 July, a west-bound train was thrown from the tracks at a switch in a suburb south of Baltimore. The engine caught fire and both the engineer and the fireman were severely injured. The strikers denied any involvement.

In Baltimore, police were dispatched to Camden Junction, Mount Clare and Riverside Station. Maryland Governor John Lee Carroll met with Vice President King of the B&O, along with a police commissioner who agreed to summon the National Guard. Bells were rung across the city to summon the militia, but once again the populace were largely behind the strikers. A strike leader said: 'The working people everywhere are with us. They know what it is like to bring up a family on 90 cents a day, to live on beans and corn meal week in and week out, to run into debt at the stores until you cannot get trusted any longer, to see the wife breaking down under privation and distress, and the children growing up sharp and fierce like wolves day after day because they don't get enough to eat.'[12] The *Sun* reported: 'One by one the shops have become wholly or partly silent, and very many men, especially in South Baltimore, are without work or the means of providing for their families. This state of affairs is confined not alone to railroad shops, but to other workshops, and a great deal of distress exists among the workingmen of all kinds.'[13]

On 18 July, the railroad strikers in Baltimore printed and circulated a list of their grievances:

They had submitted to three reductions of wages in three years; that they would have acquiesced in a moderate reduction; that they were frequently sent out on a trip to Martinsburg, and there detained four days at the discretion of the company, for which detention they were allowed pay but two days' time; that they were compelled to pay their board during the time they were detained, which was more than the wages they received; that they had nothing left with which to support their families; that it was a question of bread with them; that when times were dull on the road they could not get more than fifteen day's work in a month; that many sober, steady economical men became involved in debt last winter; that honest men had their wages attached because they could not meet their expenses; that by a rule of the company any man who had his wages attached should be discharged; that this was a tyranny to which no rational being should submit, and that it was utterly impossible for a man with a family to support himself and family at the reduced rate of wages.

Instructions were given to the regimental commanders of the Maryland National Guard to keep their men at the ready. General Barry, commander at Fort McHenry in Baltimore, received marching orders for seventy-five men to move to Martinsburg to address ongoing disturbances there. They departed by rail, and were joined by eight companies of federal troops from Washington, D.C.

By the end of 19 July, the strike had spread from Baltimore to Chicago. It involved multiple rail companies, and had grown to include a variety of mechanics, artisans and laborers. General violence threatened to break out in Pittsburgh and the city was blockaded. A committee representing the strikers departed Baltimore to ensure solidarity along the line in demanding $2 per hour. The city was peaceful, but anxious.

By Friday, 20 July, around 250 trains sat idle in Baltimore. The B&O requested that Governor Carroll move state troops from Baltimore to Cumberland, where the situation had deteriorated. That afternoon Brigadier General James R. Herbert was ordered to muster the troops of the 5th and 6th Regiments, Maryland National Guard, to their respective armouries in preparation. With knowledge that groups of workers had been dispersed along the lines to impede traffic, including the movement of troops, he issued a simultaneous declaration to the people of the state: 'I ... by virtue of the authority vested in me, do hereby issue this my proclamation, calling upon all citizens of this State to abstain from acts of lawlessness, and aid lawful authorities in the maintenance of peace and order.'[14]

Crowds had gathered at four different points in the city, and along the route it was believed the soldiers would take to embark on their trains. Mayor Ferdinand Latrobe read the riot act and ordered the crowds to disperse, but to no effect. Police commissioners ordered the closing of all barrooms and saloons. That evening, as many workers in the city were ending their shifts, the alarm was sounded to gather the troops of the 5th and 6th Regiments. It proved counterproductive as it attracted yet more people onto the streets to witness the unfolding spectacle.

Up to 250 men of the 5th Regiment mustered at their armoury on the corner of Fifth and Front streets. Each man was equipped with a Springfield breech-loading rifle, and twenty rounds of ammunition. They began their march toward Camden Station, intending to board a train to Cumberland.[15] Onlookers had gathered to watch the procession, and at first cheered the troops. But the mood turned ugly as the crowd were joined by 'a rough element eager for disturbance; a proportion of mechanics either out of work or upon inadequate pay, whose sullen hearts rankled; and muttering and murmuring gangs of boys, almost outlaws, and ripe for any sort of disturbance'.[16] The soldiers were attacked by crowds throwing bricks and stones and forced to halt with several casualties. They formed up across the width of the street, fixed bayonets and advanced toward their objective. Shots were fired at the troops, but all successfully moved through the crowd and to the station.

At the same time, the soldiers of the 6th Regiment began leaving their armoury on the second and third floors of a warehouse, with the only exit being a narrow stairway through which no more than two men could walk abreast. They were met by a jeering crowd of up to 4,000, some of whom hurled paving stones through the armoury windows. Additional police were sent for, but they too were forced to shelter alongside the soldiers.

Colonel Peters ordered three companies of 120 men of the 6th to march to Camden Station. They were again pelted with stones by the crowd who believed the soldiers had been issued with blank cartridges. The troops opened fire and the frightened crowd retreated. Given a temporary reprieve, the troops continued their march. They were then attacked in the rear and made to halt by the pressing of the crowd. Without orders, some soldiers fired on the crowd, killing one and wounding several. The mob shrank back, and the soldiers continued until they reached the offices of the *Baltimore American* newspaper where they stopped and, under orders, fired two volleys into the crowd, causing several fatalities. They were forced to halt a third time, and again fired on the crowd, killing two men and one boy, before moving on to the station. Meanwhile, the men of the 5th and 6th regiments met at Camden Station along with some 200 police. Governor Carroll and Mayor Latrobe, B&O Vice President King, General Herbert and his staff, and a number of police commissioners there decided that conditions were too dangerous to send any troops away to Cumberland.

The train intended for the transportation of the troops was ready for departure, but the crowd bombarded it with stones, disabling it, and driving off both its engineer and fireman. The tracks were torn up and by 10 p.m. the mob that had gathered at the station, and which filled the streets for several blocks, had swollen to around 5,000. The soldiers and police drove them to the far end of the station where they set fire to passenger cars, the dispatcher's office, and the roundhouse. Some firefighters dispatched to the scene were driven off, and others had their hoses cut when they attempted to set up their pumps, but under the protection of the police and soldiers the flames were extinguished. That night Governor Carroll requested federal assistance from President Rutherford B. Hayes, convinced by the day's events that the state forces were insufficient. The men of the 5th and 6th stayed at the depot throughout the night and into the next morning.

Sources differ on the total casualties that day. One account had ten militiamen killed, but others suggested that only one was killed and more than twenty seriously wounded. In their struggle to enter Camden Station, the 5th suffered sixteen to twenty-four casualties, none serious.[17] Between nine and twelve of the rioters were killed, and thirteen to forty injured. Through the early hours of that Saturday, many from the 6th Regiment deserted, until only eleven were left, who were then incorporated into the ranks of the 5th. Governor Carroll recalled: ' … the slender force at my command was incompetent to protect the city, or to carry a sense of security to those who had a right be secured …' That morning, all business remained suspended. The bars in Baltimore remained closed, and a guard of soldiers and police protected workers as they set about the task of repairing the tracks and restoring the station to operating order. Toward nightfall, a battery of artillery was stationed at the depot. In a proclamation President Hayes urged 'all good citizens ... against aiding, countenancing, abetting or taking part in such unlawful proceedings, and I do hereby warn all persons engaged in or connected with said domestic violence and obstruction of the laws to disperse and retire peaceably to their respective abodes on or before twelve o'clock noon of the 22[n]d day of July.'

After dark, a mob of 2,500 to 3,000 gathered at Camden Station, jeering the soldiers. The rioters injured several members of the militia, damaged engines and train cars, and burned portions of the station.[18] The crowd grew increasingly restless until the soldiers guarding the area around the depot were assaulted with stones and pistols once again. The sentinels were called in, the soldiers assembled, and the command given to prepare to fire. The crowd, by now familiar with what was to follow, dispersed. The troops fixed bayonets, and briefly struggled with the remnants who tried, but failed, to break the line. There was a brief exchange of gunfire. Police officers, backed by the bayonets of the soldiers, advanced on the crowd and each officer arrested one man, who was then taken into the station, disarmed, and held there. As a tactic it was largely successful, and the area around the station was largely cleared, though sporadic gunfire was heard throughout the night. Between 165 and 200 were detained. Four, including one police officer, were injured in the exchange of fire, and several who resisted arrest were beaten severely.[19]

At the foundry near the Carey Street Bridge a crowd of over 100 gathered and threatened to set fires. A contingent of the 5th arrived, and a volley fired over the heads of the crowd proved sufficient to dissuade further onslaughts. An unsuccessful attempt was made to burn a B&O transportation barge at Fell's Point and sixteen were arrested. That night, three separate attempts were made to set fire the 6th Regiment armoury which, with its first floor full of dry fabrics and other furniture-making material, was highly vulnerable to arson. None were successful. Just before midnight, 120 marines arrived at the station and reported to the governor, who ordered them to set about capturing the mob leaders. Governor Carroll telegraphed President Hayes that order had been restored in the city.

However, in the early hours of Sunday morning, a thirty-seven-car B&O train full of coal and oil was set ablaze. Fifty marines were dispatched to the scene. Those cars which had not yet caught fire were detached from those burning, and by the time the flames were extinguished between seven and nine cars had been destroyed at a cost of $12,000. The mills and lumber yard of J. Turner & Cate, near the Philadelphia Wilmington & Baltimore rail depot, were then set afire. The entire property, extending over a full city block, was destroyed.

The following morning, the first passenger trains left the city and continued running throughout the day. Shortly after, General Hancock arrived, followed by 360 to 400 federal troops from New York and Fort Monroe, who relieved those guarding Camden Station. They brought with them two 12-pounder artillery pieces. Around noon, General Abbot arrived with a battalion of around 100 engineers. As the group advanced toward the armoury of the 6th Regiment, where they were to be quartered, they were met by a crowd of 500. Jeers turned to missiles until one soldier, Private Corcoran, was struck in the head and wounded. Abbott gave orders that his men were to halt and fix bayonets, and the crowd scattered.

Throughout that day and the previous, up to 500 new special police were sworn in, doubling the size of the police force. Each was provided with a badge and a revolver. The recently arrived regulars brought the garrison of federal troops in the city to between 700 and 800, in addition to the police, newly appointed special police, and national guardsmen. The vessels *Powhatan* and *Swatara* were also on hand with their 500 marines. Court was held all that day in the southern district, and 195 charges of riot and seventeen charges of drunkenness were dealt with. That night the city was quiet. General Hancock was directed to move his men to Pittsburgh, where other riots were ongoing. Abbott's engineer corps took over the armoury and helped create a company of artillery armed with two howitzers, 2,000 rounds of ammunition, and 250 muskets. The governor and adjutant general put out a call for volunteers to fill two new regiments – the 7th and 8th – with 1,000 men each. General Howard was chosen to command the 7th, and General Charles E. Phelps the 8th. The following day those who were left of the original 6th Regiment would disband. The armoury of the 6th remained guarded by a single police officer.

Although widespread violence had ceased, a pronounced military presence in the city remained and the strikes continued. With freight transport via rail stopped, commerce in the city was forced to rely on supplies carried by water or those driven by cart. Dozens of ships remained idle in the harbour for lack of goods to transport, and stevedores remained out of work. The stoppage of coal threatened all manufacturing, and the gas supply on which the city depended for lighting. The *Sun* reported 3,000 draymen, 600 oil men, and 1,500 stevedores out of work due to the embargo. The stoppage of freight threatened the city's food supply.

On Thursday 26 July a committee from the engineers, firemen, brakemen and conductors met with Governor Carroll. They presented him with a list of their unanimously adopted demands. The governor said he had no power to satisfy them, but he assured them that he intended to enforce the law and put down violence by any means necessary. The committee in turn assured Carroll that they had no connection with the violence, but merely intended to stop work until their demands were met. Carroll replied: 'You have more to do than simply abstain from riotous proceedings. You must not stand behind riots and let violators of the law promote the destruction of property. You are responsible for the violence that has been done, whether you were actually engaged in it or not. You on your part must drive away from you the evil-disposed people who have done so much harm, and discountenance in the plainest way everything tending to violence.'

The next day, some railways throughout the country resumed traffic, though the B&O remained idle. B&O Vice President King published a reply to the demands of the strikers, saying that they simply could not be met for lack of work and low prices for hauling freight. He wrote: 'The experience of the last ten days must satisfy everyone that if freight trains are stopped on the Baltimore and Ohio Railroad, the city of Baltimore is not only deprived of the great commercial advantages which she has heretofore enjoyed, but the entire community is made to feel that all business must be seriously crippled and the price of all kinds of family supplies greatly increased.' Later that evening, the company said that while it would not negotiate on the matter of the 10 per cent wage reduction, it would 'be pleased to address itself to the investigation of any of the minor grievances of which the men complained'. A vote was taken and the company's proposals were rejected unanimously.[20]

A military force gathered at Camden Station in the morning of Saturday 29 July included 250 federal troops, 250 men of the 5th Maryland Regiment, and 260 policemen. Under this guard, freight traffic once again resumed in and out of Baltimore, and eight trains in total were sent out. Strikers were present, but peaceful, and some returned to work. As business resumed, stalled products poured through the city, including 4 million gallons of petroleum, 1.25 million bushels of wheat, 250,000 gallons of coal oil, 1,463 head of cattle, and 90 carloads of coal.

Those strikers who still held out declared that they would not interfere, but asserted that the company would be unable to find sufficient workers without them, and that by remaining united they could yet see their terms met. They were given notice to report to work on Monday 30 July or be sacked. Most chose discharge, but the company had little trouble in acquiring the workers needed to run the trains.[21]

On Wednesday 1 August, the *Baltimore American and Commercial Advertiser* summarised the situation:

> The strikers have gained absolutely nothing by the movement. The ten per cent reduction has been enforced by the four trunk lines, and the only concessions were those that might have been had for asking, without the loss of a single day's work. Such of the strikers as were caught committing criminal acts are now under arrest, and the great majority of the rest are most anxious to resume their places. Some of the railroad companies have discharged every man that took part in the strike, while others have only dropped the ringleaders, and have held out inducements to the others to return to work.

By the time peace was completely restored in the city, the cost to the state was $85,000. Later that year, the B&O agreed to a number of reforms including paying a crew a quarter of a day's pay if the train they were working was cancelled, and passes were to be given for working men who had long layovers. They were minor concessions, hard won.

However, the Great Upheaval was far from over, and a great deal more blood was shed. Across New York state there were strike actions in Albany, Rochester, Syracuse and Buffalo. Workers in industries other than railroads still attacked them because of how they cut through the cities and dominated city life. Pittsburgh, Pennsylvania, became the site of the worst violence of related strikes. Thomas Alexander Scott of the Pennsylvania Railroad, contemporarily described as one of the first robber barons, suggested that the strikers should be given 'a rifle diet for a few days and see how they like that kind of bread'. As in some other cities, local law enforcement officers refused to fire on the strikers. Several state militia units were ordered into service, including the 3rd Pennsylvania Infantry Regiment under the command of Colonel George R. Snowden.

By the morning of Saturday the 21st, it had become clear that many of the Pittsburgh police and local militia sided with the strikers. Many of the militia ordered to muster at the rail yards never arrived. Others stacked their arms. One officer reported: 'You can place little dependence on the troops of your division; some have thrown down their arms, and others have left, and I fear the situation very much.' Another said: 'Meeting an enemy on the field of battle, you go there to kill. The more you kill, and the quicker you do it, the better. But here you have men with fathers and brothers and relatives mingled in the crowd of rioters. The sympathy of the people, the sympathy of the troops, my own sympathy, was with the strikers proper. We all felt that these men were not receiving enough wages.'[22] The militiamen chatted to friends and relatives in the crowd, and shared out hardtack. There was a party atmosphere. A lawyer told one trooper: 'You may be called upon to clear the tracks down there.' The reply was: 'They may call me and they may call pretty damn loud before they will clear the tracks.'[23]

The *Pittsburgh Leader* quoted a 'representative workingman' to warn of trouble ahead:

This may be the beginning of a great civil war in this country, between labor and capital. It only needs that the strikers should boldly attack and rout the troops sent to quell them – and they could easily do so if they tried. The workingman everywhere should join and help. The laboring people, who mostly constitute the militia, will not take up arms to put down their brethren. Will capital, then, rely on the United States Army? Pshaw! These ten or fifteen thousand available men would be swept from our path like leaves in the whirlwind. The workingman of this country can capture and hold it if they will only stick together. Even if so-called law and order should beat them down in blood ... we would, at least, have our revenge on the men who have coined our sweat and muscles into millions for themselves, while they think dip is good enough butter for us.[24]

The crowd controlled the railroad switches and people rode the line through the city free of charge. Militia officers refused to clear the crossings with artillery. Adjutant General J. W. Latta ordered General Brinton along with his First Division, Pennsylvania National Guard, to report to Pittsburgh. Around 600 militia arrived late lunchtime, bringing two Gatling guns. Twenty rounds of ammunition were distributed to each man. A steel manufacturer warned railroad officials not to send in the newcomers against the strikers until his workforce was back on the factory floor. He said: 'I think I know the temper of our men pretty well, and you would be wise not to do anything until Monday. If there's going to be firing, you ought to have at least ten thousand men, and I doubt if even that many could quell the mob that would be brought down on us.' The railroad official replied: 'We must have our property.' He predicted that 'the Philadelphia regiment won't fire over the heads of the mob'. The scene was set for massacre and retribution.

Mid-afternoon, an order was given for the sheriff and his deputies, accompanied by National Guard troops, to move on the outer depot of the Pennsylvania Railroad and arrest the group's leaders. They found a crowd of 2,000, with another 10,000 nearby. Attempts to serve the sheriff's writs met with derision and the troops were sent forward to disperse the crowd. Some strikers attempted to take rifles from the soldiers, and one was injured in the advance of bayonets. Some protesters began to throw rocks and fire pistols at the troops; several men were injured, at least one seriously. The troops returned fire and used their bayonets, beginning with a single unordered shot, and continuing in a volley for nearly ten minutes. When the firing ceased, an estimated twenty men, women and children had been killed, with another twenty-nine wounded.[25] 'The sight presented after the soldiers ceased firing was sickening,' reported the *New York Herald*; the area 'was actually dotted with the dead and dying'. Rather than quell the uprising, these actions infuriated the strikers, who retaliated and forced the militia to take refuge in a railroad roundhouse.

One reporter wrote:

The news of the slaughter of the mob spread through the city like wild-fire, and produced the most intense excitement. The streets were rapidly crowded, and the wildest rumors prevailed. When the news reached the large number of rolling-mill hands and workmen in the various shops of the city, they were excited to frenzy, and by eight o'clock the streets of the central portion of the city were alive with them. A large crowd broke into the manufactory of the Great Western Gun-Works, and captured 200 rifles and a quantity of small-arms, and various other crowds sacked all the other places in the city where arms were exposed for sale, getting about 300 more. Among them were 1000 mill hands from Birmingham, on the south side.[26]

The rioters fell upon the rail yards, set fire to train cars and engines, and prevented any effort at extinguishing them, in some cases at gunpoint.

The city populace mobilised in fury against those responsible for the slaughter – the incomer militia and the railroad officials. Pittsburgh militiamen actively joined the crowd after seeing Gatling guns trundle towards the scene of the action. Workers rushed from the factory floor to collect pistols, muskets and even butcher knives from their homes. Six hundred men from nearby Temperanceville marched in with a full band and colours. Civil authority collapsed, and the mayor refused to call in the police or to address the crowd himself. The Philadelphia militia's success in clearing through the crowd at such cost was a pyrrhic victory as even trainmen who had previously refused to join the strike now refused to run the stalled trains. The strike remained unbroken.

A group of Philadelphia National Guard retreated and took refuge in the roundhouse at the train depot. Several thousand strikers surrounded the building. For a time, the mob avoided the position for fear of the garrison opening fire. The soldiers saw that a captured artillery piece was positioned within a hundred yards of the roundhouse; they concentrated fire around it to prevent the rioters using it. Fifteen men were killed around the cannon.

The soldiers' shooting initially dissuaded the attackers, but they soon regrouped, and returned fire with pistols and muskets. They eventually resolved to burn the roundhouse. As one member of the mob phrased it: 'We'll have them out if we have to roast them out.' Rail cars containing oil, coke, and whisky were set ablaze and rolled downhill toward the round house, which began to slowly burn.[27] But as evening approached, the crowd broke, and the troops made an orderly escape, pursued by up to 1,000 men, and under harassing fire. According to the legislative report in 1878, the National Guard forces 'were fired at from second-floor windows, from the corners of the streets ... they were also fired at from a police station, where eight or ten policemen were in uniform'. Three troops were killed during the march, as were some protesters. The pursuit broke off after the party crossed the Allegheny River; the troops continued to march until well into the following evening, when they bivouacked near Sharpsburg. The city's outraged population had indeed routed the military, but at a terrible cost – at least forty dead and many more wounded.

The burning of railroad property continued. By 7 a.m. on Sunday 22nd, the fires extended from Millvale Station to 20th Street. US Commissioner of Labor Carroll D. Wright later testified that riots were, in some instances, aided by agents of the railroad company, attempting to destroy aging and soon-to-be replaced cars that they could then charge to the county purse. Widespread looting continued. Hundreds were engaged in breaking into train cars and distributing their contents, with occasional assistance from police. The crowd stopped firemen saving a grain elevator even though it was not owned by the railroad, saying: 'It's a monopoly and we're tired of it.'[28] A burning rail car was run into the Union Depot and the building set alight. Looters turned their attention to the Cincinnati & St Louis Railroad, and when the goods there were carried away, it too was set on fire. The city fire department remained on duty throughout the conflagration, and concentrated their efforts on private property along Liberty Street, as they were continuously prevented by the mob from accessing the burning railroad facilities. By Monday morning 194 locomotives, more than 2,000 cars and all railroad buildings had been destroyed.[29]

Meanwhile, in Philadelphia, strikers battled local militia and set fire to much of Center City before Governor John Hartranft used federal troops to put down the uprising. Workers in Reading, Pennsylvania's third-largest industrial city at the time, also broke out into a strike. This city was home of the engine works and shops of the Reading Railroad, against which engineers had struck since April 1877. State militia shot sixteen citizens. Workers burned down the only railroad bridge offering connections to the west to prevent local militia from being mustered to actions in Harrisburg or Pittsburgh. Authorities used state militia, local police and the Pinkertons in an attempt to break the strike.[30] Reading Railroad management mobilised a private militia to shoot ringleaders.[31]

In the railroad town of Allegheny, on the pretext that the governor was outside the state, strikers announced that the state militia had no legal authority and proposed to treat them as a 'mob'. The strikers broke into the local armoury, dug rifle pits and trenches, set up patrols and warned 'civilians' to stay away.[32] They took over management of the railways and, for a time, the trains ran smoothly for the benefit of local people rather than shareholders. It was an effective transfer of power, copied in Columbia, Meadville and Chenago, Pennsylvania. In Buffalo, New York state, the militia was scattered by an armed crowd who seized and barricaded the Eric roundhouse.[33]

On 25 July, 1,000 men and boys, many of them coalminers, marched to the Reading Railroad Depot in Shamokin. They looted the depot when the town announced it would pay them only $1 a day for emergency public employment. A strike leader told a meeting: 'While it is hot we can keep the ball rolling.' The mayor, who owned coalmines, organised a city militia and called in seven companies of the National Guard. They marched through a tenement district to clear the tracks and were stoned by the occupants. The soldiers, without orders, opened fire and killed eleven people. As in Pittsburgh, the local people were enraged and fought back, wounding twenty with stones and bullets. They broke open an arsenal and took sixty rifles. The following day the companies which had conducted the massacre were again stoned and turned towards the crowd. A newly arrived body of troops told them: 'If you fire at the mob, we'll fire on you.'[34]

In Scranton, railway strikers held a mass meeting and resolved to demand a pay rise 'in order to supply ourselves and our little ones with the necessaries of life'. General Manager William Walker Scranton replied that same day, insisting that 'nothing in the world would give me more pleasure,' but continued: 'With the present frightfully low prices of iron and steel rails it is utterly impossible for us to advance wages at all ... Our steel works, as everybody knows, are now idle because we have no work to do there. Until the reduction of ten per cent on the 10th of this month there has been no reduction in your wages for nearly a year, while during that time there has been a falling off in the prices we get for iron and steel of over twenty-five per cent. I think you ought to consider these things fully and reflect whether the little work we can give you is not better than no work at all. I assure you when prices will warrant it we shall be very glad to pay wages in proportion.'

Mayor McKune created a force of armed special police to help maintain order, a 116-strong group named the 'Scranton Citizens'

Corps'.[35] McKune met on 27 July with representatives of the Brotherhood of Trainmen and the firemen and brakemen who agreed to return to work at their previous wages. Soon after, the mill workers returned to work, with assurances from W. W. Scranton. The Citizens' Corps assembled in the Forest & Stream Sportsman's Club and acquired 350 guns as well as ammunition.

Rumours spread that the strike was weakening. Volunteers took over the mine pumps, which had been abandoned by the miners, in order to prevent flooding of the tunnels. The Citizens' Corps prepared for a possible armed confrontation, drilled by those of its members who were Civil War veterans. The group used the mine company store owned by W. W. Scranton as their headquarters. A dispatch on 29 July summarised: 'The entire Lackawanna region is idle. Week before last this region sent nearly 150,000 tons of coal to market. Last week it did not send any ... The situation here is absolutely painful, and there is no knowing what moment an outbreak will occur.'

On 30 July, due to the efforts of Mayor McKune, who assured the strikers that railway traffic would resume, the strikers from the Delaware, Lackawanna & Western Railroad returned to work at their old wages. The miners scorned the capitulation of the railway workers. Governor Hartranft went from Harrisburg to Scranton with a force of militiamen and regulars. At breakfast time on 1 August, up to 5,000 strikers converged on an open space near the city's iron mills. An activist showed a forged letter claiming that Lackawanna Iron and Coal Company would reduce wages to 35 cents per day. The rumour spurred an angry protest, and the crowd moved against the Lackawanna Iron and Coal facilities. They routed other workers and injured some. In response, Scranton led an assembly of his own employees and the Citizens' Corps. McKune issued the proclamation: 'I hereby order all places of business to be immediately closed and all good citizens to hold themselves in readiness to assemble at my headquarters, at the office of the Lackawanna Iron and Coal Company, upon a signal of four long whistles from the gong at the blast furnaces.' The night passed relatively quietly. Two spies were apprehended hiding in a lumber box wagon, attempting to judge the strength and activity of the Citizens' Corps. They were questioned and released with assurances that the corps was well prepared for any attack. In the early morning an attack was attempted on W. W. Scranton's residence, but was averted by patrols.

The mayor confronted the crowd and urged them to halt but was knocked down. Cries went up from the crowd, 'The Mayor is killed!' but he escaped with the aid of a priest. The Citizens' Corps marched on, assailed with jeers of 'See the damn vigilantes! We'll take their guns!' Several were struck and knocked down by stones and clubs, with shouts of 'Go for their guns, they have only blank cartridges; kill the sons-of-bitches.' Pistols were fired and one of the posse was wounded in the knee.

Samuel Crothers Logan wrote:

> The storm which had been gathering for more than two hours burst at once, with a violence that threatened the sweeping of the whole city with destruction. A shout was raised: 'Go for the shops' and 'clean out the black-legs' [those who had returned to work during the strike]; and immediately the crowd began to move ... It was at once revealed, through the telescopes of the watchers all along the avenue, that these crowds were armed with clubs, which were shaken in the fury of violence. It was afterwards learned that a store down the valley had been robbed by men on their way to this meeting, showing that, at least some of them had come prepared for mischief.[36]

The corps, led personally by Scranton and armed with new rifles, killed four and wounded up to fifty more. Steven Phillips would die six days later from injuries sustained in the confrontation. Charles Dunleavy, Patrick Lane and Patrick Langan were killed at the scene. 'Seeing the attack at the rear, and the stones flying from the open lot, and hearing the crack of the pistol shots, the Mayor threw up his hands, waved a bloody kerchief with which he had wiped his face, and shouted, "Fire, Boys!" Whether the soldiers, or their sergeant, heard the command of the Mayor is more than doubtful. The men at the rear of the column, finding no alternative left them, opened fire "as by a single impulse".'[37]

Pennsylvania Governor Hartranft declared Scranton to be under martial law. On 2 August around 3,000 troops of the Pennsylvania National Guard First Division arrived from Pittsburgh under the command of Major General Robert Brinton. The troops arrested an estimated seventy activists *en route*, and forced those apprehended to repair places where the railroad tracks between the cities had been destroyed.

The Miner's Executive Committee opened a store for families, stocked by the donations of local businessmen and farmers, to relieve those who were suffering as negotiations to end the strike continued. A meeting of local businessmen at the Anthracite Club resolved that the men of the corps should be commended for their 'courageous efforts' in dispersing the mob and averting calamity, and that they would 'stand shoulder and purse if need be in their defense'. Governor Hartranft arrived in the city along with his staff and 800 men of the Pennsylvania National Guard Second Division, under the command of General Henry S. Huidekoper. W. W. Scranton wrote: 'The sullen determination of the strikers in the recent struggle is shown most forcibly by the fact that despite the powerful protection now here for those who desire to pursue their peaceful avocations, none of the miners have returned to work, and the mine pumps are still worked by the bosses and clerks in the employ of the companies ... They will be peaceable while the soldiers are here, but when they go away, they will have many a grievance to redress from their standpoint.'[38]

The Pennsylvania State forces were joined on 6 August by seven companies of US Regulars under Lieutenant Colonel Brennan, and on 9 August by the Third US Infantry Regiment under Lieutenant Colonel Henry Marrow. On 10 August, General Huidekoper and his state forces departed.

By 8 October, some of the miners of the Pennsylvania Coal Company, who were forced to join the strike by the actions of that July, resolved to return to work, but were prevented two days later when the only line of transportation for their coal was burned by the remaining strikers. By this point 'outrages' were being committed on a daily basis: 'Placing obstructions upon the railroads, burning buildings, firing upon watchmen and pump engineers at the mines, and the robbing of arms in the neighborhood.'[39]

On 11 October, W. W. Scranton convinced some to return to work in the Pine Brook mine, and posted a notice that any miner who did not do so the following day would no longer be employed by the company. Many did return, and worked under the guard of two companies of soldiers. That evening word came that a mob of some 500 were approaching the city with intent to 'fix the black legs' at Pine Brook. Men of the guard were assembled at the mine and stood guard till morning. Every night following the 12th, at the request of the mayor, a forty-man garrison stood at the ready. On 16 October the miners held a meeting and unanimously voted to return to work. They did so beginning the next day, having won nothing in concessions.[40]

A coroner's jury indicted twenty-two members of the Citizens' Corps on charges of 'wilful murder'. The arrest warrants were placed in the custody of constables, with orders to execute them. General Huidekoper dispatched troops to take control of the prisoners. This was done primarily to ensure the safety of the men, as it was believed that those who had been in the mob, and compatriots of those slain, intended to do them harm. As W. W. Scranton wrote of the situation: 'They hold that we are guilty of murder, and with their aldermanic jury's verdict to back them, they would hold a court of Judge Lynch and hang the unfortunate one of us who got into their clutches without an hour's delay, providing they didn't first tear him to pieces.' The accused were transferred to the custody of the mayor and sheriff and taken by train to appear before the court in Wilkes-Barre, Pennsylvania.[41] Transportation by wagon was believed to be too dangerous. Again, as W. W. Scranton phrased it, 'the whole neighborhood is filled with Molly Maguires'.

Each man was subsequently released 10 August on $3,000 bail.[42] The charge of murder was later amended to manslaughter by grand jury indictment. The trial was convened 26 November under Judge Harding, with the widow of Patrick Langan, one of those slain on 1 August, named as prosecutor. Of the twenty subpoenaed by the prosecution to bear witness to the peaceful nature of the protest, only six appeared to testify. Three admitted to seeing violence committed by the mob prior to the shooting. Many more testified on behalf of the accused. In his closing remarks for the defence, Stanley Woodward concluded: 'We therefore hold that there was a riot, and that these men here charged were in the full heroic performance of their duties as citizens when this unfortunate event occurred. But the blood of these victims must be upon their own heads.'[43] That day the jury returned verdicts of not guilty on all charges.

W. W. Scranton filed libel suits in 1879 against Aaron Augustus Chase, editor of the *Scranton Daily Times*, and state Judge William Stanton. The suits were related to 'inflammatory articles' published in August 1878, charging W. W. Scranton with the 'crime of murder' during the 1877 strike. Stanton had been sitting judge in 1877 and was arrested for libel in the Scranton case after being implicated by witnesses; he was alleged to have written an 'incendiary' piece in the *Advocate*, 'calculated to incite the killing of Mr. Scranton'.[44]

Two separate trials were held: in September 1879 Chase was found guilty and sentenced to a $200 fine and thirty days' imprisonment. Stanton was acquitted in his own trial, but was forced to resign from the judgeship. One observer stated that 'the one great trouble here in Scranton is our population, an excess of miners for the work to be done'.[45]

Jeremy Brecher wrote: 'By now, the movement was no longer simply a railroad strike. With the battles between soldiers and crowds drawn from all parts of the working population, it was increasingly perceived as a struggle between workers as a whole and employers as a whole. This was now reflected in the rapid development of general strikes.'[46] Around Pittsburgh, workers joined in enthusiastically. In McKeesport the strike spread from tube workers to workers at a rolling mill, a car works and a planning mill. They moved on to Andrew Carnegie's giant steelworks where the workers downed tools and joined them.[47] In Buffalo, New York, a general strike closed tanneries, hog yards, canal works, coal yards, mills and a nut-and-bolt factory. Factories and shops were shuttered in Harrisburg, Pennsylvania. In Columbus a crowd shouting 'Shut up or burn up' closed mills and clay and pipe works.

Rail traffic in Chicago was paralyzed when angry mobs of unemployed citizens wreaked havoc in the rail yards, shutting down both the Baltimore and Ohio and the Illinois Central railroads. Soon, other railroads throughout the state were brought to a standstill, with demonstrators shutting down railroad traffic in Bloomington, Aurora, Peoria, Decatur, Urbana and other rail centres throughout Illinois. In sympathy, coal miners in the pits at Braidwood, LaSalle, Springfield and Carbondale went on strike as well. In Chicago, the Workingman's Party organised demonstrations that drew crowds of 20,000 people.

Judge Thomas Drummond of the Court of Appeals for the Seventh Circuit, who was overseeing numerous railroads that had declared bankruptcy, ruled that 'a strike or other unlawful interference with the trains will be a violation of the United States law, and the court will be bound to take notice of it and enforce the penalty'. Drummond told federal marshals to protect the railroads, and asked for federal troops to enforce his decision: he subsequently had strikers arrested and tried them for contempt of court.[48]

The mayor of Chicago, Monroe Heath, recruited 5,000 men as volunteer militia, asking for help in restoring order. They were partially successful, and shortly thereafter were reinforced by the arrival of the National Guard and federal troops, mobilised by the governor. On 25 July, violence between police and the mob erupted, with events reaching a peak the following day. These blood-soaked confrontations between police and enraged mobs are known as the Battle of the Viaduct as they took place near the Halsted Street viaduct. The headline of the *Chicago Times* screamed, 'Terrors Reign, The Streets of Chicago Given Over to Howling Mobs of Thieves and Cutthroats'. Order was finally restored. An estimated twenty men and boys died, none of whom were law enforcement or troops; scores more were wounded; and the loss of property was valued in the millions of dollars.

On 21 July, disgruntled workers in the industrial rail hub of East St Louis, Illinois, halted all freight traffic, with the city remaining in the control of the strikers for almost a week. The local Workingman's Party led a group of approximately 500 men across the Missouri River in an act of solidarity with the nearly 1,000 workers on strike. The strike on both sides of the river was ended after the governor appealed for help and gained the intervention of some 3,000 federal troops and 5,000 deputised special police. Bosses organised reliable employees into armed units. These forces killed at least eighteen people in skirmishes around the city and on 28 July they took control of the Relay Depot and arrested around seventy strikers.

The general strike reached the South, often starting with black workers and spreading to whites.[49] Rail workers in Marshall, Texas, were supported by black longshoremen in nearby Galveston. Fifty black sewer workers in Galveston struck for more pay and were in turn supported by whites. Both strikes were, in the short term at least, successful.

But overall the strikers failed to hold what they won. Brecher wrote: 'Having shattered the authority of the status quo, they faltered and fell back, unsure of what to do. Meanwhile, the forces of law and order – no longer cowering in the face of overwhelming force – began to organize.'[50] All strikes lost momentum when President Hayes sent federal troops from city to city. The federal forces were stretched because most of the army was tied up suppressing Native American uprisings in New Mexico and the Dakotas, and pursuing Chief Joseph's Nez Pierces towards the Canadian border. The enlisted men had not been paid for months and many, having been driven into the army by unemployment, were sympathetic to working white men. But there were no mutinies, and the army succeeded where militia had failed. The troops suppressed strike after strike, until at last, approximately forty-five days after it had started, it was over. President Hayes noted in his diary: 'The strikers have been put down by *force*.'[51]

No complete accounting of the economic losses caused by this strike exists. It is known that the engineers' and firemen's brotherhoods lost approximately $600,000 over the forty-five days of the strike. The Burlington Railroad suffered losses of at least $2.1 million. Strikers in Pittsburgh burned in total thirty-nine buildings, 104 engines, forty-six to sixty-six passenger cars, and between 1,200 and 1,383 freight cars. Damage estimates ranged from $5 million to $10 million.[52]

Brecher wrote: 'The Great Upheaval was in the end thoroughly defeated, but the struggle was by no means a total loss. Insofar as it aimed at preventing the continued decline of workers' living standards, it won wage concessions in a number of cases and undoubtedly gave pause to would-be wage-cutters to come, for whom the explosive force of the social dynamite with which they hampered had now been revealed. Insofar as it aimed at a workers' seizure of power, its goal was chimerical, for the workers as yet formed only a minority in a predominantly farm and middle-class society. But the power of workers to virtually stop society, to counter the forces of repression, and to organise co-operative action on a vast scale was revealed in the most dramatic form.'[53]

Union organisers planned for their next battles while politicians and business leaders took steps to prevent a repetition of the chaos. Unions became better organised as well as more competent, and the number of strikes increased. The Knights of Labor grew to be a national organisation of predominately Catholic workers, numbering 700,000 by the early 1880s. During that decade nearly 10,000 strike actions and lockouts took place. In 1886 alone nearly 700,000 workers went on strike. Business leaders strengthened their opposition to the unions, often firing men who tried to organize or join them. Nonetheless, the labour movement continued to grow.

Many states enacted conspiracy statutes. States formed new militia units and constructed National Guard armouries in numerous industrial cities. For workers and employers alike, the strikes had shown the power of workers in combination to challenge the status quo. A state militiaman in Pittsburgh, ordered to break the 1877 strike, pointed out that the workers were driven by 'one spirit and one purpose among them – that they were justified in resorting to any means to break down the power of the corporations'. Attempts to utilise local militia to quell violent outbreaks in 1877 highlighted their ineffectiveness, and in some cases their propensity to side outright with strikers and rioters. In response, as earlier riots in the mid-1800s had prompted the modernisation of police forces, the violence of 1877 provided the impetus for the formation of the modern National Guard, 'to aid the civil officers, to suppress or prevent riot or insurrections'.

* * *

Seventeen years later history came close to repeating itself. The Pullman Strike pitted the newly formed American Railway Union (ARU) against the Pullman Company, the main railroads, and the federal government under President Grover Cleveland and shut down much of the nation's freight and passenger traffic west of Detroit.

The conflict began in the 'company town' of Pullman, Chicago, on 11 May 1894 when nearly 4,000 factory employees of the Pullman Company began a wildcat strike in response to recent reductions in wages. The owner, industrialist George Pullman, aimed to hire African Americans to undercut wages even further[54] without reducing the rents paid on company-owned homes. Pullman owned pretty much everything in the town – homes, land, churches and stores. The minister of the local Methodist-Episcopal church recorded: 'After deducting rent the men invariably had only from one to six dollars or so on which to live for two weeks. One man had a pay check in his possession of two cents after paying rent ... He has it framed.'[55] When the company laid off workers and lowered wages, it did not reduce rents – the company refused to let their workers buy or own their own homes, while it also levied exorbitant rates on water and gas supplies – and the workers called for a strike even though they had not yet formed a union. Founded in 1893 by Eugene V. Debs, the ARU was an organisation of unskilled railroad workers designed to alleviate workers' sufferings by uniting them. Debs put it simply: 'The forces of labor must unite. The dividing lines must grow dimmer day by day until they become unperceptible (*sic*), and then labor's hosts marshalled under one conquering banner, shall march together, vote together and fight together, until working men shall receive and enjoy all the fruits of their toil.'[56]

Debs brought in ARU organisers to Pullman and signed up many of the disgruntled factory workers. When the company refused recognition of the ARU or any negotiations, ARU called a strike against the factory, but it showed no sign of success.[57] To win, Debs called a massive boycott against all trains that carried a Pullman car, starting on June 26, 1894. Within four days, 125,000 workers on twenty-nine railroads had 'walked off' the job rather than handle Pullman cars.[58] All 26 rail roads out of Chicago were paralyzed. The strike at its peak involved some 260,000 workers in 27 states and territories, of whom around half were non-ARU members who came out in sympathy. The Baltimore and Ohio and the Big Four Railroad could move barely a tenth of their normal traffic. Debs wrote later that the strike was effectively won within four days as far as beating the railroad companies was concerned, leaving 'the combined corporations paralyzed and helpless.'[59]

But the Railroad Brotherhoods and the American Federation of Labor (AFL) opposed the boycott, and the General Managers Association of the railroads coordinated the opposition. The railroads began hiring strike-breakers, which increased hostilities. Many black workers were recruited and crossed picket lines, as they feared that the racism expressed by the ARU would lock them out of another labour market. This added racial tension to the union's predicament.[60]

On 29 June 1894, Debs hosted a peaceful meeting to rally support for the strike from railroad workers at Blue Island, Illinois. Afterward, groups within the crowd became enraged and set fire to nearby buildings and derailed a locomotive.[61] Elsewhere, sympathy strikers prevented transportation of goods by walking off the job, obstructing railroad tracks, or threatening and attacking strike-breakers. This increased the demand for federal action to end a crisis which dovetailed with the ongoing miners' strike. The *New York Times* regarded it as 'the greatest battle between labor and capital that has ever been inaugurated in the United States', while the *Chicago Tribune* said that it had 'attained the dignity of an insurrection'.

Under direction from President Grover Cleveland, US Attorney General Richard Olney set out to crush the strike. Olney had been a railroad attorney and continued to receive a $10,000 retainer from the Chicago, Burlington and Quincy Railroad which was higher than his official $8,000 salary. Olney obtained an injunction in federal court barring union leaders from supporting the strike and demanding that the strikers cease their activities or face being fired. Olney told reporters: 'We have been brought to the ragged edge of anarchy and it is time to see whether the law is sufficiently strong to prevent this condition of affairs.' Debs and other leaders of the ARU ignored the injunction, and federal troops were called up to enforce it, overriding the objections of the Illinois governor. Debs called a general strike of all union members in Chicago, but this was opposed by Samuel Gompers, head of the AFL, and other established unions, and it failed.[62]

Until federal troops arrived in Chicago, the strike had been almost entirely peaceful. Debs and other leaders had warned that violence would play into the hands of the companies. But another ARU official warned that 'the very sight of a blue coat arouses their anger; they feel it is another instrument of oppression that has come, and they are liable to do things they would not do if the blue coats were kept away'.[63] Debs himself said: 'The first shot fired by the regular soldiers at the mob here will be the signal for a civil war. I believe that as firmly as I believe in the ultimate success of our course. Bloodshed will follow, and 90% of the people of the US will be arrayed against the other 10%.'[64]

On the night of 4 July crowds gathered to overturn boxcars and destroy railroad property. Most were not railway workers but the unemployed and immigrants of the general working class. Their numbers swelled the following day and around 10,000 congregated at the stockyards and moved up the Rock Island Line. That night a fire destroyed seven structures at the World's Columbian Exhibition. The morning after that an Illinois Central railroad agent shot two members of the crowd. The crowd retaliated by burning 700 cars at the Panhandle yards, in total causing $340,000 worth of damage.[65] Armed forces occupying Chicago totalled 14,000, including federal troops, state militia and deputy marshals. During mayhem which flared across the city, they killed up to thirty people and seriously wounded fifty-three. On 7 July National Guardsmen, after having been assaulted, fired into a mob, killing at least four people and wounding many others. The bloodshed continued when two more people were killed by troops in Spring Valley, Illinois.

City by city, the federal forces broke the ARU efforts to shut down the national transportation system. Thousands of US Marshals and some 12,000 army troops, commanded by Brigadier General Nelson Miles, took action. President Cleveland wanted the trains moving again, based on his legal, constitutional responsibility for the mails. His lawyers argued that the boycott violated the Sherman Antitrust Act, and represented a threat to public safety. The arrival of the military and the subsequent deaths of workers in violence led to further outbreaks of violence.[66]

News reports and editorials depicted the boycotters and strikers as foreigners who contested the patriotism expressed by the militias and troops involved, as numerous recent immigrants worked in the factories and on the railroads. The editors warned of mobs, aliens, anarchy and defiance of the law. Debs was arrested on federal charges, including conspiracy to obstruct the mail as well as disobeying an order directed to him by the Supreme Court to stop the obstruction of railways and end the boycott. He was defended by Clarence Darrow who argued that it was the railways, not Debs and his union, that met in secret and conspired against their opponents. Sensing that Debs would be acquitted, the prosecution dropped the charge when a juror took ill. Although Darrow also represented Debs at the United States Supreme Court for violating the federal injunction, Debs was sentenced to six months in prison. The ARU then dissolved.[67]

The Pullman workers held out, even after militia were sent in as guards at the works. But once the wider railroad strike was defeated, owner Pullman rehired workers on his own terms under the gun-barrels of the militia.[68] In the strike's aftermath, however, the state ordered the company to sell off its residential holdings so that it could no longer keep its stranglehold on rents. In the decades after its boss died (1897), Pullman remained the area's largest employer before closing in the 1950s.

While serving his six-month term in the jail at Woodstock, Debs and his ARU comrades received a steady stream of written material from socialists around the country. He recalled several years later: '... I began to read and think and dissect the anatomy of the system in which workingmen, however organised, could be shattered and battered and splintered at a single stroke.' Debs was visited in jail by Milwaukee socialist newspaper editor Victor Berger, who 'came to Woodstock, as if a providential instrument, and delivered the first impassioned message of Socialism I had ever heard'.[69] Berger left him a copy of *Das Kapital* and 'prisoner Debs read it slowly, eagerly, ravenously'.[70] Debs emerged from jail at the end of his sentence a changed man. Following his release from jail in 1895, Debs became a committed advocate of socialism, helping in 1897 to launch the forerunner of the Socialist Party of America. He ran for president in 1900 for the first of five times as head of the Socialist Party ticket. He died in 1926. In 1894, in an effort to conciliate organised labour after the strike, President Grover Cleveland and Congress designated Labor Day as a federal holiday. Legislation for the holiday was pushed through Congress six days after the strike ended.[71]

And what of Jay Cooke, the devout Episcopalian former rail baron whose greed had kick-started the depression and subsequent mayhem? By 1880 Cooke had met all his financial obligations, and through an investment in the Horn Silver Mine in Utah had again become wealthy. He died in 1905, renowned as a philanthropist for founding several churches and a girls' school.

4

The Haymarket Affair

'many voices raised to justify a dark deed'

In November 1887, a twenty-year-old Chicago newspaper sketch artist called Art Young was filled with trepidation about being sent to draw the mass hanging of supposed anarchists and bombers. Years later he wrote: 'They were all young men, except Fielden who appeared to be in his forties. Even the beard worn by Schwab and Lingg's moustache could not disguise their youthfulness. And now word came of an explosion in the jail – that Lingg had put a bomb into his mouth and lighted the fuse and was dying. I was chilled with the horror of the story as details kept coming in. Suffering untold agony with his face terribly mutilated, Lingg remained conscious while three physicians worked over him, and lived six hours.'[1] It was one way of escaping the scaffold and the noose.

It was also an extraordinary footnote in what became known as 'The Haymarket Affair', or 'The Frame-Up'. The bloody events that led up to the suicide and executions proved a pivotal moment for the US labour movement and still draw controversy today.

* * *

After the Great Depression, Chicago was a magnet for thousands of German and Bohemian immigrants employed at about $1.50 a day for sixty hours during a six-day work week.[2] Attempts to fight for better conditions were met with sackings, lock-outs and blacklisting. Private security forces used ethnic tensions to divide and rule. They were in turn opposed by socialist and anarchist organisations during the economic slowdown up to 1886, and soon numbered several thousand mostly immigrant, workers who read, or contributed to, the German-language newspaper *Arbeiter-Zeitung*, or Workers' Times, edited by August Spies, a thirty-year-old former upholsterer turned radical labour activist. Some anarchists armed themselves with guns and explosives. Such militants believed that the seizure of major industrial plants would spark a popular revolution.[3]

In October 1884, a convention of the Federation of Organized Trades and Labor Unions set 1 May 1886 as the deadline for a standard eight-hour working day. They prepared a general strike as the deadline approached. On the appointed day thousands walked out, 10,000 in Milwaukee alone.[4] In Chicago, the centre of agitation, up to 40,000 workers laid down their tools, and many more supported rallies, including a march on the city's lumber yards.[5]

On 3 May, striking workers gathered near Chicago's McCormick Harvesting Machine Company plant when unionised moulders had been locked out since early February. The mainly Irish American workers had come under attack from Pinkerton guards during an earlier strike action in 1885. Strike-breakers were under protection from a garrison of 400 police officers. Half of the replacement workers defected to the general strike on 1 May, and McCormick workers continued to maintain strong picket lines.

Speaking to a rally outside the plant, Spies told them to 'hold together, to stand by their union, or they would not succeed'.[6] When the end-of-the-workday bell sounded, however, a group of workers surged to the gates to confront the strike-breakers. Despite calls for calm by Spies, the police fired on the crowd. Two McCormick workers were killed (although some newspaper accounts said there were six fatalities). Spies would later testify, 'I was very indignant. I knew from experience of the past that this butchering of people was done for the express purpose of defeating the eight-hour movement.'

Outraged local anarchists quickly printed and distributed flyers calling for a rally the following day at Haymarket Square, a bustling commercial district. Printed in German and English, the fliers claimed that the police had murdered the strikers on behalf of business interests. The first batch of flyers contain the words 'Workingmen Arm Yourselves and Appear in Full Force!' Spies insisted he would not speak at the rally unless the words were removed from the flier. All but a few hundred of the fliers were destroyed, and new flyers were printed without the offending words. More than 20,000 copies of the revised flyer were distributed.[7]

The rally began peacefully under a light rain on the evening of 4 May. Spies and other leaders spoke from the bed of an open wagon to a crowd estimated variously between 600 and 3,000. A large number of police officers watched from nearby. Spies said: 'There seems to prevail the opinion in some quarters that this meeting has been called for the purpose of inaugurating a riot, hence these warlike preparations on the part of so-called "law and order". However, let me tell you at the beginning that this meeting has not been called for any such purpose. The object of this meeting is to explain the general situation of the eight-hour movement and to throw light upon various incidents in connection with it.'[8]

After an hour of speeches, the crowd was so calm that Mayor Carter Harrison, who had stopped by to watch, walked home early. The British socialist Samuel Fielden delivered a brief address. Many of the crowd had already left as the weather was deteriorating. A reporter alleged that Fielden's words grew 'wilder and more violent as he proceeded'.[9] At about 10.30 p.m., just as Fielden was finishing his speech, police arrived *en masse*, marching in formation towards the speakers' wagon, and ordered the rally to disperse.[10] Fielden insisted that the meeting was peaceful. Police Inspector John Bonfield proclaimed: 'I command you [addressing the speaker] in the name of the law to desist and you [addressing the crowd] to disperse.'

A home-made bomb – dynamite encased in brittle metal – was thrown into the path of the advancing police.[11] Its fuse briefly sputtered, then the bomb exploded, killing policeman Mathias J. Degan instantly. Shrapnel mortally wounded six other officers. Art Young wrote: 'From above or behind the wagon a whizzing spark; a tremendous explosion; many policemen falling; their comrades firing into the panic-stricken crowd, killing and wounding.'[12] Witnesses indeed later insisted that immediately after the blast there was a flurried exchange of gunshots between police and demonstrators.[13] Accounts vary widely as to who fired first and whether any of the crowd fired at the police. There is evidence that the police fired on the fleeing demonstrators, reloaded and then fired again, killing four and wounding as many as seventy people. Inspector Bonfield wrote that he 'gave the order to cease firing, fearing that some of our men, in the darkness might fire into each other'. An anonymous police official told reporters: 'A very large number of the police were wounded by each other's revolvers. ... It was every man for himself, and while some got two or three squares away, the rest emptied their revolvers, mainly into each other.'[14] A *New York Times* article, headlined 'Anarchy's Red Hand', read: 'The villainous teachings of the Anarchists bore bloody fruit in Chicago tonight and before daylight at least a dozen stalwart men will have laid down their lives...'[15]

In all, seven policemen and at least four workers were killed. Another policeman died two years after the incident from complications related to injuries received on that day. About sixty policemen were wounded in the incident. Police captain Michael Schaack later wrote that the number of wounded workers was 'largely in excess of that on the side of the police'.[16] The *Chicago Herald* described a scene of 'wild carnage' and estimated at least fifty dead or wounded civilians lay in the streets.[17] It is unclear how many civilians were wounded since many were afraid to seek medical attention, fearing arrest.[18]

A harsh anti-union clampdown followed the Haymarket incident. The entire immigrant community, particularly Germans and Bohemians, came under suspicion. Police raids were carried out on homes and offices of suspected anarchists. Chicago police squads conducted an eight-week shakedown and a small group of anarchists were discovered to have been engaged in making bombs on the day of the incident.[19] Young wrote of a 'hue and cry – widespread police raids; arrests of hundreds of men and women known as or suspected to be Anarchists, Socialists, or Communists; announcements of the discovery of various dynamite "plots"...'[20] Union organisations such as the Knights of Labor were quick to disassociate themselves from the anarchist movement and to repudiate violent tactics as self-defeating. Many workers believed there had been a conspiracy involving the Pinkertons, pointing to the agency's history of violent methods to discredit workers.[21] The police, however, believed in a planned anarchist conspiracy. They raided the offices of the *Arbeiter-Zeitung*, arresting its editor August Spies, editorial assistant Michael Schwab and Adolph Fischer, a typesetter. A search of the premises resulted in the discovery of the 'revenge' flyer.[22]

On 7 May police searched the premises of Louis Lingg, a twenty-two-year-old German-born anarchist, where they found bomb-making materials. Lingg's landlord William Seliger was also arrested but cooperated with police and was not charged. An associate of Spies, Balthazar Rau, was traced to Omaha and brought back to Chicago. After interrogation, Rau offered to cooperate with police. He alleged that the defendants had experimented with dynamite bombs and accused them of having published what he said was a code word, 'Ruhe' ('peace'), in the *Arbeiter-Zeitung* as a call to arms at Haymarket Square.[23]

Rudolf Schnaubelt, the police's lead suspect as the bomb thrower, was arrested twice early on and released. By 14 May, when it became apparent he had played a significant role in the event, he had fled the country.[24] On 4 June 1886, seven suspects were indicted by the grand jury and stood trial for being accessories to the murder of Degan.[25] Of these, only two had been present when the bomb exploded – rally speakers Spies and Fielden, who were stepping from the improvised platform when the bomb went off. Two others, the typesetter Fischer and prominent activist Albert Parsons, had been present at the beginning of the rally but had left and were at Zepf's Hall, an anarchist rendezvous, at the time of the explosion. Parsons, believing that the evidence was weak or non-existent, had turned himself in to show solidarity with the accused. Spies's assistant editor Michael Schwab was also arrested even though he was speaking at another rally at the time of the explosion. Others not directly tied to the Haymarket rally, but arrested because they were notorious for their militant radicalism, included George Engel, who had been home playing cards on the fateful day, and Lingg, the bomb maker denounced by his associate, Seliger. Another defendant who had not been present was Oscar Neebe, an editorial associate. Of the eight defendants, five – Spies, Fischer, Engel, Lingg and Schwab – were German-born immigrants.

The trial, presided over by Judge Joseph Gary, began on 21 June 1886 and, exceptionally for the time, lasted until 11 August. It was also notable for the hostility displayed towards the defendants by the public, the media and the judge, a former carpenter who constantly ruled for the prosecution and who denied a motion that the defendants be tried separately.[26] Selection of the jury was extraordinarily difficult, lasting three weeks; nearly a thousand persons were called. All union members and anyone who expressed sympathy toward socialism were dismissed. In the end a jury of twelve was seated, most of whom confessed prejudice against the defendants. The prosecution, led by Julius Grinnell, argued that since the defendants had not actively discouraged the person who had thrown the bomb, they were therefore equally responsible as conspirators.[27] The jury heard the testimony of 118 people, including fifty-four members of the Chicago Police Department and the defendants Fielden, Schwab, Spies and Parsons.

Press coverage was uniformly hostile to the defendants. The *Chicago Times* described the defendants as 'arch counselors of riot, pillage, incendiarism and murder'; other reporters described them as 'bloody brutes', 'red ruffians', 'dynamarchists', 'bloody monsters', 'cowards', 'cutthroats', 'thieves', 'assassins', and 'fiends'.[28]

Art Young wrote:

> Newspaper editors and public men generally cried for a quick trial of the defendants and prompt execution of the guilty, and here was every reason to believe from the published reports that the accused deserved to be hanged. Public opinion was formed almost solely by the daily press, and in its columns evidence was steadily piled up against these labour agitators. Parsons had disappeared on the night of the bombing – police all over the country were watching for him; was not his flight confession of guilt? Rudolph Schnaubelt also was gone; he had been arrested twice and questioned briefly, but had been released – and Captain Schaak was incensed at the 'stupidity' of the detectives who had let him go.
>
> Like the great mass of the Chicagoans; I was swayed by these detailed reports of the black-heartedness of the defendants. Outstanding business and professional men and prominent members of the clergy denounced the accused, who were now all lumped together as 'Anarchists,' and condemned the seven Haymarket killings as the 'the most wanton outrage in American history.' In the bloody and gruesome descriptions of the tragedy of May 4, the city's people forgot the needless killing of the six workers by the police on May 3. I too saw 'evidence' against Parsons in his running away: He had spoken at the mass meeting, and the explosion had come only a few minutes after he left – and then he had vanished. Innocent men do not run away when a crime has been committed (so my youthful mind naively reasoned then): they stay and face the music.[29]

Police investigators under Captain Michael Schaack had a lead fragment removed from a policeman's wounds chemically analysed. They reported that the lead used in the casing matched the casings of bombs found in Lingg's home. A metal nut and fragments of the casing taken from the wound also roughly matched bombs made by Lingg.

Schaack concluded that the anarchists had been experimenting for years with dynamite and other explosives, refining the design of their bombs before coming up with an effective device.[30]

Young wrote:

Shortly after the jury had been selected, I was assigned to make some pictures of scenes in the courtroom. The place was crowded, but I managed to get a seat with the reporters at a table near the defense attorneys. The prosecution was putting in its case, and there were continual objections by the defense to the line of questioning and the frequent side remarks to the jury by Julius S. Grinnell, the state's attorney. Usually these objections were overruled, in a rasping voice, by Judge Joseph E. Gary; it occurred to me then that I'd hate to be tried before such a snarling old judge. It was common knowledge that it had been difficult to find reputable and competent criminal attorneys in Chicago willing to defend the accused's cause which was too unpopular, editorial notice had been plainly served that only a pariah and an enemy of society would try to save those men from the gallows. In the face of this warning three courageous members of the bar, who hitherto had handled only civil cases, had agreed to undertake the Anarchists' defense. William P. Black was chief of these; a captain in the Union Army during the Civil War, he was known as a fighter; tall, dark, and handsome, with a pronounced jaw that shook a short beard, he was often the center of all eyes in court. Assisting Black were William A. Foster, said to be capable as a finder of evidence, and Sigismund Zeisler, an earnest and studious young man with a blond Van Dyke beard, red lips, and wavy hair.

On the other side of this desperate contest was Grinnell, the state's attorney, who was understood to aspire to the governor's chair, and several assistants, whose names got into print much less often than Grinnell's. He had a fresh, healthy face and a big well curled mustache. Frank S. Osborne, jury foreman, was chief salesman for Marshall Field & Co. and the other eleven 'good and true' answered to these descriptions; former railroad-construction contractor; clothing salesman; ex-broker from Boston; school principal; shipping clerk; traveling paint salesman; bookkeeper; stenographer for the Chicago & Northwestern Railway; voucher clerk for the same railroad; hardware merchant; seed salesman. All the defendants were neatly dressed. They sat in their chairs with dignity, and with the elegant self-assurance of men who expected to be exonerated if they got justice. There was a breathless tension to the court proceedings, the air electric. Grinnell talked much about 'protecting society and government against enemies bent on their destruction.' Captain Black was often on his feet with objections.[31]

The jury returned guilty verdicts for all eight defendants. Before being sentenced, Neebe told the court that Schaack's officers were among the city's worst gangs, ransacking houses and stealing money and watches. Schaack laughed and Neebe retorted, 'You need not laugh about it, Captain Schaack. You are one of them. You are an anarchist, as you understand it. You are all anarchists, in this sense of the word, I must say.' Judge Gary sentenced seven of the defendants to death by hanging and Neebe to fifteen years in prison.

The sentencing provoked outrage within the labour movement, and worldwide condemnation. The trial was widely believed to have been a serious miscarriage of justice and was condemned by celebrated attorney Clarence Darrow, and playwrights Oscar Wilde and George Bernard Shaw. But sympathy for the condemned was limited in the popular imagination; the bombing had sparked widespread public fear and revulsion against the strikers and general anti-immigrant feeling. The journalist George Frederic Parsons identified the fears of middle-class Americans concerning labour radicalism, and asserted that the workers had only themselves to blame for their troubles.[32]

The case was appealed in 1887, first to the Illinois Supreme Court, then to US Supreme Court. After such fruitless appeals were exhausted, Illinois Governor Richard James Oglesby commuted Fielden's and Schwab's sentences to life in prison on 10 November 1887. On the eve of his scheduled execution, as the sketch artist Art Young fretted, Lingg committed suicide in his cell with a smuggled blasting cap which he reportedly held in his mouth like a cigar and which blew off half his face.[33]

Young wrote:

Butch White, the city editor, assigned me to go to the county jail and make pictures of the prisoners. The jail is in the rear of and adjacent to the criminal courts building in which the trial had been held. Despite the newspaper stories of plans for an attempted rescue of the seven men, no special precautions seemed to be taken by the guards inside. After my newspaper credentials had established my identity at the entrance, I climbed the iron stairs up to the tier where the Anarchists were confined, and was allowed to roam freely there while I drew my sketches. Other visitors were there, and they looked into the cells of the Anarchists curiously, as one might gaze at animals in a zoo. Parsons sat writing at a table piled with books and papers. He reminded me of a country editor – and he had edited a paper in Waco, Tex., before he came to Chicago. Adolph Fischer, who had been a printer on the *Arbeiter Zeitung*, looked like an eagle – light-haired, eager, and appearing as hopeful as he had been in court. George Engel, also a German printer, had less the appearance of an intellectual than the others. His eyes seemed dull, as if feeling had gone from him. Michael Schwab, spectacled associate editor and editorial writer, had a sad face. Samuel Fielden, a bearded ex-Methodist preacher born in England, was a familiar speaker in halls, and working-class street meetings, with the voice and intensity of a born orator. August Spies, editor of the *Arbeiter Zeitung*, was strikingly handsome, straightforward in his talk. But it is Louis Lingg that I remember best in thinking back to that visit to the jail; my memory picture of him is clearest because the sun was shining in his cell as I sketched him. Only twenty-two, and blond, he had a look of disdain for all. He sat proudly in his chair, facing me with unblinking eyes. Silent as though he might have been saying: 'Go ahead. Do what your masters want you to do. As for me, nothing matters.'[34]

The next day four defendants – Engel, Fischer, Parsons, and Spies – were taken to the gallows in white robes and hoods. They sang the *Marseillaise*, the anthem of the international revolutionary movement. Family members who attempted to see them for the last time were arrested and searched for bombs, although none were found.

In the moments before the men were hanged, Spies shouted, 'The time will come when our silence will be more powerful than the voices you strangle today.' Witnesses reported that the condemned men did not die immediately when they dropped, but strangled to death slowly, a sight which left the spectators visibly shaken.[35] Young, who has proved to be a reliable witness, recalled: 'Three hundred policemen had formed a cordon around the jail, a block away from it on all sides, keeping the curious crowds on the outside of a line of heavy rope. Only those persons who could satisfy the police that they had bona fide passports could get through. Once a newspaperman got into the jail, the police would not let him out – though he could send copy to his office by messengers who waited at the entrance. The hanging proceeded efficiently from the viewpoint of the authorities. When the four men had dropped from the scaffold and the doctors had pronounced all of them dead, the tension of months had suddenly gone. All over town that afternoon there were drunken policemen, in and out of the saloons.'[36]

Notwithstanding the convictions for conspiracy, no actual bomber was ever brought to trial, 'and no lawyerly explanation could ever make a conspiracy trial without the main perpetrator in the conspiracy seem completely legitimate.'[37]

On 26 June 1893, the progressive governor of Illinois, John Peter Altgeld, himself a German immigrant, signed pardons for Fielden, Neebe and Schwab, calling them victims of 'hysteria, packed juries, and a biased judge' and noting that the state 'has never discovered who it was that threw the bomb which killed the policeman, and the evidence does not show any connection whatsoever between the defendants and the man who threw it'.

Altgeld also faulted the city of Chicago for failing to hold Pinkerton guards responsible for repeated use of lethal violence against striking workers.[38] Altgeld was subsequently defeated in his re-election bid. Historian Carl Smith wrote: 'The visceral feelings of fear and anger surrounding the trial ruled out anything but the pretense of justice right from the outset.' But in 2011, labour historian Timothy Messer-Kruse concluded: 'The tragic end of the story was the product not of prosecutorial eagerness to see the anarchists hang, but largely due to a combination of the incompetence of the defendants' lawyers and their willingness to use the trial to vindicate anarchism rather than to save the necks of their clients.'[39]

The Haymarket Affair was a setback for the American labour movement and its fight for the eight-hour day. Yet it also strengthened its resistance, especially in Chicago. The Knights of Labor doubled its membership, reaching 40,000 in autumn 1886.[40] In 1889, American Federation of Labor president Samuel Gompers wrote to the first congress of the Second International meeting in Paris. He informed the world's socialists of the AFL's plans and proposed an international fight for a universal eight-hour work day.

Speculation on the identity of the bomb-thrower has continued ever since. Suspects include the activist Rudolph Schnaubelt, who fled the

US before trial; the German shoemaker George Schwab; the teamster and farmer George Meng; an agent provocateur working for either the police or the Pinkertons; a disgruntled worker who hated the police; the carpenter Thomas Owen; Reinold 'Big' Krueger, who was killed by police either in the melee after the bombing or in a separate disturbance the next day; and a 'mysterious outsider' reported by a saloon-keeper. We'll never know.

Police captain Michael Schaack, who had led the investigation, was dismissed from the police force for allegedly having fabricated evidence in the case but was reinstated in 1892. Judge Joseph Gary was in 1888 appointed by the Supreme Court to the Appellate Court for the First District of Illinois. He returned to the Cook County Superior Court in 1897. Both the Republicans and the Democrats nominated him each time he ran for judge, a position he held continuously from 1863 to 1906. He was the oldest judge on the circuit when he died in 1906.

Haymarket had a profound impact on socialist movements across the globe. Labour studies professor William J. Adelman wrote: 'No single event has influenced the history of labor in Illinois, the United States, and even the world, more than the Chicago Haymarket Affair. It began with a rally on May 4, 1886, but the consequences are still being felt today. Although the rally is included in American history textbooks, very few present the event accurately or point out its significance.'[41]

And on May Day 2015, the British Labour MP Stephen Pound wrote:

> There has been so much written about the Haymarket Affair and there is still a huge amount of confusion as to whether spies pretending to be anarchists, pretending to be undercover Pinkerton's men, pretending to be German socialists, but actually agents provocateurs were anything other than cruelly ill-treated workers who wanted nothing more than the eight-hour day. The utterly macabre hanging of four of the defendants dressed in white robes and hoods still haunts, as does the almost unbelievable prejudice shown by the Judge and the very carefully chosen jury. We also remember the rallying cry; 'eight hour day with no cut in pay' and I can almost hear the slogan being shouted by Chicago's swelling throng. To commemorate the foul miscarriage of justice perpetrated on the Haymarket defendants does seem appropriate and while the

judge and jury have been forgotten; August Spies, Albert Parsons, Adolph Fischer and George Engel will always remembered. It is hard to realise nowadays how influential the Haymarket Square trial was at the time and the international sense of revulsion was reflected by George Bernard Shaw and Oscar Wilde ... A fitting footnote to the whole awful business occurred on the 41st anniversary in 1927 when a tram driver rammed the vast monument topped with the statue of a Chicago policeman in Haymarket Square. Anyone looking at a picture of the statue will note that the officer's right arm is raised in what looks exactly like a Nazi salute. The tram driver said that he was sick and tired of seeing that policeman with his arm raised and the whole edifice has been moved a number of times since and I believe that today it is either inside the headquarters of the Chicago police department or within the police academy grounds.[42]

But perhaps the last word should go to Art Young, writing in 1939:

All the news stories I read then and nearly all the talk I heard about the case then indicated that the executed men were guilty. Not for years did I have an opportunity to see and study the other side of the picture. So when, a short time later, I was asked to draw a cover for an anti-Anarchist pamphlet, I readily assented. Its title was *Justice Triumphant Over Anarchy*, and it upheld the hangings. If the dead can hear, I ask their pardon now for drawing that cartoon. I was young and was misled by the clamor of many voices raised to justify a dark deed.[43]

5

The Pinkerton Rebellion

'a disdain for the public conscience...'

The Pinkerton Detective Agency, once the world's biggest, has long been associated with Western mythology, and with good deeds. Pinkerton agents were hired to track down such outlaws as Jesse James, and Butch Cassidy and the Sundance Kid, generally unsuccessfully. On 17 March 1874, two Pinkerton detectives and a deputy sheriff, Edwin P. Daniels, ran into associates of the Younger brothers; one Pinkerton was killed in the ensuing shootout. After a bank robbery in Union, Missouri, the Pinkerton detective Chas Schumacher trailed the gang and was killed. Pinkertons were also hired for transporting money, gold and high-quality merchandise between cities and towns, which made them vulnerable to outlaws. Given the dangers, agents were well paid and well armed.

But during the period of the Wild West and beyond, the vast bulk of Pinkerton work was the business of strike-breaking. They were involved, often brutally, in coal, iron and lumber disputes in Michigan, Illinois, New York, Pennsylvania and West Virginia, plus the 1877 Great Railway Strike and the 1921 Battle of Blair Mountain. Undercover infiltration and intimidation, the threat and use of heavy violence, jury-tampering and bribery, sabotage and downright assassination were their stock in trade. Their main opponents were not the Wild West outlaws of romance, but half-starved strikers and poverty-stricken immigrants.

However, things did not always go their way.

* * *

Glasgow-born Allan J. Pinkerton emigrated to the US in 1842, aged twenty-three, and aided escaped slaves on the 'Underground Railway'. An encounter with a gang of counterfeiters – who were arrested – led to his appointment in 1849 as the first police detective in Cook County, Illinois. In 1850, he partnered with Chicago attorney Edward Rucker in forming the North-Western Police Agency, which later became Pinkerton & Co., and finally the Pinkerton National Detective Agency.

The agency solved a series of train robberies during the 1850s, first bringing Pinkerton into contact with Abraham Lincoln, then a rail company's lawyer. Although Pinkerton had supported black emancipation and the rights of workers, demand for more nefarious services outstripped his conscience. Historian Frank Morn wrote: 'By the mid-1850s a few businessmen saw the need for greater control over their employees; their solution was to sponsor a private detective system.'

During the first two years of the Civil War, Pinkerton was head of the Union Intelligence Service and was instrumental in foiling an attempt on Lincoln's life in Baltimore. His agents became adept at working undercover as Confederate sympathisers. Under the alias of Major E. J. Allen, Pinkerton himself undertook several missions. He was then hired by the railroads to chase train robbers, but his failure to capture Jesse James saw his reputation plummet. His opposition to labour unions emerged during this period. In 1872, the Spanish government hired Pinkerton to help suppress a revolution in Cuba. This he did, despite knowing that the regime's record did not sit well with his avowed opposition to slavery. His agency grew as widespread strikes made the hiring of labour spies big business.

During the 1870s, the Philadelphia and Reading Railroad hired the Pinkertons to probe the labour unions in the company's mines. Agent James McParland infiltrated the Molly Maguires, (*see Chapter 3*) leading to their extermination by foul means. Pinkerton wrote in 1878 of his 'extensive and perfected detective system', adding that 'my agencies have been busily employed by great railway, manufacturing and other corporations, for the purpose of bringing the leaders and instigators [of strikes] to the punishment they so richly deserve. Hundreds have been punished. Hundreds more will be punished.'

Allan Pinkerton died in Chicago on 1 July 1884, most probably by slipping on a flagstone and biting his tongue, leading to gangrene.

At the time of his death, he was working on a system to centralise all criminal identification records, the beginnings of a database currently maintained by the FBI. After his death, the agency continued to operate and became a major force against the labour movement, to the disgust of generations of working people. It was aided by the cash-strapped Department of Justice, which sub-contracted Congress orders to form a sub-organisation devoted to 'the detection and prosecution of those guilty of violating federal law'.[1]

During the 1886 railway strike, McParland worked undercover for railroad tycoon Jay Gould. A local socialist wrote after one court case in which the Pinkerton was presumed to have perjured himself: ' ... he will do anything, no matter how low or vile, to accomplish his purpose ... There is not today, in the United States outside prison walls, a more conscienceless and desperate criminal than McParland.'

Allan Pinkerton had left the agency to his two sons. The brothers opened their fourth office in Denver in order to compete with their new rivals, the Thiel Detective Agency, and assigned Charles O. Eames to head it. When it appeared that Eames was running the western branch dishonestly, they told McParland to investigate. He discovered extensive abuses against clients and everyone was fired except for McParland and Charlie Siringo. McParland was made superintendent of the Pinkertons' western division.

In April 1891, Mrs Josephine Barnaby was murdered by poison. McParland tricked Thomas Thatcher Graves, her accused murderer, into traveling from Rhode Island to Denver where he was arrested and convicted of the crime. McParland also hired gunman Tom Horn (later executed for murder in Wyoming), who, while working for Pinkerton, killed seventeen men, according to a count by Siringo.

McParland continued enthusiastically to infiltrate and disrupt the newly formed unions. He successfully placed numerous spies within the Western Federation of Miners (WFM), and more into the United Mine Workers. Some of McParland's agents took part in the WFM Colorado strike, and one was charged with sabotaging the union's relief programme. WFM secretary Bill Haywood wrote of such dirty tricks, which were common:

> I had been having some difficulty with the relief committee of the Denver smelter men. At first we had been giving out relief at such a rate that I had to tell the chairman that he was providing the smelter men with more than they had had while at work. Then he cut down

the rations until the wives of the smelter men began to complain that they were not getting enough to eat. Years later, when his letters were published in *The Pinkerton Labor Spy*, I discovered that the chairman of the relief committe [*sic*] was a Pinkerton detective, who was carrying out the instructions of the agency in his methods of handling the relief work, deliberately trying to stir up bad feeling between the strikers and the relief committee.[2]

It was against such a backdrop that the agency was awarded the contract to break a steel strike, leading to incidents which became infamous and which were variously known as the Pinkerton Rebellion, or the Homestead Massacre.

Carnegie Steel introduced new technology during the 1880s, allowing the company to supply armour plate to the US Navy at premium prices. As production speeded up, and mills expanded, the labour force also grew, but with cheaper workers less skilled than the existing members of the Amalgamated Association of Iron and Steel Workers (AA), a craft union established in 1876. The AA's membership was concentrated west of the Allegheny Mountains and the first test of strength came on 1 January 1882 with a strike at the giant Homestead works to prevent management from including a non-union 'yellow dog' clause in the workers' contracts. Violence occurred on both sides, with the company bringing in numerous strike-breakers. The strike ended on 20 March in a complete victory for the union.[3]

When negotiations for a new three-year collective bargaining agreement failed, the AA called another strike in 1889. The strikers seized the town and made common cause with various immigrant groups and repelled a trainload of strike-breakers on 10 July. When the sheriff returned with 125 newly deputised agents two days later, the strikers rallied 5,000 townspeople and the company backed down.[4] The AA effectively ran the Homestead plant. AA membership doubled, and the local union treasury had a balance of $146,000. Relationships between workers and managers grew tense.[5] The scene was set for another confrontation, and while earlier large-scale strikes elsewhere had proved largely leaderless and disorganised, this would be different.

Multi-millionaire Andrew Carnegie placed financier, property developer and industrialist Henry Clay Frick in charge of his company's operations in 1881. The son of a failed businessman, Frick had initially made his fortune turning coal into coke for steel manufacture. His company employed 1,000 workers and controlled 80 per cent of the coal output in Pennsylvania. Frick had met Carnegie in New York while on his honeymoon. The two formed a partnership to ensure an unbroken supply of coke to Carnegie's mills. The partnership was uneasy, but they agreed that top priority must be to break the union at Homestead, even though Carnegie had previously condemned the use of strike-breakers and told associates that no steel mill was worth a single drop of blood. 'The mills have never been able to turn out the product they should, owing to being held back by the Amalgamated men,' Frick complained in a letter to Carnegie.[6]

In 1889 Carnegie imposed a 25 per cent pay cut and tried to set individual contracts. The workers immediately went out on strike. The company hired Pinkerton detectives as guards and tried to bring in strike-breakers, but were defeated by mass picketing. Frick wrote: 'The posse taken up by the sheriff – something over 100 men – were not permitted to land on our property; were driven off with threats of bodily harm, and it looked as if there was going to be great destruction of life and property.'[7] The company signed a three-year contract with the AA, but behind the scenes made preparations for a future confrontation. Carnegie ordered the Homestead plant to stockpile products so the plant could weather a future strike. He also drafted a notice (which Frick never released) withdrawing recognition of the union.[8]

With the collective bargaining agreement due to expire on 30 June 1892, Frick and the leaders of the local AA entered into negotiations in February. With the steel industry doing well and prices higher, the AA asked for a wage increase; it represented about 800 of the 3,800 workers at the plant. Frick immediately countered with a 22 per cent wage decrease that would affect nearly half the union's membership. Carnegie encouraged Frick to use the negotiations to break the union: ' ... the Firm has decided that the minority must give way to the majority. These works, therefore, will be necessarily non-union after the expiration of the present agreement.'[9] Carnegie, a pacifist, purposefully avoided the moral dilemmas raised by the Homestead strike by beginning a European vacation before the strike began. When questioned in Scotland about Frick's actions, Carnegie washed his hands of any responsibility and declared that Frick was in charge.[10]

Frick wrote to Robert Pinkerton to hire 300 guards for Homestead, saying: 'The only trouble we anticipate is that an attempt will be made to prevent such men with whom we will by that time have made satisfactory arrangements from going to work, and possibly some demonstration of violence upon the part of those whose places have been filled, or most likely by an element which usually is attracted to such scenes for the purpose of stirring up trouble...' The private army was to assemble in Ohio, taken by train to a point below Pittsburgh, and then shipped down the Ohio River to Homestead. The Pinkertons had the manpower and expertise, it was assumed, to crush any resistance. After all, the agency had helped break strikes in around seventy disputes. Its 2,000 active detectives and 30,000 reserves was larger than the nation's standing army.[11]

Frick announced on 30 April 1892 that he would bargain for twenty-nine more days. If no contract was reached, Carnegie Steel would cease to recognize the union. Frick locked workers out of the plate mill on the evening of 28 June. When no collective bargaining agreement was reached on 29 June, Frick locked the union out of the rest of the plant. A high fence was topped with barbed wire, sniper towers with searchlights were constructed and high-pressure water cannons were placed at each entrance. All aspects of the plant were protected, reinforced or shielded.

At a mass meeting on 30 June, local AA leaders announced that the company had broken the contract by locking out workers a day before the contract expired. The Knights of Labor, representing the mechanics and transportation workers, agreed to walk out alongside the skilled workers of the AA who struck in sympathy the same day.[12] A packed meeting at the Opera House voted overwhelmingly for action – the unskilled and semi-skilled feared that if the company won, their wages would be cut as well.

The Declaration of the Strike Committee read:

The employees in the mill of Messrs. Carnegie, Phipps & Co., at Homestead, Pa., have built there a town with its homes, its schools and its churches; have for many years been faithful co-workers with the company in the business of the mill; have invested thousands of dollars of their savings in said mill in the expectation of spending their lives in Homestead and of working in the mill during the period of their efficiency ... Therefore, the committee desires to express to the public as its firm belief that both the public and the employees aforesaid have equitable rights and interests in the said mill which cannot be modified or diverted without due process of law; that the employees have the right to continuous employment in the said mill during efficiency and good behaviour without regard to religious, political or economic opinions or associations; that it is against public policy and subversive of the fundamental principles of American liberty that a whole community of workers should be denied employment or suffer any other social detriment on account of membership in a church, a political party or a trade union; that it is our duty as American citizens to resist by every legal and ordinary means the unconstitutional, anarchic and revolutionary policy of the Carnegie Company, which seems to evince a contempt [for] public and private interests and a disdain [for] the public conscience...

The strikers secured a steam-powered river launch to patrol the Monongahela River alongside the plant's premises. Men divided themselves into units along military lines, with three divisions or watches splitting the day into eight-hour shifts. Picket lines were thrown up around the plant and the town. The commanders of each division had eight captains, trusted men from each of the eight local lodges. Each captain had personal charge over such posts as the river front, the water gates and pumps, the railway stations and the plant's main gates. Pickets were ordered to report in every thirty minutes. Eight hundred foreign workers, Slavs and Hungarians, were held back as a reserve brigade under the command of two Hungarians with two interpreters.[13] Ferries and trains were watched. Strangers were challenged and if no suitable explanations for their presence was forthcoming, they were escorted outside the city limits. Telegraph communications with AA locals in other cities were established to monitor the company's attempts to hire replacement workers. Reporters were issued special badges which gave them safe passage through the town. Tavern owners were told to prevent excessive drinking.[14]

Frick was also busy. He placed advertisements for replacement workers in newspapers in the Eastern and Midwestern states, and even Europe. Frick sought several times to have the Pinkerton agents deputised, as attacking duly deputised county law enforcement officers would provide grounds for claiming insurrection.[15] On 4 July, Frick formally requested that Sheriff William H. McCleary intervene to allow supervisors access to the plant. McCleary dispatched eleven deputies to the town to post handbills ordering the strikers to stop interfering with the plant's operation. The strikers tore them down, herded the deputies onto a boat and sent them downriver to Pittsburgh. Frick ordered the construction of a solid board fence topped with barbed wire around mill property, which the workers quickly dubbed 'Fort Frick'. And the Pinkertons were summoned.

The 300 'detectives' assembled on the Davis Island Dam on the Ohio River about 5 miles below Pittsburgh at 10.30 p.m. on 5 July 1892. They were given Winchester rifles, placed on two specially equipped barges and towed upriver. The barges, bought specifically for the Homestead lockout, contained sleeping quarters and kitchens and were intended to house the agents for the duration of the strike. Frick planned to open the works with non-union men early the following morning after the Pinkerton men had broken through the picket lines. With the mill ringed by striking workers, the agents would access the plant grounds from the river.[16]

The AA had learned of the Pinkertons' mission as soon as they had left Boston. A small flotilla of union boats went downriver to meet the barges. Strikers on the steam launch fired a few random shots at the barges, then withdrew – blowing the launch whistle to alert the plant. The strikers blew the plant whistle at 2.30 a.m., drawing thousands of men, women and children. The Pinkertons attempted to land under cover of darkness about 4 a.m. A large crowd of families had kept pace with the boats as they were towed by a tug into the town. A few shots were fired at the tug and barges, but no one was injured. The crowd tore down the barbed-wire fence and strikers and their families surged onto the Homestead plant. Some in the crowd threw stones at the barges, but leading strikers shouted for restraint.[17]

The Pinkerton agents attempted to disembark. A striker lay on the gangplank, and when the first Pinkerton detective attempted to shove him aside, the union man shot him in the thigh, knocking him backwards.[18] Then all hell broke loose. John T. McCurry, a boatman on the steamboat *Little Bill*, later testified: 'The armed Pinkerton men commenced to climb up the banks. Then the workmen opened fire on the detectives. The men shot first, and not until three of the Pinkerton men had fallen did they respond to the fire. I am willing to take an oath that the workmen fired first, and that the Pinkerton men did not shoot until some of their number had been wounded.' But McCurry's claims were tainted – he was indirectly employed by Pinkerton and, having been wounded himself in the melee, had a grudge against the steel men.

The *New York Times* reported that the Pinkertons opened fire and wounded William Foy, 'a worker'.[19] Regardless of which side fired first, the first two individuals wounded were Frederick Heinde, captain of the Pinkertons, and Foy. The Pinkerton agents aboard the barges then fired into the crowd, killing two and wounding eleven. The crowd responded, killing two and wounding twelve. The tit-for-tat firefight continued for about ten minutes.[20]

The strikers continued to fire on the barges sporadically. Periods of calm were interspersed with mutual fusillades. Some union members fired, generally aimlessly, from rowboats and the steam-powered launch. Homestead burgess John McLuckie issued a proclamation at 6 a.m. asking for townspeople to help defend the peace. Over 5,000 people crowded on the overlooking hills. Six miles away in Pittsburgh, thousands of steelworkers gathered in the streets, listening to accounts of the attacks at Homestead; hundreds began to move toward the town with a wild array of weapons to assist the strikers.[21]

After a few more hours under a blisteringly hot July sun, the strikers attempted to burn the barges. They seized a raft, loaded it with oil-soaked timber and floated it downriver. There was some panic on board, and a Pinkerton captain threatened to shoot anyone who fled, but the fire burned itself out before it reached the barges. The strikers then loaded a railroad flatcar with drums of oil and set it afire. The flatcar stopped at the water's edge and burned itself out. Dynamite was thrown at the barges, but little damage was done. Early that afternoon the workers poured oil onto the river, but attempts to light the slick failed.[22] A 20-pounder used in town celebrations, and a smaller cannon from the local museum, were trained on the barges, but to little effect. A gas main was directed at the barges and ignited, but the result was more akin to firecrackers than an actual explosion.

The AA worked behind the scenes to avoid further bloodshed. Outgoing AA international president William Weihe asked to meet Frick, but the latter refused. The strike leaders knew that the more chaotic the situation became, the more likely it was that Governor Robert E. Pattison would call out the state militia. Sheriff McCleary initially resisted attempts to call for state intervention, and Pattison urged him to exhaust every effort to restore the peace.[23]

At 4 p.m., events at the mill quickly began to wind down. More than 5,000 men – most of them armed mill hands from the nearby South Side, Braddock and Duquesne works – arrived at the Homestead plant. Weihe wanted to prevent further trouble and, having again been snubbed by Frick, urged the strikers to let the Pinkertons surrender, but he was shouted down. Weihe tried to speak again, but this time his pleas were drowned out as the strikers bombarded the barges with fireworks left over from the recent Independence Day celebration. Hugh O'Donnell, a heater in the plant and head of the union's strike committee, then spoke to the crowd. He demanded that each Pinkerton be charged with murder, forced to turn over his arms and then removed from the town. The crowd shouted their approval.[24]

The Pinkertons, too, wished to surrender and their commanders faced mutiny. Most of those on board were not regular Pinkertons, but guards hired under false pretences and shipped to Homestead at gunpoint.[25] At 5 p.m., they raised a white flag and two agents asked to speak with the strikers. O'Donnell guaranteed them safe passage out of town. Upon arrival, their arms were stripped from them. As the Pinkertons crossed the grounds of the mill, the crowd formed a gauntlet through which the agents passed. Men and women threw stones, spat on them and beat them. Several Pinkertons were clubbed into unconsciousness. A striker seized a Pinkerton agent's rifle and attempted to break it in two. He succeeded in shooting himself in the stomach and died. A woman poked out an agent's eye with her umbrella. Almost none of those who ran the gauntlet emerged unscathed. Members of the crowd ransacked the barges, then burned them to the waterline.[26]

The casualty lists remain controversial, but reliable sources suggest that forty strikers and pickets were shot, and nine died; among the Pinkertons, twenty were shot, seven killed and almost all the remainder hurt to differing degrees. The nation's media, and others from much farther afield, descended on the town. The reports they filed varied wildly in support of one side of the other. But sheet music for a newly penned song – '*Father Was Killed by the Pinkerton Men*' – sold out swiftly.[27]

Sheriff McCleary and Weihe agreed a 'civilised' transfer of the detained Pinkertons. A special train arrived at 12.30 a.m. and McCleary accompanied the battered and subdued agents to Pittsburgh.[28] When the Pinkertons arrived in the city, state officials declared that they would not be charged with murder, as had been agreed by the union side, and were released.

The strike committee tried by telegram to persuade Governor Pattison that law and order had been restored in the town. Although

Pattison had ordered the Pennsylvania militia to muster, he had not formally charged it with doing anything because of his fear that, as the union controlled Homestead with the overwhelming support of its citizens, the outcome could be a bloodbath. Pattison again refused to order the town taken by force, saying: 'I am of the opinion that there would not have been a drop of blood shed if the proposition had been accepted to let the locked-out men guard the plant.' But once initial emotions had faded, Pattison came under intense political pressure to act. He had been elected with the backing of a Carnegie-supported political machine, and he could no longer refuse to protect Carnegie interests.

The Pennsylvania National Guard arrived on 12 July. Its resources were massive – following the 1887 Great Upheaval it had been greatly expanded and could muster 8,000 officers and men armed with Springfield .45 rifles and Gatling guns. The steelworkers resolved to meet the militia amicably, hoping to establish good relations with the troops. But the militia managed to keep its arrival in the town a secret almost to the last moment. Mid-morning on 12 July, in a deliberate subterfuge, they arrived at the small Munhall train station near the Homestead mill, rather than the downtown train station as expected. Their commander, Major General George R. Snowden, a lawyer and Civil War veteran, made it clear to local officials that he sided with the owners. He said of the strikers: 'Pennsylvanians can hardly appreciate the actual communism of these people. They believe the works are theirs quite as much as Carnegie's.'

When Hugh O'Donnell, the head of the union's strike committee, attempted to welcome Snowden and pledge the cooperation of the strikers, Snowden told him that the strikers had not been law abiding, and that 'I want you to distinctly understand that I am the master of this situation'. More than 4,000 soldiers surrounded the plant. Within twenty minutes they had displaced the picketers. By way of intimidation, another 2,000 troops camped on the high ground overlooking the city.[29]

The company quickly brought in strike-breakers and restarted production under the protection of the militia. Despite the presence of AFL pickets in front of several recruitment offices, Frick easily found others to work the mill. He quickly had built bunk houses, dining halls and kitchens to accommodate the newcomers, many of them black, who arrived on 13 July. Within two days, the mill furnaces were relit.

When a few workers attempted to storm into the plant, militiamen fought them off and wounded six with bayonets. But all was not well inside the plant. A race war between non-union black and white workers broke out.[30] The town was placed under martial law, further disheartening the remaining strikers

The strike had by then spread to other Carnegie works in and around Pittsburgh. Workers at the Union Iron Mill and at the Beaver Falls mills declared they would not return until Frick ended his lockout of their comrades at Homestead. The strike dragged on for four months. Workers at Duquesne joined the AA, but in August the state militia escorted strike-breakers into the plant and suppressed a riot.[31]

Back at Homestead, Frick struggled to recruit the most highly trained steelworkers needed to fully restore plant operations. In some cases they were shanghaied under false pretences. In Cincinnati, for example, fifty-six were offered good pay at another Carnegie plant and placed on a train; it was only when the doors and windows were locked that guards told them they were destined for Homestead. They fought with the guards and forced open doors, and only twenty-one were left when the train reached Homestead. A strike-breaker later reported that, once there, 'we were made prisoners in the works and guarded like convicts. The more ignorant were told by the foreman that if they ventured outside the union men would shoot them like dogs … At least half of them are sick from heat, bad water and poor food.'[32]

Strikers bombarded the plant with leaflets offering reluctant scabs good treatment and their train fares home if they walked out. There was a mass exodus for the door, but not enough left to halt production. Even Frick was impressed by the strikers' resilience, saying: 'The firmness with which these strikers hold on is surprising everyone.'[33] But outside influences came into play.

The nation again focused on Homestead when, on 23 July, the New York anarchist Alexander Berkman tried to assassinate Frick. He entered Frick's office, armed with a revolver and a sharpened steel file. Frick started to rise from his chair while Berkman fired point-blank. A bullet hit Frick in the left earlobe, penetrated his neck near the base of the skull, and lodged in his back. The impact knocked Frick down, and Berkman fired again, striking Frick again in the neck. Carnegie Steel vice president John George Alexander Leishman grabbed Berkman's arm and prevented a third shot.[34] Frick was seriously wounded, but all three men crashed to the floor in a violent embrace. Berkman managed to stab Frick four times in the leg with the steel file before finally being subdued by other employees. Frick was back at work in a week; Berkman was found guilty of attempted murder and was sentenced to twenty-two years.

The Berkman assassination bid undermined public support for the union and prompted the final collapse of the strike. O'Donnell was sacked as chair of the strike committee when he proposed to return to work at the lower wage scale if the unionists could get their jobs back. On 12 August, the company announced that 1,700 men were working at the mill and production had resumed at full capacity. The national AFL refused to intervene. The union voted to go back to work on Carnegie's terms; the strike had failed and the union had collapsed.[35]

The company took the war to the courts. On 18 July, sixteen of the strike leaders were charged with conspiracy, riot and murder, remanded in custody for the night and forced to post a $10,000 bond. Most of the men could not raise the bail bond and went to jail or into hiding. The union retaliated by charging company executives with murder. The company men, too, had to post a $10,000 bond, but they were not forced to spend any time in jail. A compromise was eventually reached whereby both sides dropped their charges, with some exceptions.[36] Only four workers were ever tried on the actual charges filed by the state. Three of them were found innocent of all charges but Hugh Dempsey, the leader of the local Knights of Labor District Assembly, was found guilty of conspiring to poison non-union workers at the plant – despite the state's star witness recanting his testimony on the stand. Dempsey served a seven-year prison term.

Public support for the strikers evaporated. The AFL refused to call for a boycott of Carnegie products in September 1892. Wholesale crossing of the picket line occurred, and the state militia pulled out on 13 October, ending the ninety-five-day occupation. The AA was nearly bankrupted by the action. With only 192 out of more than 3,800 strikers present, the Homestead chapter of the AA voted narrowly to return to work on 20 November 1892.

The strike at Beaver Falls gave in the same day as the Homestead lodge. The AA affiliate at Union Mills held out until 14 August 1893. But by then the union had only fifty-three local members. The union had been broken. Jeremy Brecher wrote: 'In the final analysis, the strikers were defeated by the new technology of the steel industry. In earlier days, it had been impossible to run the mills without the skilled men of the Amalgamated ... But with the increasing mechanization of the mills, employers could start up with new men and only a nucleus of experienced workers. The new giant corporations with many plants could easily shift work from a struck plant to an unstruck one and be relatively unscathed by a strike.'[37] Most steel companies enforced wage decreases similar to those imposed at Homestead.[38]

An organising drive at the Homestead plant in 1896 was crushed by Frick. In May 1899, 300 Homestead workers formed a new AA lodge, but Frick ordered the Homestead works shut down and the unionisation effort collapsed. De-unionisation efforts began against the AA in 1897 when Jones and Laughlin Steel refused to sign a contract. By 1900, not a single steel plant in Pennsylvania remained unionised. Many lodges disbanded, their members disillusioned. AA membership sagged to 10,000 in 1894 from its high of over 24,000 in 1891. A year later, it was down to 8,000. A 1901 strike against Carnegie's successor company, US Steel, collapsed. By 1909, membership in the AA had sunk to 6,300. A nationwide stoppage in 1919 was also crushed.

Frick prospered. He bought the private Pullman railroad car *Westmoreland* for nearly $40,000. It featured a kitchen, pantry, dining room, servant's quarters, two staterooms, and a lavatory. He frequently used it to travel between his residences in New York, Pittsburgh and Massachusetts.[39] Frick and his wife booked tickets to travel back to New York on the inaugural trip of the *Titanic* in 1912. The couple cancelled after Adelaide sprained her ankle in Italy and they missed the voyage. Henry Clay Frick died of a heart attack on 2 December 1919, weeks before his seventieth birthday.[40]

A bridge over the Monongahela River near the site of the Homestead battle is named Pinkerton's Landing Bridge in honour of the dead on one side of the Homestead Strike, or Pinkerton Rebellion.

***

The Pinkertons remained very much in business despite the humiliation of Homestead. They continued to be involved in the suppression of organised labour, but 1893 legislation ruled that under federal law an 'individual employed by the Pinkerton Detective Agency, or similar organization, may not be employed by the Government of the United States or the government of the District of Columbia'. The agency temporarily switched from industrial guardianship and protection rackets to the more honest pursuit of criminals and murderers.

In 1895, detective Frank Geyer tracked down the killer of the three Pitezel children, leading to the eventual trial of H. H. Holmes, arguably America's first known serial killer in the modern sense. Holmes had taken over a Chicago pharmacy and built it into an elaborate maze of death traps to which he lured numerous victims during the 1893 Columbian Exposition. Some of these rooms had gas jets so that Holmes could asphyxiate his victims. There were also trapdoors and chutes so that he could move the bodies down to the basement where he could burn the remains in a kiln. Pinkertons had previously apprehended Holmes in 1894 in Boston on an outstanding warrant for insurance fraud. Holmes would later confess to murdering the two Pitezel girls by forcing them into a large trunk and gassing them. Geyer found the decomposed bodies in a Toronto cellar. He followed Holmes to Indianapolis where he discovered the Pitezel boy's remains in a chimney. Holmes' murder spree finally ended when he was arrested in Boston on 17 November 1894.[41] In October 1895, Holmes was put on trial for the murder of Benjamin Pitezel, and was sentenced to death. Following his conviction, Holmes confessed to twenty-seven murders in Chicago, Indianapolis and Toronto. He was paid $7,500 by Hearst newspapers in exchange for his confession, which was quickly found to be mostly nonsense. Later it was argued that he may have killed up to 200 people in his Chicago 'house of horror' but that is now regarded as a wild exaggeration, partially based on Holmes's own fantasies. On 7 May 1896, Holmes was hanged in Philadelphia County Prison.

At the beginning of November 1913, a strike by streetcar workers of the Indianapolis Traction and Terminal Company brought the city to a standstill, caused severe state-wide rail disruption, and interrupted the city elections. The company had previously employed spies to infiltrate the union, but they failed to prevent an outbreak of rioting when strike-breakers were brought in to operate the trams. The city police refused orders to combat the rioters as the violence worsened. The company hired 300 professional strike-breakers through the Chicago Pinkerton office.

On the afternoon of 2 November, police chief Martin Hyland ordered a police escort to take the Pinkertons from Union Station to the company's maintenance building. The police broke a path through the strikers, but another riot erupted as the Pinkertons attempted to restore transit service. Whenever the strike-breakers launched a streetcar from the storage barns, the strikers attacked them with rocks and bricks. They boarded the streetcars, dragged the crews from the cars and set the cars on fire. After the destruction of six cars, the strike-breakers abandoned their attempts.[42] Chief Hyland and many officers were sympathetic to the strike, but the local judicial magistrates were not. Union members who were arrested faced fines up to $50, while the arrested strike-breakers were immediately acquitted by a local judge.

On 3 November, Sheriff Porttens deputised 2,000 men to help the Pinkertons. The police were able to hold back the crowd at first by liberally using their clubs. The rioters increased the intensity of their attack, and men on the rooftops began throwing stones and bricks. The greatly outnumbered police abandoned their posts and the strike-breakers fled into the storage buildings. People in the crowd opened fire, killing one of the strike-breakers and injuring others. By the end of 3 November, after two days of protecting the cars, less than fifty policemen remained on duty in the city. Without police protection, the Traction and Terminal Company shut down operations and refused to restart them until adequate protection could be provided.[43]

On 4 November, bands of pro-union men went on the rampage, vandalised property, burnt streetcars, harassed public officials, and effectively shut down much of the city in the worst violence of the strike.[44] A group of about 1,500 men began marching towards the electric distribution centre used to power the entire streetcar system, and the remaining police opened fire. Several were injured, and the crowd was driven away. Between 8,000 and 10,000 rioters flooded Illinois Street, the main business district, setting fires. The Pinkertons made another attempt to move the streetcars into their car-houses to protect them from being vandalised. Rioters attacked the policemen protecting the strike-breakers, and the police clubbed the rioters to drive them back. The rioters fled, and the police resumed their attempt to move the cars only to have the rioters renew the attack. Pinkertons opened fire on the crowd; four rioters were killed. The rioters eventually overpowered the police and strike-breakers and forced them to abandon their efforts.[45]

The Indianapolis Merchants' Association and other business leaders petitioned Governor Ralston to call out the Indiana National Guard. Members of both parties accused the union leaders of trying to prevent their voters from reaching the polls.[46] Ralston, after much prevarication, declared martial law. He mobilised 2,200 Guardsmen, assembling them in the city's armoury and in the basement of the Indiana Statehouse.

Companies of troops protected the important areas of the city and patrols enforced a curfew. Armed companies set up Gatling guns around the headquarters of the Traction and Terminal Company, but Ralston refused a request from company leaders that he order the guard force to operate the streetcars; Ralston instead insisted that business leaders allow him to act as an arbiter between the company and the strikers.

Ralston promised the union that he would withdraw the troops and draft legislation to reform working conditions if the men showed good faith and returned to work.[47] The following day the union and company agreed to later submit all grievances to the Indiana Public Service Commission for arbitration, and agreed to abide by its verdict. The arrangement was submitted to a workers' vote and was approved unanimously.

The Pinkerton strike-breakers were escorted out of the city by the National Guard on 8 November. They left by train to return to Chicago. The same day, the employees returned to work and normal operations resumed. The strike had lasted eight days, four strikers and two strike-breakers had been killed, several others shot, and hundreds on both sides were injured during the clashes. The events were the 'greatest breakdown in public order ever seen in Indianapolis' according to historian William D. Dalton.[48]

Meanwhile, for the Pinkertons it was business as usual, and McParland was at the centre of more controversies. When Charlie Siringo wrote his memoirs, published in 1915, about working for the Pinkerton Agency for twenty years, he accused McParland of ordering him to commit voter fraud in the re-election attempt of Colorado Governor James Peabody. He declared the agency 'corrupt' and guilty of not just election fraud but also of jury tampering, fabricating confessions, providing false witnesses, bribery, intimidation, and hiring cold killers for its clients. The agency suppressed Siringo's books, in one case with an accusation of libel. Historian MaryJoy Martin wrote: 'McParland would stop at nothing to take down [unions such as the Western Federation of Miners] because he believed his authority came from "Divine Providence". To Carry out God's Will meant he was free to break laws and lie until every man he judged evil was hanging on the gallows. Since his days in Pennsylvania he was comfortable lying under oath.' McParland died on 18 May 1919 in Denver's Mercy Hospital. He left a widow, Mary, but no children.

The Pinkertons continued to be associated with strike-breaking in the public consciousness and continued operating the dark arts of industrial spying and infiltration. That only changed in 1937 following revelations of the La Follette Civil Liberties Committee investigating anti-union malpractice.[49] It revealed that the agency was still receiving hundreds of thousands of dollars yearly for supplying leading corporations with labour spies. According to the committee, the Pinkertons had a gross annual income of over \$2 million in 1934 and Robert A. Pinkerton, by now the head of the agency, received from it in dividends alone \$129,500 in 1935, a sum much greater than the salary of the President of the United States.

Pinkerton's criminal detection work also suffered from the police modernisation movement, which saw the rise of the Federal Bureau of Investigations. The agency had little option but to concentrate on company protection services. In July 2003, Pinkerton was acquired by Securitas, one of the world's largest security companies.

Edward Zane Caroll Judson, who went by Ned Buntline. Under this *nom de plume* he did more than anybody to advance the dime novel, and also endeavoured to whip up anti-immigrant rhetoric through a series of doomed newspaper ventures.

John Morrissey, connected criminal, champion boxer, leading Dead Rabbit gangster, state senator and member of the US House of Representatives. (Courtesy of the Library of Congress)

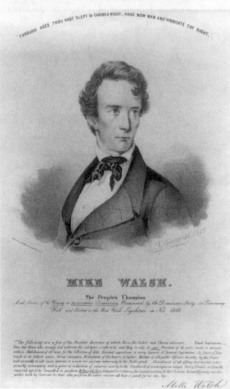

Mike Walsh was one of the earliest leaders of the Bowery Boys, and became a kind of martyr figure among the white workingmen of New York during his periods of incarceration. (Courtesy of the Library of Congress)

New York's Bowery neighbourhood in Manhattan, a notorious den of gangsters at the turn of the twentieth century and proud home of the Bowery Boys. (Courtesy of the Library of Congress)

A depiction from the *Illustrated London News* of a pitched battle during the Draft Riots in New York between rioters and soldiers of the Union Army.

Above left: The depiction in *Harper's Weekly* of Maryland National Guard's Sixth Regiment fighting its way through downtown Baltimore during the Great Upheaval. (Courtesy of the Library of Congress)

Above right: The infamous Pinkerton agent James McParland, who infiltrated the 'Molly Maguires' on behalf of Franklin B. Gowen of the Philadelphia and Reading Coal and Iron Company. His testimony alone led numerous union men to the gallows on trumped-up charges. (Courtesy of the Library of Congress)

Below: The burning of Pennsylvania Railroad and Union Depot in Pittsburgh during the Great Upheaval, as depicted in *Harper's Weekly* in July 1877. (Courtesy of the Library of Congress)

Striking workers during the Pullman strike of 1893. (Courtesy of the Library of Congress)

Living conditions were dreadful among the poor at the time of the Pullman strike. (Courtesy of the Library of Congress)

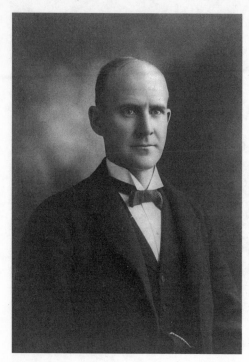

Left: Eugene V. Debs, founder of the American Railway Union. Debs became the reluctant leader of the Pullman strike, having first tried to dissuade the workers. He was imprisoned for his role and became a socialist while incarcerated, going on to found the International Workers of the World and be the five-time presidential candidate for the Socialist Party of America. (Courtesy of the Library of Congress)

Below: Pullman strikers outside the Arcade Building in Pullman, Chicago. (Courtesy of the Abraham Lincoln Historical Digitization Project)

Right: The first flyer to advertise the labour demonstration at Haymarket on 4 May 1886 was highly controversial for the language it used, calling on working men to arm themselves and 'come in full force'. It was quickly withdrawn, but too late. (Courtesy of the Library of Congress)

Below: Haymarket as it appeared in the late nineteenth century. The bomb that was thrown into the throng of police and demonstrators kicked off gun battles that killed several people. (Courtesy of the Library of Congress)

Attention Workingmen!

GREAT

MASS-MEETING

TO-NIGHT, at 7.30 o'clock,

AT THE

HAYMARKET, Randolph St., Bet. Desplaines and Halsted.

Good Speakers will be present to denounce the latest atrocious act of the police, the shooting of our fellow-workmen yesterday afternoon.

Workingmen Arm Yourselves and Appear in Full Force!

THE EXECUTIVE COMMITTEE.

Achtung, Arbeiter!

Große

Massen-Versammlung

Heute Abend, ½8 Uhr, auf dem

Heumarkt, Randolph-Straße, zwischen Desplaines u. Halsted-Str.

☞ Gute Redner werden den neuesten Schurkenstreich der Polizei, indem sie gestern Nachmittag unsere Brüder erschoß, geißeln.

☞ Arbeiter, bewaffnet Euch und erscheint massenhaft!

Das Executiv-Comite.

Left: A *Harper's* front page for 1892 reporting on the Homestead massacre, also known as the Pinkerton Rebellion. Demonstrations representing the Amalgamated Association of Iron and Steel Workers turned deadly after a lockout by the Carnegie Steel Company, with Pinkertons trading fire with strikers. (Courtesy of the Library of Congress)

Below: Hard, underpaid labour on the sugar plantations of Louisiana in the late 1800s led to conflicts which eventually mutated into race war and lynchings, demonstrating the fine line between economic and racial conflict at the time. (Library of Congress)

Above: Chicago in 1900, a powder keg for social unrest. (Courtesy of the Library of Congress)

Below left: Jack Johnson, whose comfortable defeat of Great White Hope James J. Jeffries sparked race riots and lynchings. (Courtesy of the Library of Congress)

Below right: Ida B. Wells, an investigative journalist and early leader in the Civil Rights Movement. Born into slavery, one of her many contributions to American social justice came in the form of eyewitness reports she gathered of the massacre in East St Louis in 1917. (Courtesy of Library of Congress)

IDA B. WELLS.

Above: The silent protest that took place in New York in solidarity with the victims of the East St Louis riots. (Courtesy of the Library of Congress)

Below: Little Italy in Manhattan, *circa* 1900. Italian enclaves such as this popped up in numerous cities and saw the steady growth of organised crime centred on Sicilian families. (Courtesy of the Library of Congress)

Above: The docks in New Orleans. A great deal of goods were trafficked through here, making it a key battleground for various organised crime groups. (Courtesy of the Library of Congress)

Right: After the slaying of police chief David Hennessy was attributed to 'dagoes', various suspects were pulled from jail after some were acquitted. They were lynched by a mob of thousands that counted prominent citizens among its number. (Courtesy of the Library of Congress)

Giuseppe 'the Clutch Hand' Morello, the first boss of the Morello crime family, now known more widely as the Genovese family.

William Flynn, who pursued members of the Morello gang, partnered up with police detective Joe Petrosino, who was later murdered, likely on Giuseppe Morello's orders. Here Petrosino is pictured with two other police officers escorting Mafia hitman Petto 'the Ox', one of Giuseppe's enforcers. (Courtesy of the Library of Congress)

Members of the Camorra gang on Navy Street. In 1916 they invited six Morello leaders to discuss peace terms on their turf; though only two Morello men showed up, the two were gunned down. One was the Morellos' top man, Nick Terranova.

Downtown Boston in 1917. (Courtesy of the Library of Congress)

State Guardsmen are briefed during the Boston Police Strike of 1919, in which police officers demanded recognition for their trade union and improved wages and working conditions. The striking officers were depicted uncharitably in the press, and President Calvin Coolidge improved his public image through the ostensibly firm position he took. (Courtesy of the Massachusetts Digital Commonwealth)

A strike leader addresses demonstrators in Gary, Indiana. (Courtesy of the Library of Congress)

Thomas Felts, right, and D. O. Baldwin, left, of the Baldwin–Felts Detective Agency, which was instrumental in strike-breaking activities and violent confrontations with union members. Their actions were central to the battles of Matewan and Blair Mountain. (Courtesy of the Library of Congress)

Sid Hatfield, chief of police for Matewan, West Virginia. After Baldwin–Felts men evicted a number of miners from their homes in Matewan, Hatfield confronted the detectives and a gun battle ensued in which the Baldwin–Felts men were driven off. He was killed in broad daylight attending court where he was to be tried for conspiracy.

Troops camped at Blair Mountain during the hostilities.

The landscape around Blair Mountain even today gives an impression of the difficulty of the combat that took place there. (Courtesy of the Library of Congress)

6

Race War

'(shot down) like so many cattle.'

Lynchings and mass racial violence were not the sole preserve of the Deep South. In the East and central USA there were bouts of utter carnage. Blacks were hanged from lampposts, kicked to death, their homes burnt out and, on at least one occasion, their neighbourhoods bombed from the air. Almost all were intrinsically linked to the battles between organised labour and capitalism following the Civil War due to the flood of relatively cheap labour when emancipated slaves, and their children and grandchildren, came onto the market in cities which embraced the transatlantic version of the Industrial Revolution. The outcomes were far bloodier, and lasted longer, that anything seen in Britain or continental Europe.

However, there were earlier race riots in which African Americans were not the main target. As we have seen, during the early to mid-nineteenth century, violent rioting occurred between Protestant 'Nativists' and recently arrived Irish Catholic immigrants. The West, of course, was not immune to such turmoil – the San Francisco Vigilance Movements of 1851 and 1856, seen by many as establishing law and order in the face of government corruption, systematically attacked first Irish immigrants, and later Mexicans, Chileans who came as miners during the California Gold Rush, and Chinese workers tunnelling through mountains to build the first transcontinental railway. But the scale of such pogroms was far greater in the East, and most often directed against blacks who had swapped slavery for paid work.

In 1887, for example, workers at sugar plantations in Louisiana, organised by the Knights of Labor, went on strike for an increase in their pay to $1.25 a day. Most of the workers were black, but some were white, infuriating Governor Samuel Douglas McEnery, who declared that 'God Almighty has himself drawn the color line'. McEnery served as Louisiana governor from 1881 until 1888, and was a US Senator from 1897 until 1910, which shows how popular his views were among white voters.

The Knights of Labor was the largest of the American labour organisations during the 1880s, and the first to champion the rights of black workers. The collapse of the National Labor Union in 1873 left a vacuum for workers looking for organised support. The Knights of Labor was founded as a secret society by a small group of Philadelphia tailors at the end of 1869, reached 28,000 members in 1880, then jumped to 100,000 in 1884. By 1886 some 20 per cent of all workers were affiliated with the organisation, ballooning to nearly 800,000 members.[1] The Knights of Labor elected as their leader Terence V. Powderly, a visionary with a coherent agenda to improve the lot of the workers. The body grew rapidly.[2] It was open to all workers and its members included low-skilled workers, railroad workers, immigrants and steel workers.[3] Rejecting socialism and anarchism, its members demanded the eight-hour day, and promoted republicanism. In some cases, it acted as a labour union, negotiating with employers. In 1887 the Knights of Labor organised a major three-week sugar strike against Louisiana cane plantations during the critical harvest season. The outcome was a massacre.

Enmities in Louisiana, a former slave state, ran deep. After emancipation, planters complained bitterly about having to negotiate with representatives of black workers. One of the richest, Alexander F. Pugh, wrote: 'Negroes and federal officers took up too much time in negotiating new labor contracts. Part of the delay was occasioned by the fact that the Negroes were dissatisfied with the settlements from the past year, and additional delays were brought about because of changes in labor rules and regulations.'[4] Pugh wrote in his diary: 'I have agreed with the Negroes today to pay them monthly wages. It was very distasteful to me, but I could do no better. Everybody else in the neighborhood has agreed to pay the same, and mine [laborers] would listen to nothing else.'[5]

The sugar cane harvest and processing involved a large labour force pushed to physical extremes. Sugar plantations were described as 'factories in the field' and had high death rates before and after the abolition of slavery.[6] Workers were forced by owners to accept scrip for pay which had already been cut because of a declining international market. The 'pasteboard tickets' were redeemable only at company stores, which operated at high profit margins. The plantation kept the books, and often illiterate workers were permanently in debt. Required by law to pay off the debt, workers became essentially bound to the plantation. Effective slavery had returned to the area. The Knights of Labor exposed the blatant injustice and regional recruitment soared.[7]

In October 1877, the millionaire planter Duncan F. Kenney had founded the state-wide Louisiana Sugar Producers' Association (LSPA) of 200 of the largest planters in the state, and served as its president. The association lobbied the federal government for sugar tariffs, and also adopted a uniform pay scale. They withheld 80 per cent of the wages until the end of the harvest season, in order to keep workers on the plantations until the crop was in. The workers resisted, but the state government supported the powerful planters, sending in state militia and using convict labour from prisons to harvest and process the cane.

In late October labour representatives delivered demands to the LPSA that included an increase in wages to $1.25 a day, bi-weekly payments, and wages in currency instead of tickets or scrip. As the LPSA ignored the demands, the Knights of Labor called a strike for 1 November, timed to coincide with the critical 'rolling period' of the crop, in Lafourche, Terrebonne, St Mary, and Assumption parishes. Most plantations fell idle. The stoppage threatened the entire sugar cane harvest for the year. It was the largest labour action ever seen in the industry, involving an estimated 10,000 workers, nine-tenths of them black.

The militia suppressed strikers in St Mary parish, resulting in up to twenty killed or wounded on 5 November in the black village of Pattersonville. The militia protected some 800 contract workers brought to Terrebone parish, and helped capture and arrest fifty strikers, most for union activities. The strike collapsed, and workers returned to the plantations. The workers prevented the local sheriffs from evicting anyone from the plantation-owned cabins they lived in, so the state again sent in the Louisiana militia. They evicted the workers at gunpoint and helped scab replacements get safely to the fields. The strikers, with nowhere to go, gathered in Thibodaux. The state militia withdrew, leaving it to local officials to manage an increasingly dangerous situation.

Parish District Judge Taylor Beattie, who owned Orange Grove Plantation and was a member of the LPSA, set up a 'Peace and Order Committee' in Thibodaux, in all but name a vigilante murder squad for vested interests. He declared martial law and recruited 300 white men for his committee to serve as a paramilitary force. He ordered blacks within the city limits to show a pass to enter or leave. Beattie was an ex-Confederate, an ex-slaveholder and a former member of the Knights of the White Camelia, set up to violently suppress black Republicans voting during Reconstruction. Beattie ordered the paramilitary to close the entrances to the city on the morning of 22 November and stand guard. The strikers resisted and fired on two of the pickets, injuring both. After hearing reports of strikers firing into operating sugar mills, whites in Thibodaux organised vigilante squads to guard the town, claiming that the strikers were intent on 'burning it down'. Whites rode through the neighbourhood firing their weapons, sparking understandable panic. Strikers and their family members were rounded up; many were told to 'run for their lives' and then executed.[8] They targeted known and suspected Knights of Labor organisers. Blacks were murdered on town streets and in the surroundings woods and swamps where they had tried to hide. Bodies were left in shallow graves.

A black newspaper in New Orleans described the scene:

'Six killed and five wounded' is what the daily papers here say, but from an eye witness to the whole transaction we learn that no less than thirty-five Negroes were killed outright. Lame men and blind women shot; children and hoary-headed grandsires ruthlessly swept down! The Negroes offered no resistance; they could not, as the killing was unexpected. Those of them not killed took to the woods, a majority of them finding refuge in this city (New Orleans).[9]

According to historian Rebecca Jarvis Scott, 'no credible official count of the victims of the Thibodaux massacre was ever made; bodies continued to turn up in shallow graves outside of town for weeks to come'. Eric Arnesen wrote that local white residents privately admitted more than fifty workers were murdered in Thibodaux, but the total was uncertain. Along the Bayou Lafourche, black oral history has told of hundreds of casualties, including wounded and missing. James Keith Hogue attributes fifty deaths to the three-day attacks by the paramilitaries, saying that, in addition, numerous Knights of Labor organisers disappeared over the next year.

After the massacre, the organisation of sugar workers was suspended, and plantation workers returned to the fields under the owners' terms. White Democrats, who dominated the state legislature, soon passed laws for disenfranchisement of blacks, racial segregation and other Jim Crow rules. There was no more effort to organise sugar workers until the 1940s. The frail structure of the Knights of Labor, battered by charges of failure and violence, began to disintegrate. Most members abandoned the movement, leaving at most 100,000 in 1890. Remnants continued in existence until 1949, when the group's last fifty-member local dropped its affiliation.

For many decades the Thibodeaux massacre was virtually erased from state histories. But at the time the massacre caused a furore in the small-circulation, black radical press. An anonymous article headlined 'Red-Handed Murder: Negroes Wantonly Killed at Thibodaux, La.' thundered:

Murder, foul murder has been committed and the victims were inoffensive and law-abiding Negroes. Assassins more cruel, more desperate, more wanton than any who had hitherto practiced their nefarious business in Louisiana have been shooting down, like so many cattle, the Negroes in and around Thibodaux, Lafourthe parish, La.

For three weeks past the public has been regaled, daily, with garbled reports of the troubles existing between the laborers and planters in the sugar district. Strange to say not one of these reports, excepting two, exculpated the Negroes from any desire, or any intention so far as their actions could be judged, of resorting to violence and bloodshed in order to secure the just and equable demand made by them for an increase of wages. Militia from different portions of the State have been on duty in the threatened section, and during all of this time the only acts and crimes of an outrageous character committed were so committed by either the troops, sugar planters or those in their hire. The Negroes during all of the time behaving peaceably, quietly and within the limits of the law, desiring only to secure what they asked and demanding what they had and have a perfect right to do – an increase of wages.

The planters refused to accede to their requests and at the same time ordered them from the plantations. At this juncture, and especially was it the case at both Thibodaux and Houma, the Knights of Labor, to which organization most of the laborers belong, hired all the empty houses in the above towns they could, and there quartered the homeless blacks. Such unexpected action maddened the planters and their followers, (some excepted) and as a [con]sequence they resorted to arms and every other devilish device which the ingenuity of a few chosen spirits could devise in order to force the Negroes to work for the wages offered.

With an obstinacy worthy of the righteousness of their cause the Negroes quartered in Thibodaux refused to accede to the planters. Such being the case, the planters determined to kill a number of them, thus endeavouring to force the balance into submission. The militia was withdrawn to better accomplish this purpose, and no sooner had they departed for home than the preparation for the killing of the Negroes began. Last Sunday night, about 11 o'clock, plantation wagons containing strange men fully armed were driven into Thibodaux and to Frost's restaurant and hotel and there the strangers were quartered. Who they were and where they came from, no one, with me exception of the planters and Judge Taylor Beattie, seemed to know; but it is a fact that next day, Monday, [martial] law was declared and these cavalcades of armed men put on patrol duty and no Negro allowed to either leave or enter the town without shooters, insolent and overbearing toward the Negroes, doing all in their power to provoke a disturbance ... Finding that the Negroes could not be provoked from their usual quiet, it was resolved that some pretext or other should be given so that a massacre might ensue.

It came: Tuesday night the patrol shot two of their number, Gorman and Molaison, and the cry went forth 'to arms, to arms! the Negroes are killing the whites!' This was enough. The unknown men who by this time had turned out to be Shreveport guerrillas, well versed in the Ouachita and Red River plan of killing 'niggers,' assisted by Lafourthe's oldest and best, came forth and fired volley after volley, into the houses, the churches, and wherever a Negro could be found.

Such is a true tale of affairs as enacted at Thibodaux. To read it makes the blood of every man, black or white, tingle if his system is permeated with one spark of manhood. To even think that such disregard of human life is permitted in this portion of the United States makes one question whether or not the war was a failure? Citizens of the United States killed by a mob directed by a State judge, and no redress for the same! Laboring men seeking an advance in wages, treated as if they were dogs! Black men whose equality before the law was secured at the point of the bayonet shown less consideration than serfs? This is what is being enacted in Louisiana today ... At such times and upon such occasions, words of condemnation fall like snow-flakes upon molten lead. The blacks should defend their lives, and if they needs must die, die with their faces toward their persecutors fighting for their homes, their children and their lawful rights.[10]

A modern account summed up: 'This strike took place at a time when the labor movement was a completely new idea, and anything must have seemed possible to those workers who began to dream of a better life. Their dreams, not yet dimmed by cynicism, recuperation, or fear, could only be destroyed by barbaric brutality on the scale of the Thibodeaux massacre. The next attempt to organize sugarcane workers in southeast Louisiana came in the 1950s, long after this first bloody battle in cane country, because they cannot kill an idea.'[11]

***

White-on-black race riots if anything got bloodier after the turn of the century. The Atlanta race riot of 1906 was contemporarily described in the media as a 'racial massacre of negroes'.[12] The full death toll remains unknown, but 'officially' at least twenty-five blacks[13] and two whites were killed. Unofficial reports ranged up to 100. Some blacks were hanged from lampposts.[14]

The Atlanta elite considered their city to be a prime example of how whites and blacks could live together in racial harmony, but racial tensions between workers were exacerbated by the black franchise. African Americans stood for office and opened successful businesses, several steps too far for city rulers. There was increased competition between blacks and whites for jobs and that heightened class distinctions.[15]

The gubernatorial election of 1906 in which M. Hoke Smith and Clark Howell competed for the Democratic nomination saw tensions boil over. Both candidates wanted to disenfranchise black voters because they felt that they could hand the election to the other candidate. Hoke Smith was a former publisher of the *Atlanta Journal*, while Clark Howell was the editor of the *Atlanta Constitution*.

Both newspapers fomented racial hatred for political ends, spreading the fear that whites would not be able to maintain the current social order. In print, bars that were run and frequented by black citizens were attacked as 'dives' of iniquity decorated by portraits of nude white women. Police reports of white women allegedly sexually molested and raped by black men[16] were heavily reported, usually with little or no foundation.

In addition to the political debates waged in the *Journal* and the *Constitution*, other newspapers, especially the *Atlanta Georgian* and the *Atlanta News*, carried stories throughout the year about alleged assaults on white women by black men. The media provoked anger and hatred in its white readers with editorials, and cartoons linking blacks to rising crime, particularly rape, and 'exposing' the desire of 'uppity' blacks to achieve equality with whites. By late September, after newspaper reports of four separate alleged assaults – none of them substantiated – by blacks on white women circulated in Atlanta, mob violence erupted[17] on the afternoon of Saturday 22 September. Extra editions of these accounts, sensationalised with lurid details and inflammatory language intended to inspire fear if not revenge, circulated, and soon thousands of white men and boys gathered in downtown Atlanta. City leaders, including Mayor James G. Woodward, sought to calm the increasingly indignant crowds but failed to do so. By early evening, the crowd had become a mob; from then until after midnight, they surged down Decatur Street, Pryor Street, Central Avenue, and throughout the central business district, assaulting hundreds of blacks. They attacked black-owned businesses, smashing the windows of black leader Alonso Herndon's barbershop and, as Herndon had gone home, killing the barbers in a shop across the road. The crowd also attacked streetcars, entering trolley cars and beating black men and women; at least three men were beaten to death.[18] *Le Petit Journal* reported: 'Black men and women were thrown from trolley-cars, assaulted with clubs and pelted with stones. An unknown and disputed number of blacks were killed and many injured.' Finally, the militia was summoned around midnight, and streetcar service was suspended. The mob showed no signs of letting up, however, and the crowd was dispersed only once a heavy rain began to fall around 2 a.m. Atlanta was then under the control of the state militia.

On Sunday, 23 September, the Atlanta newspapers reported that blacks were no longer a problem for whites because Saturday night's violence had driven them off public streets. While the police, armed with rifles, and militia patrolled the streets and key landmarks and guarded white property, blacks secretly obtained weapons to arm themselves against the mob, fearing its return. White vigilante groups invaded some black neighbourhoods.

The following day a group of African Americans held a meeting in Brownsville, about 2 miles south of downtown Atlanta and home to the historically black Clark College and Gammon Theological Seminary. The blacks were heavily armed. When Fulton County police learned of the gathering, they launched a raid; a shootout ensued, and an officer was killed. In response, three companies of heavily armed militia were sent to Brownsville, where they seized weapons and arrested more than 250 African American men. Sporadic fighting continued throughout the day.

Walter White, the future head of the NAACP, the National Association for the Advancement of Colored People, gave the best eyewitness account:

> The unseasonably oppressive heat of an Indian summer day hung like a steaming blanket over Atlanta. My sisters and I had casually commented upon the unusual quietness. It seemed to stay Mother's volubility and reduced Father, who was more taciturn, to monosyllables. But, as I remember it, no other sense of impending trouble impinged upon our consciousness. I had read the inflammatory headlines in the *Atlanta News* and the more restrained ones in the *Atlanta Constitution* which reported alleged rapes and other crimes committed by Negroes. But these were so standard and familiar that they made – as I look back on it now – little impression. The stories were more frequent, however, and consisted of eight-column streamers instead of the usual two or four-column ones.
>
> Father was a mail collector. His tour of duty was from three to eleven P.M. He made his rounds in a little cart into which one climbed from a step in the rear. I used to drive the cart for him from two until seven, leaving him at the point nearest our home on Houston Street, to return home either for study or sleep. That day Father decided that I should not go with him. I appealed to Mother, who thought it might be all right, provided Father sent me home before dark because, she said, 'I don't think they would dare start anything before nightfall.' Father told me as we made the rounds that ominous rumors of a race riot that night were sweeping

the town. But I was too young that morning to understand the background of the riot. I became much older during the next thirty-six hours, under circumstances which I now recognize as the inevitable outcome of what had preceded.

One of the most bitter political campaigns of that bloody era was reaching its climax. Hoke Smith had fought for legislation to ban child labor and railroad rate discriminations. He had denounced the corrupt practices of the railroads and the state railway commission, which, he charged, was as much owned and run by northern absentee landlords as were the railroads themselves. He had fought for direct primaries to nominate senators and other candidates by popular vote, for a corrupt practices act, for an elective railway commission, and for state ownership of railroads – issues which were destined to be still fought for nearly four decades later by Ellis Arnall. For these reforms he was hailed throughout the nation as a genuine progressive along with La Follette of Wisconsin and Folk of Missouri.

To overcome the power of the regular Democratic organization, Hoke Smith sought to heal the feud of long standing between himself and the powerful ex-radical Populist, Thomas E. Watson. Watson was the leader of an agrarian movement in the South which, in alliance with the agrarian West, threatened for a time the industrial and financial power of the East. He had made fantastic strides in uniting Negro and white farmers with Negro and white industrial workers. He had advocated enfranchisement of Negroes and poor whites, the abolition of lynching, control of big business, and rights for the working man. He had fought with fists, guns, and spine-stirring oratory in a futile battle to stop the spread of an industrialized, corporate society.

His break with the Democratic Party during the 1890s and the organization of the Populist Party made the Democrats his implacable enemies. The North, busy building vast corporations and individual fortunes, was equally fearful of Tom Watson. Thus was formed between reactionary Southern Democracy and conservative Northern Republicanism the basis of cooperation whose fullest flower is to be seen in the present-day coalition of conservatives in Congress. This combination crushed Tom Watson's bid for national leadership in the presidential elections of 1896 and smashed the Populist movement. Watson ran for president in 1904 and 1908, both times with abysmal failure. His defeats soured him to the point of vicious acrimony. He turned from his ideal of interracial decency to one of virulent hatred and denunciation of the 'nigger.' He thus became a naturally ally for Hoke Smith in the gubernatorial election in Georgia in 1906.

The two rabble-rousers stumped the state screaming, 'Nigger, nigger, nigger!' Some white farmers still believed Watson's abandoned doctrine that the interests of Negro and white farmers and industrial workers were identical. They feared that Watson's and Smith's new scheme to disfranchise Negro voters would lead to disfranchisement of poor whites. Tom Watson was sent to trade on his past reputation to reassure them that such was not the case and that their own interests were best served by now hating 'niggers.'

Watson's oratory had been especially effective among the cotton mill workers and other poor whites in and near Atlanta. The *Atlanta Journal* on August 1, 1906, in heavy type, all capital letters, printed an incendiary appeal to race prejudice backing up Watson and Smith which declared: 'Political equality being thus preached to the negro in the ring papers and on the stump, what wonder that he makes no distinction between political and social equality? He grows more bumptious on the street, more impudent in his dealings with white men, and then, when he cannot achieve social equality as he wishes, with the instinct of the barbarian to destroy what he cannot attain to, he lies in wait, as that dastardly brute did yesterday near this city, and assaults the fair young girlhood of the south ... '

At the same time, a daily newspaper was attempting to wrest from the *Atlanta Journal* leadership in the afternoon field. The new paper, the *Atlanta News*, in its scramble for circulation and advertising took a lesson from the political race and began to play up in eight-column streamers stories of the raping of white women by Negroes. That every one of the stories was afterward found to be wholly without foundation was of no importance. The *News* circulation, particularly in street sales, leaped swiftly upward as the headlines were bawled by lusty-voiced newsboys. Atlanta became a tinder box.

Fuel was added to the fire by a dramatization of Thomas Dixon's novel *The Clansman* in Atlanta. (This was later made by David Wark Griffith into *The Birth of a Nation*, and did more than anything else to make successful the revival of the Ku Klux Klan.) The late Ray Stannard Baker, telling the story of the Atlanta riot in *Along the Color Line*, characterized Dixon's fiction and its effect on Atlanta and the South as 'incendiary and cruel.' No more apt or accurate description could have been chosen.

During the afternoon preceding the riot little bands of sullen, evil-looking men talked excitedly on street corners all over downtown Atlanta. Around seven o'clock my father and I were driving toward a mail box at the corner of Peachtree and Houston Streets when there came from near-by Pryor Street a roar the like of which I had never heard before, but which sent a sensation of mingled fear and excitement coursing through my body. I asked permission of Father to go and see what the trouble was. He bluntly ordered me to stay in the cart. A little later we drove down Atlanta's main business thoroughfare, Peachtree Street. Again we heard the terrifying cries, this time near at hand and coming toward us. We saw a lame Negro bootblack from Herndon's barber shop pathetically trying to outrun a mob of whites. Less than a hundred yards from us the chase ended. We saw clubs and fists descending to the accompaniment of savage shouting and cursing. Suddenly a voice cried, 'There goes another nigger!' Its work done, the mob went after new prey. The body with the withered foot lay dead in a pool of blood on the street.

Father's apprehension and mine steadily increased during the evening, although the fact that our skins were white kept us from attack. Another circumstance favored us – the mob had not yet grown violent enough to attack United States government property. But I could see Father's relief when he punched the time clock at eleven P.M. and got into the cart to go home. He wanted to go the back way down Forsyth Street, but I begged him, in my childish excitement and ignorance, to drive down Marietta to Five Points, the heart of Atlanta's business district, where the crowds were densest and the yells loudest. No sooner had we turned into Marietta Street, however, than we saw careening toward us an undertaker's barouche. Crouched in the rear of the vehicle were three Negroes clinging to the sides of the carriage as it lunged and swerved. On the driver's seat crouched a white man, the reins held taut in his left hand. A huge whip was gripped in his right. Alternately he lashed the horses and, without looking backward, swung the whip in savage swoops in the faces of members of the mob as they lunged at the carriage determined to seize the three Negroes.

There was no time for us to get out of its path, so sudden and swift was the appearance of the vehicle. The hub cap of the right rear wheel of the barouche hit the right side of our much lighter wagon. Father and I instinctively threw our weight and kept the cart from turning completely over. Our mare was a Texas mustang which, frightened by the sudden blow, lunged in the air as Father clung to the reins. Good fortune was with us. The cart settled back on its four wheels as Father said in a voice which brooked no dissent, 'We are going home the back way and not down Marietta.' But again on Pryor Street we heard the cry of the mob. Close to us and in our direction ran a stout and elderly woman who cooked at a downtown white hotel. Fifty yards behind, a mob which filled the street from curb to curb was closing in. Father handed the reins to me and, though he was of slight stature, reached down and lifted the woman into the cart. I did not need to be told to lash the mare to the fastest speed she could muster.

The church bells tolled the next morning for Sunday service. But no one in Atlanta believed for a moment that the hatred and lust for blood had been appeased. Like skulls on a cannibal's hut the hats and caps of victims of the mob of the night before had been hung on the iron hooks of telegraph poles. None could tell whether each hat represented a dead Negro. But we knew that some of those who had worn the hats would never again wear any.

Late in the afternoon friends of my father's came to warn of more trouble that night. They told us that plans had been perfected for a mob to form on Peachtree Street just after nightfall to march down Houston Street to what the white people called 'Darktown,' three blocks or so below our house, to 'clean out the niggers.' There had never been a firearm in our house before that day. Father was reluctant even in those circumstances to violate the law, but he at last gave in at Mother's insistence. We turned out the lights early, as did all our neighbors. No one removed his clothes or thought of sleep. Apprehension was tangible. We could almost touch its cold and clammy surface. Toward midnight the unnatural quiet was broken by a roar that grew steadily in volume. Even today I grow tense in remembering it.

Father told Mother to take my sisters, the youngest of them only six, to the rear of the house, which offered more protection from stones and bullets. My brother George was away, so Father and I, the only males in the house, took our places at the front windows of the parlor. The windows opened on a porch along the front side of the house, which in turn gave onto a narrow lawn that sloped down to the street and a picket fence. There was a crash as Negroes smashed the street lamp at the corner of Houston and Piedmont Avenue down the street. In a very few minutes the vanguard of the mob, some of them bearing torches, appeared. A voice which we recognized as that of the son of the grocer with whom we had traded for many years yelled, 'That's where that nigger mail carrier lives! Let's burn it down! It's too nice for a nigger to live in!' In the eerie light Father turned his drawn face toward me. In a voice as quiet as though he were asking me to pass him the sugar at the breakfast table, he said, 'Son, don't shoot until the first man puts his foot on the lawn and then – don't you miss!'

The mob moved toward the lawn. I tried to aim my gun, wondering what it would feel like to kill a man. Suddenly there was a volley of shots. The mob hesitated, stopped. Some friends of my father's had barricaded themselves in a two-story brick building just below our house. It was they who had fired. Some of the mobsmen, still bloodthirsty, shouted, 'Let's go get the nigger.' Others, afraid now for their safety, held back. Our friends, noting the hesitation, fired another volley. The mob broke and retreated up Houston Street.

In the quiet that followed I put my gun aside and tried to relax. But a tension different from anything I had ever known possessed me. I was gripped by the knowledge of my identity, and in the depths of my soul I was vaguely aware that I was glad of it. I was sick with loathing for the hatred which had flared before me that night and come so close to making me a killer; but I was glad I was not one of those who hated; I was glad I was not one of those made sick and murderous by pride.[19]

City officials, businessmen, clergy, and – hypocritically – the press called for an end to violence, because it was damaging Atlanta's image as a thriving New South city. The riot had been covered throughout the US and internationally. Fears of continued disorder prompted some white civic leaders to seek a dialogue with black elites, creating the false hope among mainstream Northern whites that racial reconciliation was possible in the South without national intervention. Such ersatz hopes, however, exacerbated black social divisions, leaving the city among the most segregated and socially stratified in the nation. Black businesses were dispersed to the east, where the district Sweet Auburn soon developed and flourished.[20]

Newspaper accounts at the time and subsequent scholarly treatments of the riot vary widely on the number of casualties. Estimates range from twenty-five to forty African American deaths, although the city coroner issued only ten death certificates for black victims. Most accounts agree that only two whites were killed, one of whom was a woman who suffered a heart attack on seeing the mob outside her home.[21]

The *New York Times* reported that when the mayor was asked as to the measures taken, he replied: 'The best way to prevent a race riot depends entirely upon the cause. If your inquiry has anything to do with the present situation in Atlanta, then I would say the only remedy is to remove the cause. As long as the black brutes assault our white women, just so long will they be unceremoniously dealt with.'[22] The *Charleston News and Courier* wrote: 'Separation of the races is the only radical solution of the negro problem in this country. There is nothing new about it. It was the Almighty who established the bounds of the habitation of the races. The negroes were brought here by compulsion; they should be induced to leave here by persuasion.'

A grand jury was convened in Fulton County and laid the blame squarely on press rabblerousing: 'Believing that the sensational manner in which the afternoon newspapers of Atlanta have presented to the people the news of the various criminal acts recently committed in this county has largely influenced the creation of the spirit animating the mob of last Saturday night; and that the editorial utterances of *The Atlanta News* for some time past have been calculated to create a disregard for the proper administration of the law and to promote the organization of citizens to act outside of the law in the punishment of crime.'[23]

Some black Americans agonised over their opinions on the necessity of armed self-defence. Harvard-educated W. E. B. Du Bois stated after the Atlanta riot: 'I bought a Winchester double-barrelled shotgun and two dozen rounds of shells filled with buckshot. If a white mob had stepped on the campus where I lived I would without hesitation have sprayed their guts over the grass.'[24] In later years Du Bois argued that organised political violence by black Americans was folly, but in response to real-world threats on black people, he 'was adamant about the legitimacy and perhaps the duty of self-defense, even where there [might be a] danger of spill-over into political violence'. Efforts to promote racial reconciliation and understanding included the creation of the Commission on Interracial Cooperation in 1919.[25]

However, increased segregation, the loss of short-lived voting power, the rise of the Ku Klux Klan and other white supremacist organisations, lynchings (nearly 3,500 African Americans were so murdered between 1882 and 1968),[26] the lack of social and economic opportunities in the South, and such tragedies as those seen in Atlanta and elsewhere led to a massive upheaval with huge outcomes in the industrialised United States.

* * *

Historian Nicholas Lemann wrote that the Great Migration was 'was one of the largest and most rapid mass internal movements in history – perhaps the greatest not caused by the immediate threat of execution or starvation. In sheer numbers it outranks the migration of any other ethnic group – Italians or Irish or Jews or Poles – to [the United States]. For blacks, the migration meant leaving what had always been their economic and social base in America and finding a new one.'[27]

The Great Migration was the movement of at least 6 million African Americans from the rural South to the urban, industrialised North and Midwest of America from around 1910. Until then, more than 90 per cent of the African American population lived in the American South.[28] By the end, a bare majority of 53 per cent remained in the South, while 40 per cent lived in the North, and 7 per cent in the West. African Americans had become an urbanised population.

The Great War which devastated Europe from 1914 saw a boom in American manufacturing, and the armaments and meatpacking industries expanded. Their bosses were keen to attract cheap labour to maximise their profits. The steady arrival of poor Southern blacks provided that supply. Fifty years after a bloody civil war had resulted in emancipation, the South remained a bad place for blacks. Jim Crow laws kept them poor and powerless and maintained segregation in schools, restaurants, hotels and transport vehicles. Literacy tests and property qualifications denied them the vote. Their plight was exacerbated by falling cotton prices between 1913 and 1915 and severe floods which destroyed the homes and fields of black farmers along the Mississippi. African Americans moved from all fourteen states of the South, especially Alabama, Texas, Mississippi, Louisiana and Georgia. Big cities were the principal destinations throughout the two phases of the Great Migration: New York and Chicago, followed in order by Philadelphia, St Louis, Detroit, Pittsburgh and Indianapolis.[29] Almost half of those who migrated from Mississippi ended up in Chicago, while those from Virginia tended to move to Philadelphia, with the closest cities attracting the most migrants. Labour shortages in Northern factories due to war service meant thousands of jobs available to African Americans in steel mills, railroads, meatpacking plants, and the automobile industry. Northern companies offered special incentives to encourage black workers to relocate. In 1900–01, Chicago had a total population of 1,754,473; by 1920, the city had added more than a million residents.[30]

Because the migrants concentrated in the big cities, their influence was magnified. Cities that had been virtually all white at the start of the century became centres of black culture and politics. The northern 'Black metropolises' set up newspapers, businesses, jazz clubs, churches, and political organisations that provided the staging ground for new forms of racial politics and new forms of black culture. Educated African Americans were better able to obtain jobs, eventually gaining a measure of class mobility, but because so many people migrated in a short period of time, the African American migrants were often resented by the urban European American working class which felt threatened by the influx of new competition for jobs. Tensions were often most severe between ethnic Irish, defending their recently gained positions and territory, and recent immigrants and blacks. African Americans moved as individuals or small family groups. There was no government assistance, but Northern industries such as the railroads, meatpacking and stockyards, paid for transportation and relocation.

Populations increased so rapidly among both African American and new European immigrants that there were housing shortages in most major cities. The newer groups were forced to compete for the oldest, most rundown housing. Ethnic groups created territories which they defended against change. Discrimination often restricted African Americans to crowded neighbourhoods. The more established populations of cities tended to move to newer housing as it was developing in the outskirts. Migrants often encountered residential discrimination, in which white homeowners and realtors prevented migrants from purchasing homes or renting apartments in white neighbourhoods. Since African American migrants retained many Southern cultural and linguistic traits, such cultural differences created a sense of 'otherness'.

* * *

In 1908 Jack Johnson became the first African American world heavyweight boxing champion. Racial tensions sparked widespread violence outside the ring.

The son of slaves, Johnson grew up in Galveston, Texas, and in his teens learnt to punch strong and fast. He made his debut as a professional boxer in November 1898 and moved swiftly up the ranks within the largely segregated sport until he won the world heavyweight title from Canadian Tommy Burns in Sydney, Australia, on Boxing Day 1908.

White Americans were outraged and called for a 'Great White Hope' to take back the crown in the name of racial superiority. Before one bout, the *New York Times* thundered: 'If the black man wins, thousands and thousands of his ignorant brothers will misinterpret his victory as justifying claims to much more than mere physical equality with their white neighbors.' White contenders took him on, but were, repeatedly and often literally, floored. In 1910, former undefeated heavyweight champion James Jeffries was persuaded out of retirement to challenge Johnson, tempted from his alfalfa farm by a bounty rumoured to be $120,000. It was to be the 'Fight of the Century'.

Racial tension was brewing leading up to the fight and to prevent any harm to either boxer, guns were prohibited within the arena, as was the sale of alcohol or anyone under the effects of alcohol. On 4 July, in front of 20,000 people, in a purpose-built ring in Reno, Nevada, Jeffries' corner threw in the towel after the white veteran had been knocked down twice. Jeffries took defeat gracefully, saying: 'I could never have whipped Johnson at my best. I couldn't have hit him. No, I couldn't have reached him in 1,000 years.' White fans were not so gracious. That Fourth of July evening, when blacks celebrated with parades, race riots erupted in New York, Pittsburgh, Philadelphia, New Orleans, Atlanta, St Louis, Little Rock and Houston. At least twenty people were killed across twenty-five states and hundreds more were injured. Unlike many other race riots, not all the victims were black.

Race War

The *United Press* news agency reported from New York:

When news that Johnson had defeated Jeffries flashed over the wires last night, riots between whites and blacks followed in a dozen cities of the country, and reports this morning increase the number and add to the list of injured. Eleven riot calls were reported to police in New York within little more than an hour after the bulletin boards and extras announced the decision. One negro was clubbed to death and more than 100 were beaten up, while a number of whites are suffering from knife and bullet wounds. In the Tenderloin a negro was seized by angry whites and strung up to a lamppost. He was nearly dead when the police cut him down. At 135th and 8th in the better class negro quarter a mob of white men stormed a street car, pulled a negro into the street and kicked and beat him. Police rescued the negro. Another mob attempted to lynch a negro buying a paper. The negro drew a stiletto and held the mob off until police arrived. In the 'black and tan' and 'San Juan hill' negro sections mobs set fire to a negro tenement house, hurled stones at windows, and tried to keep the occupants in by blocking the exits. The fire department routed the mob. Smaller riots were of frequent occurrence throughout the night and early morning.

Two fatally hurt, two hospitals crowded with injured, and 236 prisoners in the city jails, summed up the result of the all-night rioting in Washington. Mobs at times estimated at 7,000 persons rushed through the streets. In Pittsburgh there were three riots. Street cars were blocked and police had to club their way through the negro section.

In Atlanta, a negro yelled 'Hurrah for Johnson' on a crowded downtown street and was instantly attacked by half a dozen white men. Police rescued him. Blacks in Wilmington, Delaware, attacked a white man following an argument over the fight. A crowd of white men then chased the blacks several blocks and bombarded a house in which one took refuge. At Columbus, Ohio, the entire negro population, numbering 20,000, celebrated the Johnson victory. About 400 men and women paraded through the streets with a band. There was fighting all along the line of march. Several were injured, but the police finally prevented trouble and allowed the march to continue into the negro section.[31]

In Ulvadia, Georgia. it was reported: 'The negroes came into the town today and started drinking heavily. Their noisy conduct angered the citizens and a posse formed to "Clean out the camp". The whites opened fire on the negroes killing three. The other negroes fled into the woods.' In Roanoke, Virginia, a newspaper reported: 'One white man, Joe Chockely, has a bullet wound in his skull and probably fatally wounded is a net result of clashes here tonight following the announcement that Jack Johnson defeated Jeffries. The trouble started when a negro just heard the news from Reno said; "Now I guess the white folks will let the negroes alone." A white man replied "no" and the two clashed. Police had difficulty landing the negro in jail, being compelled to draw their revolvers. Later a negro shot Chockely and escaped.'

In Houston, a black man, Charles Williams, had his throat fatally cut by a white man on a street car when he cheered for Johnson. In Washington, D.C. the white Thomas Mundle, an enlisted man of the Marine corps, had his throat cut by a negro and died. Joseph Benham, another white man, got into a fight with a negro and was stabbed to death. In New York a black waiter, George Crawford, had his head beaten in with a baseball bat during an argument with a white man over the fight. The assailant escaped, and Crawford died in hospital. In Mounds, Illinois, the media reported: 'One dead and one mortally wounded is the result of an attempt by four negroes to shoot up the town in honor of Jack Johnson's victory at Reno tonight. A negro police officer was killed when he attempted to arrest them.' In Philadelphia a white man was stabbed to death by a black man, while in Shreveport, Louisiana, a black man was shot in the face by a white man. The victims in both cases died.[32] The reports of violence dominated the news pages for weeks before flickering out.

Many states and cities banned the exhibition of the grainy, silent film of the Johnson–Jeffries fight. Attempts were made to erase all coverage of Johnson's victory. On 10 June 1946, Johnson died in a car crash in North Carolina after speeding angrily from a diner that refused to serve him. However, Johnson's skill as a fighter and the money that it brought made it impossible for him to be ignored by the Establishment. In terms of fame, notoriety and celebrity, he foreshadowed Muhammad Ali.

* * *

A terrified black man ran out of his burning home and was shot down by several whites, one of whom wore short trousers. Enraged working-class white men burned and beat and shot and lynched any black man who dared to walk the streets of East St Louis. Black women and girls were stripped and beaten by white women and girls who finished them off with their shoe heels. The black quarter was gutted in America's worst race riot of the twentieth century. Broken, bereaved families trudged across the Missouri River to find sanctuary, to little avail.[32] But the outrage sparked by the atrocity helped the difficult birth of an organised civil rights movement. Much of what we now know about the events of July 1917 in East St Louis is due to the eyewitness reports gathered from refugees by campaigning black journalist Ida Bell Wells. Her own story can serve as an illustration of the long struggle running up to the massacre and beyond.

Her parents were slaves and she was born on 16 July 1862, shortly before President Abraham Lincoln's proclamation of emancipation, in Holly Springs, Mississippi. She was taught at the Freedman's School, Shaw University, and when she was sixteen her parents and her ten-month-old brother died in the yellow fever epidemic which swept the South. After their funeral it was decided that the six remaining children would be split among various branches of the family. Ida was horrified at the thought and to keep the family together she dropped out of college and found work as a teacher in a black school. She and her grandmother raised the other children alone. Later Ida moved to Memphis and attended summer sessions at the well-respected Fisk University in Nashville. There she became a radical concerned with both racial and female suffrage. Aged twenty-four, she wrote: 'I will not begin at this late day by doing what my soul abhors, sugaring men, weak deceitful creatures, with flattery to retain them as escorts or gratify a revenge.'[33]

More than seventy years before the more famous Rosa Parks case, she was dragged from a train because she refused to give up her seat to a white man and move to an overcrowded blacks-only carriage. She hired a Memphis lawyer to sue the Chesapeake, Ohio and Southwestern Railway for breach of 1875 legislation banning racial discrimination on public transport. When her black lawyer was paid off by the railway company she hired a white attorney. She won her case in December 1884 and was granted a $500 settlement. That, however, was reversed two years later by the Tennessee

Supreme Court.[34] The case made her a local celebrity and, while still teaching elementary pupils, she became a reporter for the *Evening Star* newspaper, and wrote a weekly column for the *Living Way* periodical. She gained a wider reputation for highlighting racial injustice and in 1989 she became editor and co-owner of the magazine *Free Speech*, which was housed in the Beale Street Baptist Church in Memphis.[35]

In 1892 a Memphis grocery store owned by three of Ida's black friends, Thomas Moss, Calvin McDowell and Henry Stewart, was regarded as taking business from a white-owned store. Their grocery was besieged by a white mob and in the altercation three white men were shot and injured. The three black storekeepers were jailed on trumped-up charges of raping a white woman. Another, larger mob broke them out and killed them in an open field, urged on by numerous onlookers. Ida, in a *Free Speech* article, urged blacks to leave Memphis, saying: 'There is only one thing left to do, save our money and leave a town which will neither protect our lives or property, nor give us a fair trial in the courts, but takes us out and murders us in cold blood when accused by white persons.'[36] Some followed her advice, but others stayed and boycotted white businesses. Ida bought a pistol and began researching the fresh outbreak of lynching which terrorised blacks across the South. In one article she implied that some such murders followed consensual sex between black men and white women. The white populace was enraged at the supposed slur on their women and, while Ida was away, the *Free Speech* office was destroyed.

Ida went first to Philadelphia and then to New York where she joined *The Age*. During one speaking engagement she broke down in tears when recalling the lynching of her three friends. She became the head of the Anti-Lynching Crusade. In an article she concluded that lynchings were rarely caused by the alleged rape of white women, as their perpetrators claimed, but by efforts by white supremacists to deter black economic, commercial and educational progress. She moved to Chicago where she met and married black lawyer and *Chicago Conservator* owner Ferdinand Barnett. They had four children. Although distracted by family life, she continued to focus on women's groups and the anti-lynching movement, and embarked on speaking tours of the US, Britain and Europe. She shocked initially sceptical audiences with her graphic stories of the treatment of black Americans. She returned to Chicago where she reported on racial tensions between a growing black population and immigrants from Europe who were in competition for the new industrial jobs. From Chicago she again travelled South when similar tensions erupted on the banks of the Missouri River. On the bridge across it she was met by a tide of frightened blacks clutching what pathetic belongings they could carry. They, she quickly realised, were the lucky ones.

East St Louis, Illinois, was a racial tinderbox in 1917. On the far shore of the Missouri its twin city of St Louis was cosmopolitan with an international name, having hosted the World Fair and the Olympic Games in 1904. East St Louis was built around heavy industry, the railway and the meat trade. Industry had mushroomed after the Civil War, but many businesses over-extended their credit and were poorly equipped to weather the economic recession which followed the Panic of 1873. East St Louis's industries and transport links proved particularly vulnerable. Railway companies slashed the pay of some of their workers and sacked the rest, breeding unrest and trade union organisation among the white working class. A wave of strikes crippled the railways in 1877, and the one in East St Louis itself was marked by a 'bloodless, efficient and quick' takeover of the city's commerce and transportation systems. The strikers, largely German immigrants, formed a commune which halted all freight railway traffic. The strike spread to the meatpacking houses and the national stockyard. At one plant the strikers allowed 125 cattle to be butchered in return for 500 cans of beef for their families. The strike ended peacefully, leaving a legacy of organised labour militancy. That legacy would prove to have both good and bad consequences.

In East St Louis, white residents, trade unionists, workers and community leaders had been taken aback by the speed and scale of the black influx. In 1910 just 10 per cent of the city's 59,000 residents were black, and they were heavily segregated, out of sight in ghettos, their children educated in negro schools despite Illinois state laws prohibiting separate school systems. By 1916 the proportion had doubled, with up to 2,000 more arriving each month.

Many blacks who flocked to the Democrat-run boomtown were Lincoln Republicans who got caught up in the bitter 1916 elections. Some were accused of dodging residency rules to illegally vote Republican. Democrat leaders accused their opponents of buying black votes. Republican businessmen responded by boosting black recruitment in their factories and stock yards. Democrats in turn spread false stories that the incomers were responsible for a surge in crime. Police chief Ransom Payne, a leading Democrat, reported that he had received a letter from Tennessee law officers that 'bad niggers' had seen rich pickings in East St Louis and migrated there to plunder. Lurid newspaper reports added to the sense of a city under siege by alien incomers. Democrat President Woodrow Wilson warned of election fraud by 'conscienceless agents of sinister forces'. He sent Justice Department agents to interrogate 'colonized' blacks. Republican National Committee chairman William Wilcox responded by branding the whole controversy a 'bold attempt to disenfranchise Negro voters by the Democrats who have long been expert in the disenfranchisement of Negroes in the South'.

Come election day, however, the supposed avalanche of black Democrat votes did not materialise. Illinois did go Republican, but East St Louis and St Clair county voted solidly Democrat. Nonetheless the controversy, fuelled by smears and fears, had raised the temperature of bigotry and hatred. Anti-black sentiment increased heavily within the trade union movement. Historian Elliott Rudwick wrote: 'During the months after the election local organized labour leaders, who had supported President Wilson, took a leaf out of the Democratic Party's campaign handbook, and anti-Negro propaganda emanated from the economic as well as the political front.'[37]

During a series of strikes before and after the election, the company bosses exploited tension by persuading many poor blacks to become 'replacement workers'. The union men saw them as 'scabs'. Before 1913 the Aluminium Ore Company, a major employer, had initially employed only white workers, and blacks were still rare in April 1916 when the plant employed 1,900 men. The company refused to recognise the local union, the Aluminium Ore Employees Protective Association (AOEPA). Its white members went on strike and quickly forced the management to capitulate. The bosses responded to their humiliation by recruiting black non-union men to limit the impact of future strike action. By February 1917 they totalled 470, a quarter of the workforce. In almost every case black recruits replaced dismissed union activists and former strikers.

When spring arrived the AOEPA affiliated to the American Federation of Labor (AFL) and the management accused them of being in the pay of the German Kaiser, intent on disrupting the supply of war equipment to the US army and navy. The union walked out, taking with them half of the white workforce. At first production nose-dived even as the non-striking whites and blacks crossed the picket lines daily. Aluminium Ore superintendent C. B. Fox imported professional strike-breakers from New York, and a detective agency. He also 'borrowed' a supply of US government rifles and ammunition from a shooting club run by officers of the local Chamber of Commerce. And he successfully demanded two companies of the Illinois National Guard to patrol his plants and 'guard against property damage by persons who are sympathisers with the German cause'. A Federal Court judge issued a restraining order on the union in response to Fox's claim it was led by 'alien enemies'. The union continued to picket for the next two months, but the strike was effectively broken and none of the strikers were taken back. Emotions were as taut as a guitar string.

On 28 May around sixty delegates of the East St Louis Central Trades and Labor Union lodged a formal protest against black incomers with the city council under Democrat Mayor Fred Mollman. They declared: 'Negro and cheap foreign labor is being imported by the Aluminium Ore Company to tear down the standard of living of our citizens. Imported gunmen, detectives and federal injunctions are being used to crush our people.' Mollman assured them that the council was drawing up plans to limit the black tide. Whites in the packed auditorium shouted: 'East St Louis must remain a white man's town.' Lawyer Alexander Flannigan whipped them into a frenzy by declaring: 'There is no law against mob violence.' A rumour spread that a black robber had shot dead a white man. The crowd yelled: 'Lynch him!' Others demanded: 'Close the pawnshops and take the guns away from the Negroes.'

Mayor Mollman, a bit late in the day, pleaded with them to go home, but he was shouted down. The mob, by now up to 3,000 strong, rushed downtown, beating every black person in their way. They pulled down the overhead wheel trolleys of streetcars and attacked black passengers. Near Broadway they attacked a restaurant, a barbershop and saloons frequented by blacks, gutting several buildings. A few young black men resisted in one skirmish, but generally they simply tried to escape. They were chased down in ones and twos, kicked, beaten and left bleeding in gutters. The police transported some of the injured blacks to hospital, but took others to their HQ and charged them with carrying concealed weapons inside their bloodied clothes. Most police stood by and ignored the actions of the white mob. Police detectives Samuel Coppedge and Frank Wadley did, however, prevent rioters burning down several black homes on Third and Missouri Avenue.

Mollman called Major R. W. Cavanaugh, commanding officer of the National Guardsmen stationed in the city since the start of the Aluminium Ore strike. Cavanaugh told him he lacked the authority to redeploy his men from company property to defend black citizens and stifle the riot. Mollman, by now in a state of near panic, got the same response when he asked the Illinois National guard HQ in Springfield to deploy 200 troops. White mobs rampaged until the early hours of 29 May. Drink and fatigue finally sent them home, but they promised to arm themselves for another attack, jeering: 'We'll burn the Negroes out and run them out of town.'[38] Several hundred blacks carried suitcases across the Missouri bridge to St Louis. They were not molested.

Illinois Governor Frank Lowden finally despatched six companies of National Guardsmen to the city. Their priority appeared to be to disarm blacks preparing to defend their families and property against further attack. Throughout the day hundreds of whites watched ominously as police and Guardsmen disarmed blacks and paraded them in and out of police stations. A few whites were also disarmed, including union official Charles Lehman, who was arrested for carrying a gun and ammunition. It was not enough.

Before sundown a white mob descended on the gates of the meatpacking plants. They waited for black employees to finish work, and then forced them to run a gauntlet. One by one the black labourers were beaten to the ground. A block away a packaging worker was shot. Shortly afterwards a contingent of Guardsmen arrived and were greeted by a flurry of shots fired into the air by white youths. The Guardsmen ostentatiously loaded their rifles and the whites disappeared, moving back into black neighbourhoods where they joined others hurling anything they could get their hands on. Rudwick wrote: 'Windows in homes were shattered and shots were exchanged on both sides. A few blocks away on Illinois and Summit avenues hundreds of shots were fired by blacks and whites. At Third and Summit Avenue, several (black) shacks were literally torn to pieces, a few dwellings were set on fire, and oil-soaked rags were found outside several others.' The Guardsmen quelled a second night's rioting at about midnight. Police chief Payne arrested several Guardsmen, however, for actively leading attacks on blacks. Most of the black casualties were not newcomers, but well-established East St Louis residents and small businessmen.

Over the two nights around 6,000 blacks left the city precincts and trudged either into the countryside or across the Missouri bridge. Over the following fortnight most were persuaded to return to their homes and business premises. The black backlash which law-abiding whites feared most did not materialise. By 10 June Governor Lowden had withdrawn all Guardsmen, apart from two companies at the Aluminium Ore plant. Many people, mainly blacks, had been injured and much property had been damaged or destroyed. But no-one had died. The peace did not last long.

In early June white pickets had attacked black 'scabs' at Aluminium Ore and the police again arrested black victims for carrying concealed weapons. The beatings continued day after day and, given the police's refusal to protect them, the remaining National Guard escorted blacks between home and workplace.

On 17 June several hundred whites badly beat a sixty-year-old black man who refused to give up his streetcar seat to a white woman. He survived, barely. Later that month a black delegation led by Dr LeRoy Bundy and Dr L. B. Bluitt, physicians to the blacks of St Clair County, warned Mayor Mollman that black patience was fast running out – there was a very real danger in future of a black victim shooting a white assailant. Such an incident, they predicted, would spark race war. Mollman expressed 'surprise and dismay' as he believed that race relations had improved since the previous disturbances. Rudwick wrote: 'Mollman's professed ignorance was one more proof that as a city official he often postponed making unpleasant decisions. He and his political machine wanted to maintain the support of both the lower-class whites and the blacks. To avoid offending white laborers he refused to protect blacks, but he also did not wish to alienate black voters.' Mollman told the delegation that their complaints would be investigated thoroughly. The two doctors were unimpressed. Mollman summoned police chief Payne who insisted that his officers were doing their full duty.

Four days later, in the early evening of Sunday 1 July, a black man was beaten near Tenth and Bond Avenue, and it was reported that he had shot and wounded his attacker. Later that night a black woman in a torn dress told a crowd of black men that whites had beaten her and several others. The blacks threatened retaliation. Shortly before midnight a Ford car full of whites fired shots into black homes along Market Street. Residents returned fire as the

Ford drove away. What happened next was a tragedy born of a highly volatile situation.

Police chief Payne was told that armed blacks were 'on a rampage'. He despatched a white ford car carrying a driver and two detectives dressed in civilian clothes in the front seat, and uniformed officers in the back. *St Louis Republic* reporter Roy Albertson was on the running board. The two detectives were Samuel Coppedge and Frank Wadley who in May had chased off a white mob intent on burning black homes. Albertson reported: '(We) turned into Bond Avenue from Tenth, meeting more than 200 rioting negroes ... who without a word of warning opened fire.' The reporter later admitted that the firing could have been due to local blacks mistaking the police Ford for the one which a few hours earlier had peppered their homes with shot. The fusillade killed Coppedge instantly and Wadley died the next day from several gunshot wounds.[39]

The bullet-ridden and blood-soaked car was parked in front of the police station, drawing crowds of white people. Their anger reached fever pitch when they read Albertson's inflammatory account in the first edition of his newspaper the following day. They vowed bloody revenge. At 9 a.m. a meeting at the Labor Temple agreed that the killing of the two officers was final proof that 'black armies' were mobilising to massacre the whites. White merchants and businessmen urged Mollman to deputise a citizen army to prevent another riot, but the mayor declared himself ill and refused to leave the safety of his office. The previous night he has called for six militia companies from Springfield but only two arrived, and those not until late afternoon of Monday 2 July. By then it was too late.

The Labor Temple mob headed towards Broadway, a major streetcar transfer point, and shot a black man. Armed groups of up to twenty-five whites attacked streetcars and clubbed and stoned black passengers of all ages and both sexes. The kerbs were lined with thousands of white onlookers displaying 'good humour ... like waiting for a church parade'. They applauded the spectacle and encouraged the carnage as the area between Broadway and Illinois was turned into a 'bloody half-mile'.

A few whites who tried to aid injured blacks were hissed by white women who threatened them with penknives and hat pins. A white businessman who simply stood and watched said later: 'If you had been there you would have been just as big a coward as the rest of us.' A few black men held their arms up in surrender but were clubbed down by rifle butts. Mary Howard watched white women stop cars and pull off black women for beatings. 'One woman's clothes they tore off entirely,' she told reporter Ida Wells, 'and then they took off their shoes and beat her over the face and head with their heels. Another woman who got away ran down the street with every stitch of clothing torn off her back, leaving only her shoes and stockings on.'[40] Another observer reported that when blacks fell, 'young girls got blood on their stockings while kicking the victims and the sight amused the rioters'. Injured black women begged for mercy but white women laughed as they beat their faces and breasts with stones and sticks. The *New York Times* reported: 'Ten or fifteen young girls about eighteen years old chased a negro woman at the Relay Depot ... The girls were brandishing clubs and calling upon the men to kill the woman.' Their victim was allegedly a known prostitute frequented by white men. Other observers saw girls clawing at the eyes of dying victims.

In the early afternoon several beaten black men lying in pools of their own blood were calmly executed by gunmen. The mayhem spread and the killing of blacks became indiscriminate. The rioters made no apparent effort to target the blacks involved in the shooting of the detectives, preferring more defenceless prey. Several fatalities were among the oldest and most respected blacks in the city.[41]

The mobs descended on the black neighbourhoods they had tried to destroy in May. One rabble-rouser shouted: 'They got Sam and Frank ... we'll get them.' Black homes were torched and their residents picked off one by one as they tried to escape the flames. An ambulance crew who tried to take a bloodied black man to hospital was warned off and the mob threw the injured black into the flames where he perished. An observer noted: 'This was not the hectic raving demonstration of men suddenly gone mad.' It was a coolly calculated slaughter. *Post-Despatch* reporter Paul Anderson witnessed six murders, in every one of which the black victim was defenceless and begging for mercy. Death was often not enough, and corpses were remorselessly kicked and clubbed to a pulp. A barely-alive black man was strung up on a clothesline dangling from a telegraph pole, but the cord broke. A journalist appealed to National Guardsmen to intervene, but they were 'not interested'. The mob got a stronger rope and put it around his neck. The journalist reported: 'One of the lynchers stuck his fingers inside the gaping scalp and lifted the negro's head by it, literally bathing his hand in the man's blood. "Get hold and pull for East St Louis," called the man as he seized the other end of the rope. The negro was lifted to a height of about seven feet and the body left hanging there for hours.'[42]

An eighteen-year-old black, Jimmie Eckford, sent to collect a chicken from a grocery, was knocked off his bicycle and hit on the head with a brick. He staggered into a nearby yard occupied by a white family to seek refuge. The mob threatened to torch the house and the occupants threw the boy back into the street. 'He was kicked and stamped on and beaten till they knocked the teeth from his head and killed him,' said Mary Howard.

Most blacks were passive, scared and intent only on escaping over the Missouri. A steady stream of refugees, some carrying bundles of hastily salvaged belongings, tramped across the bridge running another gauntlet of abuse. One witness told Ida Wells that she saw whites snatch a baby from a mother's arms and toss it in the river. They then killed the mother, her husband and her other child.[43]

Mary Howard, witness to so many atrocities, was arrested by Guardsmen who forced their way into her house in a fruitless search for weapons. A white *Chicago Herald* reporter described the National Guardsmen charged with protecting the blacks as 'lax and cruelly good-natured'. In one instance, he wrote, 'a corpulent (black) woman brought up the rear of the procession and for several blocks a white boy, one of a gang of stone-throwing mischief-makers, who followed every squad, was beating her with an iron bar at intervals of a few yards. She did not dare to protest or resist. She was too frightened to scream. At last a white man, probably a non-resident of East St Louis, called the attention of a Guardsman to the outrage, and he laughingly drove the boy off.'[44] There were several reports of Guardsmen actively joining the rioters. Ida Wells reported that a black commercial building containing a grocery and a barber shop was invaded, ransacked and two blacks driven out: 'There they were shot down and left to be burned alive. The shots were fired from militia rifles by khaki-uniformed men. Dozens of men who saw it done proclaimed it so, slapped their thighs and said the Illinois National Guard was alright.' Joe Avant was with around twenty other blacks who went to their usual after-work café when six Guardsmen and four policemen opened fire indiscriminately, wounding six, one of them fatally. They searched the terrified customers and confiscated pocket knives.

Another white reporter, the *Post-Dispatch*'s Carlos Hurd, wrote that in the downtown district possession of a black skin that afternoon was a death warrant. He saw black men stoned to death and the bodies of five more hanging from lampposts. He saw a dying man try to raise himself on one elbow before a well-dressed young white man crushed his skull with a flat stone. He reported that the slogan of that day was 'Get a nigger', followed by 'Get another'. He heard a rattle of gunshots when a black man tried to escape his burning home: 'He laid on the pavement, a bullet wound in his head and his skull bare in two places. At every movement of pain which showed that life remained, there came a terrific kick in the jaw or the nose or a crashing stone from some of the men who stood over him. At the corner, a few steps away, were a sergeant and several Guardsmen. The sergeant approached the ring of men around the prostrate black. 'This man's done for,' he said. 'You'd better get him away from here.' No one made a move to lift the blood-covered form, and the sergeant walked away, remarking when questioned about an ambulance that 'the ambulances quit coming'. However, an undertaker's ambulance did come fifteen minutes later and took away the lifeless black who had in the meantime been further kicked and stoned.'[45]

At 4 p.m. a black man was shot down on the corner of Sixth Street and Broadway. Hurd reported: 'One of those firing on him being a boy in short trousers. The driver of the ambulance that came was not permitted to remove the body and it layed for an hour beside the streetcar tracks seen by the passengers of every passing car.' Nearby a black in critical condition was found in a sewer, having been beaten with paving stones and thrown in eleven hours earlier. He was pulled out, but it is not known whether he survived. Railway worker William Lues was on his way home from work when the mob shot him 'to pieces' and dragged his body around the streets at the end of a rope. Blacks, dead and alive, had their fingers cut off as trophies. Others were chased into the Cahokia River and picked off by gunmen for sport. Some who managed to struggle to the shore were stoned to death by white children. An elderly black woman, aged between seventy and eighty, was beaten almost to death by women, and then finished off by men.

Many of those blacks who escaped the burning district were rounded up by Guardsmen and marched to the police station, although many could barely walk because of their beatings. The crowd pelted them with bricks which they were unable to dodge because they were hemmed in by the militia's bayonets. A handful of whites were arrested.

The *Associated Press* reported that one of the white detainees was overheard saying: 'I have killed my share of Negroes today. I have killed so many that I am tired and somebody else can finish them off.' But when Captain O. C. Smith of the F police company went to the station to formally charge the boaster, he had already been released.

The square block of Eight and Broadway was 'burnt to an ash heap'. Three children died inside one burning shack, including the one-year-old son and two-year-old daughter of William Forest. The coroner later found that they had been shot in the head.

All witnesses reported that local firemen, boosted from crews across the river in St Louis, did their utmost to douse the fires, but were repeatedly chased off by the crowds. The riots climaxed at around 6 p.m. as more National Guardsmen – not locals – arrived and patrolled the intersections between the black neighbourhoods and the city centre. They escorted hundreds of tired, terrified blacks to the relative safety of the City Hall auditorium.

Estimates of the number of blacks killed range from fifty to 140, with around 100 hospitalised and many more who tended their own wounds. Around 6,000 were left homeless and property loss was estimated at $3 million. Seven whites were killed, some of them accidentally by fellow rioters. The riots badly hit trade between the two cities either side of the Missouri. The St Louis Chamber of Commerce reckoned that more than 100,000 tons of goods and materials normally sent across the bridge were halted. St Louis shipping companies complained that their black workers were too scared to unload goods on the eastern shore. The Armour meatpacking plants, also hit by the reluctance of black labourers to report for work, reported a 50 per cent drop in cattle killed and a 70 per cent fall in hogs butchered. The Southern Railway Company's warehouse was destroyed along with over 100 carloads of merchandise valued at £500,000. A whites-only theatre was also consumed by the flames. The burnt-out district remained a wasteland, but black refugees slowly filtered back to where the jobs were.[46]

An East St Louis Chamber of Commerce delegation, mostly outraged by the damage to property rather than the human toll, met Mayor Mollman on 6 July and demanded the resignation of the police chief. They accused Mollman himself of allowing a 'reign of lawlessness'. Chamber vice president Maurice Joyce said: 'We have a police department that is incompetent and inefficient, if not worse. Not only was the word sent out that law would not be rigidly enforced but the impression was allowed to spread that law violators would be winked at.'[47]

African Americans across the US were badly shaken by the riots and the calculated slaughter, and they joined whites in demanding answers. Some black reporters searched for a conspiracy to weaken the war effort against Germany, others saw efforts by Southern businessmen to stop the migration of cheap black labour. But most blacks blamed the organised labour movement which excluded them from membership and called them 'scabs' when they tried to feed their families. The Boston Equal Rights League told AFL president Samuel Gompers that the 'bloodiest, most murderous massacre of coloured Americans in the country's history at East St Louis was committed by labor unionists'. Civil rights leader W. E. B. Du Bois said that the victims were killed because they were black and strike-breakers. The black *Atlanta Independent* editorialised: 'What shall we do to be saved? If we don't work in the South we are jailed; if we do work in the North we are mobbed.' A black minister about to see service as a military chaplain, quoted by Rudwick, asked how his nation could go to war in Europe when there was 'so much filth in her backyard'.[48] That became a common theme, with newspaper editorials thundering at the hypocrisy of claiming to fight for peace overseas while permitting a race war at home. President Wilson was condemned as the biggest hypocrite of all, and his subsequent behaviour added weight to that charge.

On 25 July, Wilson federalised the Illinois National Guard in East St Louis, a measure that ensured they were exempt from service in the trenches of Europe. But he ignored several appeals to appoint a federal grand jury to investigate the race riot. His secretary, Joseph Tumulty, told reporters that the details of the riot were so sickening he could not bear to read them. The *New York Evening Post* saw Wilson's failure to condemn the rioters showed that he remained at heart a Southern racist. Wilson's silence and equivocation was in sharp contrast to the attitude taken by his predecessor, Theodore Roosevelt, who condemned the 'appalling brutality' displayed at East St Louis. AFL President Gompers, who was sharing the same platform, interpreted that as hostility to organised labour. He said that racial violence, although obviously to be deplored, was due to bosses importing blacks and strike-breakers. Roosevelt, ever the grandstander, strode over to him and shook his fist in the union leader's face. He roared that he would never accept 'apologies for the brutal infamies imposed on coloured people.'

The most eloquent reaction, however, and one which gave voice to the emergent black protest, came from Marcus Garvey, the Jamaican-born orator and civil rights campaigner who had arrived in the US from England the previous year. In a speech just four days after the event he aroused the passions of those for whom East St Louis was just another manifestation of long-term injustice:

> The East St Louis riot, or rather massacre, of Monday 2nd, will go down in history as one of the bloodiest outrages against mankind for which any class of people could be held guilty. This is no time for fine words, but a time to lift one's voice against the savagery of a people who claim to be the dispensers of democracy. I do not know what special meaning the people who slaughtered the Negroes of East St Louis have for democracy of which they are the custodians, but I do know that it has no literal meaning for me as used and applied by these same lawless people. America, that has been ringing the bells of the world, proclaiming to the nations and the peoples thereof that she has democracy to give to all and sundry, America that has denounced Germany for the deportations of Belgians into Germany, America that has arraigned Turks at the bar of public opinion and public justice against the massacres of the Armenians, has herself no satisfaction to give 12 million of her own citizens except the satisfaction of a farcical inquiry that will end where it began, over the brutal murder of men, women and children for no other reason than that they are black people seeking an industrial chance in a country that they have laboured for over three hundred years to make great. For three hundred years the Negroes of America have given their life blood to make the Republic the first among the nations of the world, and all along this time there has never been even one year of justice but, on the contrary, a continuous round of oppression. At one time it was slavery, at another time lynching and burning, and at the present date it is wholesale butchery. This is a crime against the laws of humanity. It is a crime against the laws of the nation. It is a crime against Nature. And a crime against the God of all mankind.[49]

Uncomfortably for modern perceptions, Garvey also blamed immigrants: 'It is strange to see how the real American white people, the people who are direct descendants from the Pilgrim Fathers, allow the alien German, the Italians and other Europeans who came here but yesterday, to lead them in bloody onslaught against the Negroes who have been here for over three hundred years.' But his appeal for simple justice and freedom from oppression was understood clearly from New York tenements and Chicago factories to the cotton fields of the South and ranches of the West. On 28 July around 10,000 black people marched down New York's Fifth Avenue in silent protest. The men dressed in black, the women and children in white. The event was organised by Harlem community groups and the NAACP.

The state authorities asked Ida Wells to compile a report based on her interviews with around fifty witnesses. She concluded that no organised effort was made to protect black people or disperse the mobs. The police and Guardsmen were indifferent, or inactive, or actively encouraged the 'barbarians'. Her report was held under seal by the government as classified information. It was not declassified until 1986.

More recent academic studies mainly blamed white industrial workers for the savagery, but also pinpointed the city's saloon culture, links between organised crime and local politicians and businessmen, the presence of female rioters who stirred up their drunken menfolk, and efforts by blacks to arm themselves in self-defence. Historian William Tuttle concluded that large-scale racial violence was 'embedded deep in the social, economic and political structures' of American cities, North and South. Charles Lumpkins saw the riots as an effort to prevent African Americans organising to obtain the civil rights promised them after the Civil War:

In the late 19th century, African Americans in East St Louis were busy building institutions and expanding their political influence. (They) established a vibrant community in a border region where Northern industrial and Southern folk cultures overlapped. Like those in Ohio River border cities such as Pittsburgh and Cincinnati, black East St Louisians confronted varying patterns of racism, cleaved into social classes, and engaged in many forms of political action. (They), like those in Chicago, Cleveland, Detroit and other industrializing Midwest cities, lived and worked among white people, but apart from them. After 1870, black East

St Louisian men voted and exercised other rights of citizenship; all black residents availed themselves of integrated public transportation and, earlier than black Americans in other cities, entered industrial employment in appreciable numbers ... In East St Louis black people did more than just react to white hostility, they organised their community to advance their interests. They built institutions and a rich urban culture ... Their leaders did succeed in winning a certain level of patronage as well as appointive and elective offices. But this success in the political arena concerned white political bosses ... Unsure of the outcome of this struggle, certain politician-businessmen decided to employ mass racial violence to eliminate the threats they had perceived from rapid shifts in East St Louis's political culture between 1915 and mid-1917. White machine politicians, through their proxies, unleashed murderous anti-black violence to terrorize African Americans into leaving the city *en masse*. It was an American pogrom, or ethnic cleansing...[50]

All of which is true, to a certain degree. And it is easy now to blame crooked politicians and unscrupulous bosses. But ordinary, white working-class men, women and children who inflicted such horrors on ordinary, black working-class men, women and children must shoulder their burden of guilt.

President Wilson and his Attorney-General, Thomas W. Gregory, agonised over legal precedents for an inquiry and judicial prosecutions, but ultimately ignored the 1866 Civil Rights Act which allowed prosecutions of those conspiring to violate rights guaranteed in the US Constitution, regardless of colour. Congress, however, launched a federal investigation which lasted a month. The hearings resulted in no civilian prosecutions or militia courts-martial, but Mayor Mollman and his private secretary, Maurice Ahearn, were accused of malfeasance in public office.[51] It was suspected, but not proved, that Mollman's failure to act was due to his sympathies with, or allegiance to, those who sought to drive out the blacks. Ahearn was found to have ordered the police and militia to destroy cameras, 'thus preventing moving picture men from photographing the mobs'. The report added: 'No man gave greater assistance to the rioters, and assured them more safety from prosecution, than did Ahearn when he ordered that photographers be denied their free right to take pictures.' Little was said about the rights of black families to live, unmolested, in their own homes. The final official report rebuked the East St Louis Establishment, saying that 'the activities of employers, labor organisers and politicians created a milieu which made the race riot possible'. No one was prosecuted for murder, assault or arson.

However, the report did put the emerging American superpower on notice of the true volatility of racial disharmony, and of the emergence of an angry and organised civil rights movement. In East St Louis blacks returned and rebuilt their homes and communities with an overriding sense of racial solidarity. They used their votes to get patronage. They forged alliances with immigrant groups and became involved in organised labour after the Congress of Industrial Organizations opened its doors to black members. And both locally and nationally they became active in the fight for genuine equality.

Ida Wells-Barnett was active in that fight until 1933 when she died, aged sixty-six. Playwright Tazewell Thompson wrote of her: 'A woman born in slavery, she would grow to become one of the great pioneer activists of the civil rights movement. A precursor of Rosa Parks, she was a suffragist, newspaper editor and publisher, investigative journalist, Co-founder of the NAACP, political candidate, mother, wife, and the single most powerful leader in the anti-lynching campaign.'[52] She had herself written: 'One had better die fighting against injustice than die like a dog or a rat in a trap.'

* * *

In the summer and early autumn of 1919, race riots swept more than three dozen cities; in most cases, whites attacked African Americans, but in some cases many black people fought back, notably in Chicago. The highest number of fatalities occurred in the rural area around Elaine, Arkansas, where five whites and an estimated 100–240 black people were killed.[53] Civil rights activist and author James Weldon Johnson coined the term 'Red Summer'. As a field secretary of the National Association for the Advancement of Colored People since 1916, he organised peaceful protests against the racial violence of that summer.[54] Following the war, rapid demobilisation of the military without a plan for absorbing veterans into the job market, and the removal of price controls, led to unemployment and inflation that increased competition for jobs. In some cities, blacks were hired as strike-breakers.[55] Authorities viewed with alarm African Americans' advocacy both of racial equality and the rights of the working man. In a private conversation in March 1919, President Woodrow Wilson said that 'the American Negro returning from abroad would be our greatest medium in conveying bolshevism to America.'[56]

Early in 1919, Dr George Edmund Hayes, director of Negro Economics for the Department of Labor, wrote: 'The return of the Negro soldier to civil life is one of the most delicate and difficult questions confronting the Nation, north and south.'[57] One black veteran wrote to the editor of the *Chicago Daily News* saying the returning black veterans 'are now new men and world men, if you please; and their possibilities for direction, guidance, honest use, and power are limitless, only they must be instructed and led. They have awakened, but they have not yet the complete conception of what they have awakened to.'[58]

W. E. B. Du Bois, an official of the NAACP and editor of its monthly magazine, saw an opportunity: 'By the God of Heaven, we are cowards and jackasses if now that the war is over, we do not marshal every ounce of our brain and brawn to fight a sterner, longer, more unbending battle against the forces of hell in our own land.'[59] In May 1919, following the first serious racial incidents, he published his essay 'Returning Soldiers': 'We return from the slavery of uniform which the world's madness demanded us to don to the freedom of civil garb. We stand again to look America squarely in the face and call a spade a spade. We sing: This country of ours, despite all its better souls have done and dreamed, is yet a shameful land ... We return. We return from fighting. We return fighting.'

Between 1 January and 14 September 1919, white mobs lynched at least forty-three African Americans, with sixteen hanged and others shot; another eight men were burned to death. The states appeared powerless or unwilling to interfere or prosecute such mob murders. President Wilson received a telegram: 'The National Association for the Advancement of Colored People respectfully enquires how long the Federal Government under your administration intends to tolerate anarchy in the United States?'[60]

Warnings of civil catastrophe went unheeded. After a riot instigated on 10 May in Charleston, South Carolina, the city imposed martial law. Isaac Doctor, William Brown and James Talbot, all black men, were killed. Five white men and eighteen black men were injured. A naval investigation found that four American sailors and one civilian – all white – initiated the riot.[61] In early July, a white race riot in Longview, Texas, led to the deaths of at least four men and destroyed the African American housing district in the town. In Washington, D.C., starting 19 July, white men, many in the military and in uniforms of all three services, responded to the rumoured arrest of a black man for rape of a white woman with four days of mob violence against black individuals and businesses. They rioted, randomly beat black people on the street, and pulled others off streetcars for attacks. When police refused to intervene, the black population fought back. Troops tried to restore order as the city closed saloons and theatres to discourage assemblies, but a summer rainstorm had more of a dampening effect. When the violence ended, a total of fifteen people had died: ten white people, including two police officers; and five black people. Fifty people were seriously wounded and another 100 less severely wounded. It was one of the few times in such twentieth-century riots when white fatalities outnumbered those of blacks. In Norfolk, Virginia, a white mob attacked a homecoming celebration for African American veterans of the war. At least six people were shot, and the local police called in Marines and Navy personnel to restore order.

There were also race riots involving murder, injuries and destruction of black property in Sylvester, Georgia (10 May), Putnam County, Georgia (29 May), Monticello, Mississippi (31 May), New London, Connecticut (13 June), Memphis, Tennessee (13 June), Annapolis, Maryland (27 June), Macon, Mississippi (27 June), Bisbee, Arizona (3 July), Scranton, Pennsylvania (5 July), Dublin, Georgia (6 July), Philadelphia, Pennsylvania (7 July), Coatsville, Pennsylvania (8 July), Tuscaloosa, Alabama (8 July), Baltimore, Maryland (11 July), Port Arthur, Texas (15 July), New Orleans, Louisiana (23 July), Darby, Pennsylvania (23 July), and Hobson City, Alabama (26 July).

That was when the NAACP sent a telegram of protest to President Wilson about

> ... the shame put upon the country by the mobs, including United States soldiers, sailors, and marines, which have assaulted innocent and unoffending negroes in the national capital. Men in uniform have attacked negroes on the streets and pulled them from streetcars to beat them. Crowds are reported ... to have directed attacks against any passing negro ... The effect of such riots in the national capital upon race antagonism will be to increase bitterness and danger of outbreaks elsewhere. National Association for the Advancement of Colored

People calls upon you as President and Commander in Chief of the Armed Forces of the nation to make statement condemning mob violence and to enforce such military law as situation demands ... [62]

The summer's greatest violence occurred during rioting in Chicago's Southside, where both blacks and Irish were crowded into substandard housing. The Irish had been in the city longer and were organised around athletic and political clubs which fiercely defended their territory and political power against all newcomers.[63] A combination of ethnic gangs and police neglect strained race relations even further.[64] At the same time, African American veterans exhibited greater militancy and pride having served their country. Younger black men rejected the passivity traditional in the South and promoted armed self-defence and control of their neighbourhoods.

Longstanding racial tensions exploded in five days of violence that started on 27 July 1919. On that hot summer day, on a segregated Southside Chicago beach, a white man threw rocks at black swimmers in the water, which resulted in seventeen-year-old Eugene Williams' death as he paddled a makeshift raft into 'white territory'. Witnesses pointed out the killer to a policeman, who refused to make an arrest, but instead arrested the complainant. An indignant black mob attacked the officer. White mobs began pulling black people off trolley cars, attacking black businesses, and beating victims with baseball bats and iron bars. Having learned from the East St Louis riot, the city closed down the streetcar system, but the rioting continued. At one point, a white mob threatened Provident Hospital, many of whose patients were African American. The police successfully held them off.

The *Chicago Daily Tribune*, generally antagonistic to African Americans, reported:

Two colored men are reported to have been killed and approximately fifty whites and negroes injured, a number probably fatally, in race riots that broke out at south side beaches yesterday. The rioting spread through the Black Belt and by midnight had thrown the entire south side into a state of turmoil. Among the known wounded are four policemen of the Cottage Grove avenue station, two from west side stations, one fireman of engine company No. 9, and three women. A colored rioter is said to have died from wounds inflicted by Policeman John O'Brien, who fired into a mob at Twenty-ninth street and Cottage Grove avenue. The body, it is said, was spirited away by a colored man.

So serious was the trouble throughout the district that Acting Chief of Police Alcock was unable to place an estimate on the injured. Scores received cuts and bruises from flying stones and rocks, but went to their homes for medical attention. Minor rioting continued through the night all over the south side. Negroes who were found in street cars were dragged to the street and beaten. They were first ordered to the street by white men and if they refused the trolley was jerked off the wires. Scores of conflicts between the whites and blacks were reported at south side stations and reserves were ordered to stand guard on all important street corners. Some of the fighting took place four miles from the scene of the afternoon riots.[65]

There were rumours that several blacks had been drowned in the lakeside incident. Police dragged the shore and found Williams' body, although he was not immediately identified.

The *Daily Tribune* went on:

John O'Brien, a policeman attached to the Cottage Grove avenue station, was attacked by a mob at Twenty-ninth and State streets after he had tried to rescue a fellow cop from a crowd of brawling Negroes. Several shots were fired in his direction and he was wounded in the left arm. He pulled his revolver and fired four times into the gathering. Three colored men dropped. When the police attempted to haul the wounded into the wagon the Negroes made valiant attempts to prevent them. Two were taken to the Michael Reese hospital but the third was spirited away by the mob. It was later learned that he died in a drug store a short distance from the shooting.

Fire apparatus from a south side house answered an alarm of fire which was turned in from a drug store at Thirty-fifth and State streets. It was said that more than fifty whites had sought refuge here and that a number of Negroes had attempted to 'smoke them out.' There was no semblance of a fire when the autos succeeded in rushing through the populated streets.'
Charles Cromier was sitting in his window at 2839 Cottage Grove avenue watching the clashing mobs. A stray bullet lodged

169

in his head and he fell back into the room. Spectators saw him being helped to a chair by a woman.

After the shoreside 'battle royal', blacks 'turned on Policeman Callahan and drove him down Twenty-ninth street. He ran into a drug store at Twenty-ninth street and Cottage Grove avenue and phoned the Cottage Grove avenue police station. Riot calls were sent to the Cottage Grove avenue station and more reserves were sent into the Black Belt. By this time the battling had spread along Cottage Grove avenue and outbreaks were conspicuous at nearly every corner. Meanwhile the fighting continued along the lake. Miss Mame McDonald and her sister, Frances, had been bathing with a friend, Lieut. Runkie, a convalescing soldier. A colored woman walked up to the trio and made insulting remarks. Runkie attempted to interfere, but the colored woman voiced a series of oaths and promptly struck the soldier in the face. Negroes in the vicinity hurled stones and rocks at the women and both were slightly injured.'

One report stated:

In less than a half hour after the beach outbreak, Cottage Grove avenue and State street from Twenty-ninth south to Thirty-fifth were bubbling caldrons of action. When the situation had gotten beyond the control of the Cottage Grove police, Acting Chief of Police Alcock was notified. He immediately sent out a call to every station in the city to rush all available men to the Black Belt. Before they arrived colored and white men were mobbed in turn. The blacks added to the racial feeling by carrying guns and brandishing knives. It was not until the reserves arrived that the rioting was quelled.

News of the afternoon doings had spread through all parts of the south side by nightfall, and whites stood at all prominent corners ready to avenge the beatings their brethren had received. Along Halsted and State streets they were armed with clubs, and every Negro who appeared was pommeled. Lewis Phillips, colored, was riding in a Thirty-ninth street car, when a white man took a pot shot from the corner as the car neared Halsted street. Phillips was wounded in the groin and was taken to the Provident hospital. Melvin Davies, colored, of 2816 Cottage Grove avenue, was waiting for a Thirty fifth street car at Parnell avenue when he was slugged from behind. His assailant disappeared.[66]

The initial casualty list illustrates the nature of the fighting. It included: Policeman John O'Connell, white, knocked down and beaten; Policeman John Callahan, white, beaten and bruised by mob; Policeman Thomas J. Gallagher, white, scalp wounds; Edward Hausner, white, cut about legs and face; Arthur Carroll, white, head bruised by stone; James Crawford, coloured, shot through abdomen, 'probably will die, taken to Michael Reese hospital'; Charles Cormier, white, shot in head by stray bullet; William Long, white, cut in head and back; Joseph Wiggins, coloured, beaten about head; Phil Griffin, coloured, shot in both legs; George Stauber, white, beaten and cut; Herman Rabisohn, white, bruised by missiles; John O'Neil, white, struck on head by brick; Walter Carson, white, face cut by rock; William Cheeshire, white, stabbed in face; Anton Dugo, white, shot in leg; William Soott, coloured, scalp wounds; Miss Mamie Mcdonald, white, head cut by brick; Miss Frances Mcdonald, sister, back injured by rock; Mrs Gladys Williams, white, face bruised by stone; Melvin Davis, coloured, beaten while waiting for Halsted street car; Harry Speez, coloured, knocked unconscious by whites at Thirty-first and Halsted streets; Lewis Phillips, coloured, shot in groin while riding in Thirty-ninth street car; Frank Walls, white, pipeman of Engine company 9, struck in neck by rock; Evelyn Boyde, white, hit on face and hip by stones; Frances Boyde, sister, knocked down by rock; Lewis B. Knight, white, beaten about head with club.[67] Inevitably, given the circumstances, many of the black casualties went unreported.

During the riot, Chicago Mayor William Hale Thompson played a game of brinksmanship with his Illinois counterpart Frank Lowden. Thompson refused to ask Lowden to send in the militia for four days, even though Lowden had deployed the force in the city, ready to intervene.[68] Future mayor Richard J. Daley, then aged seventeen, was an active member of the Irish Hamburg Athletic Club, which a post-riot investigation named as instigators in attacks on blacks. Daley's political career never suffered and he served as mayor for twenty-one years.

Sections of the Chicago economy were shut down for several days during and after the riots, as plants were closed to avoid interaction among feuding groups.[69] Mayor Thompson drew on his association with this riot to influence later political elections.[70]

The Chicago riot lasted almost a week, ending only after the government had deployed nearly 6,000 National Guard infantrymen. They stationed them around the Black Belt to prevent any further white attacks. By the evening of 30 July, most violence had ended. Newspaper accounts noted numerous attempts at arson; for instance, on 31 July, more than thirty fires were started in the Black Belt before noon and rioters stretched cables across the streets to prevent fire trucks from entering the areas. There were also sporadic violent attacks in other parts of the city, including the Chicago Loop. At least thirty-eight people died, twenty-three blacks and fifteen white, and another 537 were injured, two-thirds of them African American. Patrolman John W. Simpson was the only policeman killed in the riot. Approximately 1,000 residents, mostly African Americans, were left homeless because of the fires. Many African American families had left by train before the rioting ended, returning to their families in the South.

Chief of Police John J. Garrity, closed 'all places where men congregate for other than religious purposes' to help restore order. Governor Lowden authorised the deployment of the 11th Illinois Infantry Regiment and its machine gun company, as well as the 1st, 2nd and 3rd reserve militia; the four units totalled 3,500 men. The Cook County Sheriff Sherriff deputised between 1,000 and 2,000 ex-soldiers to help keep the peace. With the reserves and militia guarding the Black Belt, the city arranged for emergency provisions to provide its residents with fresh food. White groups delivered food and supplies to the line established by the military; the deliveries were then distributed within the Black Belt by African Americans. While industry was closed, the packing plants arranged to deliver pay to certain places in the city so that African American men could pick up their wages.

Once order was restored, Lowden was urged to create a state committee to study the cause of the riots. Lowden proposed forming a committee to write a racial code of ethics and to draw up racial boundaries for activities within the city. The Cook County Coroner's Office undertook seventy day sessions, twenty night sessions and 450 witness examinations. Southside youth gangs, including the Hamburg Athletic Club, were later found to have been among the primary instigators of the racial violence. For weeks, in the spring and summer of 1919, they had been anticipating, even eagerly awaiting, a race riot and on several occasions they had tried to precipitate one.

The conduct of the white police force was criticised during and after the riots. State's Attorney Maclay Hovne accused them of exclusively arresting African American rioters, while refusing to arrest whites. Roaming gangs of Bridgeport whites, who were mostly ethnic Irish, perpetrated much of the violence. The *New York Times* coverage during the riot clearly conveyed that whites were responsible for planned large-scale arson against black areas and for numerous mob attacks. Because of early police failures to arrest whites, no white Chicagoans were convicted of any of the murders, and most of the deaths were not even prosecuted. One man was prosecuted for Williams' death, but was acquitted.

At the Union Stock Yard, one of Chicago's largest employers, all 15,000 African American workers were initially expected to return to work on Monday, 4 August 1919. But after arson near white employees' homes near the Stock Yard the day before, the management banned all African American employees for fear of further rioting. Governor Lowden insisted that the troubles were related to labour issues rather than race. Nearly one-third of the African American employees were non-union and were resented by union employees. Black workers were kept out of the stockyards for ten days because of continued unrest. On 8 August 1919, about 3,000 non-union blacks showed up for work under protection of special police, deputy sheriffs, and militia. The white union employees threatened to strike unless such security forces were discontinued.[71]

At the end of July, the Northeastern Federation of Colored Women's Clubs, at an annual convention, denounced the rioting and burning of negroes' homes and asked President Wilson 'to use every means within your power to stop the rioting in Chicago and the propaganda used to incite such'.[72] At the end of August, the NAACP protested again to the White House, noting the attack on the organisation's secretary in Austin, Texas, the previous week. This was the occasion of their aforementioned question to President Wilson: 'The National Association for the Advancement of Colored People respectfully enquires how long the Federal Government under your administration intends to tolerate anarchy in the United States?'[73]

There were further race riots in Newberry, South Carolina (27 July), Bloomington, Illinois (28 July), Syracuse, New York (31 July), Philadelphia (31 July), Hattesburg, Mississippi (4 August), Texarkana, Texas (6 August), and New York City (21 August).

On 30 August, in Knoxville, Tennessee, a white mob gathered after a black suspect was arrested on suspicion of murdering a white woman. They stormed the county jail searching for the prisoner. They did not find him but liberated sixteen white prisoners, including suspected murderers. They moved on and attacked the African American business district, leaving at least seven dead and wounding more than twenty people.[74] At the end of September, another race riot in Omaha, Nebraska, erupted (see Appendix 2). Despite the premise of this book, racial warfare indeed spread to the Midwest.

Given the numbers involved, the Elaine race riot in rural Philips County, Arkansas, from 30 September to 1 October 1919, was arguably the deadliest racial conflict in United States history. In the heart of cotton country, African Americans outnumbered whites by ten to one and by three to one in the county overall.[75] Most blacks worked as sharecroppers, while white landowners controlled the economic power; a familiar story, as we have seen.

Black farmers began to organise in 1919 to try to negotiate better conditions, including fair accounting and timely payment of monies due them. Robert L. Hill, a black farmer, had founded the Progressive Farmers and Household Union of America, and was working with farmers throughout Phillips County. Its purpose was 'to obtain better payments for their cotton crops from the white plantation owners'. Whites often tried to disrupt such organising and threatened farmers. The union had hired a white law firm headed by Ulysses S. Bratton, a former assistant federal district attorney, in the capital of Little Rock to represent the black farmers in getting fair settlements for their 1919 cotton crops.

Around 100 African American farmers, led by Hill, met at a church in Hoop Spur, near Elaine. Armed guards protected the meeting. When two deputised white men and a black trustee arrived at the church, shots were exchanged. W. D. Adkins, one of the white men, was killed and the other white man wounded; it was never determined who shot first. The black trustee raced back to Helena, the county seat of Phillips County, and alerted officials. A posse was dispatched and within a few hours hundreds of white men began to comb the area for blacks they believed were launching an insurrection. Allegations surfaced that the white posse and US soldiers who were brought in to put down the so called 'rebellion' had massacred defenceless black men, women and children.[76]

Whites also requested help from Arkansas Governor Charles Hillman Brough, citing a 'Negro uprising'. Sensational newspaper articles published by the *Little Rock Gazette* and others reported that an 'insurrection' was occurring, and that blacks had planned to murder white leaders. Brough contacted the War Department and requested Federal troops. After considerable delay, nearly 600 US troops arrived, finding the area in chaos. White men roamed the area randomly attacking and killing blacks of any age and either sex. Fighting lasted for three days before the troops disarmed both parties and arrested 285 black residents, putting them in stockades for investigation and protection.

An estimated 100 to 237 African Americans and five whites were killed, and more wounded. A dispatch from Helena to the *New York Times*, datelined 1 October, said: 'Returning members of the [white] posse brought numerous stories and rumours, through all of which ran the belief that the rioting was due to propaganda distributed among the negroes by white men.'[77] The next day's report added detail: 'Additional evidence has been obtained of the activities of propagandists among the negroes, and it is thought that a plot existed for a general uprising against the whites.' A white man had been arrested and was 'alleged to have been preaching social equality among the negroes'. Part of the headline was 'Trouble Traced to Socialist Agitators'.[78] A few days later a *Western Newspaper Union* dispatch was captioned 'Captive Negro Insurrectionists'.[79]

Governor Brough appointed a Committee of Seven to investigate, composed of prominent local white businessmen. Without talking to any of the black farmers, they concluded that the sharecroppers' union was a socialist enterprise and 'established for the purpose of banding negroes together for the killing of white people'.[80] The NAACP promptly released a statement from a contact in Arkansas providing another account of the origins of the violence: 'The whole trouble, as I understand it, started because a Mr. Bratton, a white lawyer from Little Rock, Ark., was employed by sixty or seventy colored families to go to Elaine to represent them in a dispute with the white planters relative to the sale price of cotton.' It referred to a report that quoted Bratton's father: 'It had been impossible for the negroes to obtain itemized statements of accounts, or in fact to obtain statements at all, and that the manager was preparing to ship their cotton, they being sharecroppers and having a half interest therein, off without settling with them or allowing them to sell their half of the crop and pay up their accounts ... If it's a crime to represent people in an effort to make honest settlements, then he has committed a crime.'[81]

NAACP Field Secretary Walter White, who was of mixed race, was sent from New York City to Elaine in October 1919 to investigate events. After a few days, and despite holding legitimate credentials, he heard from a train conductor that his life was in danger. The conductor told the young man that he was leaving 'just when the fun is going to start', because they had found out that there was a 'damned yellow nigger passing for white and the boys are going to get him'. When White asked what the boys would do to the man, the conductor told White that 'when they get through with him he won't pass for white no more!' Nevertheless, White had time to talk with both black and white residents in Elaine, and in a subsequent report characterised the violence as 'an extreme response by white landowners to black unionisation'.[82]

The only men prosecuted for these events were 122 African Americans, with seventy-three charged with murder. Twelve were quickly convicted and sentenced to death by all-white juries for the murder of the first white deputy at the church. Others were as rapidly convicted of lesser charges and sentenced to prison. During appeals, the death penalty cases were separated, with six convictions being overturned at the state level because of technical trial details. These six defendants were quickly retried in 1920 and convicted again, but the state supreme court overturned the verdicts, based on violations of the Due Process Clause of the 14th Amendment and the 1875 Civil Rights Act, due to exclusion of blacks from the juries. The lower courts failed to retry the men within the two years required by Arkansas law, and they were released in 1923.

Protests and appeals to the federal government continued for weeks. A letter in late November from the National Equal Rights League appealed to President Wilson's international advocacy for human rights: 'We appeal to you to have your country undertake for its racial minority that which you forced Poland and Austria to undertake for their racial minorities.'

A report by Dr George Edmund Haynes of October 1919 was a call for national action; it was published in the *New York Times* and other major newspapers. He noted that lynchings were a national problem. As President Wilson had noted in a 1918 speech, from 1889 to 1918, more than 3,000 people had been lynched; 2,472 were black men, and fifty were black women. Haynes said that states had shown themselves 'unable or unwilling' to put a stop to lynchings, and seldom prosecuted the murderers. He connected the lynchings to the widespread riots in 1919:

> Persistence of unpunished lynchings of negroes fosters lawlessness among white men imbued with the mob spirit, and creates a spirit of bitterness among negroes. In such a state of public mind a trivial incident can precipitate a riot. Disregard of law and legal process will inevitably lead to more and more frequent clashes and bloody encounters between white men and negroes and a condition of potential race war in many cities of the United States. Unchecked mob violence creates hatred and intolerance, making impossible free and dispassionate discussion not only of race problems, but questions on which races and sections differ.[83]

In mid-summer, in the middle of the Chicago riots, a federal official told the *New York Times* that the violence resulted from 'an agitation, which involves the I.W.W., Bolshevism and the worst features of other extreme radical movements'.[84] In response, some black church leaders asked black people to shun violence in favour of 'patience' and 'moral suasion'.[85] In August the *Wall Street Journal* editorialised: 'Race riots seem to have for their genesis a Bolshevist, a Negro, and a gun.' The *Times* saw 'bloodshed on a scale amounting to local insurrection' as evidence of 'a new negro problem' because of 'influences that are now working to drive a wedge of bitterness and hatred between the two races'. Until recently, the *Times* said, black leaders showed 'a sense of appreciation' for what whites had suffered on their behalf in fighting a civil war that 'bestowed on the black man opportunities far in advance of those he had in any other part of the white man's world'. The *Times* continued:

> Every week the militant leaders gain more headway. They may be divided into general classes. One consists of radicals and revolutionaries. They are spreading Bolshevist propaganda. It is reported that they are winning many recruits among the colored race. When the ignorance that exists among negroes in many sections of the country is taken into consideration the danger of inflaming them by revolutionary doctrine may [be] apprehended ... The other class of militant leaders confine their agitation to a fight against all forms of color discrimination. They are for a program on uncompromising

protest, 'to fight and continue to fight for citizenship rights and full democratic privileges'.

As evidence of militancy and Bolshevism, the *Times* named W. E. B. Du Bois and quoted his editorial in *The Crisis*: 'Today we raise the terrible weapon of self-defense ... When the armed lynchers gather, we too must gather armed.' When the *Times* endorsed Haynes' call for a bi-racial conference to establish 'some plan to guarantee greater protection, justice, and opportunity to negroes that will gain the support of law-abiding citizens of both races', it endorsed discussion with 'those negro leaders who are opposed to militant methods'.[86]

In mid-October government sources provided the *Times* with evidence of Bolshevist propaganda appealing to America's black communities. This account set communist propaganda in the black community into a broader context, since it was 'paralleling the agitation that is being carried on in industrial centres of the North and West, where there are many alien laborers'. The *Times* described newspapers, magazines, and 'so-called "negro betterment" organizations' as the way propaganda about the 'doctrines of Lenin and Trotzky' was distributed to black people. It cited quotes from such publications, which contrasted the recent violence in Chicago and Washington, D.C. with 'Soviet Russia, a country in which dozens of racial and lingual types have settled their many differences and found a common meeting ground, a country which no longer oppresses colonies, a country from which the lynch rope is banished and in which racial tolerance and peace now exist'. The *Times* noted a call for unionisation: 'Negroes must form cotton workers' unions. Southern white capitalists know that the negroes can bring the white bourbon South to its knees. So go to it.'

On 17 November, Attorney General A. Mitchell Palmer reported to Congress on the threat that anarchists and Bolsheviks posed to the government. More than half the report documented radicalism in the black community and the 'open defiance' black leaders advocated in response to racial violence and the summer's rioting. It faulted the leadership of the black community for an 'ill-governed reaction toward race rioting ... In all discussions of the recent race riots there is reflected the note of pride that the Negro has found himself, that he has "fought back," that never again will he tamely submit to violence and intimidation.' It described 'the dangerous spirit of defiance and vengeance at work among the Negro leaders'.[87] The Red Summer was over, but its aftermath continued to be brutal.

On 31 May and 1 June 1921, for example, the white community of Greenwood in Tulsa, Oklahoma, rioted, killing up to 300 black people. The attack, carried out on the ground and by air, destroyed more than thirty-five blocks of the district, at the time the wealthiest black community in the nation. That bloody incident is outside the remit of this book, but an account is given in Appendix 3.

It was a long, hard road before the fight was won and segregation outlawed. Many others took up the civil rights flag and many more lost their lives, including Martin Luther King. But without the passions inflamed by the massacres in East St Louis, Chicago, and dozens more cities, it would have taken longer. And Barack Obama might not have reached the White House.

7

The Early Mafia

'Who killa de chief?'

New Orleans police chief David Hennessy, a man who, many thought, had previously got away with murder, was shot by several gunmen as he walked home from work on the evening of 15 October 1890. He had been caught up in a feud between the Provenzano and Matranga families from Sicily, business rivals on the city waterfront. When asked who had shot him, Hennessy reportedly whispered to police Captain Billy O'Connor: 'Dagoes.'

Italians were rounded up but when the murder trial partially collapsed, the accused were subjected to the biggest mass lynching of whites in American history. The city fathers, the public and the press generally approved because of anti-immigrant hysteria, and the term 'Mafia' became widespread.

***

The original Mafia was born in the upheaval of Sicily's transition out of feudalism in 1812. Previously, the nobility owned most of the land and ruled through their private armies, but they then sold or rented to private citizens. The 1860 annexation of the island by mainland Italy accelerated the process, creating a huge boom in landowners – from 2,000 in 1812 to 20,000 by 1861. The surge in both commerce and a rapacious landowning class caused innumerable disputes which needed settling, but the law and its enforcers were thinly spread and deeply corrupt. Some towns did not have any permanent police force and were only visited every few months by some troops to collect malcontents, leaving criminals to operate with impunity in the interim.[1] Banditry, rising food prices, the loss of public and church lands, and the loss of feudal commons pushed many desperate peasants to steal.

In the face of rising crime, booming commerce, and inefficient authorities, property owners turned to extra-legal arbitrators, alleged protectors and enforcers who eventually organised themselves into the first Mafia clans. They operated a massive protection racket, which may initially have helped the downtrodden but quickly developed into a criminal organisation that often worked with the landed gentry to keep down the peasantry. Mike Dash wrote eloquently: 'It rooted and took shape in a land of stark beauty, grinding poverty and frequent violence, insinuating its way into the fabric of the island until it exercised a malign, corrupting influence over most aspects of civilian life.'[2]

The US Mafia emerged in impoverished Italian immigrant neighbourhoods in New York's East Harlem, Lower East Side and Brooklyn, in other areas of the East Coast, and several other major metropolitan areas, including New Orleans during the late nineteenth century, following waves of Italian immigration from Sicily and other regions of southern Italy. It had its roots in the Sicilian Mafia but gradually merged with Neapolitan, Calabrian and other Italian criminal groups. The term 'Mafia' was originally used in Italy by the media and law enforcement to describe criminal groups in Sicily. The term is derived from the word 'Ma'afir' a term rooted in Arabic and meaning 'shelter' or 'place of refuge'. Like the Sicilian Mafia, the American Mafia did not use the term to describe itself. Neither group has a formal name and instead used the term *cosa nostra* (Italian for 'our thing').

The earliest Italian incomers, particularly to New York, were from the northern industrial cities, bringing with them much-needed skills and a middle-class sensibility. They were generally welcomed, but that changed in the 1880s when poorer Italians from the south and Sicily began to enter in ever-increasing numbers, driven out of their homelands by grinding poverty, high and unfair taxation, military conscription and a series of natural disasters including drought and volcanic eruptions. They were largely unskilled and ill-prepared for cultural assimilation; few spoke English or mixed outside their native communities and many had little intention of doing so. During that phase, less than half applied for US citizenship because their intention was to work hard, spend little and, eventually, return home. That was resented by many others in the American melting pot.

There was also, undoubtedly, an influx of criminals ready to exploit their own countrymen. Sicilian authorities issued passports to known murderers to get rid of them. Nineteen male Italians out of twenty passing through the Ellis Island immigration post were found to be carrying personal weapons, not all of them for their own protection. The similarities and complexities of Italian names caused chaos – when the immigrant vessel SS *Belgravia* underwent a check, one in six of the passengers were found to have given false names or bogus personal backgrounds. Such problems were sorted by the greasing of official palms. Law-abiding families were tarred with the same brush as the criminals, with the *New York Herald* complaining that 'the scum of Southern Europe is dumped on the nation's door in rapacious, conscienceless, lawbreaking hordes'.[3] The U.S. Bureau of Immigration classified northern and southern Italians as two different races, exacerbating public perceptions. Between 1890 and 1910, for example, Sicilians made up less than 4 per cent of the white male population yet were roughly 40 per cent of the white victims of lynch mobs.[4]

The first published account of the Mafia in the US was in spring 1869 when the *New Orleans Times* reported that the city's Second District had become overrun by 'well-known and notorious Sicilian murderers, counterfeiters and burglars, who, in the last month, have formed a sort of general co-partnership or stock company for the plunder and disturbance of the city'. Emigration from southern Italy to the Americas was primarily to Brazil and Argentina, and New Orleans had a heavy volume of port traffic to and from both destinations.

Mafia groups became influential in the New York City area, gradually progressing from small neighbourhood operations in poor Italian ghettos to citywide and eventually national organisations. As in Sicily, the society claimed to protect poor Italians, but preyed almost exclusively on Italian communities.[5] Giuseppe Morello, whose grandson and namesake was to become even more notorious, was the first known Mafia member to reach the US.[6] He and six other Sicilians fled to New York after murdering eleven wealthy landowners, and the chancellor and a vice chancellor of a Sicilian province. He was arrested in New Orleans in 1881 and extradited to Italy.

From 1890 to 1900, 655,888 Italian immigrants arrived in the US, of whom two-thirds were men. The immigrants populated various US cities, forming 'Little Italies' subdivided into regional groupings. Italian neighbourhoods typically grew in the older areas of the cities, suffering from overcrowded tenements and poor sanitation. Their closed communities created little more than a microcosm of the society they had left in Europe and criminals exploited this, extorting the more prosperous Italians in their neighbourhood. A crime that would eventually snowball into an epidemic was known as 'The Black Hand'.[7] The extortions were done anonymously by delivering threatening letters demanding money, signed with crudely drawn symbols, such as a knife or a skull. One such letter said: 'If you have not sufficient courage you may go to people who enjoy an honorable reputation and be careful as to whom you go. Thus you may stop us from persecuting you as you have been adjudged to give money or life. Woe upon you if you do not resolve to buy your future happiness, you can do from us by giving the money demanded.' People paid the Black Hand extortionists as American law had no understanding, or power, to help them. A letter that appeared in the *New York Times* said:

My name is Salvatore Spinelli. My parents in Italy came from a decent family. I came here eighteen years ago and went to work as a house painter, like my father. I started a family and I have been an American citizen for thirteen years. I had a house at 314 East Eleventh Street and another one at 316, which I rented out. At this point the 'Black Hand' came into my life and asked me for seven thousand dollars. I told them to go to hell and the bandits tried to blow up my house. Then I asked the police for help and refused more demands, but the 'Black Hand' set off one, two, three, four, five bombs in my houses. Things went to pieces. From thirty-two tenants I am down to six. I owe a thousand dollars interest that is due next month and I cannot pay. I am a ruined man. My family lives in fear. There is a policeman on guard in front of my house, but what can he do? My brother Francesco and I do guard duty at the windows with guns night and day. My wife and children have not left the house for weeks. How long can this go on?

The *Cosmopolitan* reported: 'No Italian is too lonely or too poor to embark as a Black-Hander. A sheet of paper, pen and ink, and enough knowledge of Italian to scrawl a few lines of demand and the accompanying threat are all that is necessary.' A strong fear was instilled in the communities, and Italian folklore spoke of gangsters being able to 'cast the evil eye' and to possess other 'magical powers';

such fables, mixed with the reality of bombings and murders, only helped to compound the effectiveness of the Black Hand legend.[8]

Meanwhile, in New Orleans, David C. Hennessy was building a career targeting Italian criminals. His father, David Snr, was a Union cavalry veteran of the Civil War who became a member of the Metropolitan Police, a New Orleans force under the authority of the governor of Louisiana. It was considered a form of occupation army by local white supremacists because they protected the right of African Americans to vote. He was murdered in a bar in 1869 by a fellow member of the Metropolitan Police[9] when David was eleven. Hennessy joined the New Orleans police force as a messenger in 1870. While only a teenager, he caught two adult thieves in the act, beat them with his bare hands, and dragged them to the police station. He made detective at the age of twenty. With his cousin Michael Hennessy, he arrested the notorious Italian bandit and fugitive Giuseppe Esposito in 1881. Esposito was wanted in Italy for numerous crimes, including kidnapping a British tourist and cutting off his ear. Esposito was deported to Italy, where he was given a life sentence.[10]

Competition between the rival factions within the forces of law and order again became bloody. In 1882, Hennessy was tried for the murder of New Orleans Chief of Detectives Thomas Devereaux on Halloween the previous year. Devereaux was the chief suspect in the murder of Robert Harris, another New Orleans police detective. At the time, Hennessy was challenging Deveraux for the position of chief. Hennessy argued that he shot his rival in the head in self-defence and was found not guilty.[11] The verdict was controversial, and Hennessy left the department and joined a private security firm given police powers by the city. He handled security for the New Orleans World Fair of 1884–85. The *New York Times* noted that Hennessy's men were, 'neatly uniformed and are a fine-looking and intelligent body of men, far superior to the regular city force'.[12]

In 1888, Joseph A. Shakespeare, the nominee of the Young Men's Democratic Association, was elected Mayor of New Orleans with Republican support. The son of a Swiss Quaker, Shakespeare had previously been mayor for a short but turbulent term in which he had tried and failed to break the power of 'the Ring', a scandal-plagued local political machine. He had increased the city's revenue by selling the Carrollton Street Railroad franchise and by allowing illegal gambling operations to operate as long as they made regular payments to the city treasury. This time around he had again promoted himself as a reform candidate again opposing the Ring. And, as before, he was supported by members of the conservative Bourbon business elite. His election was characterised by the presence of armed bands of men from both the reform and Ring camps.[13]

Shakespeare promptly appointed Hennessy as his police chief. Hennessy inherited a police force that was incompetent and corrupt. Under his supervision, it began to show signs of improvement.[14] As the youngest chief of police in the USA, he was handsome, shrewd, courageous and a teetotaller in a city of hard drinkers. He had a reputation, rare in police circles at the time, for personal probity and integrity. But he was far from perfect. He made arrests without bothering overmuch about procedures, was involved in squalid internal police feuds, and met relatives and cronies in the private Red Light club. While popular with the public, he had no shortage of enemies.[15]

Over the following eighteen months, Hennessey was increasingly involved in the Provenzano–Matranga feud over control of the Italian fruit trade on the docks. Both families were Sicilian. Hennessy, by then thirty-two, put several of the Provenzanos in prison after a crew of Matranga stevedores were ambushed and three men wounded in a post-midnight fusillade, and their appeal trial was coming up. However, Hennessy had been planning to offer new evidence at the trial which would clear the Provenzanos and implicate the Matrangas. If true, this would mean that the Matrangas, and not the Provenzanos, had a motive for his murder.[16] The Provenzano patriarch, Joe, was a regular at the Red Light. Joe was believed to have been involved in the murders of three men in the Italian Quarter, including that of a longshoreman whose torso was found stuffed into a greasy sack. But Hennessy was more concerned about the Matrangas, who paid their stevedores half that of their rivals because of alleged links to Sicilian crime lords.[17]

The Italian authorities had provided information that Salvatore Marino, a leading member of the Stoppaglieri crime syndicate in Monreale, Sicily, whose trial for murder had collapsed after a bribed court official burnt the prosecution files, had fled to New Orleans a decade before. He died of yellow fever, but not before boasting of his influence on the Matrangas. Joe Provenzano, admittedly not an unbiased source, told reporters that there were around twenty Stoppaglieris working for the Matrangas. He went on: 'They're the committee, and there are at least 300 greenhorns who've got to do anything the leaders say. They pay them $10, $20 or $100 to get a man out of the way, and if the man they order to kill someone won't do it, they have him killed so he can't tell anything to the police. They've got the Mafia Society everywhere ... in San Francisco, St Louis, Chicago, New York and here.'[18]

Hennessy's secretary, George Vandervoort later revealed that his boss had amassed incriminating files on the Matranga brothers and on Joe Macheca, the head of a fruit shipping line who had first subcontracted work to the Provenzanos before switching to the Matrangas to maximise profits, giving the latter family a virtual monopoly of the fruit trade from South America. Vandervoort said of Hennessy: 'He dug deeper into the order than any outsider had ever dared, and when he was up to see me he said he had evidence to uproot the Mafia in this country. He had ascertained facts that would have uncloaked their band of assassins and would have sent a great crowd to the penitentiary for perjurers.'[19]

Two days before the Provenzano trial, Hennessy attended the New Orleans Police Board, chatted to colleagues in his office, and shared a late-night plate of oysters with a police friend. Close to midnight he trudged through a heavy mist towards the small house he shared with his mother, his vision impaired by his open umbrella. It is unlikely that he even saw five men hunched in the shadows before they opened fire with heavy-calibre weapons. A revolver bullet punched through his chest, bisected a lung and touched the membrane of his heart. More bullets slammed into his elbow and broke a bone in his leg, while his right side was spattered by buckshot. Hennessy was knocked backwards, but after a few seconds he raised himself to his feet, drew his own gun, and limped after his fleeing attackers. After firing two futile shots, he collapsed for a second time. He was found by his friend Billy O'Connor, with whom he had shared oysters just minutes before. Hennessy whispered: 'They gave it to me ...and I gave it them back as best I could.' He then hissed the soon-to-be notorious reference to 'Dagoes'.[20] He was awake in hospital for several hours after the shooting, and spoke to friends, but did not name the shooters. The next day complications set in and he died.[21]

Mike Dash reported: 'Hennessy's men had passed a miserable night dredging the muddy gutters along Girod Street in search of the murder weapons; by dawn they were all for picking up some suspects first and worrying about their stories later.'[22] Despite the lack of any firm evidence, or testimony from the victim, it was widely believed that Hennessy's killers were Italian assassins. Since then, many historians have questioned this assumption.[23] However, at the time, local papers such as the *Times-Democrat* and the *Daily Picayune* freely blamed 'Dagoes' for the murder.[24] The pressure to catch his killers was intense. Mayor Shakespeare fanned the flames. He told the police to 'scour the whole neighbourhood. Arrest every Italian you come across.' Previously he had described the New Orleans Italian immigrant community as 'the most idle, vicious and worthless people among us … They are filthy in their persons and homes and our epidemics nearly always break out in their quarter. They are without courage, honor, truth, pride, religion or any quality that goes to make good citizens.'

Within twenty-four hours, at least forty-five people had been arrested.[25] By some accounts, as many as 250 Italians were rounded up.[26] They included a twelve-year-old boy wrongly identified as a lookout. Most were eventually released for lack of evidence. Local Italians were afraid to leave their homes for several days after the murder, but eventually the furore died down and they returned to work.

Nineteen men were ultimately charged with the murder, or as accessories, and held without bail in the Parish Prison. A push-cart pedlar was arraigned because he failed to turn up at the usual time. Pietro Monasterio, a shoemaker, was arrested because he lived across the street from where Hennessy was standing when he was shot. Antonio Marchesi, a fruit peddler, was arrested because he was a friend of Monasterio's and 'was known to frequent his shoe shop'.[27] Emmanuele Polizzi was arrested when a policeman identified him as one of the men he had seen running from the pitch-black scene of the crime. But more credible suspects included Charles Matranga, who was charged with plotting the murder, and several of the Matrangas' friends and workers. Joe Macheca, regarded as the most powerful Italian in the city, was also picked up.

A few days after Hennessy's death, Mayor Shakespeare gave a speech declaring that Hennessy had been 'the victim of Sicilian vengeance' and calling upon the citizenry to 'teach these people a lesson they will not forget'.[28] He appointed a Committee of Fifty to investigate 'the existence of secret societies or bands of oath-bound assassins … and to devise necessary means and the most effectual and speedy measures for the uprooting and total annihilation' of any such organisations. On 23 October, the committee published an open letter to the Italian American community encouraging them to inform on each other anonymously. The letter ended on a menacing note: 'We hope this appeal will be met by you in the same spirit in which we issue it, and that this community will not be driven to harsh and stringent methods outside of the law, which may involve the innocent and guilty alike ... Upon you and your willingness to give information depends which of these courses shall be pursued.'[29] The letter was signed by the committee's chairman, Edgar H. Farrar, who later served as president of the American Bar Association.

The Committee of Fifty hired two private detectives to pose as prisoners and try to get the defendants to talk about the murder. They did not obtain any useful information and were not asked to testify at the trial. Only Polizzi, who appeared to be mentally ill, said anything to incriminate himself, and his confession was deemed inadmissible. Meanwhile, the defendants were subject to extremely negative pre-trial publicity. Across the country, newspapers ran headlines such as 'Vast Mafia in New Orleans' and '1,100 Dago Criminals'.[30] Several shotguns were found near the scene of the crime. One was a muzzle-loader, a type which was widely used in New Orleans and throughout the South but which police claimed was a 'favourite' of Italians. Another had a hinged stock. Local newspapers reported that such guns were imported from Italy; in fact they were manufactured by the W. Richards Company.[31]

Spurred to action by the popular accounts of Hennessy's murder, a twenty-nine-year-old newspaper salesman named Thomas Duffy walked into the prison on 17 October 1890, sought out Antonio Scaffidi, whom he had heard was a suspect, and shot him in the neck with a revolver. Scaffidi survived the attack, only to be doomed later. Duffy was eventually convicted of assault and sentenced to six months in prison.[32]

A trial of nine of the suspects began on 16 February 1891, and concluded on 13 March 1891, with Judge Joshua G. Baker presiding. The defendants were represented by Lionel Adams of the law firm Adams and O'Malley, and the state by District Attorney Charles A. Luzenberg. Jury selection was a time-consuming process: hundreds of prospective jurors were rejected before twelve people were found who were not opposed to capital punishment, were not openly prejudiced against Italians, and were not of Italian descent themselves.

The trial was a farce, the evidence presented often weak or contradictory. The murder had taken place on a poorly lit street on a damp night, in a notoriously corrupt city, and the eyewitness testimony was unreliable. Suspects were identified by witnesses who had not seen their faces, but only their clothing. Captain Billy O'Connor, the witness who claimed to have heard Hennessy blame 'Dagoes' for the assassination, was not called to testify. There were numerous other discrepancies and improprieties. At one point, two employees of the defence law firm were arrested for attempting to bribe prospective jurors. Polizzi broke down in the dock and claimed that Matranga and Macheca were joint leaders of the city Mafia, but his outburst made little impact because he was clearly insane – he spent the rest of the trial either slumped in a chair or trying to bite passing court officials. Afterwards, when federal district attorney William Grant looked into the case, he reported that the evidence against the men was 'exceedingly unsatisfactory' and inconclusive. He could find no evidence linking any of the accused to the Mafia, or to any attempts to bribe the jury. The bribery charges were eventually dismissed.[33] Matranga and Macheca produced a dozen witnesses to testify that they had both been at the opera at the time of Hennessy's murder, an alibi which the prosecution claimed had been bought.

Matranga and another man were cleared by the judge's direction, and four more were found not guilty by the jury. The jury asked the judge to declare a mistrial for the other three, as they could not agree on a verdict. Despite the acquittals, they were not released, and all nine men were sent back to the prison pending an additional charge of 'lying in wait' with intent to commit murder.[34] The jurors were given the option to leave by a side door but chose to walk out the front door and face the angry crowd. Several defended their decision to reporters, arguing that they had 'reasonable doubt' and had done what they thought was right. Some were harassed, threatened, fired from their jobs, and otherwise vilified for failing to convict the Italians.

The 150-strong Committee on Safety met that evening to plan their response. The following morning an advertisement appeared in local newspapers calling for a mass meeting at the statue of former Speaker of the House of Representatives Henry Clay, near the prison. Citizens were told to 'come prepared for action'. The *Daily States* editorialised: 'Rise, people of New Orleans! Alien hands of oath-bound assassins have set the blot of a martyr's blood upon your vaunted civilization! Your laws, in the very Temple of Justice, have been bought off, and suborners have caused to be turned loose upon your streets the midnight murderers of David C. Hennessy, in whose premature grave the very majesty of our American law lies buried with his mangled corpse – the corpse of him who in life was the representative, the conservator of your peace and dignity.'[35]

As thousands of demonstrators gathered near the Parish Prison, Pasquale Corte, the Italian consul in New Orleans, appealed to Louisiana governor Francis T. Nicholls to prevent an outbreak of violence. The governor declined to take any action without a request from Mayor Shakespeare, who had gone out to breakfast and could not be reached.[36] Meanwhile, at the Clay statue, attorney William S. Parkerson was telling the people of New Orleans to 'set aside the verdict of that infamous jury, every one of whom is a perjurer and a scoundrel'. Witnesses recalled that his 'eyes snapped fire'. When the speech was over, the crowd marched to the prison, chanting, 'We want the Dagoes.' Inside, as the mob was breaking down the door with a battering ram, prison warden Lemuel Davis let the nineteen Italian prisoners out of their cells and told them to hide themselves as best they could in the cell blocks.[37]

Although the estimated 8,000 demonstrators armed with guns, knives and staves outside the jail gave the sense that the lynching was a spontaneous outburst, and contemporary reports speak of the mob going 'mad', the killings were in fact carried out by a relatively small, disciplined 'execution squad' led by Parkerson and three other city leaders: Walter Denegre, lawyer; James D. Houston, politician and businessman; and John C. Wickliffe, editor of the *New Delta* newspaper. Up to sixty, allegedly all hand-picked by Parkerson, entered the prison after a rear door was breached and, while others guarded all exits, methodically combed the prison buildings.[38]

Macheca, cornered in his cell, tried to defend himself with an Indian club, but was shot dead. Terrified non-Italian convicts pointed out the hiding places of six of the targets who were then lined against a wall and blasted with shotguns, tearing their bodies apart. At least 100 shots were fired in that incident alone. The mentally ill Polizzi was hauled outside, hanged from a lamppost, and shot around thirty times. Antonio Bagnetto, the fruit peddler, was hanged from a tree and shot. In all, eleven were killed. The bullet-riddled bodies of Polizzi and Bagnetto were left hanging for hours.[39] Parkerson was carried in triumph on the shoulders of his men. The lawyer piously declared: 'Mob violence is the most terrible thing on the face of the earth. You have performed your duty. Now go to your homes, and if I need you, I will call you.'

Not all his targets had been killed. Charles Matranga had hidden under the floorboards of a closet in the jail's women's section and escaped. He and the other survivors were set free after the lynching, and the charges against those who had not been tried were dropped. Matranga returned to work as a stevedore and carried on living openly in the city until his retirement in 1918.[40] But while murderous passions had quickly simmered down, the debate over the justification or otherwise of the killings carried on in print and in the courts. It emerged that Polizzi had a police record, having reportedly cut a man with a knife in Austin, Texas, several years earlier. Two others had police records in Italy: Geraci had been accused of murder and had fled before he could be tried, and Comitz had been convicted of theft. Incardona was wanted in Italy as a petty criminal[41] Three of the men – Comitz, Monasterio, and Traina – had not applied for US citizenship and could still be considered Italian subjects. All of those lynched were Sicilian immigrants except for Macheca, a Louisiana native of Sicilian descent, and Comitz, who was from the Rome area.

American newspapers were largely sympathetic to the lynchers, and anti-Italian in tone. Shortly after Hennessy's death, the *Daily States* informed readers that the suspects were 'a villainous looking set' and described their appearance in racist terms, concluding, 'They are not Italians, but Sicilians.' The victims were presumed to have been involved with the Mafia and therefore deserving of their fate. A *New York Times* headline announced, 'Chief Hennessy Avenged ... Italian Murderers Shot Down.'[42] An editorial the next day vilified Sicilians in general: 'These sneaking and cowardly Sicilians, the descendants of bandits and assassins, who have transported to this country the lawless passions, the cut-throat practices, and the oath-bound societies of their native country, are to us a pest without mitigation. Our own rattlesnakes are as good citizens as they ... Lynch law was the only course open to the people of New Orleans.'[43] A *Boston Globe* front-page headline read, 'STILETTO RULE: New Orleans Arose to Meet the Curse.' Not all editors were convinced of the mob's innocence, however. The *Charleston News and Courier* argued that murder by vigilantes was no more acceptable than any other kind. The *St. Louis Republic* wrote that the men were killed 'on proof of being "dagoes" and on the merest suspicion of being guilty of any other crime'.[44]

A grand jury convened on 17 March 1891. Judge Robert H. Marr, presiding, was a long-time personal friend of several members of the lynch mob.[45] On 5 May 1891, the grand jury concluded that several jurors in the Hennessy case had been bribed. No proof was offered, and no criminal charges were pursued. The grand jury claimed that it could not identify the participants in the lynching. In the same report, the lynching was described as a 'gathering' of 'several thousands of the first, best, and even the most law-abiding, of the citizens of this city'. No one was indicted. Only Thomas Duffy, the newspaper salesman who had shot Scaffidi in October, had been penalised. In fact, in an ironic twist, Duffy was serving time in Parish Prison at the time of the lynching.

In his 1977 book *Vendetta*, Richard Gambino noted that Hennessy had a colourful past which provided any number of possible motives, none of which the police chose to investigate. Shortly after the lynching, the city passed an ordinance handing over control of all New Orleans dock work to the newly formed Louisiana Construction and Improvement Corporation, a business headed by several of the lynch mob leaders. Italian waterfront merchants and workers, who had been making remarkable economic progress up to then, were thus eliminated as competitors.

After the Hennessy case, at least eight more men of Italian descent were lynched in Louisiana. In each case, local authorities claimed to be unable to identify anyone involved.[46] For decades, Italian Americans were taunted in the streets with the words: 'Who killa de chief?'

The incident strained relations between the US and Italy. The Italian government demanded that the lynch mob be brought to justice and reparations be paid to the dead men's families. When the US refused, Italy recalled its ambassador from Washington in protest. The US followed suit, recalling its legation from Rome. Diplomatic relations remained at an impasse for over a year. There were even rumours of war. When President Benjamin Harrison agreed to pay a $25,000 indemnity to the victims' families, Congress tried unsuccessfully to intervene, accusing him of 'unconstitutional executive usurpation of Congressional powers'.[47]

The contrasting American and Italian attitudes toward the lynchings are perhaps best summarised by Theodore Roosevelt, then serving on the US Civil Service Commission. He wrote to his sister Anna Roosevelt Cowles: 'Monday we dined at the Camerons; various dago diplomats were present, all much wrought up by the lynching of the Italians in New Orleans. Personally, I think it rather a good thing, and said so.'[48]

Mayor Shakespeare was narrowly defeated for re-election in 1892, with the Italian vote a decisive factor. Shakespeare ran for a third term in 1892, but by then his reputation as a reformer was tarnished, and he was defeated by Ring candidate John Fitzpatrick, who had strong pro-labour credentials. Shakespeare died in New Orleans in 1896. Gaspare Marchesi, who survived by hiding in the prison while his father was lynched, was awarded $5,000 in damages in 1893 after suing the city of New Orleans.[49]

The death of Hennessy became a rallying cry for law enforcement and nativists to halt the immigration of Italians into America. Henry Cabot Lodge claimed that 'the paupers and criminals of Europe' were 'pouring into the United States' and proposed a literacy test to keep out the poorest immigrants. The Hennessy case gave rise to the now-familiar stereotype of the Italian American mafioso. Journalists of the time used the word 'Mafia' loosely to sell newspapers, often linking the crimes of individual Italians to organised crime when no evidence of such a connection existed. After the lynching, newspapers circulated wild rumours that thousands of Italian Americans were plotting to attack New Orleans and were wrecking railroads in New York and Chicago. The press reported that the defence lawyers in the Hennessy case were paid by the Mafia, when in fact Italian-language newspapers in cities across the country had raised funds for the men's legal defence. That said, however, the dawn of a new century brought evidence that, whatever people called it, organised crime was in the ascendancy.

***

Pasquarella Spinelli, middle-aged, plump and barely literate, was one of the richest people in New York, worth, it was said, $300,000. She owned a large stable located at 334 E108th Street, and had interests in several other businesses, including leasing tenements in Harlem, moneylending, and the management of the Rex, the largest Italian vaudeville theatre in Manhattan.[50] Police suspected, but never bothered to prove, that her main income was from the proceeds of crime. One such deal was with Nick Terranova, who ran the Morello clan's lucrative horse theft racket, and she allowed him to use the stables to conceal the steeds at a rate of $5 a day per animal. Horse theft was a big business. In 1909 it was estimated that 800 horses were stolen in the city, at a value of around $300 each. Owning a large stable in which one could temporarily house stolen horses whilst they were clipped, put the owner in a powerful position in the criminal world. The stable was described in the press as 'a rambling one storey structure, built partially of sheet iron, packing boxes, discarded odds and ends of house wreckage – doors for instance with hinges still on them yet. It is a rabbit warren which shelters two or three junk shops, a wheelwrights, a blacksmiths, a boarding stable and a hay and grain store.' The building became known as the 'Murder Stables', allegedly the scene of, or dumping ground for, innumerable mob executions, although the numbers cited were perhaps press hyperbole.[51] Spinelli's career ran parallel to the rise of organised crime in New York.

The first boss of the Morello crime family was Giuseppe 'the Clutch Hand' Morello (2 May 1867–15 August 1930). His nickname came from having a one-fingered, deformed right hand that resembled a claw. He was born in Corleone, Sicily.[52] His *Mafioso* father died in 1872 and his mother remarried a year later to Bernardo Terranova, a member of the Corleone Mafia. The Morello and Terranova children grew up together and Giuseppe's stepfather facilitated his early induction into the local *cosca*, or Mafia clan.[53]

Morello emigrated in 1892 after becoming a suspect in a murder in Corleone and after his counterfeiting ring had been exposed.[54] He was prosecuted *in absentia* for counterfeiting and sentenced to six years. Morello's three half-brothers Nicolò, Vincenzo and Ciro, his stepfather Bernardo, and most of his other near-relatives arrived in New York on 8 March 1893. In the mid-1890s, Morello moved to Louisiana in search of employment and was joined by the other members of the Morello–Terranova family. The following year they moved to Texas and farmed cotton.[55] After contracting malaria in 1897, he returned to New York where Morello lost investments in a saloon and a date factory. In 1898, Morello's wife Maria Rosa Marvalisi died. In the early 1900s Morello married Nicolina 'Lena' Salemi, who stayed with him for the rest of his life. In 1902, he acquired a saloon at 8 Prince Street in Manhattan which was to become a meeting place for members of his gang, known as the 107th Street Mob, which would later evolve into the Morello crime family. In 1903, Ignazio 'the Wolf' Lupo, the Sicilian Mafia boss in Little Italy, married Morello's half-sister Salvatrice. Crime was by now very much a family affair.

In just three years, Jack Dash wrote, 'Giuseppe Morello assembled the first Mafia gang in Manhattan. It was only a small group of men at first, but they were all utterly loyal to him, and if the branch of the Stoppaglieri in New Orleans had claim to be the first *cosca* in the country, Morello's family boasted a vastly more significant distinction. It survived. It grew and changed over the years, fighting and merging with other groups until the outward traces of its early days were lost ... the Morellos were the first family of organised crime in the United States.'[56]

Family businesses included extortion, loan sharking, Italian lottery, robbery and counterfeiting. Illegally earned money was then legitimised by legal businesses such as stores or restaurants, making them the first crime family to organise money laundering on a substantial scale. They also introduced new ways of extorting small amounts of money every week from business owners in exchange for 'protection', as opposed to the theft of large amounts which might bankrupt them. This technique was adopted from the small-scale Black Hand gangsters whose operations ran, to some extent, in tandem.

In January 1908, a bomb blew open the front of an Italian Bank, Pasquale Pati & Son, on Elizabeth Street. Pati was the most successful Italian banker in New York, with his wealth estimated at half a million dollars. His bank displayed piles of money behind their secured windows as proof of their ability to pay depositors. The son, Salvatore Pati, who was in the bank at the time of the bombing, managed to secure the money while the bomb throwers escaped into the crowds on Elizabeth Street. The bomb was not an attempt at robbery, but a warning from the Black Hand after Pati had publicly announced he would have no truck with gangland extortion. After the explosion, nervous depositors began to withdraw their money, and in the next four weeks over $400,000 in deposits were removed. On 6 March 1908, three armed men entered the bank, but escaped empty handed when Pati shot one them; the would-be robber later died in hospital.

Pati began to receive more death threats. He was forced to close the bank just two weeks later, after he learned a group of men had attempted to set fire to his family home in Brooklyn. He pinned a note to the front of the bank reading: 'The clientele of this bank be calm and trustworthy, as the banker, Pasquale Pati, has long been obliged to absent himself to protect his existence and family.' A crowd rushed to the next-largest Italian bank, F. Acritelli & Son, which was then also forced to close. A police guard was provided for both banks. Three days later, after Pati had not reappeared, the director of the Italian Chamber of Commerce was appointed receiver of the bank by the US Circuit Court. Pati, who had built his business up over seventeen years having started as a cobbler before moving into grocery and real estate, was a ruined man.[57]

Morello kept a lower profile, preferring the technique that 'you have to skim the cream off the milk without breaking the bottle.' Mike Dash wrote: 'The Clutch Hand understood instinctively how to go about making cash, making the threat of violence behind a veneer of bonhomie and adding refinements of his own.' His tactics may have been more sophisticated than the Black Hand mobsters, but that was due to common sense rather than any finer feelings. He demonstrated time and again that, stripped of the veneer, his methods 'exploited the weak and dealt in fear'.[58]

Morello's empire was underpinned by his merciless ordering of death sentences against everyone who dared to face him. Lupo, his main enforcer, was responsible for more than sixty murders in a ten-year killing spree. The Morello family would frequently employ the notorious barrel murder system, dumping dismembered corpses into large wooden barrels. The barrels would then be thrown into the sea, left on a random street corner, abandoned in a back alley or shipped to non-existent addresses in another city. One such murder, that of forty-three-year-old Manhattan newcomer Benedetto Madonia, became notorious. Madonia had been dragooned into Morello's counterfeiting operation by thugs who threatened both himself and his wife and had allegedly broken the code of silence. On the chilly night of 14 April 1903, he was eating his supper in a dank room behind a Little Italy tavern when the door burst open and several mobsters entered. Their leader was Morello himself, flanked by an enforcer known as Petto the Ox. Morello signalled with his good hand and two men dragged Madonia to his feet. Morello barked insults at the terrified Sicilian, who was then dragged towards a rusty sink. His head was jerked back by his hair, exposing his throat. A third man drew a 14-inch stiletto blade sideways above Madonia's Adam's apple, stopping only at the top of his spine. The Ox completed the job with his own knife, almost removing head from body. Blood pumped into the sink; not a drop fell on the floorboards. The body was stuffed into a commercial barrel and taken by cart to an East 11th Street lumber yard. An arm and a leg projected from the barrel when it was found the following morning by a cleaning woman. That was almost certainly deliberate as Morello wanted it found as a warning to others.[59]

Morello either ordered, or was implicated in, a string of murders, not all of whose victims ended in barrels. Jewellery pedlar Meyer Weisband was found stuffed into a trunk on the docks in January 1901, his throat cut and his teeth knocked out, possibly having committed the sin of demanding payment from his Sicilian customers. The following year the Italian banker Louis Troja, believed to be the richest man in Harlem, was bludgeoned to death in his office.[60] The list went on and on.

Morello was unchallenged as leader, with Lupo his deputy, and the gang members obeyed orders without question. They were paid as little as $10 a day to run local scams and extort protection money. One of the few to later testify in court, Ralph Daniello, said:

> Sometimes the system does not run smoothly. Then there is trouble – and death. Sometimes the leaders of one district look with envious eyes on the wealth made in the other; sometimes an outsider tries to squeeze in. Sometimes one of the leaders tries to depose his fellow boss and get a larger share of the spoils himself. Sometimes a gambling house owner forgets to give over a share of his winnings. Then one of the leaders would call one of us into his house. 'This man is in the way,' the boss would say, naming someone. 'He interferes. Go get him.' We went. We did not dare protest. It was the other man's life or ours. For the murder, we did not get a cent, but we knew that if we returned to headquarters without finishing it, that same day would see our end. We lived in constant terror.[61]

Many assassinations were bungled by ill-trained thugs, but others involved a great deal of planning. A freelance Italian hold-up man foolish enough to rob known gangsters on the street wore a chainmail vest for protection; he was tailed for days until he stepped out of his apartment without his armour and was immediately shot dead. Rival extortionist Giuliano Sperlozza, a known enemy of the Morellos, was so terrified he hid for days in a windowless room deep within his tenement. An infiltrator gained access to the long hallway and chalked an 'O' halfway up the hiding-place door. A sniper then fired a bullet through a tenement window which travelled along the corridor, through the 'O' and into the seated target.[62] By 1905, Morello had created the largest, most influential Sicilian crime family in New York City and was recognised as *capo di tutti capi* (boss of bosses) by Mafia leaders in other US cities.

The media were not blind to the upsurge in gangsterism. At the height of the Morello family's reign, the *Herald* reported:

> There is a wood on the outskirts of New York where certain trees are almost cut in twain by the leaden slugs which have been

fired into targets nailed to them. It is there that they become proficient with the revolver and the shotgun with the barrel sawn off short. When a man is marked for death his assassins learn the street which he passes through most frequently on his way home at night. Then an apartment or a stable with a window facing the street is selected ... Some night when the victim is strolling homeward the ugly snub-nosed barrels are thrust through the window, which has been kept open just wide enough day and night. There is a squeeze on the trigger, the roar of the explosion to which Harlem's 'Little Italy' is becoming accustomed, and by the time the police enter the building from which the shot was fired, there is nothing but a few empty bottles, a table and a chair, and the smell of stale tobacco smoke.[63]

For the Morello gang, counterfeiting was always the most lucrative racket, but also the one that drew the most attention from the authorities, in particular from William Flynn, who would later precede J. Edgar Hoover as head of the FBI. At the time, Flynn was the head of the Secret Service's New York bureau and had been pursuing Morello for the Madonia barrel murder. New York-born, and a former plumber and jailor, he knew the city's backstreet warrens and the people who inhabited them. He carefully built up a network of contacts and informants and managed through gentle coercion alone to 'turn' at least one Morello gang member. Flynn collaborated with police detective Joe Petrosino, who was murdered in 1909 in Palermo, Sicily, where he was tracing the backgrounds of the gangster families. Petrosino's murder was never officially solved, but Flynn had no doubt that the hit had been ordered by Giuseppe Morello. By late 1909 Flynn was ready to act.

He and his men raided Morello's ramshackle tenement apartment on the night of 15 November. They found him and his half-brother Nick Terranova fast asleep on adjoining mattresses. They woke groggily as they were pinioned to the floor. Under Morello's pillow there were four loaded revolvers, while under Terranova's there were five. Flynn reported later: 'One might compare Giuseppe to a one-man war, and I frequently wondered why he didn't fear himself at times.' Several other gang members were also arrested before the raiding party was confronted by Morello's wife Lina, holding her infant daughter in one hand, a knife in the other. Flynn recalled: 'Morello's wife made herself extremely unpopular with us by drawing a wicked knife. It took two of us to get it away from her. Bereft of the knife, she subsided into tears.'[64] Three 'Black Hand' letters to other Mafia bosses demanding enormous sums of money were found inside the nappy of one of the Morello infants.

Morello and seven other gang members were locked up that night. The enforcer Lupo was picked up without a whimper as he strolled close to his apartment on 8 January 1910. He was unarmed; in his pockets were a nail file and $7. Bail was set at the unheard-of sums of $10,000 for Morello and between $7,500 and $5,000 for the other gang members. They could not raise such sums and stayed in their cells, preparing for the trial and fabricating alibis with those on the outside. Their associates imposed stiff, compulsory levies on Italian businesses to pay for the court costs and lawyers' fees.[65]

The trial involved more than sixty witnesses, some of whom were faced with death threats inside and outside the courtroom. But despite the gangsters' ferocious reputations, the jury rejected manufactured alibi evidence. Morello was sentenced to twenty-five years' hard labour, later reduced to twenty, and a $500 fine for counterfeiting. Lupo got thirty years and a similar fine. The others got sentences ranging from fifteen to eighteen years. Morello maintained his position as the head of his crime family for the first year of his sentence, during which time he hoped his conviction would be overturned on appeal. His appeals were not immediately successful, and Morello became depressed as he lost his official position as boss of New York and all the influence he once held. Nick Terranova took over control.

It was during this period that the 'Murder Stables' came to notoriety. On 29 October 1911, the daughter of Pasquarella, Nellie Lenere, walked into the E104th Street police station and claimed 'a man had met with accident in her home.' The police discovered the body of Frank 'Chick' Monaco, a well-known Harlem gangster. He had been stabbed twenty-five times in the back. Lenere claimed she had killed him as he tried to rob the family safe. Her story did not match the dead man's autopsy – and her clothes were too clean for such butchery. The police suspected she was, through fear, shielding the real killers. Under cross-examination, she claimed that Monaco had lured her to a cottage in Westchester, where she was robbed and held for two days. Lenere was eventually acquitted by the Coroner's jury due to a lack of evidence.

In 1912, Nicholas Terranova opened a blacksmith shop in the stables. Antonio Comito, in testimony to the Secret Service in 1910, said that one of the Morello gang members, Nick Sylvester, 'boasted that his first sentence was for five years in the reformatory as a minor. He ran away from the reformatory in company with several other boys and got into the horse-stealing business. He was sentenced several times for small offenses and he once was arrested for carrying concealed weapons. During his imprisonment he came to know a certain Terranova, who was a half-brother of Morello, and they became fast friends. They stole horses in New York and sold them in other cities at reduced prices; or they would bring the horses to friends in the country and receive payment. He told of being arrested once when with Morello's son and brother; they had thrown a bomb into a store in Mott Street. They were let go because there were no witnesses to the crime.'[66]

Pasquarella, along with Nellie, moved to an apartment overlooking the stables yard. At around 5.30 p.m. on 20 March 1912, Pasquarella left her apartment and crossed the street to the stable. Nellie, who was still at home, heard gunshots and leapt to the window to see her mother dead with two gunshot wounds in her head and neck and two gunmen fleeing from the scene. The police concluded the killing was in revenge for the death of Monaco, as Nellie's description matched those of two of Monaco's cronies. They were never caught, but saloon-keeper Angelo Losco was later arrested. He was eventually freed only to himself be killed nine months later. Several anonymous letters sent to the district attorney claimed that Pasquarella had been killed by Aniello Prisco, because of 'her willingness to give the police information in regards to the killing of her son-in-law'.[67] Pasquarella's partner in the stables, Luigi Lazzazara, was charged with opening a stable door to allow access to the gunmen. Lazzazara had been a friend of the late Monaco and was reported to have been helping him blackmail the family, but he was later discharged. Nellie Lenere, after witnessing the murder, feared for her own life. She fled to Italy and sent back false reports of her own murder to confuse her enemies. It was later thought that she returned to New York and went into hiding.

Lazzazara took over the stables. He had previous convictions for horse theft and unlicensed firearms. Aged sixty-two, he was found stabbed to death in the early hours of 20 February 1914. Policeman Flaherty saw three men struggling at the junction of 1st Avenue and 108th Street; as he approached one man fell dead. On 9 April 1914, Giuseppe Gandolfo was mortally wounded outside the stable. He had been returning home with his son when they were both shot. Gandolfo had previously been employed at the stable by Spinelli as a blacksmith. The next owner of the 'Murder Stables', Ippolito Greco, was a saloon keeper with Morello associate Angelo Gagliano and a suspect in an earlier murder. He received a message to meet some friends at a saloon; as he left the stable with four men, including his brother Vincenzo, he was shot and killed in October 1915.

In the four years after the first murder there were numerous other killings in the same vicinity. The press linked these killings together under the same 'Murder Stables' headline, but it is likely that the other murders and shootings were linked to power struggles both within the Morello family, and between them and rival Neapolitan gangs of the Camorra.

Under Nick Terranova, the Morello clan continued its murder spree. Terranova was particularly ruthless in tracking down and having killed those who defected from the gang, or those allies who did not conform exactly to his orders. One of the latter was Joe DiMarco, a smallpox-scarred twenty-eight-year-old professional gambler and restaurateur who ran profitable card games across Italian Harlem. He had been an ally of the Morellos since 1910, but he refused to hand over the lion's share of his gambling profits to the Terranova brothers. It was rumoured that DiMarco had put out a contract on Nick Terranova, and from then his days were numbered. In April 1913 he was shot through the neck in an ambush, but survived subsequent surgery to everyone's astonishment, given the depth of his wound. He went into hiding, but a year later the Terranovas tried again. DiMarco was being shaved in a barbershop when two gunmen blasted him from the threshold before turning and running away. Covered in blood and lather, DiMarco was merely peppered by a dozen pellets.

DiMarco, perhaps by now considering himself invulnerable, opened a downtown restaurant and hired two bodyguards. In the summer of 1916, the Terranovas carefully planned one final hit. The local *Herald* correspondent reported:

> DiMarco liked to play cards, and his enemies used that fact to lure him to his death. Someone guided him to a dark little room in the rear of a tenement down in James Street in the afternoon, where it was understood there would be a poker game. DiMarco took one, or maybe two, of his bodyguards along. One, Charles Lombardi sat beside him at the poker table. ...a 'straight flush', a very unusual 'hand', was dealt to DiMarco, for that 'hand was found under

his bullet-ridden body. They believe that the dealing of that hand was the signal for the gunmen to open fire on DiMarco and his unsuspecting bodyguard. Twenty shots were fired, perhaps more … DiMarco was shot ten times and Lombardi twice.[68]

Up to ten men who had been in the room fled, leaving behind straw hats, possibly to mislead the police.

Two months later DiMarco's brother Salvatore, who was involved in Harlem coal rackets, was attacked with baseball bats off Washington Avenue. His body was found in weeds, his skull crushed like an eggshell and his throat cut for good measure. Although he was robbed of a considerable sum of money, it was widely believed that his murder had been ordered to prevent a blood feud over his brother's death.

The Terranova brothers soon had their hands full in a war with the Camorra, a secret society initially based in Naples from the 1820s who proved themselves just as ruthless as the Cosa Nostra when their members emigrated to the American eastern seaboard. Between 1900 and 1910, leading Camorrists settled across the East River, facing the Morello stronghold, and organised their criminal enterprises, primarily gambling and dealing cocaine.[69] In 1915, Brooklyn Camorra leader Pellegrino Morano began moving in on the Morello family's territory after a Neapolitan ally of the Morello family, Giosue Gallucci, was killed in East Harlem. The following year, Morello gangsters killed Camorra member Nick Del Guido. Soon after a peace conference was called between the two warring groups, but Morano refused Morello's offer and open warfare continued. The war between New York's Sicilian Mafia and Neapolitan Camorra lasted for over two years, and claimed scores of lives.

The leading Camorra gang, which used as its base a coffee shop on Navy Street, was run by 30-year-old Alessandrio Vollero, who had arrived in New York with his wife and children. He hated Nick Terranova, blaming him for the death of a close friend. Morano, meanwhile, was incensed at Morello attempts to monopolise the lottery rackets. He and Vollero joined forces to achieve a simple aim – the wiping out of the Terranovas and their Morello lieutenants. Six Morello leaders, including the three Terranova brothers, were invited to Navy Street to discuss peace terms and future co-operation. A dozen Camorra thugs were secreted around the coffee shop venue, their bullets smeared with garlic which, it was believed, would cause infection if any of their targets were merely wounded.[70]

On the warm afternoon of 7 September 1916, the assassins were dismayed when only two of the six Morello bosses showed up – Nick Terranova and his friend Eugene Ubriaco. Apparently suspecting nothing, Terranova was wholly nonchalant, enjoyed a glass of Moxie and inquired after the health of the visibly drawn and shaken waiter who served him. The two men then strolled back into the autumn sunshine. Vollero's gunmen held their fire until the two men were close, then let loose a flurry of gunshots from several different directions. Terranova crumpled into the gutter, shot six times, having only half-drawn his revolver. Ubriaco fired five of his six bullets at the attackers before himself falling, shot in the heart. He lay among shards of glass from windows broken by stray bullets.

The Morellos had lost their most effective leader, but Morano, Vollero, and several underlings were soon arrested, and in 1917 they were all convicted of murder and sentenced to life imprisonment. The war ended soon afterward, and the Neapolitan Camorra was assimilated into the Sicilian Mafia by 1919.

Newly released from Atlanta Federal Penitentiary in 1920 and trying to retake control of his empire, Giuseppe Morello was considered a threat to his former captain, now turned Mafia boss, Salvatore D'Aquila; within a year, D'Aquila ordered Morello killed. Morello, along with a number of others given a similar Mafia death sentence, fled to Sicily for a spell. One such exile, a former D'Aquila gunman, Umberto Valenti, went after Morello and his chief protector and ally, Giuseppe Masseria, in order to regain the favour of D'Aquila. A war ensued and, after much violence and some prominent deaths among the *Mafiosi* involved, Valenti was killed by Masseria gunmen in August 1922. With Valenti gone, D'Aquila's power began to lose its appearance of invulnerability. Morello, sensing his time to rule had passed and the power of Masseria was on the rise, became consiglieri to Masseria and prospered under him throughout the Prohibition years of the 1920s.

Meanwhile, from the 1890s to 1920, in New York the Five Points Gang, founded by Paul Kelly, were very powerful in the Little Italy of the Lower East Side. They were often in conflict with the Jewish Eastmans of the same area. There was also an influential Mafia family in East Harlem, while the Neapolitan Camorra was also very active in Brooklyn.

Paul Kelly was born Paolo Antonio Vaccarelli, but adopted the name when he began professional boxing after emigrating to New

York in the early 1890s. Using money gained from prize-fighting, Kelly began operating several bordellos in the Italian immigrant district east of the Bowery. Offering his services to Tammany Hall politician 'Big' Tim Sullivan, Kelly used his gang to help elect Tom Foley against incumbent Paddy Divver. The latter was a local saloon owner campaigning to keep prostitution out of the Fourth Ward during the 1901 Second Assembly District primary elections. On the day of the primary on 17 September, Kelly's gang of over 1,500 men assaulted Divver supporters, blocked polling booths, and committed numerous acts of voter fraud to win the election for Foley, such as voting several times during the day; one gang member claimed that 'I got in fifty-three votes.'[71] Foley was the challenger, not the incumbent; the Second Ward already had numerous houses of prostitution as Divver, a judge and long-time Tammany leader, was well aware. Kelly later gained control of the vice districts of the Fourth and Sixth Wards, including prostitution, and enjoyed a virtual monopoly in the Five Points.

In 1901 Monk Eastman, leader of the Eastman Gang, unusually travelling without a bodyguard, was set upon by Five Pointers when he blundered into the Bowery armed only with a pair of knuckledusters. He knocked down three of his attackers before a fourth shot him twice in the stomach. They left him for dead, but he stumbled to the nearest hospital, closing his gaping wounds with his fingers. For several weeks he lay close to death but recovered to seek revenge. After his hospital discharge, police found the body of a Five Pointer lying in a Grand Street gutter. The victim had been lured from his usual haunts by a woman and shot dead.

Herbert Asbury wrote:

For more than two years the conflict between the Eastmans and the Five Pointers raged almost without cessation, and the darkened streets of the East Side and the old Paradise Square section were filled night after night with scurrying figures who shot at each other from carriages, or from that strange new invention, the automobile, or pounced upon each other from the shelter of doorways, with no warning save the vicious swish of a blackjack or section of lead pipe. Stuss games owned by members of the Eastman clan were held up and robbed by the Five Pointers and Kelly's sources of revenue were similarly interfered with by the redoubtable Monk and his henchmen. Balls and other social functions in New Irving and Walhalla Halls were frequently interrupted while the gangsters shot out their mutual hatred without regard for the safety and convenience of the merrymakers; and the owners of dives and dance halls lived in constant fear that their resorts would be the scene of bloody combat, and so subject them to unwelcome notoriety.[72]

In 1903 Kelly was arrested for robbery with violence and served nine months. On release, he formed the Paul Kelly Association, an athletic club which he used to recruit younger criminals for his organisation. He soon opened the New Brighton Athletic Club, a two-storey cafe and dance hall at 57 Great Jones Street. Always well-dressed, Kelly spoke French, Italian and Spanish fluently, and his educated and sophisticated nature impressed many of the New York elite who flocked to the club. Kelly's organisation expanded into other parts of Manhattan and parts of New Jersey, but his urbane image alienated some top gunmen, who left for the Eastman Gang.

Eastman, whose gang of over 2,000 gunmen controlled New York's East Side, was an old-fashioned thug, the opposite of the 'cultured' Kelly. While both gangs were under the control of Tammany Hall, the two constantly fought over control of the 'neutral' territory along the Bowery. Tammany Hall called them to a sit-down meeting and ordered them to have a boxing match to settle the issue. The winner would take control of the prized neutral territory, and the war would end. Both parties agreed, and Kelly and Eastman slugged it out, but the fight ended in a draw. The gangs resumed warfare. Eastman was arrested for robbing a man on the West Side who was being tailed by detectives, and Tammany Hall, eager to end the warfare between its two affiliated gangs, refused the usual protection. Eastman was sentenced to ten years in Sing Sing.

With Eastman's arrest, Kelly completely controlled New York. He had internal competition, however, and in November 1905, two of Kelly's former lieutenants, Biff Ellison and Razor Riley, tried to kill him at his New Brighton headquarters. Kelly, drinking with bodyguards Bill Harrington and Rough House Hogan, returned their fire. The lights were shot out and for five minutes the protagonists blazed away in the darkness. Harrington died protecting Kelly, shot in the head by Riley. Their attackers escaped, and a wounded Kelly was taken to a private hospital before he could be arrested. Kelly turned himself in a month later, but charges were dropped due to his political connections. Of the assailants, Ellison was imprisoned and died insane, and Riley was found dead of pneumonia in his Chinatown basement hideout. However, the negative publicity caused Kelly's New Brighton club to be closed down for the protection of its socialite regulars, beginning the end of Paul Kelly's dominance in the New York underworld.[73]

Tammany Hall put pressure on Kelly to lower his profile as it sought to clean up the Bowery. After Kelly closed the *New Brighton*, he moved operations to the Italian immigrant communities in Harlem and Brooklyn, but his power declined, as did the influence of the Five Points gang. Nevertheless, it still attracted ambitious thugs eager to make a name for themselves. Among them was Louis Pioggi, better known as Louie the Lump, a small-statured nineteen-year-old who saw himself as an Italian Billy the Kid. On 14 May 1908 he bumped into rival gangster Kid Twist in a Coney Island dance hall. Both were competing for the affections of the pretty dancer Carroll Terry and when it became clear that she favoured the better-known Twist, Louie stormed off to a nearby saloon to drown his sorrows in neat whiskey. He was joined by Twist and henchman Cyclone Louie who, after verbally tormenting the lovesick lad, forced him to jump out of the window.

Humiliated, Louis telephoned a member of his gang council, and asked permission to kill Twist. Permission was granted, and half a dozen gunmen were sent by car to help him. Kid Twist and Cyclone Louie were still in the saloon, chuckling over their treatment of the Lump. A thug unknown to Twist walked timidly inside and told him that Carroll Terry wanted to see him outside. Twist and Cyclone dutifully stepped through the front door and were confronted by enemies on all sides. Louie the Lump shot Twist through the head with a revolver, and then through the heart as he toppled to the sidewalk. Cyclone Louie started to run but was peppered by bullets from the Five Pointers and fell across the body of his boss. Carroll Terry, who had indeed been on her way to meet Twist, was hit in the shoulder by a stray bullet. The killings took seconds, and the killers then scattered. Louie put a discouraging bullet through the helmet of a police officer before driving at speed to Manhattan. He went into hiding until political 'arrangements' could be made, then gave himself up and pleaded guilty to manslaughter. He was sentenced to eleven months in a reformatory.[74]

The power of the Five Pointers was never broken, but unwelcome publicity saw the Tammany Hall political machine pull away, with the gang's subsequent loss of influence. Kelly retained ties to his old neighbourhood, becoming a vice president of the International

Longshoremen's Association (ILA) under the name Paul Vaccarelli. He led a spontaneous port-wide strike begun in protest against a derisory, five cents-an-hour wage increase. With the support of Mayor John F. Hylan, Kelly was appointed to a commission to resolve the strike, which he ended without obtaining any concessions for the strikers. Kelly became a labour racketeer, providing muscle in disputes during the 1920s. He died of natural causes around 1936.

Two separate Mafia families emerged in New England.[75] The Boston crime family was founded in 1916 by Gaspare Messina.[76] In 1917, Frank Morelli formed the Providence, Rhode Island, crime family.[77] Morelli went on to control bootlegging and gambling operations in Maine and Connecticut. In 1924, Gaspare Messina stepped down as Boston's Mafia boss, assuming a businessman's role while working with Frank Cucchiara and Paolo Pagnotta from a grocery store on Prince Street in Boston's North End.

A report issued by the Italian White Hand Society, Chicago, 1908, offered an explanation for the rise of the American Mafia:

> To a certain type of Italian criminal, who in his native land lives in continual dread of the carabineers, the guards of public safety, the civic guards, and even the rural and forest guards, any one of whom may appear at his very bedside any hour of the night to make sure that he is at home from sunset until dawn, this country where such an abundance of guardians of the peace is replaced only by the policeman, often nothing but a creature of politics, cannot fail to appear as the promised land … To a certain type of Italian criminal, who, when mysterious crimes are committed, is liable to be locked up in jail as a suspect, sometimes even for months, simply because he is recognised as being capable of committing crime, this country, where hold-ups, thugs plying their trade in the most prominent streets, or in the elevated railroad stations and street cars, night riders and lynchers, so often escape justice, cannot fail to appear as a most fertile vineyard, easy of cultivation for one willing to take chances.

During this time, a Mafia power struggle ensued in Boston, as rival gangs fought for loansharking, illegal gambling, and bootlegging rackets. It was the last racket which, for crime lords across the nation, became the most lucrative.

* * *

On 17 January 1920, Prohibition began in the US with the 18th Amendment to the Constitution, making it illegal to manufacture, transport or sell alcohol. It was a gift to organised crime because there was little if any reduction in public demand, and any law that lacks public support is impossible to enforce. It created an atmosphere that tolerated crime as a means to provide liquor to the public, and organised crime leapt at the opportunity. The murder rate during the Prohibition Era rose from 6.8 per 100,000 individuals to 9.7, and within the first three months preceding the Eighteenth Amendment half a million dollars in bonded whiskey was stolen from government warehouses.[78] There were over 900,000 cases of liquor shipped to the borders of US cities. Criminal gangs and politicians saw the opportunity to make fortunes and began shipping larger quantities of alcohol to US cities. The majority of the alcohol was imported from Canada,[79] the Caribbean, and the American Midwest where stills manufactured illegal alcohol. Control of a vastly profitable industry, which dwarfed the protection, larceny and counterfeiting rackets of the early gangster, was handed over to the underworld. Every major city saw its streets run red with blood as rival Mafia families and their Jewish and Irish American gangster rivals battled to gain supremacy of their local liquor markets. Victorious factions went on to dominate organised crime in their respective cities, setting up the family structure of each city. Gangs hijacked each other's alcohol shipments, forcing rivals to pay them for 'protection' to leave their operations alone.

In the early 1920s, Benito Mussolini took control of Italy and waves of Italian immigrants fled fascism to the US. They were joined by more Sicilian Mafia members anxious to escape Mussolini's purges.[80] Throughout the 1920s, Italian Mafia families began waging wars for absolute control over bootlegging, raking in huge fortunes before, in many cases, meeting a violent end. In Chicago, Al Capone's family massacred the North Side Gang, an Irish American outfit. In New York City the war was initially with the Irish American White Hand Gang, but by the end of the 1920s, two factions of organised crime had emerged to fight for control of the criminal underworld, one led by Joe Masseria and the other by Salvatore Maranzano. Masseria was murdered, and Maranzano then divided New York City into five families before himself being murdered, shot and stabbed by two assassins dressed as police officers on the orders of Lucky Luciano. More murders followed, clearing out the Old Guard and creating a 'new' Mafia not so wedded to its Sicilian origins.

The Prohibition era of Al Capone, the St Valentine Day's Massacre, Elliot Ness, Lucky Luciano and the dominance, and partial dismantling, of the Mafia is outside the remit of this book. But Mike Dash wrote perceptively: '... the Mafia's standing as the most fearsome, most efficient, most iconic gang of criminals in the United States, owed as much to Morello as it did to the vastly better-known hoodlums of the Luciano generation. Mafia history, in the United States, begins not with Maranzano's murder, as it is generally written. Its roots lie several decades earlier, in the dust and blood of Corleone and in the fractured heart of the Morello family.'[81]

8

The Red Scare and the Boston Police Strike

'agents of Lenin'

A mass meeting of the Boston Police Union responded to criticism from future president Calvin Coolidge:

> When we were honorably discharged from the United States army, we were hailed as heroes and saviors of our country. We returned to our duties on the police force of Boston. Now, though only a few months have passed, we are denounced as deserters, as traitors to our city and violators of our oath of office. Among us are men who have gone against spitting machine guns single-handed, and captured them, volunteering for the job. Among us are men who have ridden with dispatches through shell fire so dense that four men fell and only the fifth got through. Not one man of us ever disgraced the flag or his service. It is bitter to come home and be called deserters and traitors. We are the same men who were on the French front.[1]

They had good reason to feel aggrieved. But so had the city's elite. For the 1919 Boston Police Strike saw a brief but deeply worrying outbreak of lawlessness which threatened everything the propertied class held dear. Moreover, this was the period of the Red Scare, and a walk-out by the forces of law and order was perceived as an opportunity for the forces of Bolshevism to destroy burgeoning, American-style capitalism. It was a time of paranoia.

The cost of living had risen by 76 per cent since 1913, while police wages had risen just 18 per cent. Soldiers returning from the war were flooding the labour market, putting downward pressure on workers' earning power. During 1919, one-fifth of the country's workers would strike. The year opened with New York's harbour workers walking out in January, followed by the dressmakers.[2] That was just the start.

The *Nation* editorialised: 'The common man, forgetting the old sanctions, and losing faith in the old leadership, has experienced a new access of self-confidence, or at least a new recklessness, a readiness to take chances on his own account. In consequence, as is by this time clear to discerning men, authority can no longer be imposed from above; it comes automatically from below.'[3]

***

The Red Scare was the product of Great War jingoism and terror of the consequences of the Russian Revolution. US government, institutions and big business saw the threat of Communism everywhere, including the trade unions and organised labour in general at a time of huge industrial, racial and social unrest. Before the war ended, President Woodrow Wilson ordered a crackdown on subversion, real and imagined, by fair means or foul. That was aided immensely during wartime by legislation covering sedition and espionage. Particular targets were foreign-born radicals and anarchists, the Socialist Party of America and the Industrial Workers of the World, known as 'Wobblies'. The immediate post-war period saw hysterical rhetoric in newspapers, illegal searches, arrests and detentions, legal intimidation, and mass deportations. Bolshevism was blamed for pretty much everything perceived to be holding back the American Dream.

On 21 January 1919, 35,000 shipyard workers in Seattle went on strike for long-delayed wage rises. The Seattle Central Labor Council gave enthusiastic support. More than 100 local unions joined a general strike on 6 February and 60,000 strikers paralysed city commerce, transport and urban services. The General Strike Committee maintained order and provided essential services.[4] The hard-line Seattle mayor, Ole Hanson, had 1,500 police and 1,500 federal troops on hand to put down any disturbances. He personally oversaw their deployment throughout the city 'The time has come,' he said, 'for the people in Seattle to show their Americanism … The anarchists in this community shall not rule its affairs.' He promised to use them to replace striking workers, but never carried out that threat.[5]

The leaders of the American Federation of Labor (AFL) feared that the general strike was turning opinion against them and felt that they would lose wartime gains.[6] The national press called the general strike 'Marxian' and 'a revolutionary movement aimed at existing government'. 'It is only a middling step,' said the *Chicago Tribune*, 'from Petrograd to Seattle.'[7] Within two days some unions drifted back to work at the urging of their leaders. Finally, on 10 February, the General Strike Committee voted to end the strike the next day.[8] The original strike in the shipyards continued.

Although his role had been, at most, peripheral, Mayor Hanson took credit for ending the five-day strike and was hailed by the press. He resigned a few months later and toured the country giving lectures on the dangers of 'domestic bolshevism'. He earned $38,000 in seven months, five times his annual salary as mayor.[9] Following his resignation, he wrote a book on the perceived radical menace which was published in January 1920. He wrote:

I am tired of reading rhetorical, finely spun, hypocritical, far-fetched excuses for bolshevism, communism, syndicalism, IWWism! Nauseated by the sickly sentimentality of those who would conciliate, pander, and encourage all who would destroy our Government, I have tried to learn the truth and tell it in United States English of one or two syllables ... With syndicalism – and its youngest child, bolshevism – thrive murder, rape, pillage, arson, free love, poverty, want, starvation, filth, slavery, autocracy, suppression, sorrow and Hell on earth. It is a class government of the unable, the unfit, the untrained; of the scum, of the dregs, of the cruel, and of the failures. Freedom disappears, liberty emigrates, universal suffrage is abolished, progress ceases ... and a militant minority, great only in their self-conceit, reincarnate under the Dictatorship of the Proletariat a greater tyranny than ever existed under czar, emperor, or potentate.[10]

He added that the fact that the general strike was peaceful only underlined its revolutionary intent:

The so-called sympathetic Seattle strike was an attempted revolution. That there was no violence does not alter the fact ... The intent openly and covertly announced, was for the overthrow of the industrial system; here first, then everywhere ... True, there were no flashing guns, no bombs, no killings. Revolution, I repeat, doesn't need violence. The general strike, as practised in Seattle, is of itself the weapon of revolution, all the more dangerous because quiet. To succeed, it must suspend everything; stop the entire life stream of a community ... That is to say, it puts the government out of operation. And that is all there is to revolt – no matter how achieved.[11]

Workers across the country struck for better pay and conditions – 10,000 woolworkers in Passaic, New Jersey; hotel workers in New York; 8,000 furriers in the same city; firemen in Cleveland; 35,000 ladies' garment workers across several eastern states; and many more localised actions. Some were successful in cutting punishing working hours.[12] The *Survey* magazine reported that 'in New York City a great variety of strikes is in progress. Cigarmakers, shirt-makers, carpenters, bakers, teamsters and barbers are out in large numbers. The most depressed trades are catching the strike infection, witness the walkout last week of women workers on feathers and artificial flowers, who want a forty-four-hour week and the abolition of home work. Even the scrubwomen employed in a downtown building put strike-breakers to rout with their mop handles.' In Chicago there were, in rapid succession, strikes by 1,700 street sweepers, 800 garbage collectors, 900 bridge labourers, 800 City Hall clerks and over 300 fire department engineers; in all, those who walked out totalled 5,000 public employees. The *Survey* reported on another strike at the Corn Products Refining Company in the Chicago suburb of Argo: 'The attempt to operate the works led to an uprising of the cosmopolitan population, which resulted in bloodshed and a great demonstration at the funeral of the men who were killed in which many returned soldiers in uniform participated.'[13] The victims had been shot by company security guards.

The Senate's Overman Committee, previously charged with investigating war-time German subversion, announced during the Seattle general strike that it would study 'any efforts being made to propagate in this country the principles of any party exercising or claiming to exercise any authority in Russia' and 'any effort to incite the overthrow of the Government of this country'. A 'volunteer spy', the New York lawyer Archibald Stevenson, testified during the subsequent hearings[14] that anti-war and anti-draft activism during the war had turned into propaganda 'developing sympathy for the

Bolshevik movement'. He added: 'The Bolshevik movement is a branch of the revolutionary socialism of Germany. It had its origin in the philosophy of Marx.' The Senators heard that Bolshevism had united many disparate elements on the left, including anarchists and socialists of many types, 'providing a common platform for all these radical groups to stand on'. Other witnesses described the horrors of the revolution in Russia and the consequences of a comparable revolution in the United States: atheism, the seizure of newspapers, assaults on banks, the abolition of the insurance industry, and even women made the property of the state.[15] On the release of the final report, newspapers printed sensational articles on the 'Red Peril'.

Some of the scaremongering proved justified, however, as 1919 witnessed several anarchist bombings. In late April, thirty-six booby-trap bombs were mailed to prominent politicians, judges and businessmen.[16] They were in identical packages, timed to arrive on May Day. Some were undelivered because the full postage had not been paid.[17] One bomb, intended for Ole Hanson, arrived early and failed to explode. On 29 April, a package sent to Senator Thomas W. Hardwick of Georgia, a sponsor of anti-anarchist legislation, injured his wife and housekeeper. The following day, sixteen packages were recognised by a vigilant New York postal clerk, and another twelve bombs were recovered before reaching their targets. In June, eight bombs containing up to 25 lbs of explosives detonated almost simultaneously in several US cities.[18] All were wrapped or packaged with heavy metal shrapnel.[19]

All of the intended targets had participated in some way with the investigation of or the opposition to anarchist radicals. The intended victims included a Massachusetts state representative and a New Jersey silk manufacturer. Fatalities included a New York City nightwatchman, William Boehner, and one of the bombers, Carlo Valdinoci, who died when the bomb he placed at the home of Attorney General Palmer exploded in his face.[20] Though not seriously injured, Palmer and his family were thoroughly shaken by the blast, and their home was largely demolished.[21] All of the bombs were delivered with pink flyers bearing the title 'Plain Words' that accused the intended victims of waging class war and promised: 'We will destroy to rid the world of your tyrannical institutions.'[22] Police and the Bureau of Investigation tracked the flyer to a print shop owned by an anarchist, Andrea Salcedo, who nevertheless escaped prosecution. Forensic and oral evidence tied the bomb attacks to the Galleanists.[23] Though some of the cabal were deported or fled of their own accord, attacks by remaining members continued until 1932.

The left in 1919 mounted especially large May Day demonstrations, and violence erupted during normally peaceful parades in Boston, New York, and Cleveland. In Boston, police tried to stop a march that lacked a permit. Both sides fought for possession of the socialists' red flags. One policeman was stabbed and killed. The former child prodigy William Sidis was arrested. He was sentenced to eighteen months under the Sedition Act. During his later trial, Sidis stated that he had been a conscientious objector to the draft, was an atheist and a socialist. Later a mob attacked the socialist headquarters. Police arrested 114, all from the socialist side. In New York, soldiers burned printed materials at the Russian People's House and forced immigrants to sing the Star-Spangled Banner.

In Cleveland, Ohio, a mob ransacked the campaign HQ of Socialist mayoral candidate Charles Ruthenberg. Mounted police, army trucks, and tanks restored order. Two people died, forty were injured, and 116 arrested. The city government immediately passed laws to restrict parades and the display of red flags. Newspapers blamed the May Day marchers for provoking the nationalists' response. The *Salt Lake City Tribune* said: 'Free speech has been carried to the point where it is an unrestrained menace.'[24]

***

Unusually, the Boston police department was under the direct control of the mayor and a commissioner appointed by the governor of Massachusetts. The mayor was responsible for the department's expenses and the physical working conditions of its employees, but the commissioner controlled operations and the hiring, training and discipline of the police officers.[25]

By 1918 the rank and file were seething with discontent, due largely to penny-pinching by the authorities. The salary for patrolmen was set at $1,400 a year. Officers had to buy their own uniforms and equipment which cost over $200. New recruits received $730 during their first year. All ranks were hit hard by post-war inflation. Ill feelings grew as police officers discovered they were earning less than an unskilled steelworker, half as much as a carpenter or mechanic and 50 cents a day less than a streetcar conductor. Boston city labourers

were earning a third more on an hourly basis.[26] Officers worked
up to ninety hours a week. They were not paid for time spent on
court appearances. They also objected to being required to perform
such tasks as 'delivering unpaid tax bills, surveying rooming houses,
taking the census, or watching the polls at election' and checking the
backgrounds of prospective jurors as well as serving as 'errand boys'
for their officers. They complained about having to share beds and the
lack of sanitation, baths, and toilets at many of the nineteen station
houses where they were required to live. The Court Street station had
four toilets for 135 men, and one bathtub. A patrolman complained:
'That was the way it was day after day, round after round. We had
no freedom, no home life at all. We couldn't even go to Revere Beach
without the captain's permission.'[27]

Boston's police officers had formed an association known as the
Boston Social Club in 1906, and in 1917 a delegation met with
Commissioner Stephen O'Meara to ask for a pay rise. He was
sympathetic, but advised them to wait for a better time. They pressed
the issue in the summer of 1918 and, near the end of the year, Mayor
Andrew Peters offered salary increases that would affect a quarter of
the officers. O'Meara died in December 1918, and Governor Samuel
McCall appointed Edwin Upton Curtis, former Mayor of Boston, as
Commissioner of the Boston Police Department.[28]

Curtis, the son of seventh-generation Bostonians, was the co-founder
of a law firm and an active Republican Party member.[29] He had also
served as Boston's Assistant US Treasurer and Collector of the Port.
He was, in all senses, an Establishment figure and a man of his time
and of his privileged class. He was not known for brooking dissent
at any level. After another meeting where Social Club representatives
repeated their salary demands, Peters said: 'While the word "strike"
was not mentioned, the whole situation is far more serious than
I realized.' He also made it clear to the rank and file that they were
not entitled to form their own union.[30] Curtis did not share his
predecessor's or the mayor's sympathy for the police, but in February
1918 he offered a wage compromise that the police rejected.

A few months later, in June 1919, the American Federation of Labor
(AFL) began to accept police organisations into their membership.
By September, it had granted charters to police unions in thirty-seven
cities, including Washington, D.C., Los Angeles, Miami, and St Paul,
though not without protests from some city officials, who opposed the
unionisation of police, firefighters, and teachers.[31] On 9 August 1919,

the Boston Social Club requested a charter from the AFL. Two days later, Curtis issued a General Order forbidding police officers to join any 'organization, club or body outside the department', making an exception only for patriotic organisations such as the American Legion. He argued that such a rule was based on the conflict of interest between police officers' duties and union membership: 'It is or should be apparent to any thinking person that the police department of this or any other city cannot fulfil its duty to the entire public if its members are subject to the direction of an organization existing outside the department ... If troubles and disturbances arise where the interests of this organization and the interests of other elements and classes in the community conflict, the situation immediately arises which always arises when a man attempts to serve two masters, – he must fail either in his duty as a policeman, or in his obligation to the organization that controls him.'[32]

On 15 August, the police received their AFL charter and the Central Labor Union of Boston welcomed the police union. Curtis refused to meet with the eight members of the police union's committee. He suspended them and eleven others who held various union offices and scheduled trials to determine if they had violated his General Order. The business community roundly applauded his tough line.

Curtis proceeded with department trials of the nineteen suspended officers and on 8 September found them guilty of union activity and extended their unpaid suspensions. The police union members immediately responded by voting 1,134 to 2 in favour of a strike to protest the commissioner's denial of their right to ally themselves with the AFL and scheduled it to start at evening roll call the next day.[33] Boston's newspapers called it 'Bolshevistic', and urged the police to reconsider. One also warned the police that their eventual defeat was guaranteed, that they would lose because 'behind Boston in this skirmish with Bolshevism stands Massachusetts, and behind Massachusetts stands America'.[34] Governor Coolidge called the strikers 'deserters' and 'traitors', and the police union responded as quoted at the beginning of this chapter. They added: 'The first men to raise the cry were those who have always been opposed to giving to labor a living wage. It was taken up by the newspapers, who cared little for the real facts. You finally added your word of condemnation...'

The Boston Police Department officers went on strike at 5.45 p.m. Of the force's 1,544 officers and men, 1,117 (72 per cent) failed to report for work.[35] Governor Coolidge assigned 100 members of the state's

Metropolitan Park Police Department to replace the striking officers, but fifty-eight of them refused to participate and were suspended from their jobs. Despite the bluster of Commissioner Curtis, the city had little police protection for the night as volunteer replacements were still being organised and due to report the next morning. Many of those who provided scab labour were students at Harvard University.[36]

Over the night of 9/10 September, the city witnessed an outbreak of hooliganism and looting. Some of it was simple rowdiness, such as youths throwing rocks at streetcars and overturning the carts of street vendors. More overtly criminal activity included the smashing of store windows and looting their displays or setting off false fire alarms. Such activity was restricted to only parts of the city and, according to the *New York Times*, 'throughout the greater part of the city the usual peace and quiet prevailed'.[37]

The president of Harvard University, Lawrence Lowell, called on more students to volunteer, as did Boston's businessmen. Crowds waited outside police stations to attack the volunteers. Cries of 'kill the cops' were heard. The Commander of Station 6 in South Boston kept his Harvard volunteers in the station in order to protect their lives. At Scollay Square, a centre of amusement halls and theatres, there were sporadic confrontations between the replacement police and the crowd, resulting in several students being cornered. When the first troop of cavalry arrived, they had to intervene to rescue groups of police. Several guardsmen were injured by rocks but, eventually, the threat of live ammunition and horsemen with swords pushed the crowd from Scollay Square. Boston became a hive of military activity, as Governor Coolidge eventually provided 5,000 State Guards. At the old armoury, near the Park Plaza Hotel, mobile units with machine guns set up headquarters.

Violence peaked during the night of 10/11 September, but by this time businesses were better prepared. Some had boarded up their windows, while others stayed open all night with armed guards visible to discourage any who sought to take advantage of the absence of law-enforcement officers. But the Guard proved inexperienced at handling crowds and quick to assert control with disregard for human life. Gunfire in South Boston left two dead and others wounded. Scollay Square was the scene of a riot where one died. The death tally ultimately reached nine.[38] Whether the crowds were threatening property or making trouble because they were in sympathy with the strikers is unknown.[39]

The *Los Angeles Times* wrote: 'No man's house, no man's wife, no man's children will be safe if the police force is unionized and made subject to the orders of Red Unionite bosses.' In Philadelphia, the *Public Ledger* reported: 'Bolshevism in the United States is no longer a specter. Boston in chaos reveals its sinister substance.'[40]

In an editorial on the first morning of the strike, the *New York Times* supported the police commissioner and said that the strikers were 'inspired unconsciously by anti-social ideals, or acting by "suggestion" of their London and Liverpool brethren', which had recently seen similar strikes. It said: 'A policeman has no more right to belong to a union than a soldier or a sailor. He must be ready to obey orders, the orders of his superiors, not those of any outside body. One of his duties is the maintenance of order in the case of strike violence. In such a case, if he is faithful to his union, he may have to be unfaithful to the public, which pays him to protect it. The situation is false and impossible ... It is the privilege of Boston policemen to resign if they are not satisfied with the conditions of their employment ... but it is intolerable that a city ... should be deserted by men who misunderstand their position and function as policemen, and who take their orders from outside ... It is an imported, revolutionary idea that may spread to various cities. There should be plain and stern law against it. It is practically an analogue of military desertion ... It ought to be punished suitably and repressed.'[41] It later called the strike 'this Boston essay in Bolshevism' and lamented the attempt of Mayor Peters 'to submit to compromise an issue that could not be compromised'.[42]

Newspaper accounts exaggerated the level of crime and violence that accompanied the strike, resulting in a national outcry. President Woodrow Wilson, speaking from Montana, branded the walkout 'a crime against civilization' that left the city 'at the mercy of an army of thugs'.[43] He said that 'the obligation of a policeman is as sacred and direct as the obligation of a soldier. He is a public servant, not a private employee, and the whole honor of the community is in his hands. He has no right to prefer any private advantage to the public safety.'

In Washington, Senator Henry Cabot Lodge said: 'If the American Federation of Labor succeeds in getting hold of the police in Boston it will go all over the country, and we shall be in measurable distance of Soviet government by labor unions.'[44] The *Ohio State Journal* opposed any sympathetic treatment of the strikers: 'When a policeman strikes, he should be debarred not only from resuming his office, but from citizenship as well. He has committed the unpardonable sin; he has forfeited all his rights.'[45]

Commissioner Curtis later praised the Guards' performance in his Annual Report: 'The whole community is now aware of the effectiveness with which the Massachusetts State Guard worked when it came into the city. I cannot add anything to the universal chorus of commendation that has greeted their work.' The morning papers following the first night's violence were full of loud complaints and derogatory terms for the police: 'deserters', 'agents of Lenin'. City life continued relatively normally, especially during daytime hours. Schools remained open. Later claims against the city for losses incurred during the two nights of disorder ran to $35,000, of which the city paid $34,000.[46]

On the evening of 11 September, the Central Labor Union considered calling a general strike in support of the striking police, more as an expression of solidarity than a declaration of serious intent. It collected the votes of its constituent unions and on 12 September announced it was delaying a decision. Their statement explained: 'We are not to act in a manner that will give the prejudiced press and autocratic employers a chance to criticize us.'[47] That same day AFL vice-president Matthew Wolf said his organisation discouraged strikes by government employees but defended their right to organise: 'All wage earners have the right to associate with one another and collectively to improve their condition.' He added: 'On the question of industrial democracy [i.e., unionisation], we find still that group of employers, Bourbonic in character, who believe democracy means for them to ruin or rule industrially. They cannot conceive that works have any right in the management of industry. ... The time has passed when any man can say that he is the ruler of the people in his employment.'[48]

AFL President Samuel Gompers quickly assessed the situation and the strength of public sentiment. On 12 September, he urged the strikers to return to work, asking the city to agree to suspend judgment on whether to recognise the police union. The police accepted Gompers' recommendation immediately. Coolidge replied with a statement of support for Curtis' hard line. Gompers telegraphed Coolidge again, this time blaming Curtis for the crisis.[49] Coolidge dismissed the commissioner's behaviour as irrelevant, because no provocation could justify the police walkout. His terse summation created his reputation on the national scene: 'There is no right to strike against the public safety, anywhere, anytime.'[50] Coolidge said he would continue to 'defend the sovereignty of Massachusetts'.

By the weekend, the State Guards had become a magnet for curious sightseers. Large crowds strolled through the city centre and thousands attended a band concert on the Boston Common. 'The shootings of the last few days for interference with guardsmen,' said the *New York Times*, 'seem to have had a marked effect.'

Coolidge said he originally hoped to reinstate the officers, stating in a telegram to a labour convention, 'I earnestly hope that circumstances may arise which will cause the police officers to be reinstated.'[51] Over the objections of Mayor Peters, Commissioner Curtis announced on 13 September that he planned to recruit a new force. He fired roughly 1,100 and hired 1,574 replacement police officers from a pool of unemployed First World War veterans. Members of the United Garment Workers refused to sew uniforms for the new hires, who had to report for work in civilian clothing.[52]

The new officers received higher salaries and more vacation days than the strikers had. They enjoyed a starting salary of $1,400 along with a pension plan, and the department covered the cost of their uniforms and equipment. The population of Boston raised $472,000 to help pay for the State Guards until new police officers could be recruited. By the end of the year the strikers had formed a new organisation called the Association of Former Police of the City of Boston.

The strike gave momentum to Coolidge's political career. In 1918, he had narrowly been elected governor. In 1919 he won 62 per cent of the votes when running against an opponent who favoured reinstating the strikers. He failed to carry Boston by just 5,000 votes, an impressive showing for a Republican in a strongly Democrat city. The *Boston Transcript* reported: 'Massachusetts is hailed today from Maine to California as the winner of a shining triumph for straight Americanism. The voting booths of the old Bay State were a battleground for the nation. The ancient faith was under fire. Law and order formed the line of cleavage. The governor was the commander-in-chief, the people of the commonwealth were the invincible army, the issue was America, and in the triumph of that issue all America triumphs.'

Coolidge himself later said, 'No doubt it was the police strike in Boston that brought me into national prominence.'[53] In a post-election congratulatory telegram President Wilson wrote: 'I congratulate you upon your election as a victory for law and order. When that is the issue, all Americans must stand together.' His role in the strike, however limited, became a prominent feature of his resume as he sought higher office. According to one obituary, 'the Boston police strike of 1919

... brought him national prominence and the nomination for the Vice Presidency' in 1920.[54] Edward Upton Curtis served as Police Commissioner until his sudden death in 1922.

The Boston Police Strike was not as bloody as events across the Atlantic the same year. English police in London and Liverpool went out to stop the suppression of their embryonic union. The strike failed miserably, but in Liverpool the absence of the constabulary led to several days of mayhem still known locally as 'The Loot'. Gunboats sailed up the River Mersey, and troops fought hand-to-hand battles with rioters and looters. At least one rioter was shot dead and others were believed to have succumbed to wounds in back alleys and tenements.[55]

The failure of the Boston strike contributed to declining union membership. The AFL revoked the charters it had granted to police unions. That ended police unionism in the US for two decades. In 1931, the Massachusetts legislature voted to allow the officers who had struck to be rehired. In 1937, Massachusetts Governor Charles Hurley, after meeting with some of the 1919 strikers, backed the decision of Police Commissioner Joseph Timilty not to reinstate them.[56]

The Boston Police Patrolman's Association was formed in 1965 following the enactment of a state statute allowing state and municipal workers to organise for the sake of collective bargaining. Not a single police officer in the US again went out on strike until July 1974, when some Baltimore police, estimated at 15 to 50 per cent of the force, refused to report for work for several days as a demonstration of support for other striking municipal unions.[57]

***

The Great Steel Strike of 1919 was an attempt by the weakened Amalgamated Association of Iron, Steel and Tin Workers (the AA) to organise effective opposition to reductions in skilled operatives. In 1892, the AA had lost a bitter strike at the Carnegie's steel mill in Homestead, Pennsylvania, which culminated with a day-long gun battle that left twelve dead and dozens wounded (*see Chapter 5*). From a high of more than 24,000 members in 1892, union membership had sunk to less than 8,000 by 1900. The AFL began organising unskilled iron and steel workers into federal unions in 1901. Many local federal unions became deeply entrenched in the workplace.

The strike which began on 22 September 1919 was backed by 98 per cent of the union membership – over 400,000 – despite initial opposition from the AFL leadership. It shut down half the steel industry, including almost all mills in Chicago, West Virginia, Pennsylvania, Lackawanna (New York) and Ohio.[58]

The owners fought back with a propaganda blitz that exposed AFL National Committee co-chairman William Z. Foster's radical past as a Wobbly. The steel companies played on Nativist fears by noting that a large number of steelworkers were immigrants. Public opinion quickly turned against the striking workers. State and local authorities prohibited mass meetings. Police attacked pickets and thousands were jailed. After strike-breakers and police clashed with trade unionists in Gary, Indiana, the army took over the city on 6 October and martial law was declared. In western Pennsylvania there was a reign of terror. Sheriff Haddock of Allegheny County banned all outdoor meetings and deputised 5,000 armed strike-breakers. The Interchurch World Movement reported after an independent inquiry:

> In Monessen, where the strikers held out for a long time, with the exception of the arrest of many Russians on vague charges of 'radicalism', the policy of the State Police was simply to club the men off the streets and drive them into their homes. Very few were arrested. In Braddock, however, where some of the mills were partly operating, the State Police did not stop at mere beating. Ordinarily, when a striker was clubbed on the street, he would be taken to jail, kept there over night, and then to Squire or the Burgess would fine him from $10 to $60. In Newcastle, the Sheriff's deputies carried the Braddock policy much further. Many of those arrested in Newcastle, who had lived in the town almost all their lives, were charged with being 'suspicious' persons and were ordered not to be released until the strike was over.

Others were released in Newcastle after they furnished bail ranging from $5000 to $2,500 each. The other towns in western Pennsylvania generally followed one of the methods described here.[59] 'Contemporary author William Z. Foster wrote that the State Police admitted they felt free to use brutal methods against the strikers, many of whom they knew from their own communities, because 'they realise fully that they can depend upon trade-union leaders to hold the strikers in check from adopting measures of retaliation.'[60]

Former steelworker Joe Rudiak, the son of Polish immigrants, recalled his memories of the 1919 steel strike as a young boy.

His father was blacklisted for acknowledging his support of the union, and from such experiences, he explained, unionism got 'embedded in you'. He went on:

> And then the steel strike came along and we were thrown out of the company house. And with the help of his friends that were union minded and all that, they built us a house ... I was about eight years of age. And I've seen strikers being beaten by the coal and iron police – state police. And also this is the first time I ever heard the word scab. In fact, I believe possibly that one of the boys' godfather – we called him a scab. And, there was marching going on and everything. You were bound to get some of that into you and you seen people take sides. I didn't see scabs to [*sic*] in because I was a youngster. My uncle – well, I would say cousin – spent eighteen months in the Western Penitentiary. He was involved in at that time the 1919 steel strike. He was involved in upsetting the suburban street car hauling scabs in from the country. And he was given a stiff sentence of eighteen months because he wouldn't turn stool pigeon. So, you're living in his house and you're listening to the language and they're talking about so-and-so, why, and all that. And you're in the corner and there's company there and different things and you're listening and now it's getting embedded in you. And I happen to just fall into that. And having a little bit of a cultural background as far as music was concerned, you know, and then finally, you had to go into the union.[61]

The companies brought in between 30,000 and 40,000 blacks and Hispanics to work in the mills. Company spies also spread rumours that the strike had collapsed elsewhere, and they pointed to the operating steel mills as proof that the strike had been defeated.[62] Congress conducted its own investigation, focused on radical influence upon union activity. In that context, US Senator Kenneth McKellar, a member of the Senate committee investigating the strike, proposed making one of the Philippine islands a penal colony to which those convicted of an attempt to overthrow the government could be deported.[63] The strike collapsed on 8 January 1920, although it dragged on in isolated areas like Pueblo and Lackawanna.[64]

The day before the strike, Attorney General A. Mitchell Palmer had invoked the Lever Act, a wartime measure that made it a crime to interfere with the production or transportation of necessities.

The law, meant to punish hoarding and profiteering, had never been used against a union. Certain of united political backing and almost universal public support, Palmer obtained an injunction on 31 October.[65] He claimed the severely ill president had authorised the action, following a meeting in the presence of his doctor.[66] Palmer also lied that the entire cabinet had backed his request for an injunction. Samuel Gompers protested that President Wilson and members of his cabinet had assured the AFL when the Act was passed that it would not be used to prevent strikes by labour unions.

Palmer was fast making a name for himself through his well-publicised crackdown on alleged Bolsheviks among the immigrant community. An initial raid in July 1919 against a small anarchist group in Buffalo failed when a federal judge tossed out his case. In August, he organised the General Intelligence Unit within the Department of Justice and recruited J. Edgar Hoover, a recent law school graduate, to head it.[67] Hoover studied arrest records, subscription records of radical newspapers, and party membership records to compile lists of resident aliens for deportation proceedings. Stung by criticism that he was moving too slowly against radicals, Palmer launched his campaign against them with two sets of police actions known as the Palmer Raids in November 1919 and January 1920. Federal agents supported by local police rounded up large groups of suspected radicals, often based on membership in a political group rather than any action taken. Undercover informants and warrantless wiretaps helped to identify several thousand suspected leftists.

The dismissal of most of the cases by Acting Secretary of Labor Louis Freeland Post limited the number of deportations to 556. Civil libertarians, the radical left, and legal scholars raised protests, but a public swayed by newspaper scaremongering broadly supported the raids. Officials at the Department of Labor, especially Post, asserted the rule of law in opposition to Palmer's anti-radical campaign. Post faced a Congressional threat to impeach or censure him. He successfully defended his actions in two days of testimony before the House Rules Committee in June 1919 and no action was ever taken against him. Palmer testified before the same committee, also for two days, and stood by the raids, arrests, and deportation program. Much of the press applauded Post's work at Labor, while Palmer, rather than President Wilson, was largely blamed for the negative aspects of the raids.

On 21 December, the army transport ship *Buford*, a veteran of the Spanish–American War which the press nicknamed the 'Soviet

Ark', left New York harbour with 249 deportees. Of those, 184 were expelled because of their membership in the Union of Russian Workers, an anarchist group that was a primary target of the November raids. Others belonged to radical organisations but disclaimed knowledge of the organisation's political aims and had joined to take advantage of educational programs and social opportunities.[68] Others on board included the well-known radical leader Emma Goldman, who had been convicted of interfering with military recruitment in 1917. A 'strong detachment of marines' numbering fifty-eight enlisted men and four officers, made the journey and pistols were distributed to the crew.[69] Its final destination was unknown as it sailed under sealed orders. Even the captain only learned his final destination while in Kiel harbour for repairs since he found it difficult to make arrangements to land in Latvia.

On 7 January 1920, at the first session of the New York State Assembly, Speaker Thaddeus C. Sweet attacked its five socialist members, declaring they had been 'elected on a platform that is absolutely inimical to the best interests of the state of New York and the United States'. The Socialist Party, Sweet said, was 'not truly a political party', but was rather 'a membership organization admitting within its ranks aliens, enemy aliens, and minors'. It had supported the revolutionaries in Germany, Austria and Hungary, he continued, and consorted with international socialist parties close to the Communist International.[70] The assembly suspended the five by a vote of 140 to 6, with just one Democrat supporting the socialists.

The assembly's action was attacked from all sides. The former Republican governor, Supreme Court Justice and presidential candidate Charles Evan Hughes defended the socialist members: 'Nothing … is a more serious mistake at this critical time than to deprive socialists or radicals of their opportunities for peaceful discussion and thus to convince them that the Reds are right and that violence and revolution are the only available means at their command.'[71] Democratic Governor Al Smith denounced the expulsions: 'To discard the method of representative government leads to the misdeeds of the very extremists we denounce and serves to increase the number of enemies of orderly free government.'[72] Hughes also led a group of leading New York attorneys in a protest that said: 'We have passed beyond the stage in political development when heresy-hunting is a permitted sport.'[73] However, newspapers continually reinforced their readers' views by presenting a vivid threat of imminent conflict with the Soviet Union.[74]

Within Attorney General Palmer's Justice Department, the General Intelligence Division (GID), now headed by J. Edgar Hoover, had become a storehouse of information about radicals in America. It had infiltrated many organisations and, following the raids of November 1919 and January 1920, it had interrogated thousands of those arrested. Although agents knew there was an enormous gap between what the radicals promised in their rhetoric and what they were capable of accomplishing, they nevertheless told Palmer they had evidence of plans for an attempted overthrow of the US government on May Day 1920.[75]

With Palmer's backing, Hoover warned the nation to expect the worst: assassinations, bombings and general strikes. Palmer issued his own warning on 29 April 1920, claiming to have a 'list of marked men'[76] and said domestic radicals were 'in direct connection and unison' with European counterparts with disruptions planned for the same day there. Newspapers stirred up more paranoia. Localities prepared their police forces and some states mobilised their militias. Boston police mounted machine guns on automobiles and positioned them around the city.[77]

The date came and went without incident. Hypocritically given their previous anti-Red hyperbole, newspapers mocked Palmer and his 'hallucinations'. Clarence Darrow called it the 'May Day scare'.[78] The *Boston American* assessed the attorney general on 4 May:

> Everybody is laughing at A. Mitchell Palmer's May Day 'revolution.' The joke is certainly on A. Mitchell Palmer, but the matter is not wholly a joke. The spectacle of a Cabinet officer going around surrounded with armed guards because he is afraid of his own hand-made bogey is a sorry one, even though it appeals to the humor of Americans. Of course, the terrible 'revolution' did not come off. Nobody with a grain of sense supposed that it would. Yet, in spite of universal laughter, the people are seriously disgusted with these official Red scares. They cost the taxpayers thousands of dollars spent in assembling soldiers and policemen and in paying wages and expenses to Mr. Palmer's agents. They help to frighten capital and demoralize business, and to make timid men and women jumpy and nervous.[79]

Once Palmer's warnings of a May Day revolution proved farcical, the anti-Bolshevik hysteria wound down quickly.[80] In testimony before

Congress on 7–8 May, Louis Freeland Post defended his release
of hundreds seized in Palmer's raids so successfully that attempts
to impeach or censure him ended.[81] Later in the month, a dozen
prominent lawyers endorsed a report that condemned Palmer's Justice
Department for the 'utterly illegal acts committed by those charged
with the highest duty of enforcing the laws' including entrapment,
police brutality, prolonged incommunicado detention, and violations
of due process in court.[82] The Massachusetts Federal District Court
ordered the discharge of twenty more arrested aliens. The conservative
Christian Science Monitor found itself unable to support Palmer
any longer, writing on 25 June: 'What appeared to be an excess of
radicalism … was certainly met with … an excess of suppression.'[83]
Leaders of industry voiced similar sentiments, and warned that
Palmer's clearly unjust activities had created more radicals than they
suppressed. One called the Justice Department's work evidence of
'sheer Red hysteria'.[84]

At the Democratic National Convention in July, Palmer never
had a chance at winning the nomination.[85] Coolidge, famous for
his opposition to the right of police to strike, won a place on the
Republican ticket, but the party's nominee, and the eventual winner
of the 1920 election, was the Senator from Ohio, Warren G. Harding.
He sounded a very different note in mid-August when he said that
'too much has been said about Bolshevism in America. It is quite true
that there are enemies of Government within our borders. However,
I believe their number has been greatly magnified. The American
workman is not a Bolshevik; neither is the American employer an
autocrat.'

When another anarchist bomb exploded on Wall Street in September
1920, newspaper response was comparatively restrained. 'More bombs
may be exploded,' wrote the *New York Times*, 'other lives may be
taken. But these are only hazards of a war which … must be faced
calmly.' If anarchists sought to make people fearful, 'by keeping cool
and firm we begin their defeat'.[86]

9

Matewan and the Battle of Blair Mountain

'vicious, strife-promoting and un-American.'

Sid Hatfield was the tough, violent sheriff of the ramshackle mining town of Matewan in Mingo County, West Virginia. He was volatile, bad-tempered and vengeful, and was reported for laughing insanely as he battered a defenceless suspect. He was a semi-literate mountain man, a person of 'primitive scruples and dubious attainments'. He was a killer who reflected the place and the time. He was also an unlikely working-class hero, as unlike most lawmen in the America of 1920, he was on the side of the working man, 'his' people. Most notably, he defended them on a dusty sidewalk, both six-guns blazing.

And he became a martyr in the mine wars which drew a line in the sand to protect workers as US-style capitalism and industrialisation changed the face of the world.

* * *

Hatfield was hewn from the rough, lonely mountains of West Virginia. His high cheekbones and close-set piercing eyes marked him out, if anyone doubted it, as a member of the Hatfield clan whose feud with the McCoys raged along the border with Kentucky before the turn of the twentieth century. That feud tells us a lot about the people who scraped a living in such rugged terrain and who eventually rose up in open revolt.

The roots of the antagonism went back to the Civil War when a McCoy patriarch joined the Union side and was murdered on his return.[1]

229

There was also bad blood when a Hatfield wanted to marry into the rival clan but was refused. In 1873 a dispute, supposedly about the ownership of a stray hog but really concerning property lines, led to litigation and murder. Another inter-clan love tryst sparked more violence. Both families ambushed each other as they went about their work and household chores. The murderers were in turn murdered. During the 1880s the feud claimed more than a dozen lives. In 1888 Wall Hatfield and several others were put on trial in partisan Kentucky for the murder of Alifair McCoy who had been shot while escaping from a house torched by the Hatfields. Seven were imprisoned for life and an eighth, Ellison Mounts, variously described as a simpleton and a psychopath, was hanged the following February. As public executions were banned in Kentucky, the scaffold was erected at the bottom of a hill in Pileville so that thousands could witness the condemned man's death by looking over the surrounding wood-plank fence. The two families agreed to an uneasy peace in 1891.[2]

As the Hatfields and McCoys were killing each other, a far bigger conflict was growing. In March 1883 the first carload of coal was taken from Pocahontas to Tazewell, Virginia, on the newly constructed Norfolk and Western Railway. The line opened the vast coalfields of south-western West Virginia and the population of the sparse backwoods exploded. Thousands of European immigrants and black refugees from the Southern states rushed in to fill the new boom towns offering decent wages and cheap accommodation around the pit heads. These towns were almost exclusively company-owned.

The *State Archives* reported:

> Miners worked in company mines with company tools and equipment, which they were required to lease. The rent for company housing and the cost of items from the company store were deducted from their pay. The stores themselves charged over-inflated prices, since there was no alternative for purchasing goods. To ensure that the miners spent their wages at the store, coal companies developed their own monetary system. Miners were paid by scrip, in the form of tokens, currency or credit, which could only be used at the company store. Even when wages were increased, companies simply increased prices to balance what they had lost in pay.

Such were the benefits of capitalism in the raw. It was a monopoly that increased exploitation and prompted the lyrics to the classic country song by Tennessee Ernie Ford:

Some people say a man is made outta mud
A poor man's made outta muscle and blood
Muscle and blood and skin and bones
A mind that's a-weak and a back that's strong

You load sixteen tons, what do you get
Another day older and deeper in debt
Saint Peter don't you call me 'cause I can't go
I owe my soul to the company store (chorus)[3]

Under the system of cribbing, workers were paid on the basis of coal
tonnage mined. Each car brought out of the mines supposedly held
2,000 pounds, but unscrupulous bosses – the majority – altered the cars
so that they could carry much more. Miners were also cheated when
company weightmen deducted pay for slate and rock mixed in with
the coal, using their own arbitrary but company-biased judgements.
Mine safety was also a major concern and the coal companies of West
Virginia had the worst safety record of any mining state. America's
worst mining disaster hit at Monagh, Marion County, in 1907, killing
361 people. It has been statistically shown that a West Virginia miner
had less chance of survival than a US soldier in the trenches at the
tail-end of the First World War.

The combination of exploitation and hazard led to the creation of
small unions specific to mining states, or even individual counties. After
several false starts they finally combined into the United Mineworkers of
America, formed in Columbus, Ohio, in 1890. By the end of that decade
the fledgling union had organised strikes in Pennsylvania, Ohio, Indiana
and Illinois. Attempts to organise in West Virginia failed until 1902 when
the union was partially recognised in the Kanawha-New River coalfield.
In response the coal companies formed the Kanawha County Coal
Operators' Association the following year. It hired private 'detectives'
from the Baldwin-Felts Agency in Bluefield as mine guards. Their real job
was to harass, intimidate, drive out and even kill union organisers. They
had the law on their side. The companies had introduced the infamous
'yellow dog' contract which forbade workers joining a union, and which
was repeatedly upheld by state courts. The bosses put deputy sheriffs
on their payroll. But their most effective tool in breaking strikes and
preventing unionisation was Baldwin-Felts itself.

The agency was formed in 1900 by a partnership between William
Baldwin, the Norfolk and Western railroad's chief special agent,

and Thomas Felts, a former law officer who had taken Wild West-style frontier justice to the borders of eastern Kentucky and West Virginia. In polite society they were both regarded as upstanding citizens – both had banking interests and Felts served two terms as a state senator. They employed gun thugs from both sides of the law, still hazy territory. The agency's first task was to protect railway property by guarding payrolls, keeping order on trains, and investigating wrecks and robberies. They branched out into legalised bounty-hunting.[4] Their 1912 pursuit of Floyd Allen, a Virginia farmer and feud-pursuer, and his family after a courtroom shootout during which the judge and four others were killed, made them national news. During the epic chase agency operatives beat witnesses, tortured those suspected of harbouring the fugitives, intercepted US mail, illegally confiscated horses, and committed numerous state and federal crimes, but no matter. They were successful.[5]

However, it was in the coalfields that Baldwin-Felts excelled. They served as mine guards, enforcers, assassins and spies, infiltrating union meetings. They saw their duty as preserving law and order at a time when there was no state police force, but they were strange lawmen. Baldwin-Felts hired notorious thugs, bullies, criminals, hoodlums. Howard Lee, later to become West Virginia's attorney general, wrote: 'They were fearless mountain men, many with criminal records, whose chief duties were to keep the miners intimidated, to beat up, arrest, jail and even kill if necessary any worker or visitor suspected of union activities around the camps.'[6]

As a result of such tactics, by 1912 the union had lost control of the Kanawha coalfield and had failed to penetrate the rest of West Virginia's southern mining areas. The same year the UMWA miners on Paint Creek, Kanawha County, demanded pay rises to match those of neighbouring, non-unionised areas. When that was rejected they walked out, beginning one of the most violent strikes in American history. It spread along nearby Cabin Creek and the strikers extended their demands to the right to unionise, an end to the monopoly of the company store, a ban on cribbing, and an end to bullying by thugs dressed as guards. The operators responded by hiring more Baldwin-Felts men to evict striking miners and their families from their company homes. The families set up tent colonies which were repeatedly attacked and ransacked by agency guards. Union leaders arrived, including the fiery and foul-mouthed Irishwoman Mary 'Mother' Jones, who brought with them large quantities of weapons and ammunition.[7] On 2 September Governor William E. Glasscock imposed martial law. Over 1,200 state militia were sent in to disarm both miners and guards. They failed to prevent open warfare and numerous violent clashes. In February 1913 an armoured train nicknamed 'the Bull Moose Special' roared through the strikers' tent encampment at Holly Creek. On board were coal boss Quin Morton and county sheriff Bonner Hill. Guards opened fire from the moving train, killing striker Cesco Estep. Morton wanted to 'go back and give them another round' but Hill talked him out of it. In retaliation, miners attacked a mine-guard encampment at Mucklow. Over several hours of gunfighting at least sixteen people died, most of them guards.

A few days later Mother Jones was placed under house arrest for inciting riot. She was sixty-eight and suffering from pneumonia, but Governor Glasscock refused to release her. So did his successor, Henry D. Hatfield, who was sworn in on 4 March. Governor Hatfield issued a series of settlement terms, including a nine-hour working day, the right to buy goods other than in company stores, and an end to discrimination against union miners. But he failed to address the right to organise and the employment of the hated agency guards. He ordered the striking miners to accept his terms or be deported out of the state. After more violence the strike was settled towards the end of July after the Baldwin-Felts men were removed from Paint and Cabin creeks. A commission ruled against the brutal methods employed by the mine guards. Its report said: 'We find that the system employed was vicious, strife-promoting and un-American.' No man worthy of the name likes to be guarded by another armed with blackjacks, revolvers and Winchesters while earning his daily bread. It is repugnant to the spirit of the labouring man and we believe the opinion of the American people. We are therefore unanimously of the opinion that the mine guard system as presently constituted should be abolished.' The recommendation was ignored.

The strike, then, brought few real improvements to the lives of miners in West Virginia, but it produced a number of future labour leaders. The young rank-and-file activists ousted corrupt UMWA chiefs and instead elected Frank Keeney as district president in 1916 along with Fred Mooney as secretary-treasurer. Both were to play key roles in the mine war to come.

Before their elevation, other coalfields suffered sporadic outbreaks of violence. The worst was the Ludlow Massacre in Colorado on 20 April 1914 when the state's National Guard attacked an encampment of striking miners. The bloody events began when the Guardsmen approached the camp, which was occupied mainly by Greek immigrant workers. The installation of a machine-gun post on an overlooking ridge provoked a shootout. The Guardsmen were joined by mine guards, including Baldwin-Felts men, and the fighting raged throughout the day. The tent town was set ablaze. During the battle four women and eleven children took refuge in a pit beneath one tent. Their charred bodies were later uncovered. The youngest victim was three-month-old Elvira Valdez. Luckier families escaped when a freight train blocked the machine gun's arc of fire. Three captured miners were later found shot dead. Their bodies lay alongside the Colorado and Southern railway tracks for three days as militia officers refused to permit their removal.[8] Following the massacre up to 1,000 enraged miners attacked mine after mine, driving off or killing the guards and setting fire to the buildings. At least thirty-five more people died over ten days of fighting.[9] President Woodrow Wilson sent in federal troops who disarmed miners, militia and guards. Despite such belated even-handedness, the strike in pursuit of union recognition was crushed. Subsequent official reports put the overall death toll between sixty-nine and 199.

US entry into the First World War in 1917 saw a boom in the coal industry with increased demand to fuel the war machine, increased wages and relative peace on the home front.[10] The end of that conflict, however, brought recession. Operators laid off miners and tried to take wages back to pre-war levels. During the war the operators in southern West Virginia had strengthened their grip and by 1919 the country's largest non-unionised coal region comprised the counties of Logan and Mingo. Local historian Cabell Phillips summed up the tinderbox situation:

Unionisation spread by a sort of slow and bloody osmosis from Pennsylvania into Indiana and Illinois, but the further south it reached, the heavier the opposition it met. In West Virginia by 1917 a sort of Mason–Dixon line had been established roughly along the line of the Kanawha River; coal fields in the counties to the north were generally unionised, those to the south were not. This gave the southern operators an economic whip hand over their northern competitors – they paid lower wages and they were immune to the shutdowns frequently enforced by the UMEA in the other fields. For good reason, then, the northern operators were almost as eager as the unionists to have the rich coal lands south of the Kanawha organised, and they secretly conspired to that end. For equally good reasons the southern operators were determined to keep the organisers out, and they had public opinion, which had just discovered the Bolshevik menace, in their favour.[11]

The union targeted Logan and Mingo as its top priority. The Logan operators, linked commercially to the steel and railway empires, through bribes and advancement bought the state house in Charleston and most law officers. They paid County Sheriff Don Chafin to keep out union organisers. He hired a small army of deputies, paid directly by the operators' association, and together they beat up and arrested anyone suspected of even attending union meetings. Despite such intimidation, hundreds of miners joined the union. They were sacked and evicted from company houses. Tent towns occupied by 1,500 miners and their families were attacked by Chafin's army, together with Baldwin-Felts men. Canvases were slashed and peppered with shotgun pellets, contents ransacked, supplies destroyed. Men and boys were pursued through woods, beaten to a pulp and arrested for assault. The bones of some of them lie there still.[12]

At the end of August 1919 rumours spread beyond the county of the atrocities committed by Chafin and his thugs. Armed miners congregated at Marmet for a march on Logan, swelling to a 5,000-strong throng. The union's Frank Mooney persuaded most to hold back in return for a promised government investigation into the abuses. Around 1,500 miners did start the march but then turned back. Another commission was appointed to consider allegations of brutality used against miners and union organisers. It ruled against the union. The coal bosses cut wages in the southern counties, while the US Coal Commission handed pay rises to unionised miners in other fields. The non-union miners of Mingo County went on strike in early May 1920. Mooney and fellow union official Bill Blizzard addressed 3,000 miners at Matewan. Over the next two weeks about half joined the UMWA. The operators called in Baldwin-Felts.

The agency already had an undercover presence in Matewan. Charles Everett Lively rented the ground floor of the UMWA's offices in the town, which he and his wife ran as a restaurant. He was thirty-four with five children, and a union activist who knew Hatfield and striking miners well. He was born and raised in West Virginia and started work in a coal mine at thirteen. In 1902 he joined the

UMWA at Blackband, Kanawha County. He surreptitiously signed up to Baldwin-Felts early in 1913 and his dual work took him all over the mining states. He worked as a miner and agency spy in Illinois, Oklahoma and Kansas. In Colorado, during a miner's strike, he was elected UMWA vice-president at the La Veta union local. His track records, contacts and the proximity of his restaurant, within earshot of union meetings, made him a valuable Baldwin-Felts asset. At a subsequent Senate hearing, following Lively's testimony regarding his past as both a union activist and an agency spy, Senator McKellar said: 'I will say that it violated every idea of right that I ever had. I never would have believed that a thing like this would happen, and I am not surprised that you are having trouble down there in Mingo County.' Lively was unapologetic, saying that he saw nothing wrong in working for the 'secret service'. He added: 'I was conscious of the fact that one wrong move on my part and a rifle bullet would ring out and I would be no more.'

The strike-breakers were led by Thomas Felts' brothers, Albert and Lee. They and their men swept through the county in what Howard Lee later described as a 'campaign of assault, intimidation and terrorism without parallel in the history of American industrial struggle'. More tent communities were destroyed, their occupants chased into gullies and ravines by riflemen. On 19 May 1920 Albert and Lee Felts, with ten or eleven other gunmen, entered Matewan to evict striking miners. The scene was set for a bloodbath.

* * *

The county was known as 'Bloody Mingo' long before the mining wars. Cabell Phillips wrote: 'Though the American frontier had all but vanished by the time the twentieth century began, the code of the frontier still prevailed in the rugged, isolated mountain enclave. Fierce pride, quick suspicions and short tempers called for the settlement of disputes on a personal basis, and life was held to be much less dear than a mountain-man's sense of his own independence and dignity.'

Such was certainly true of Sid Hatfield, who was born in 1893 in the razor-sharp hills surrounding the town. He was made sheriff of Matewan aged twenty-six after more than a decade of raising hell himself. Townsfolk reported that he could fight like a bearcat and was skilled at using his nickel-plated revolvers. A schoolteacher who watched him beat a man half to death was both horrified and astonished that he never stopped laughing as he used his fists and boots. For that reason he was nicknamed Smilin' Sid. Although a tough, maybe brutal, lawman, he was personally affronted at the intimidation and treatment of miners he regarded as his constituents, and that sense of outrage was shared by the town mayor, Cabell Testerman. Both had contested the legality of evictions by the Stone Mountain Coal Company and had applied for a warrant to arrest the incoming Baldwin-Felts detectives.[13]

Hatfield, a silver star on his chest and six-guns on his hips, confronted the Felts brothers and their gang at the train depot after they had carried out, unhampered, a number of evictions and were waiting for the next train out. Hatfield clapped his hand on Albert Felts' shoulder and told him that he and his men were guilty of carrying guns without authorisation in the town and that the arrest warrants were on their way. Albert pulled from his pocket an arrest warrant for Hatfield, saying: 'I can return the compliment.' The argument, on the surface good-natured, was carried into Tom Chambers's hardware store where a crowd of miners had gathered. Some of them, according to a witness, had their hands in their pockets 'as if on a revolver'. Mayor Testerman was called to adjudicate and promptly declared the Felts warrant to be a forgery. Miner Isaac Brewer said the warrant 'might have been written on a piece of gingerbread' and laughed in Albert's face. It is not clear who fired the first shot – although it was alleged that Hatfield fired at point-blank range – but within seconds Albert was dead on the sidewalk outside the store and the portly Mayor Testerman was fatally wounded.[14]

Detective G. B. Hildebrand, who had been hired by the agency just the day before, reported: 'Albert Felts dropped, just dropped down in just a moment, and then the shots were coming, it seemed to me from all directions.' As Felts crumpled against the doorway, Testerman doubled up in pain and staggered, unnoticed at first, around the corner. Outside the Becker and Hines drugstore he muttered 'I'll be damned,' spun around and dropped in the street. His killer may have been C. B. Cunningham, Albert's second-in-command, who had been standing close behind and who fired at least one shot before being riddled with gunfire. He fell dead, his head across his boss's legs. Isaac Brewer was shot in the chest, possibly by Felts, possibly by Cunningham. Hatfield, a gun in both hands, rushed out of the store.[15]

On the street there was pandemonium. The Baldwin-Felts men were at a disadvantage – having thought they were done for the day, several detectives had broken down their rifles and wrapped them in paper, while others had packed their revolvers in their briefcases. Some panicked, others recovered quickly. Lee Felts blazed away with two pistols as he stood his ground near the post office. Miner Art Williams, according to witnesses, fired one shot into Albert Felts' lifeless head before firing unsuccessfully at Lee. Williams pointed out Lee to fellow striker Reece Chambers, distinctive in a red sweater, and shouted: 'There! Shoot that goddamned son-of-a-bitch! I want one of his guns!' Chambers fired. Lee dropped to the ground, and Williams took the gun he coveted. He moved down a side street and outside the doctor's surgery he ran into detective O. E. Powell, who was reeling after another miner had smashed a bottle of chloroform over his head. Williams shot the detective in the back of the head.[16]

Williams continued to the town bank where he fired at wounded detective A. J. Boorher. The stricken man refused to fall until he was hit by a rifle shot from army veteran Fred Burgraff. Reece Chambers said: 'There lies one of them goddamned dogs.' He, Hatfield, Burgraff and others followed another wounded detective, Princeton deputy sheriff J.W. Ferguson. He took refuge in the home of Bill Duty and when Hatfield and the others burst in he pleaded for mercy before bolting out of the back door. He was climbing the garden fence when he was picked off by Burgraff using his US Army rifle. Ferguson toppled into McCoy Alley. Mrs Duty handed his black hat to Cora Humbard who placed it on the dead man's chest.[17]

The Anderson brothers, detectives both, tried to enter a building but it was locked against them. They were luckier next door where a miner's wife gave them refuge. When the train they had been expecting just minutes before steamed out of town, they leapt aboard the last carriage. They escaped with fellow detective Oscar Bennet who had gone to buy cigarettes before the shooting began. He observed the brief battle from the station while fearfully tearing up his identification papers. Detective Hildebrand, who had been in the store when the first man fell, also escaped. He darted around a corner, his hat pierced by gunshot, and climbed through a window into a coal storage house. He hid in an empty barrel for several hours before walking brazenly out of town along the railway tracks, whistling all the time. Fellow detective John McDowell got clear by swimming across the Tug River to Kentucky, rifle bullets splashing around his head.[18]

Mayor Testerman, still conscious, was treated by the local doctor before being put on a train to Welch, a town with better medical facilities. He died on the way, repeating several times with his last gasps: 'Why did they shoot me? I can't see why they shot me.'[19] Two miners, Bob Mullins and Tot Tinsley, were also among the fatalities. Isaac Brewer recovered from his wound, as did four other citizens shot in the melee, Sam Arters, Will Reyer, James Chanbers and Bill Bowman. That night the bodies of the Felts brothers and five other detectives were thrown into a boxcar and taken to Williamson. They were seen there after midnight by a vengeful Thomas Felts. He noticed injuries to Albert's arm and later said that the body looked as if it had been 'dragged through cinders'.

The following day the *Williamson News* headlined:

A Terrible Calamity Brings Instant Death.
Seven Baldwin-Felts Detectives Killed on the Spot.
Mayor of Matewan, C. C. Testerman, Killed and Others.

Consternation was created in the minds of all our people yesterday evening by a telephone message from Matewan that Mayor Testerman, Albert Felts, and perhaps many others had been shot in the streets of the city shortly after four o'clock. Telephone communication with Matewan became impossible, and rumors of general shooting and rioting spread like wildfire. Sheriff G. T. Blankenship quickly gathered a small company of deputies and was able to catch No. 16, which brought him to the scene very shortly after the shooting occurred.

Sheriff Blankenship was followed to Matewan in an hour or two by several automobile loads of deputies who had been mustered by Deputy Sheriff Tony Webb.

Strictly accurate reports of just what took place are not now available. It is probably that the true details will never be known, for from the firing of the first shot the confusion was so great and excitement so general that even those who witnessed the tragedy are at a loss to describe it.

According to citizens who were present, the detectives were awaiting the arrival of No. 16, on which they intended leaving town. Mayor Testerman was talking to Detective Albert Felts about the release of Policeman Hatfield, who was alleged to be in the custody of the detectives. A crowd had congregated about the station and in the street across the railroad. The first shot was fired without warning, and the shooting instantly became general.

Mayor Testerman and Mr. Felts were the first to fall, and the seven Baldwin-Felts men were shot as they tried to make their escape, according to onlookers. The twelve or fifteen detectives, it is said, fled toward the river and some of them succeeded in crossing to the Kentucky side. According to one report one of the detectives was shot while attempting to swim the river. Two of the detectives are said to have run to the tunnel just below Matewan and flagged No. 16, when the train came through a half hour later, and secured the protection of Sheriff Blankenship until the train left Matewan. These two men, and according to most reports, all the other detectives have now left this section and proceeded to Bluefield. It is said that all the detectives but one have now been accounted for. It is thought that this man may be the one some observers say was shot in the river.

Sheriff Blankenship is now on the scene, and reports that there have been no further disturbances of any importance.

Passenger trains were notified to run through Matewan without stopping last night, but the city is now quiet and train will stop as usual today.

The Baldwin-Felts men are said to have come to Matewan for the purpose of evicting from company houses miners who had joined the United Mine Workers of America. It is stated on good authority, however, that proper warrants for the evictions had not been issued by the civil authorities.

Last night Matewan was a seething mass of humanity bearing firearms. This morning it is quiet, with but few people on the streets.

Several members of the state constabulary have arrived in Williamson this morning, and it is said that by tonight about forty of them will be here.

The bodies of the seven detectives who were killed were brought to Williamson last evening on No. 1, and taken to the Ball Morgue for autopsy and embalming.

Seven men lie dead in our city today who yesterday were well and in the prime of life.

Little is known of them here except that they were detectives and were not afraid to face death in the discharge of the duties of their calling. Yet not one of the thinking people of this section but will sincerely mourn the death of these men and sympathize with those who loved them.

These men did not come here, probably, with any idea of bringing peace and better counsel to the tortured miners and mining interests of Mingo county, but it may yet be that by their deaths they have sobered the reckless ones and brought all to a more wholesome view of the troubles which exist.

These seven have paid dearly for their participation in Mingo county's troubles and we have only sorrow for their untimely taking off.

Matewan loses one of its most valuable and respected citizens in the death of Mayor C. C. Testerman. Mr. Testerman was elected mayor of Matewan last fall, and had always discharged the duties of his office in an efficient and public-spirited way.

The report that Mayor Testerman died instantly when shot yesterday, was not true. He was taken in an unconscious condition to Welch and died at the hospital there at 11:50 last night.

The many friends of the mayor in this county and elsewhere will extend their sincerest sympathy to his bereaved family.

It is very quiet in Williamson today. All the talk of our people is of the tragedy at Matewan. This should be a lesson to us all. May such a deadly combat never occur again in our midst.[20]

Felts vowed revenge and was helped by a flood of information from informants, company spies, and eyewitnesses. Some claimed that Hatfield had himself shot Mayor Testerman. That seemingly bizarre claim was given some credence a week later when the sheriff and Testerman's widow Jesse were caught in a Huntington hotel and charged with 'improper relations'. The couple had already bought a licence and married the following day on their release from jail. But to the miners, their families and the poor of West Virginia, Hatfield was a hero – a lawman who had refused to be bought and who had turned on their oppressors, a mountain man who had ambushed the ambushers. Sympathies and loyalties, however, differed from town to town and from county to county, and that proved crucial in subsequent court hearings.[21]

A grand jury issued indictments against Hatfield and twenty-one miners for conspiring to murder the Baldwin-Felts men. Thomas Felts was gratified by that, but outraged when the same grand jury issued indictments against four of the surviving detectives for the murder of Testerman and the two dead miners. The four were tried in Greenbriar County where there were few miners and many company interests, and duly acquitted. Hatfield and the miners were then acquitted in turn by a sympathetic jury in Bloody Mingo. Hatfield said: 'It's good to know you have so many friends.'

The bloodletting continued, with witnesses and accused on both sides attacked or assassinated.[22] In May 1920 Bud McCoy, an employee of Portsmouth Solvay Co., Freeburn, was shot and killed in an ambush at Lynn by unknown assailants. In August Ansie Hatfield was killed at Matewan by a hidden assassin. In October John Yates, a blacksmith, of the Crystal Block Mining Co., at Gates, was shot and instantly killed. In November policeman Ernest Ripley was killed near Vulcan by W. T. (Taylor) Cole in a three-cornered fight between Ripley, Cole, and Bill Hatfield. Hatfield was in turn killed by Ripley. Cole was tried, convicted, and sentenced. Cole was a member of Vulcan UMWA, and was at the time a deputy sheriff under Sheriff Blankenship. George Hays and an unidentified man were killed by the accidental discharge of some high explosives at Gates on 3 January 1921. From all indications the men who were killed were intending to place the explosive and blow up a house kept as a boarding place for a number of black miners.

In February union miner William Gilliam was killed by William Trent at Chattaroy. In May Harry Staton, a merchant and prohibition agent, was killed and two miners arrested. That month three state policemen, Privates Charles Kackley and Manley Vaughan were killed in a firefight in which miner George Crum was also killed. And so it went on. According to the bosses, Hatfield was implicated in at least two of the killings.[23]

Thomas Felts remained determined to see Hatfield dead in revenge for the loss of his brothers. Coal company lawyer S. B. Avis charged Hatfield and thirty others with conspiracy concerning wider dissent and violence across the coalfields. The trial was scheduled in the company stronghold of McDowell County. Hatfield was deeply suspicious of the chosen venue, saying that if he went to McDowell he would never come back. The county sheriff was another Hatfield, but he had no sympathy for either his kinsman or for striking miners. William Hatfield did, however, promise Sid's new wife that he would guarantee his safety during the trial ... but then left town abruptly on the opening day of the trial, claiming he needed to 'take the waters' at a spa resort in Virginia.

On 21 August 1921 Hatfield, his wife and companions approached the courthouse steps. Charles Lively and other Baldwin-Felts agents were waiting. As the unarmed Sid Hatfield reached the top step they opened fire. He was hit at least four times and fell lifeless at the door in front of his wife.[24] Fellow defendant Ed Chambers was also gunned down. The *Charleston Gazette* reported under an eight-column front-page banner headline: 'Sid Hatfield lies in the morgue at Welch tonight, a smile frozen on his lips, eyes wide open, and five bullets holes in his head and chest. On the slab next to him lies the body of his friend and bodyguard, Ed Chambers. They were shot down as they mounted the steps of McDowell County Court House this morning... their wives ran screaming into the doorway of the building. Who started the shooting nobody seems to know. The true story of how the men met their death will, in all probability, always remain a secret...'[25]

Hatfield's funeral was an impressive event, with the people of Mingo county determined to give him the best possible send-off. At least 2,000 people joined the funeral procession to the hilltop cemetery. The eulogy was given by Samuel Montgomery, who said: 'There can be no peace in West Virginia until the enforcement of the law is removed from the hands of private detective agencies and from those deputy sheriffs who are paid not by the state, but by the great corporations...'

Lively and his confederates insisted that the double-killing was in self-defence. They were never prosecuted.

* * *

Hatfield's murder fanned the flames of armed insurrection. In the thirteen months since the Matewan battle, 90 per cent of Mingo miners had joined the union and were either on strike or locked out. The *State Archives* reported: 'A virtual war existed in the county. Non-union miners were dynamited, miners' tent colonies were attacked, and martial law declared on three occasions.' A week after Hatfield's death a crowd of up to 5,000 protested in the capitol grounds at Charleston. UMWA leaders Frank Keeney and Bill Blizzard urged the miners to fight with whatever means were at their disposal.

Keeney, still in his thirties, was of Irish stock, and it showed. Unlike his scrawny, inarticulate followers – the mountain men, the black descendants of slaves and the European immigrants struggling to master even basic English – he was a pugnacious and powerful orator. He had been born and raised in the hills and had spent his young adulthood digging coal. He well knew the realities of poverty, low expectations and exploitation. He was muscular, squat and square-jawed, but possessed the eloquence of an Irish rebel. He was also a shrewd and sometimes pragmatic negotiator. It was said that he could as easily rouse a rabble as sit down at a polished table with a state governor or a committee of mine owners. Both would either bend to his will or, in the case of the bosses, at least force them to reassess their opinion of him.

His principal adversary was Logan County Sheriff Don Chafin who was, as we have seen, the most hated of the company lawmen. Born in the county's Marrowbone section in 1887, he joined the forces of business, law and order as a teenager. He was elected sheriff in 1912, county clerk in 1916 and sheriff again in 1920, largely due to his Democrat and mining company sponsors. He may have felt he had some justification for the war of terror he waged against the union men. During the early days of the UMWA's drive into his county he confronted union organiser Bill Petry close to the state house in Charleston and told him to keep his men out of Logan. He warned that if they came he would 'do something about it'. Petry replied: 'Why wait, Don? We can shoot too.' Both men pulled revolvers and Chafin was shot above the heart. Holding one hand over his wound to stem the blood, Chafin walked unaided to the local hospital where he was treated. The wound was not serious, but from then on any incoming union miner or union organiser was guaranteed a rough time on his patch.[26]

Over the next two weeks, Keeney criss-crossed the state, urging miners to join a march on Logan to break Chafin's power and establish the union. Hundreds assembled at Marmet. The indomitable Mother Jones, sensing impending disaster, urged caution despite previously advocating Chafin's lynching. She held up a telegram supposedly from President Harding offering to remove the mine guards if they did not march. Keeney denounced the telegram as a fake.

On 24 August the march began as 5,000 men crossed Lens Creek Mountains. They were joined by miners from across the state. Cabell Phillips wrote:

They were a tatterdemalion lot in blue jeans, worn corduroy, bits of army khaki, slouch hats and miners' capes. Many brought their women and children along, loaded on ancient jitneys or farm wagons, or trudged on foot over the hills from as far as 50 miles away. They cooked beans and fatback over open fires and slept on the ground in a cold drizzle. Most were armed, some with pistols and shotguns, others with high-powered hunting or army rifles.

They had gathered through a spontaneous impulse and with but a vague notion of what they were going to do.[27]

One group from Kanawha County commandeered a Chesapeake and Ohio freight train, renamed the 'Blue Steel Special', to meet up with the advance column in Danville. Many were First World War veterans and organised themselves into companies broadly based on their home communities. Patrols kept watch on the roads and mountain trails, units were set up to expel troublemakers, spies, thieves, bootleggers and reporters, a mobile commissary shared out food, and a medical unit of six doctors and eight nurses joined the column to treat both wounds and dysentery. Phillips wrote: 'At the little town of Racine ... workmen getting ready for the day shift at the local mines stopped and cheered a plodding file of marchers, three or four abreast, that clogged their main street and stretched out of sight in each direction. All day long they came in a straggling, disorganised procession, hundreds upon hundreds of grim-faced, weary men and excited boys, each with a gun and a sack of provisions slung over his shoulder...' The miners waved banners and wore red bandanas, earning themselves the nickname 'red-necks'. Occasionally ragged cheers would sweep the line: 'On to Logan!' and 'Remember Sid Hatfield!'[28]

In Logan County Chafin mobilised a 2,000-strong army of deputies, detectives, mine guards, shopkeepers, clerks and state police. He even offered prisoners in his overcrowded jail freedom if they joined his ranks. One prisoner, according to the *Logan Banner*, refused to pick up a rifle and was shot 'while trying to escape'.[29]

President Harding sent First World War hero Henry Bandholtz to the scene. Bandholtz, the military commander in Washington, had the power to appeal for federal troops. He and the state governor met Keeney and Mooney in Madison and, during an acrimonious session, warned that if the march continued, the miners, and specifically the union leaders themselves, could be charged with treason. Bandholtz said that he was not interested in the merits of the dispute, only in the preservation of law and order. Keeney, faced with such massive sanction, reluctantly agreed to order the miners to turn back. He caught up with the vanguard and addressed them from the bonnet of his four-cylinder Dodge. He bellowed:

I've told you men God knows how many times that any time you want to do battle with Chafin and his thugs, I'll be right there in the front lines with you. I've been there before, and you know it. But this time you've got more than Chafin against you. You've got the Government of the United States against you. President Harding has sent an army general down here to see what the trouble is and he promised me that if you break off this march and go home, you won't be troubled by the constabulary. Now I'm telling you for your own good and for the good of the cause, you've got to do it. Break up the march. Go home. You've got Uncle Sam on your side now, and he won't let you down. You can fight the government of West Virginia, but by god you can't fight the government of the United States.

Most initially obeyed their union leader and, first in grumbling batches, then in a steady stream, they turned for home. Bandholtz sent an 'all clear' to the White House and flew back to Washington. In Logan there was a peace celebration. It was premature. Trains promised by Bandholtz to take marchers home were delayed. And Chafin was not to be denied a battle.[30]

On the night of the 27th Chafin and state police captain J. R. Brockus led a raid on a miners' camp in Sharples, just within the Logan county line. Their intention, in clear breach of Bandholtz's armistice terms, was to round up men they considered to be march ringleaders. With several hundred deputies they moved silently along the mountain trails to surround the encampment. On a ridge they collided with a number of miners. Chafin demanded that they lay down their arms, and the miners responded with a fusillade. For an hour the darkness was broken by gun flashes, the silence punctuated by gunfire, shouts and screams, as the confrontation turned into hand-to-hand combat. The deputies retreated, carrying their wounded, and the miners counted five of their own dead. Many houses were struck by stray bullets during the melee, and reports spread that women and children had been caught in the crossfire.[31] The deal with Bandholtz was broken. The march was back on. The cry was: 'We'll hang Don Chafin to a sour apple tree.' Chafin's power base of Logan again became the target of the infuriated miners. To reach it they had yet to cross Blair Mountain to the south of the town.

Colonel William Eubank of the National Guard took control of Chafin's forces and deployed them on the crest of the mountain ridge in a 15-mile battle line which commanded the passes and narrow defiles. They wore white scarves to distinguish themselves from the red-necks. Below them, in the small town of Blair, the miners

Matewan and the Battle of Blair Mountain

assembled. According to a later testimony, Bill Blizzard arrived in an automobile laden with ammunition. He told the miners: 'You now have what you need, now go and get them.' Travelling showman John Brinkman, who had joined the march, reported: 'We proceeded into the hills and slept in the mountains and next morning at daybreak the firing began...'

In fact battle had already been joined well before dawn. An advance party of around 700 miners were the first to make contact with the defenders at Dingess Run. Both sides dug in behind rocks and maintained a furious fire. The next morning, the 28th, thousands of miners poured up the slopes in earnest. Raiding parties captured four Logan deputies and the son of another deputy. That evening Baptist minister John E. Wilburn formed a small armed company of parishioners to back up the miners. He declared: 'It is time to lay down the Bible and take up the rifle.' His company killed three deputies, one of them reportedly in cold blood as he begged for his life. One of the minister's raiders, Eli Kemp, was in turn killed by Chafin's men.[32]

Over the next three days there was intense fighting along the ridge battle line, by now extending over 30 miles, and in the densely wooded valleys. The hills echoed to the sporadic bursts of rifle fire and the staccato chatter of machine guns.

Eubank hired private aircraft to bomb the miners. Most of the homemade bombs, 6-inch oil well casings packed with explosives, failed to detonate. One just missed a one-room schoolhouse being used by the miners as a hospital. It did explode, creating a crater in the adjoining field, but there were no reported casualties. One plane on a reconnaissance sortie was peppered with rifle fire from the ground and forced to retire.[33]

An Associated Press correspondent reported from the front: 'With all males from the age of fifteen to sixty under arms, children and women fleeing in panic over the line into Boone County, armed patrols arriving and departing, and every available conveyance carrying supplies to the picket posts in the hills, the Sharples-Blair sector may be compared to Belgium in the early days of the world war.'[34] A dispatch from inside Logan said: 'The city was thrown into frenzy shortly after dark last night when reports from men returning from the fighting at Crooked Creek said that the miners' forces had broken through at an important point and forced a retreat by the Logan deputies. They were driven down the hillside with an armed force on the other side of Spruce Fork Ridge. Heavy fighting continued on two other sectors of the line during the afternoon and evening. "We intend to hold our lines with all the power at our command," Colonel W.E. Eubanks said.'[35] To steady the nerves of its readers, the *Logan Banner* published Tennyson's 'The Charge of the Light Brigade'.[36]

Such relatively conventional battle movements were rare, however. The fighting was at times ferocious, but mainly it was simply uncoordinated skirmishes, hit-and-run raids, sniper fire and individual duels between rival sharpshooters. Despite the valiant charges of a few miners and some close-range gunfights, there was little face-to-face combat.[37] Visibility was so limited by the thick, late summer underbrush that few combatants actually saw the enemy. The miners, at the height of the week-long battle, mustered up to 8,000 men. They had good knowledge of the difficult terrain, a seemingly endless supply of arms and ammunition, a burning sense of injustice, and the belief that they were defending the homes, families and livelihoods. The defenders' numbers probably reached 3,000, but they had several advantages which more than made up for lack of numbers. They were better armed with regulation weapons, including machine guns, and enjoyed the dubious asset of air power. More importantly, they were dug into defensive positions, having chosen the battleground. But they were still outnumbered and stretched to breaking point along the long, serpentine front. If their line had snapped, the outcome would have been even more bloody. Such an outcome was avoided when Washington belatedly took decisive action.

By then the battle was making front-page news across the world. Initially both the miners and the militia decided to exclude the press. That, and deliberately cut telegraphs, mean that in the first few days very few reports got out. The major newspapers and agencies sent in their best war correspondents to report the extraordinary conflict, and that was enough to pressurise Harding. On 1 September the president sent federal troops from Fort Thomas, Kentucky. General Bandholtz rushed to Charleston with a presidential proclamation: 'I do hereby command all persons engaged in unlawful and insurrectionary proceedings to disperse and retire peacefully to their respective abodes.' War hero Billy Mitchell led an air squadron from Langley Field near Washington to a vacant field on the outskirts of Charleston. Several planes did not arrive, having got lost or crashed across a wide region. Gas and explosive bombs stockpiled after the end of the First World War were allegedly dropped on the miners, to little effect, around Jeffrey, Sharples and Blair townships. The government later denied that any bombs had actually been dropped, but an unexploded bomb was collected by miners and displayed to great effect at subsequent trials. It was the only time before or since that air power was used by the federal government against its own citizens. More effective were reconnaissance operations, and the thousands of copies of Harding's proclamation dropped by aircraft along the front line.

Federal troops arrived at Sharples, Jeffrey, Blair and Logan on the 3rd. In the latter their bootsteps were drowned by the cheers of the citizenry who regarded themselves as under siege. After a few delays, most of the miners, particularly the army veterans, decided they could not fire on US soldiers, and surrendered. A few stayed on Blair Mountain and continued fighting for another day before they too either surrendered or went home via unmapped forest trails. Many hid their weapons in rock crevices and disused mine shafts, ready for another day. They were still being found decades later.

New York Times war correspondent Boyden Sparks later reported that it was Bill Blizzard who persuaded the most reluctant miners to lay down their arms:

> He was young, wiry, dark-haired, cordial and convincing. He wore a weather-beaten black narrow-brimmed hat, pulled over his eyes. His suit appeared to have been slept in for a week. 'Are you the general of the miners' army?' he was asked. 'What army?' Countered Blizzard with a smile. 'I guess the boys will listen to me all right.' Then he spoke to a man standing nearby. This individual trotted away to crank up a flivver, and a few minutes later Blizzard was on his way up the line. What he did when he arrived can only be surmised, but when the Regulars moved up to Sharples at daybreak a few hours later, the miner fighters were coming out of the hills. Their red badges had been snatched off. They were simply a swarm of stubbly-faced men getting out of the hills and back to their homes. But it was Blizzard who started them out.

Sparks had been dispatched to the scene with a female reporter who was to report on human interest stories. Chris Holt, fifteen at the time, recalled that the lady was wearing a pair of riding jodhpurs which 'caused almost as much of a sensation in Sharples as the battle'. He loaded the reporters into his father's Baby Overland automobile and drove them to the front lines, where he left them. While attempting to reach the Logan lines their group was fired upon and Sparks was wounded in the leg. They were captured and thrown in jail in Logan until they could be identified. They wrote 'hair raising' articles about their adventures that weren't complimentary to either jail or jailers.

The battle claimed numerous lives, but given the density of the terrain, the confused nature of the fighting, and the exaggerations on both sides, no absolutely definitive death toll is possible. Reported fatalities on the miners' side ranged from twelve to a hundred, among Chafin's men from sixteen to fifty. The wounded can safely be counted in hundreds.[38]

Most who surrendered were sent home on trains, but those perceived to be ringleaders were marked for official retribution. Specially convened grand juries issued 1,217 indictments, including 325 for murder and twenty-four for treason. Astonishingly, but true to form, all prosecutions were instigated not by the state or the federal government, but by the lawyers of the Logan County Coal Operators. Miner Walter Allen was convicted in his absence of treason. He had skipped bail and was never seen again.

Bill Blizzard, regarded by the authorities as the general of the Blair Mountain Insurrection, was tried for treason in several venues, but no verdict was reached in any of them. Prosecution and defence attorneys agreed to move the trials to Jefferson County, in the Eastern Panhandle far from the coalfields, in the same courthouse where John Brown had been tried and condemned. Coal company attorneys comprised the prosecution team. Thomas Townsend, former Kanawha County prosecuting attorney, led the defence. The prosecution chose to try Blizzard first, believing that it was the strongest of the treason cases. The trial centred on a discussion of Blizzard's location during the movement toward Blair Mountain. Prosecution witnesses claimed that Blizzard had shadowed the marchers, periodically requesting reports and issuing orders. The defence presented witnesses claiming that Blizzard had remained in Charleston during the crisis. Questions about the reliability of some prosecution witnesses, as well as Blizzard's role in convincing the miners to lay down their arms, led the jury to acquit him on 27 May 1922.[39]

Keeney and Mooney, who had left the county during the battle, were acquitted of murder. Minister John Wilburn and his son, also named John, were convicted of murdering the Logan deputies. Both were pardoned five years into their eleven-year sentences. Many other prosecutions for murder and/or treason collapsed when chief defence attorney Harry Houston won a ruling that each miner had to be charged separately and that there had to be two witnesses to each overt act. Most treason charges were reduced to lesser offences. A factor in both the acquittals and reduced sentences was public disquiet at supposed law officers – not just guards and private detectives, but elected officials – receiving most of their pay directly from the coal companies. Chafin was forced to admit in court that while his public wages never exceeded £3,000 a year, his personal assets were worth more than a third of a million dollars. Eventually all remaining charges were dropped.

One by one the mines reopened as strikers and marchers returned to work, and as refugees came out of hiding. The federal troops stayed for a few weeks until they, too, went home. Cabell Phillips, the son-in-law of Frank Keeney, recorded:

> Peace had come to West Virginia, but it was a bitter, precarious peace that in the miners' view had been imposed by force. As so often in the past 'the law' had come down on the side of their oppressors. And in retrospect this seems to have been true. Their quarrel had not been with the federal government, but with the private operators of the coal mines and a state administration which had conspired with them to ignore miners' rights ... So from the standpoint of the miners the net result of federal intervention had been only to restore an unsatisfactory status quo. Hundreds of families continued to live meagrely in tent colonies. Thousands of miners were blacklisted from employment. The Baldwin-Felts men and sheriffs' deputies were restored to authority.[40]

The Battle of Blair Mountain was a clear defeat for the miners and for a while it halted the UMWA's efforts in the state's southern coalfields. Providing defence attorneys for the treason trials had almost bankrupted the union regionally. In West Virginia union membership tumbled from 50,000 to a few hundred by 1924. Nationally, the UMWA's membership declined from 600,000 to fewer than 100,000. Keeney and Mooney were forced out of the union by new UMWA President John Lewis, whom they had failed to consult when mobilising the miners, but Bill Blizzard remained a strong force until he was finally ousted in the 1950s.

The coal bosses only enjoyed a brief, pyrrhic victory, however. Matewan and Blair Mountain raised national awareness of the appalling conditions in the coalfields and the brutal exploitation of the miners.

Congressional investigations and lurid newspaper coverage turned the miners, in the public image, from bomb-throwing Bolsheviks into proud, independent frontier heroes battling injustice. There was huge public resentment, too, at the spectacle of mainly white Americans being tried for treason by private prosecutors hired by the mining companies on the evidence of company-bought lawmen. One commentator noted: 'The human misery of the tent colonies, the harsh peonage of the mine towns and the yellow dog contract – such discoveries outraged thousands of citizens across the country who had virtually no opinion about the labor movement but very strong ones about injustice.'

In 1933 President Roosevelt's National Industrial Recovery Act aimed to pull America out of the Great Depression. He and key economic advisors believed that unrestrained competition had helped cause the slump and that government had a critical role to play through national planning, limited regulation, the fostering of trade associations, support for 'fair' trade practices, and support for 'democratization of the workplace'. Roosevelt, himself the former head of a trade association, believed that government promotion of 'self-organization' by trade associations was the least intrusive and yet most effective method for achieving national planning and economic improvement. During key negotiations, the West Virginia mine wars were repeatedly invoked. The Act enshrined trade union rights, which allowed the UMWA to recruit across Mingo, Logan and the other counties from which it had been barred at gunpoint for so long. The abolition of the mine guard system quickly followed. The UMWA were able to confront abusive managements more successfully. Their victories in turn encouraged widespread unionisation of other industries during the 1930s and helped create such umbrella organisations as the American Federation of Labor. The outcome was a universal eight-hour day, injury compensation insurance, paid holidays and medical benefits. The mine owners won the battle of Blair Mountain, but lost the war.

The *State Archives* reported on their modern website: 'Blair Mountain stands as a powerful symbol for workers to this day. The miners who participated vowed never to discuss the details of the march to protect themselves from the authorities. For many years their story was communicated by word of mouth as an inspiration to union activists. It serves as a vivid reminder of the deadly violence so often associated with labor-management disputes. The mine wars also demonstrated the inability of the state and federal governments to defuse a violent situation short of armed intervention.'[41]

The fear of a repeat of Matewan and Blair Mountain forced US capitalism to accommodate the needs and just deserts of its workforce, particularly when the Second World War hugely boosted industrial production, followed in the war's aftermath by mass consumerism. Without such bloodshed it is doubtful whether the concept of US-wide industrial organisation would have taken hold. Other newly industrialised nations followed suit. Such disputes helped turn America into a global superpower.

But the inequalities inherent in market-force capitalism remain vividly apparent.

***

The Baldwin-Felts Detective Agency was dissolved in 1937 when both its founders were freshly in their graves. Baldwin died the year before aged seventy-five, and the agency struggled on for a few months until Felts died at sixty-nine. Their files were destroyed. The abolition of the mine guard system – together with the changing public mood – had badly hit the strike-breaking business in the southern counties. Their tough tactics had become an embarrassment to those same bosses who had once so eagerly hired their thugs.

Sheriff Don Chafin invested his company paycheques well. He bought extensive property in and around Huntington, Logan County. In later years be bought and sold coon dogs. Felled by a heart attack aged sixty-seven, he died one of the town's wealthiest men.

The UMWA won more battles in Bloody Harlan County. The mining industry which boomed in the Second World War contracted in the 1960s, forcing compromise and closures. Frank Keeney continued to fight for the miners. When the UMWA abandoned the southern counties, he tried to organise an independent union. It failed, costing him his life savings and his home. He remained in Charleston, a magnet for aging veterans of 'The March' until age and infirmity overcame them. He was the last of the Blair Mountain leaders when he died in 1969.[42]

Blair Mountain remained the site of conflict and witnessed, as Kate Sheppard wrote in November 2010, a face-off between 'a new generation of activists and several modern-day coal companies intent on bulldozing and blasting away at a historical site to access the veins of coal beneath'. Campaigners managed to get Blair Mountain listed on the National Register of Historic Places. The state of West Virginia appealed and the designation was removed a few months later. The Massey Energy Company and Arch Coal continued blasting away rock very close to the mountain while the Blair Community Centre fights to preserve the battle site.

The last survivor of the Ludlow Massacre, Mary Benich-McLeary, died of a stroke in June 2007, aged ninety-four. She was eighteen months old when the Baldwin-Felts men attacked the encampment. In the mayhem she was left behind amid the burning tents, but a teenage boy heard her screams, scooped her up and took refuge in the woods. Her family never spoke to her of the carnage.

Afterword

'they refused to reform the system in time to save it.'

As we have seen, the scale of violence was far greater east of the Mississippi/Missouri during the period when the West was won, yet the opposite appears true in the popular, and populist, imagination and recollection.

This book has never been intended in any way to denigrate the Western pioneer ethos, rather to help understand the contradictions inherent in attitudes which downplay the historic role of the East as a hotbed of violent struggle. Those contradictions played a part in the election of the 'outsider' Donald Trump, an Eastern billionaire who inherited huge wealth but who purported to be on the side of the working man. An outsider, in other words, who was part of the pampered and moneyed elite rather than the political and intellectual elite.

In April 2016, while Trump was battling Ted Cruz for the Republican nomination and Hilary Clinton was slugging it out with Bernie Saunders on the Democrat side, I travelled through the cowboy states of Montana, South Dakota and Wyoming. I received nothing but hospitality and easy friendship in poor towns where the pioneer spirit remains the ongoing culture of choice. A thirty-year-old bartender in a Billings, Montana, microbrewery summed up the Wild West appeal of both Republican Donald Trump and Democrat/socialist Bernie Sanders: 'They're outsiders. They have a populist message which goes down well in rural areas where folk feel their voice goes unheard amongst the political elite.' That was a view repeated constantly. Such states in the heart of the 'real' America provide answers to those in Britain puzzled by the appeal of Trump. America's 'rim' is the Washington-central east coast, the west coast and the southern Bible belt, but the vast tract of the Midwest regards itself as the real soul of America and its people felt disenfranchised.

The stereotypes repeated in New York, Los Angeles and London are either simplistic or untrue. The three states I visited have a complicated social history which constantly confounds analysts of the political right. Take Wyoming, for example. Steeped in conservative cowboy culture, with the Republicans dominating the state senate for eighty years, it is proud of being the first state to grant women the right to vote – suffrage for women aged twenty-one and over was agreed in 1869, fifty years before Britain, while Montana followed in 1916. The reason, according to a grizzled seventy-one-year-old Vietnam vet, was 'folk knew it was unfair, and they did something about it.' The veteran, who fitted the cinematic stereotype of a prospector or mountain man but had been fluent in seven languages as a military interpreter, pointed out that Democrat Nellie Taylor Ross was the country's first state governor in 1924 and was the first female director of the US Mint, serving from 1933 to 1953. 'Mind you,' the veteran added, 'it wasn't until 1952 that Native Americans got the vote.' The truck-stop town of Hardin, Montana, on the edge of the Crow reservation, demonstrated the poverty endemic across former native lands and beyond. Here, and in much of the three states, families have a hardscrabble life far distant from the salons of Washington and New York and the studios of Hollywood. Here poverty has given common cause to old enemies, uniting them in contempt for the Establishment. Respect for common traditions, a strong sense of local community, and a distaste for welfare are other unifying themes. 'We believe in work, not welfare,' said a motor mechanic in the foothills of the Bighorn mountains, 'and if Hilary Clinton had her way we would all either get it or pay for it.' A gambler in Deadwood, South Dakota, said: 'These are the last three states left where if you break down on the road, the next car will stop. We help each other out here.' Such self-reliance is a matter of pride – if you don't believe in big government, you shouldn't claim the benefits of big government. The same is true of attitudes to the environment – this is the territory of Yellowstone National Park, the Bighorns, the Black Hills – and people want to protect their natural heritage to a degree unheard of in most of the US, and in Britain. Although a cynic might say that they want to save animals so they can shoot them.[1]

The outcome of the 2016 presidential election, of course, was a narrow victory for a three-time bankrupt businessman and reality TV star who plugged into crude populism. Former President Bill Clinton ruefully acknowledged: 'Whether you like it or not, one of Trump's great strengths was that people understood what he had to say ... there was no government-speak.' Predictably, Wyoming backed Trump by a margin of 67 per cent to just 22 per cent for Hilary Clinton, the largest margin for any presidential candidate in the state's history. In Montana to the north, the vote was 56 per cent to 35.7 per cent.

Recently I returned to Montana and Wyoming, plus a slice of Idaho, to see whether opinions had changed well into a presidency which has seen multiple sackings within the administration, further allegations of sexual misconduct, the threat of impeachments, governance and diplomacy by late-night tweets, a nuclear stand-off with North Korea, more revelations about the involvement of the Kremlin in Trump's election, a potentially disastrous intervention in the Middle East, policy U-turns and retreats on numerous policies, tax cuts for the super-rich, spats with supposed allies including Britain and the EU, and with neighbours Mexico and Canada, and a long government shutdown over the Wall. If anything, the polarisation of attitudes had become even more deeply entrenched.

Myths and downright fantasies have deep roots across America. Following the Revolutionary War, the new nation had to create its own history. Hence, the adventurer and all-round dodgy character Christopher Columbus was first popularised by Washington Irving in his 1829 biography, a book constructed almost entirely out of romance rather than history. It spun a fable of an individual who challenged the unknown sea, as Americans confronted the promise of their own wilderness, creating a land free of kings and class prejudice. Captain John Smith's 1624 account of the Jamestown colony was devoured not because of its description of hardship and colonial greed, but because of his fabled rescue by the Red Indian princess Pocahontas, a legend that has persisted ever since. There is no evidence that the *Mayflower*'s Pilgrim Fathers ever disembarked on any rock, never mind Plymouth Rock, and the first written reference was penned 121 years later.

And before they arrived, the Thanksgiving holiday had been widely practiced in Protestant Netherlands.

There's much more. The tale that the young George Washington admitted to his father that he had chopped down a prized cherry tree as 'I can not tell a lie' was invented by Parson Mason Locke Weems in his 1806 book *The Life of George Washington: With Curious Anecdotes, Equally Honorable to Himself and Exemplary to His Young Countrymen*, and further spread by Mark Twain, the novelist. The politician/planter Patrick Henry is best known for his 1775 speech kick-starting the war for independence, saying: 'I know not what course others may take; but as for me, Give me Liberty, or give me Death!' That was written forty-two years later by another 'historian', William Wirt. There is also no evidence that Betty Ross sewed the first American flag – this attribution was first made during the 1876 centennial celebrations. Add into the mix apocryphal exploits of such invented or exaggerated characters as the New England lumberjack Jigger Johnson, the Massachusetts clipper skipper and giant Captain Stormalong, and the Jersey Devil, and we can see that Easterners have no reason to feel superior or to sneer too much at Western mythologies.

The *New York Times* bestselling author Kurt Andersen, a deep-dyed American, wrote of his country as 'the dreamworld creation of fantasists, some religious and some out to get rich quick, all with a freakish appetite for the amazing'.[2] He went on: 'Our nostalgic tic also explains a lot. Americans have always been apt to think of America as the best place on Earth – but also that it used to be so much better, more pioneering, more charming, more virtuous, more authentic. People imagined in the 1700s that it was better in the theocratic wilderness of the 1600s, then in the 1800s that it was better in the 1700s, before the racket and speed of the railroads; in the 1900s we imagined it had been so much better in the 1800s, when we still depended on guns, before we moved from farms and small towns into noisy crowded cities; today, on top of those older nostalgias, we miss the good old days when Americans worked at secure well-paying jobs for years on end. In 1900 a lot of people were nostalgic for the time when Americans were all Protestant, later for when Americans were all Christian, and now for when we were practically all white – and when men were men and women were women and the love that dared not speak its name didn't speak it.'[3] Earlier, he wrote: 'For all the actual miseries and life-or-death threats the wagon-train generations endured, they moved west with fantasies as well as pans and axes and guns, real-life characters in a narrative jury-rigged out of the romantic tales and biblical stories they'd read and heard and the pictures they'd seen. These pioneers were a tiny minority of Americans. But forests and mountains and vast grassy vistas were now a key part of the national story ... Americans living in towns and cities, in order to feel truly, virtuously American, needed nearby *reminders* of wild nature, needed to pretend they were pioneers living on the edge of the untamed.'[4]

The authors of a 1970 report to the National Commission on the Causes and Prevention of Violence wrote: 'Americans have always been given to a kind of historical amnesia that masks much of their turbulent past.'[5] W. Eugene Hollon wrote that one of the results of that amnesia has been 'a tendency to over-emphasise the violent side of the frontier, in comparison to the cities, and to give short shrift to the peaceful and orderly side. Not only have we romanticized the violent characteristics of frontier life, we have transformed them into virtues and then tried to apply them to the elimination of crime at home...'[6]

At the opening of the nineteenth century, 94 per cent of Americans lived in rural settings – by 1900 almost half lived in towns or cities. The population had grown fourteen times as large, and the economy seventy times. The concentration was still east of the Mississippi/Missouri, and it is no wonder that the real frontier was by then in the battles between burgeoning capitalism and organised labour, between white supremacists and growing racial minorities, between fathers, sons and brothers to a degree not seen since the wars between the states. These are inconvenient truths. Mass strikes and insurrections in the East have been too often ignored in favour of fantasies going back to the Pilgrims and the Founding Fathers. Jeremy Brecher wrote: 'It is at such times that the veil of stasis is rent and the opposing forces maintain and undermining the existing forms of society revealed.'[7]

The author Mike Duncan has drawn explicit parallels between ancient Rome before its fall and modern America: 'Rising economic inequality, dislocation of traditional ways of life, increasing political polarisation, the breakdown of unspoken rules of political conduct [and] a set of elites so obsessed with their own privileges that they refused to reform the system in time to save it.' Robert Harris, the author of a trilogy of novels about the Roman orator Cicero, saw much the same: 'Unscrupulous millionaires whipping up the mob to attack the elite and the whole democratic structure crumbling under that pressure...'[8]

America claims to be a 'classless' society, but the momentous upheavals of race, capital and organised labour have been airbrushed out of popular history by vested interests, resulting in a subsequent ignorance of the relatively recent past which leads in turn to aberrations such as misunderstood 'populism' and a denigration of hard-won civil and social rights. Trumpism, some might say.

It was not always so. In 1900 *The New York Post* argued that the biggest threat to the American Dream was the upsurge in the number of millionaires, which was seen as an affront to the words inscribed on the Statue of Liberty. Americans dreamt of social justice and looked to government to regulate and control rampant greed, while presidents such as Woodrow Wilson wanted America to be a beacon for democracy across the world. The various 'America First' movements corrupted such visions into isolationism, a modern form of Nativism and a narrow American identity in the most ethnically divided nation on earth. Gerard DeGroot pointed to Warren Harding's campaign to encourage only white immigration, writing: 'His supporters complained about fake news and hyphenated Americans. The similarities are hard to ignore.'[9]

And it is in the success of Donald Trump that we can see an illustration of self-delusion which again goes some way to explain the airbrushing out of popular consciousness of the Wild, Wild East. Many, including Trump's own sister, have compared the president with the nineteenth-century huckster impresario P. T. Barnum, who grew rich several times over with his freak shows, museums of curiosities, snake-oil salesmanship and downright fraud. Both recognised that audiences are less interested in reality than spectacle. Historian David McCullough said that 'Barnum was loud, brassy, full of bombast, vulgar, childish, surely just a little crooked – the ultimate, delightful phoney from a delightfully phoney era.' And Ben Macintyre wrote: 'The similarities are striking. Both Trump and Barnum exhibit the skills of born salesmen, more concerned with profitable entertainment than strict truth. Barnum said he did not care what people thought of him so long as they talked about him, a principle Trump lives by. Both men became more famous and popular with every fresh gust of notoriety.'[10] Audiences – and voters – can be 'willingly deceived' and the taming of the West provides a better, clearer, more simplistic narrative than the long, messy, sordid and brutal industrial and racial warfare which created the world's most successful capitalist economy.

For the liberal left, also, that story can make uncomfortable reading. Impoverished Irish immigrants lynched blacks from lamp-posts, trade unionists did their best to enforce colour bars, and socialist 'heroes' took backhanders. But overall, the history of the Eastern half of the nation is a story of heroism, fortitude and stamina which more than matches the pioneer spirit demonstrated on the frontier.

Appendix 1

Fatal Clashes in Industrial Disputes, 1850–1920

This cannot be a comprehensive list, as in isolated areas many fatalities went unreported, and in complex disputes many other deaths were attributed simply to murder, personal vendettas or accidents. In some instances, people later died of their wounds and their deaths were not included in official tallies. In almost all the incidents listed below, the perpetrators were police, militia, private security guards and strike-breakers.

August 1850, New York garment strike. At least two tailors died as police attacked with clubs a crowd of about 300 strikers, mostly German.

July 1851, Portage, New York, railroad strike. Two striking workers of the New York and Erie Railroad were shot and killed by police officers. Strikers were dispersed the following morning by the state militia.

May 1871, Hyde Park, Scranton, Pennsylvania, steel strike. Strikers Benjamin Davis and Daniel Jones were shot and killed by a single bullet fired under the command of William W. Scranton. Over 8,000 people attended their funeral.

July 1877, Baltimore railroad strike. During the Great Railroad Strike of 1877, National Guard regiments were ordered to Cumberland, Maryland. As they marched toward their train in Baltimore, violent street battles erupted. Troops fired on the crowd, killing ten and wounding twenty-five. In Pittsburgh, as militiamen approached and sought to protect the roundhouse, they bayoneted and fired on rock-throwing strikers, killing twenty people and wounding twenty-nine. The next day, the militia mounted an assault on the strikers, shooting their way out of the roundhouse and killing twenty more people. In Reading, Pennsylvania, a unit of the State Police marched into the Seventh Street Cut, a man-made railway ravine, and were bombarded from above with bricks and stones. They fired a rifle volley into the crowd at the far end, killing ten. The Battle of the Viaduct in Chicago was between a crowd of strikers and their supporters, and police, federal troops, and state militia at the Halsted Street Viaduct. It left thirty dead.

July 1877, East St Louis, Illinois, and St Louis, Minnesota railroad and general strike. The first general strike in the US saw 3,000 federal troops and 5,000 deputised police kill at least eighteen people in skirmishes around the city.

August 1877, Scranton, Pennsylvania, coal and railroad strike. The day after railroad workers conceded and returned to work, angry striking miners clashed with a thirty-eight-man posse partly led by William Walker Scranton, general manager of the Lackawanna Iron & Coal Company. When a posse member was shot in the knee, the posse responded by killing or fatally wounding four of the strikers. Overall, twenty to thirty were killed and thirty to seventy injured.

August 1877, Lemont, Illinois, quarry strike. Troops of the state militia faced a mob of immigrant quarrymen and their women, throwing cobblestones, and fired into the crowd. They killed two Polish strikers, Jacob Kugawa and Henry Stiller, and wounded several others with bayonets.

April 1886, St Louis, Missouri, railroad strike. Striker John Gibbons, fatally shot by a non-union switchman and private watchman in St Louis, was among the ten known casualties of the Great Southwest railroad strike.

May 1886, Chicago, machinery manufacturing strike. Four killed in McCormick Harvester dispute.

May 1886, Milwaukee, building trades strike. Around 250 state militia were ordered to shoot into the crowd as it approached the iron rolling mill at Bay View, leaving seven dead at the scene, including a thirteen-year-old boy. The *Milwaukee Journal* reported that eight more died within twenty-four hours.

November 1887, Pattersonville, Louisiana, sugar strike. Around 10,000 sugar workers, 90 per cent of them black, went on strike, and a battalion of national guardsmen supporting a sheriff's posse massacred as many as twenty people in the black village of Pattersonville.

November 1887, Thibodaux, Louisiana, sugar strike. Louisiana militia, aided by bands of prominent citizens, shot at least thirty-five unarmed black sugar workers striking to gain a dollar-per-day wage and lynched two strike leaders. No credible official count of the victims was ever made; bodies continued to turn up in shallow graves outside of town for weeks afterwards.

July 1889, Duluth, Minnesota labourer strike. Several days of street riots and strikes by unorganised city labourers saw an hour-long gun battle on Michigan Street with municipal policemen. Two Finnish strikers, Ed Johnson and Matt Black, died of their wounds, as did a young bystander hit by stray bullets. Around thirty were wounded.

April 1891, Morewood, Pennsylvania, coal strike. As a crowd of about 1,000 strikers accompanied by a brass band marched on the company store, deputised members of the 10th Regiment of the National Guard fired several volleys into the crowd, killing six strikers outright, and fatally wounding three more.

July 1892, Homestead, Pennsylvania, steel strike. An attempt by 300 Pinkerton guards hired by the company to enter the Carnegie Steel plant via the river was repulsed by strikers. In the ensuing gun battle, nine strikers and seven Pinkerton guards were shot and killed, and scores wounded.

July 1892, Coeur d'Alene, Idaho, rock mining strike. A union miner was killed by mine guards. Company guards also fired into a saloon where union men were sheltering, killing three.

June 1893, Lemont, Illinois, construction strike. Dozens were injured and five were killed when quarrymen and canal workers clashed with replacement workers, local law enforcement, and two regiments of the Illinois National Guard during construction of the Chicago Sanitary and Ship Canal.

May 1894, Uniontown, Pennsylvania, coal strike. Among many violent incidents in Illinois, Ohio, and elsewhere, five strikers were killed and eight wounded by guards near Uniontown.

July 1894, Chicago railroad strike. A mob peaking at perhaps 10,000 gathered near the shoreline in south Chicago, resulting in several days of vandalism and violence in which switchyards and hundreds of railroad cars were burnt. Thousands of federal troops and deputy marshals clashed with rioters. Thirty people killed in Chicago alone. Another forty were killed in other states.

1896–97, Leadville, Colorado, silver mining strike. Six union men were killed during the strike, by strike-breakers, police, or under mysterious circumstances. Four more union men died when they joined about fifty strikers in a night-time rifle-and-dynamite attack on the Coronado and Emmett mines. The attackers burned the Coronado shafthouse and killed a firefighter trying to extinguish the blaze.

September 1897, Latimer, Pennsylvania, coal strike. Nineteen unarmed striking Polish, Lithuanian and Slovak coal miners were killed and thirty-six wounded by the Luzerne County sheriff's posse for refusing to disperse during a peaceful march. Most were shot in the back.

October 1898, Virden, Illinois, coal strike. After union workers stopped a train transporting non-union workers, eight of the union workers were killed when guards opened fire from the train. Six guards were also killed and thirty people on both sides were wounded.

May 1899, Coeur d'Alene, Idaho, rock mining union organising drive. Following a mass attack in which a non-union ore mill was destroyed by dynamite, and two men were shot and killed by union miners, President McKinley sent in US Army troops who arrested nearly every adult male. About 1,000 men were confined in a pine board prison surrounded by a 6-foot barbed-wire fence patrolled by armed soldiers. Most were released within a week, but more than 100 remained for months, and some were held until December 1899. Three workers died in the primitive conditions.

June–September 1900, St Louis streetcar strike. The Police Board swore in 2,500 citizens in a posse commanded by John Cavender, who had played a similar role in the 1877 general strike. Posse members fatally shot three strikers returning from a picnic and left fourteen others wounded. By the time the strike ended in September, fourteen strikers had been killed.

July 1901, Telluride, Colorado, mining strike. About 250 armed miners took hidden positions around an entrance to the Smuggler-Union mine complex, and demanded that the non-union miners leave the mine. One striker and two strike-breakers died in the ensuing gunfight. Assistant company manager Arthur Collins agreed to stop work at the mine. The following year, Collins was killed by a shotgun fired through a window into his home.

July–October 1901, San Francisco waterfront strikes. The city was in a commercial standstill by late August, with hundreds of ships stacked up in the bay unable to unload, while a violent struggle played out on the streets. Four were killed, two of them strikers, and some 250 were wounded.

July–October 1902, Pennsylvania coal strike. Coal and Iron Police guarding a Lehigh Valley Coal Company colliery in Old Forge came under night-time gunfire. The guards returned fire, and the next morning immigrant striker Anthony Giuseppe was found dead from a gunshot outside the site. Striker William Durham was loitering near a non-striker's house, which had been partly destroyed by dynamite the previous week, when a soldier ordered him to halt. He refused, and the soldier shot him dead.

February 1903, Stanaford, West Virginia. A volunteer armed posse of thirty led by federal, county and labour detectives launched a dawn raid against a houseful of black striking coalminers, shooting three of them dead. Another three white strikers were also killed in related violence.

June 1904, Dunnville, Colorado, rock mining strike. On 8 June, 130 armed soldiers and deputies went to the small mining camp of Dunnville, 14 miles south of Victor, to arrest union miners. When they arrived, sixty-five miners were stationed behind rocks and trees on the hills above the soldiers. One of the miners shot at the troops, who returned fire. In seven minutes of steady gunfire, miner John Carley was killed. The better-armed soldiers prevailed, and arrested fourteen of the miners.

April–July 1905, Chicago garment workers and teamsters strike. Riots erupted on 7 April and continued almost daily until mid-July. Sometimes thousands of striking workers would clash with strike-breakers and armed police each day. When the strike ended, twenty-one people had been killed and 416 injured.

February 1907, Milwaukee, Wisconsin, ironworking strike. Strike leader Peter J. Cramer of the International Molders Union was targeted and severely beaten by labour detectives. Months later he died of his injuries.

May 1907, San Francisco streetcar strike. United Railroads contracted with the nationally known 'King of the Strikebreakers', James Farley, for 400 replacement workers. Farley's armed workers took control of the entire streetcar system. A shootout on Turk Street left two dead and about twenty injured. Of thirty-one deaths from shootings and streetcar accidents, twenty-five were among passengers.

December 1908, Stearns, Kentucky, coal organising drive. On Christmas Day US Marshals battled a number of union organisers at the McFerrin Hotel in Stearns as they sought to arrest Berry Simpson. The hotel was set ablaze by order of the marshal, leaving the hotel burned out, many wounded, and two shot dead: Deputy US Marshal John Mullins and organiser Richard Ross.

May 1909, Great Lakes maritime worker strike. Three maritime unions, primarily the Lake Seamen's Union, struck a multi-state Great Lakes shipping cartel called the Lake Carriers' Association. By late November 1909 five union members had been shot and killed by strike-breakers and private police. The strike dragged on fruitlessly until 1912.

August 1909, McKees Rocks, Pennsylvania, rock mining strike. At least twelve people died and more than fifty were wounded when strikers battled with private security agents and Pennsylvania State Police mounted on horseback.

March 1910–July 1911, Westmoreland County, Pennsylvania, coalmining strike. In Yukon township, as twenty-five sheriff's deputies and state police vainly searched a boarding house, a crowd of striking miners gathered and ridiculed them. The deputies then fired into the crowd, killing one and injuring thirty. In Export, miners who were walking home passed by coal company property. Twenty sheriff's deputies and state police attacked and severely beat them. One miner, trying to protect a child in his arms, was killed. In another incident, state police stopped four immigrant miners who did not speak English to question them. A bilingual miner came by and told the four to leave, but the troopers chased, shot and killed the fifth man, allegedly in cold blood.

July 1910, South Greensburg, striking miners had obtained a permit to march, but as they began, deputy sheriffs on horseback stopped them. In defiance of the local police chief, the deputies charged with their horses, swinging clubs and then firing into the crowd, killing a miner.

July 1910, Brooklyn, New York, sugar manufacturing strike. A striking worker, Walla Noblowsky, was shot multiple times and died instantly when a strike against the American Sugar Refining Company turned violent, with outnumbered police dodging bricks thrown from tenement roofs. Thirty more were hurt.

December 1910, Chicago garment workers strike. Two of the five fatalities were strikers killed by private detectives.

January 1912, Lawrence, Massachusetts, textile strike. A police officer fired into a crowd of strikers, killing Anna LoPizzo.

March 1912, San Diego, California, free speech protest. Michael Hoy died after a police assault in jail, and Joseph Mikolash was killed by police in the IWW headquarters.

April 1912–July 1913, Kanawa County, West Virginia, mining strike. In what became known as the 'Paint Creek Mine War', twelve miners were killed on 26 July 1912 at Mucklow. Later, the county sheriff's posse attacked the Holly Grove miners' camp with machine guns, killing striker Cesco Estep. Allegedly, many more than fifty deaths among miners and their families were indirectly caused, as a result of starvation and malnutrition.

July 1912, Grabow, Louisiana, lumber strike. Galloway Lumber Company guards fired on striking demonstrators of the Brotherhood of Timber Workers, resulting in four dead and fifty wounded.

April 1913, Hopedale, Massachusetts, automatic loom manufacturing strike. Worker Emidio Bacchiocci was killed while picketing during strike at the Draper Company.

June 1913, New Orleans banana strike. Police shot at maritime workers who were striking against the United Fruit Company, killing one and wounding two more.

June 1913, Patterson, New Jersey, textile strike. Bystander Valentino Modestino was fatally shot by a private guard, and striking worker Vincenzo Madonna was shot dead shot by a strike-breaker.

August 1913, Seeberville, Michigan, copper strike. Sheriff's deputies visited a boarding house to arrest one of the boarders who had trespassed on company property while taking a shortcut home. The suspect, John Kalan, resisted arrest and went inside. As the deputies prepared to leave, someone tossed a bowling pin at them. They deputies opened fire into the crowded home, killing Alois Tijan and Steve Putich and injuring two others. The people inside the house were unarmed.

October 1913–December 1914, Trinidad to Walsenburg, southern Colorado, coal strike. Amid escalating violence and pressure from mine operators, the governor called out the National Guard. After the Ludlow Massacre (see below), striking miners at the other tent colonies went to war for ten days. They attacked and destroyed mines, and fought pitched battles with mine guards and militia along a 40-mile front. The strike ended in defeat, and up to forty-seven are estimated to have been killed in addition to the Ludlow Massacre.

November 1913, Indianapolis streetcar strike. When strike-breakers attempted to move streetcars into their carhouses, a crowd attacked. Four were shot dead.

April 1914, Ludlow mining strike. On Greek Easter morning, 177 company guards engaged by John D. Rockerfeller Junior and other mine operators, and sworn into the state militia for the occasion, attacked a union tent camp with machine guns, then set it afire. Luka Vahernik, fifty, was shot in the head. Louis Tikas and two other miners were captured, shot and killed by the militia. Five miners, two women and twelve children in total died in the massacre.

January 1915, Carteret, New Jersey, fertiliser manufacturing strike. In an unprovoked attack, forty deputies fired on strikers, killing five, at the Williams & Clark Fertilizing Company after the strikers had stopped a train to check for strike-breakers.

July 1915, Bayonne, New Jersey, oil strike. During a strike at Standard Oil and Tidewater Petroleum, armed strike-breakers protected by police fired into a crowd of strikers and sympathisers, killing four workers.

August 1915, Massena, New York, aluminium strike. In 1915 workers revolted at the Mellon family's aluminium mill and took over the plant. New York Governor Whitman sent in three companies of the state militia, armed with bayonets, to disperse a crowd of hundreds. The following day, striker Joseph Solunski died of a gunshot wound in an Ogdensburg hospital.

January 1916, East Youngstown, Ohio, steel strike. When two trainloads of strike-breakers from the South were smuggled into the Youngstown Sheet & Tube Co. plant, angry strikers assembled at the mill gates. Guards fired into the crowd, killing three strikers.

May 1916, Braddock, Pennsylvania, steel strike. Strikers had arranged to parade outside the Carnegie Steel Co. plant, but the company stationed an armed force inside the plant. They opened fire, shooting strikers and bystanders. Two strikers were killed.

June–July 1916, Chisolm, Minnesota, iron mining strike. Virginia miner John Alar was shot and killed in a confrontation between police and pickets. Another clash between guards and several strikers left a guard and a bystander dead.

November 1916, Everett, Washington. Two hundred citizen deputies of the Snohomish County sheriff waited for the arrival by passenger ship of IWW workers coming to support local strikers and opened fire from the dock. That sparked a ten-minute gun battle after which the IWW listed five dead with twenty-seven wounded, although as many as twelve members may have been killed – some were last seen drowning in the harbour waters. According to some reports, two deputies were killed by fellow deputies.

February 1917, Philadelphia sugar strike. Mill striker Martinus Petkus was killed and many badly beaten.

May 1917, Riverside, Oregon, sheep shearing strike. A negotiator for the strikers named Shoemaker was shot and killed by a sheep rancher.

August 1919, Charlotte, North Carolina, streetcar strike. Five men were killed, and more than a dozen wounded by police guarding streetcar barns of the Southern Public Utilities Company.

1919, several steel strikes. Eighteen strikers were killed, hundreds seriously injured, and thousands jailed. In August, in Brackenridge, Pennsylvania, United Mine Workers' organiser Fannie Sellins was riddled with bullets by Steel Trust gunmen on the eve of a nationwide steel strike. Joseph Starzelski, a miner, was also gunned down that same day. In September, in Hammond, Indiana, striking workers of the Standard Steel Car Company clashed with local police and company guards sworn in as police. Three strikers and one soldier were killed, and another fifty wounded.

April 1920, Butte, Montana, copper strike. A mining strike was suppressed with gunfire when deputised mine guards suddenly fired upon unarmed picketers. Seventeen were shot in the back as they tried to flee, and one man died.

May 1920, Matewan, West Virginia, coal strike. Baldwin-Felts agents and thirteen of the mining company's managers arrived to evict miners and their families from the mine camp. Chief of Police Sid Hatfield tried to arrest the detectives for illegally evicting miners and carrying weapons. A gun battle ensued, resulting in the deaths of seven agents, two miners, and Mayor Cabell Testerman. Hatfield was later gunned down on the steps of a courthouse by company goons.

1920, Philadelphia shipping strike. Five were killed and twenty injured in a longshoremen's strike.

October 1920, Hannaford, North Dakota, railroad strike. Joe Bagley, a well-known member of the IWW, was shot and killed by Special Agent Nolan of the Great Northern railway.

December 1920, Walker County, Alabama, coal strike. Local union official Adrian Northcutt of Nauvo was summoned out of his home by soldiers of Company M of the Alabama Guard, who fired seven shots, killing him. At least sixteen people died during the strike.

Appendix 2

Omaha Race Riot

During the last phase of the Red Summer, in Omaha, Nebraska, federal investigators had noted that 'a clash was imminent owing to ill-feeling between white and black workers in the stockyards'. The major meatpacking plants hired blacks as strike-breakers in 1917, resulting in hostility among working-class whites. The reformist agenda of first-term reform mayor Edward Parsons Smith was opposed by both the city's criminal establishment led by Tom Dennison and the Omaha Business Men's Association. Smith pushed through reforms with little support from the Omaha City Council or the city's labour unions. Along with several strikes throughout the previous year, on 11 September two detectives with the Omaha Police Department's 'morals squad' shot and killed an African American bellhop.

The local media sensationalised the alleged rape of nineteen-year-old Agnes Loebeck on 25 September 1919. The following day the police arrested forty-one-year-old Will Brown as a suspect. The *Omaha Bee* publicised the incident as one of a series of alleged attacks on white women by black men. The *Bee* was controlled by a political machine opposed to the newly elected reform administration of Mayor Smith.

Early afternoon, Sunday, 28 September, a large group of white youths gathered near the Bancroft School and began a march to the Douglas County Courthouse, where Brown was being held. The march was intercepted by John T. Dunn, chief of the Omaha Detective Bureau, who attempted to disperse the crowd, but they ignored his warnings. Thirty officers guarding the courthouse bantered with the crowd until the police were convinced that they posed no serious threat. A report to that effect was made to the central police station, and the captain in charge sent fifty reserve officers home for the day.

By 5 p.m., a mob of about 4,000 whites had crowded into the street on the south side of the courthouse. They began to assault the police, pushing one through a pane of glass in a door and attacking two others who had shaken clubs at them. Officers deployed fire hoses, but the crowd responded with a shower of bricks and sticks. Nearly every window on the south side of the courthouse was broken. The crowd stormed the lower doors, and the police inside fired down an elevator shaft in an attempt to frighten them, but this further incited the mob. They again rushed the police who were standing guard outside the building, broke through their lines, and entered the courthouse through a broken basement door.

Chief of police Marshal Eberstein asked the ringleaders to give him a chance to talk to the crowd. He mounted to one of the window sills alongside one of the recognised mob chiefs, and the crowd fell briefly silent. Chief Eberstein told the mob that its mission would best be served by letting justice take its course but the crowd howled him down. They swarmed about the courthouse on all sides, snatching revolvers, badges and caps from policemen. They chased and beat every black who ventured into the vicinity. The police had lost control of the crowd.

By early evening, most of the police had withdrawn to the interior of the courthouse, joining forces with Michael Clark, sheriff of Douglas County, who had summoned his deputies to the building to prevent the capture of Brown. They formed their line of last resistance on the fourth floor. They failed. Shortly before 8 p.m., the crowd set the courthouse on fire, having tapped a nearby gasoline filling station and saturated the lower floors with the flammable liquid. Shots were fired as the mob pillaged hardware stores in the business district and entered pawnshops, seeking firearms. More than 1,000 revolvers and shotguns were stolen that night. Seven officers were wounded by gunshot, none of them seriously. The mob also suffered. Louis Young, sixteen years old, was fatally shot in the stomach while leading a gang up to the fourth floor of the building. Witnesses said the youth was the most intrepid of the mob's leaders.

Pandemonium reigned outside the building. At Seventeenth and Douglas Streets, one block from the court house, James Hiykel, a thirty-four-year-old businessman, was shot and killed. The crowd continued to strike the courthouse with bullets and rocks. Spectators were shot. Participants inflicted minor wounds upon themselves. Women were thrown to the ground and trampled. Blacks were dragged from streetcars and beaten.

About 11 p.m., when the frenzy was at its height, Mayor Edward Smith came out of the east door of the courthouse into Seventeenth Street. He had been in the burning building for hours. As he emerged from the doorway, a shot rang out. 'He shot me. Mayor Smith shot me,' a young man in a US military uniform yelled. The crowd surged toward the mayor. He fought them. One man hit the mayor on the head with a baseball bat. Another slipped the noose of a rope around his neck. The crowd started to drag him away. 'If you must hang somebody, then let it be me,' the mayor said. The mob pulled him into Harney Street. A woman reached out and tore the noose from his neck. Men replaced it. Spectators wrestled the mayor from his captors and placed him in a police automobile. The throng overturned the car and grabbed him again. Once more, the rope encircled the mayor's neck. He was carried to Sixteenth and Harney Streets. There he was hanged from the metal arm of a traffic signal tower. He was suspended in the air when State Agent Ben Danbaum drove a high-powered automobile into the throng right to the base of the signal tower. With him were three detectives who grasped the mayor and untied the noose. The detectives brought the mayor to Ford Hospital. There he lingered between life and death for several days, finally recovering. 'They shall not get him. Mob rule will not prevail in Omaha,' the mayor kept muttering during his delirium.[1]

Meanwhile, the plight of the police in the court house had become desperate. The fire had licked its way to the third floor. The officers faced the prospect of roasting to death. Appeals for help to the crowd below brought only bullets and curses. The mob frustrated all attempts to raise ladders to the imprisoned police. 'Bring Brown with you and you can come down,' somebody in the crowd shouted.

On the second floor of the building, three policemen and a newspaper reporter were imprisoned in a safety vault. The four men hacked their way out through the courthouse wall. The mob shot at them as they squirmed out of the stifling vault. The gases of formaldehyde added to the terrors of the men imprisoned within the flaming building. Several jars of the powerful chemical had burst on the stairway. Its deadly fumes mounted to the upper floors. Two policemen were overcome.

Sheriff Clark led his prisoners – 121 of them – to the roof. Will Brown became hysterical. Some black fellow prisoners tried to throw him off the roof but were foiled by two deputies. Sheriff Clark ordered that female prisoners be taken from the building due to their distress. They ran down the burning staircases clad only in prison pyjamas. Some fainted on the way down. Members of the mob escorted them through the smoke and flames.[2]

The mob poured more gasoline into the building. They cut every line of hose that firemen laid from nearby hydrants. The flames were rapidly lapping their way upward. It seemed like certain cremation for the prisoners and their protectors. Then three slips of paper were thrown from the fourth floor on the west side of the building. On one piece was scrawled: 'The judge says he will give up Negro Brown. He is in dungeon. There are 100 white prisoners on the roof. Save them.' Another note read: 'Come to the fourth floor of the building and we will hand the negro over to you.'

The mob in the street shrieked its delight. Boys and young men placed firemen's ladders against the building and climbed to the second story. One had a heavy coil of new rope on his back; another had a shotgun. A shout and a fusillade of shots were heard from the south side of the building – Will Brown had been captured. A few minutes later his lifeless body was hanging from a telephone pole at Eighteenth and Harney Streets. Hundreds of revolvers and shotguns were fired at the corpse as it dangled in mid-air. Then, the rope was cut. Brown's body was tied to the rear end of an automobile and dragged through the streets to Seventeenth and Dodge Streets, four blocks away. The oil from red lanterns used as danger signals for street repairs was poured on the corpse and set alight. Members of the mob hauled the charred remains through the business district for several hours. Sheriff Clark said that black prisoners hurled Brown into the hands of the mob as its leaders approached the stairway leading to the county jail. Clark also reported that Brown moaned, 'I am innocent, I never did it; my God, I am innocent.'

The lawlessness continued for several hours after Brown had been lynched. The police emergency automobile was burned. Three times, the mob went to the city jail. The third time its leaders announced that they were going to burn it. Soldiers arrived before they could carry out their threat. The riot lasted until 3 a.m. on 29 September. Federal troops, under command of Colonel John E. Morris of the Twentieth Infantry, arrived from Fort Omaha and Fort Crook. Troops manning machine guns were placed in the heart of Omaha's business district; in North Omaha, the centre of the black community, to protect citizens there; and in South Omaha, to prevent more mobs from forming. Major General Leonard Wood, commander of the Central Department, came the next day to Omaha by order of Secretary of War Newton D. Baker. Peace was enforced by 1,600 soldiers.

Martial law was not formally proclaimed in Omaha, but it was effectively enacted throughout the city. By the request of City Commissioner W. G. Ure, who was acting mayor, Wood took over control over the police department, too. On 1 October 1919 Brown was laid to rest in Omaha's Potters Field. The interment log listed only one word next to his name: 'Lynched'.[3]

Appendix 3

Tulsa Race Riot

On 31 May and 1 June 1921, members of the white community of Greenwood in Tulsa, Oklahoma, rioted, killing up to 300 black people. The attack, carried out on the ground and by air, destroyed more than thirty-five blocks of the district, the wealthiest black community in the US. More than 800 people were injured and more than 6,000 black residents were arrested and detained.[1] The official count of the dead by the Oklahoma Bureau of Vital Statistics was thirty-nine. In 2001 the state-appointed Tulsa Race Riot Commission recommended reparations to survivors and their descendants because the city had conspired with the mob.[2] But the massacre was long omitted from local and state histories: 'The Tulsa race riot of 1921 was rarely mentioned in history books, classrooms or even in private. Blacks and whites alike grew into middle age unaware of what had taken place.'[3]

Post-First World War north-eastern Oklahoma was racially and politically tense. The territory, which was declared a state on 16 November 1907, had received many settlers from the South who had been slaveholders before the Civil War. In the thirteen years after the declaration of statehood, thirty-one people were lynched in Oklahoma; twenty-six were black and nearly all were men and boys. The new state legislature passed racial segregation laws and voter registration rules that disenfranchised most blacks and barred them from serving on juries or holding local office. In 1916, Tulsa passed an ordinance that mandated residential segregation by forbidding blacks from residing on any block where three-quarters of the residents were white. Although the US Supreme Court declared the ordinance unconstitutional the next year, it remained on the books. Since 1915, during a time of rising unemployment, the Ku Klux Klan had been growing in urban chapters across the country, particularly since veterans had been returning from the war in Europe. By the end of 1921, of Tulsa's 72,000 residents, 3,200 were Klan members.[4]

The traditionally black district of Greenwood in Tulsa had a commercial area so prosperous that it was known as 'the Negro Wall Street'. Blacks had created their own businesses and services, including several grocery stores, two independent newspapers, two movie theatres, nightclubs, and numerous churches. Black professionals – doctors, dentists, lawyers, and clergy – served the community. Blacks selected their own leaders and raised capital there to support economic growth. In the surrounding areas of north-eastern Oklahoma, blacks also enjoyed relative prosperity and participated in the oil boom.

On Memorial Day, Monday, 30 May 1921, sometime around or after 4 p.m., nineteen-year-old Dick Rowland, a black man employed at a Main Street shine parlour, entered the only elevator of the nearby Drexel Building, at 319 South Main Street, to use the top-floor restroom, which was restricted to blacks. He encountered Sarah Page, the seventeen-year-old white elevator operator who was on duty. The building was the only one nearby with a washroom that Rowland had permission to use, and the elevator operated by Page was the only one in the building. A clerk at Renberg's, a clothing store located on the first floor of the Drexel, heard what sounded like a woman's scream and saw a young black man rushing from the building. The clerk went to the elevator and found Page in what he said was a distraught state. Thinking she had been assaulted, he summoned the authorities. The official commission report from 2000 noted that it was unusual for both Rowland and Page to be working downtown on Memorial Day, when most stores and businesses were closed. It suggested that Rowland had a simple accident, such as tripping and steadying himself against the girl, or perhaps they had quarreled.[5]

Whether – and to what extent – Dick Rowland and Sarah Page knew each other has long been a matter of speculation. Some suggested that the pair might have been lovers – a dangerous and potentially deadly relationship, but not an impossibility. Everyone who knew Dick Rowland agreed on one thing: that he would never have been capable of rape. Although the police would have questioned Page, no written account of her statement has survived. It is generally accepted that they decided that whatever happened between the two teenagers was something less than an assault. The authorities conducted a low-key investigation rather than launching a man-hunt for her alleged assailant. Afterward, Page told the police that she would not press charges. Regardless of whether assault had occurred, Rowland had reason to be fearful. He fled to his mother's house in Greenwood.

The following morning, Detective Henry Carmichael and Patrolman Henry C. Pack, one of two black officers on the city's forty-five-man police force, found Rowland on Greenwood Avenue and detained him. He was initially taken to the Tulsa city jail at First and Main. Late that day, Police Commissioner J. M. Adkison received an anonymous telephone call threatening Rowland's life and ordered him transferred to the more secure jail on the top floor of the Tulsa County Courthouse. Word quickly spread in Tulsa's legal circles. As patrons of the shine shop where Rowland worked, many attorneys knew him. Witnesses recounted hearing several attorneys defending him in personal conversations with one another. One of the men said, 'Why, I know that boy, and have known him a good while. That's not in him.'[6]

The *Tulsa Tribune*, one of two white-owned local newspapers, broke the story in that afternoon's edition with the headline 'Nab Negro for Attacking Girl in an Elevator'. The same edition included an editorial warning entitled 'To Lynch Negro Tonight'.[7] The afternoon edition hit the streets shortly after 3 p.m., and soon news of the potential lynching spread. By 4 p.m., the local authorities were on alert. White people began congregating at and near the Tulsa County Courthouse. By sunset, the several hundred whites assembled outside the courthouse as a lynch mob. Willard M. McCullough, the newly elected sheriff of Tulsa County, was determined to avoid a repeat of the lynching of white murder suspect Roy Belton in Tulsa the previous year. The sheriff put six men, armed with rifles and shotguns, on the roof, disabled the building's elevator, and had his remaining men barricade themselves at the top of the stairs with orders to shoot any intruders on sight. The sheriff went outside and tried to talk the crowd into going home, without success. About 8.20 p.m., three white men entered the courthouse, demanding that Rowland be turned over to them. Although vastly outnumbered by the growing crowd out on the street, Sheriff McCullough turned the men away.

A few blocks away on Greenwood Avenue, members of the black community were gathering, rightly believing that the terrified Rowland was greatly at risk. The community was determined to prevent the lynching but divided about the tactics to be used. Young black First

World War veterans were preparing for a battle, collecting guns and ammunition. Older, more prosperous men feared a destructive confrontation that would cost them dearly. O. W. Gurley walked to the courthouse, where the sheriff assured him that there would be no lynching. Returning to Greenwood, Gurley tried to calm the group, but failed. About 7.30 p.m., a group of thirty black men, armed with rifles and shotguns, went to the courthouse to support the sheriff and his deputies. Assuring them that Rowland was safe, the sheriff and his black deputy, Barney Cleaver, told them to return home.[8]

Having seen the armed blacks, some of the more than 1,000 whites at the courthouse went home for their own guns. Others headed for the National Guard armoury at Sixth Street and Norfolk Avenue. Major James Bell of the 180th Infantry confronted a crowd of 300 to 400 men and told them that the Guard members inside were armed and prepared to shoot anyone who tried to enter. After this show of force, the crowd withdrew. At the courthouse, the crowd had swollen to nearly 2,000, many of them now armed. Several local leaders, including Reverend Charles W. Kerr, pastor of the First Presbyterian Church, tried to dissuade mob action. The chief of police, John A. Gustafson, later claimed that he tried to talk the crowd into going home.

Anxiety on Greenwood Avenue was rising. Small groups of armed black men began to venture toward the courthouse in automobiles, partly for reconnaissance, and to demonstrate they were prepared to take necessary action to protect Rowland. Many white men interpreted these actions as a 'Negro uprising'. Eyewitnesses reported gunshots, presumably fired into the air, increasing in frequency during the evening.

In Greenwood, rumours began to fly – in particular, a report that whites were storming the courthouse. Shortly after 10 p.m., a second, larger group of around seventy-five armed black men again offered their support to the sheriff, who again declined their help. A white man is alleged to have told one of the armed black men to surrender his pistol. The man refused, and a shot was fired. That first shot may have been accidental or meant as a warning shot; either way, it was a catalyst for an exchange of gunfire.

The gunshots triggered an almost immediate response by the whites. Within seconds several whites and two blacks lay dead or dying in the street. The black contingent retreated toward Greenwood and a rolling gunfight ensued. The armed white mob pursued the black group toward Greenwood, with many stopping to loot local stores for additional weapons and ammunition. Along the way innocent bystanders, many of whom were leaving a movie house after a show, were caught up in the tumult and began fleeing. Panic set in as the white mob began firing on any blacks in the crowd. The mob also shot and killed at least one white man in the confusion.

At around 11 p.m., members of the Oklahoma National Guard unit began to assemble at the armoury. Several groups were deployed downtown to set up guard at the courthouse, police station and other public facilities. Members of the local chapter of the American Legion joined patrols of the streets. The forces appeared to have been deployed to protect the white districts adjacent to Greenwood, in apparent opposition to the black community. The Guard began rounding up blacks who had not returned to Greenwood and took them to the Convention Hall on Brady Street for detention. Many prominent Tulsa whites also participated in the riot, including Tulsa founder and KKK member W. Tate Brady, a nightwatchman. He reported seeing 'five dead negroes', including one man who was dragged behind a car by a noose around his neck.

At around midnight, white rioters again assembled outside the courthouse; it was a smaller group than previously, but more organised and determined. When they attempted to storm the building, the sheriff and his deputies turned them away. Throughout the early morning hours of Wednesday 1 June, groups of armed whites and blacks squared off in gunfights. The fighting was concentrated along sections of the Frisco tracks, a dividing line between the black and white commercial districts. A rumour circulated that more blacks were coming by train from Muskogee to help with an invasion of Tulsa. At one point, passengers on an incoming train were forced to take cover on the floor of the train cars, caught in a crossfire, with the train taking hits on both sides. Small groups of whites made brief forays by car into Greenwood, indiscriminately firing into businesses and residences. They often received return fire. Meanwhile, white rioters threw lighted oil rags into several buildings along Archer Street, igniting them.

The arson spread, mainly targeting businesses on commercial Archer Street at the southern edge of Greenwood, and crews from the Tulsa Fire Department were turned away at gunpoint. By 4 a.m., an estimated two-dozen black-owned businesses had been set ablaze. As news travelled among Greenwood residents in the early morning hours, many began to take up arms in defence of their community, while others began a mass exodus from the city.

At 5 a.m., sunrise, a train whistle was heard. Many believed this to be a signal for the rioters to launch an all-out assault on Greenwood.

A white man stepped out from behind the Frisco depot and received a fatal bullet from a sniper in Greenwood. Crowds of rioters poured from places of shelter, on foot and by car, into the streets of the black community. Five white men in a car led the charge, but were killed by a fusillade of gunfire before they had gone a block.

Overwhelmed by the sheer number of whites, more blacks retreated north on Greenwood Avenue to the edge of town. Chaos ensued as terrified residents fled for their lives. The rioters shot indiscriminately and killed many residents along the way. Splitting into small groups, they began breaking into houses and buildings, looting. Several blacks later testified that whites broke into occupied homes and ordered the residents out to the street, where they could be driven or forced to walk to detention centres. A rumour spread among the whites that the new Mount Zion Baptist Church was being used as a fortress and armoury.

Numerous eyewitnesses described airplanes carrying white assailants, who fired rifles and dropped firebombs on buildings, homes, and fleeing families. Six biplane two-seater trainers left over from the war were dispatched from the nearby Curtiss-Southwest Field outside Tulsa. Law enforcement officials later stated that the planes were to provide reconnaissance and protect against a 'Negro uprising'. Eyewitness accounts and testimony from the survivors maintained that on the morning of 1 June, the planes dropped incendiary bombs and fired rifles at black residents on the ground.[9]

In a ten-page typewritten manuscript which only surfaced in 2015, Oklahoma attorney Buck Colbert Franklin recalled standing in his office, watching 'planes circling in mid-air'. He went on: 'They grew in number and hummed, darted and dipped low. I could hear something like hail falling upon the top of my office building. Down East Archer, I saw the old Mid-Way hotel on fire, burning from its top, and then another and another and another building began to burn from their top.' What he saw was a city under siege: 'Lurid flames roared and belched and licked their forked tongues into the air. Smoke ascended the sky in thick, black volumes and amid it all, the planes—now a dozen or more in number—still hummed and darted here and there with the agility of natural birds of the air.' Making his way outside, Franklin found the source of the strange sound that had peppered his building. 'The side-walks were literally covered with burning turpentine balls. I knew all too well where they came from, and I knew all too well why every burning building first caught from the top.' Franklin reported the droning of planes, the spattering of turpentine balls as they rained down upon homes and hospitals, offices and shops, the roar of the conflagration that eventually consumed the district. He added: 'I paused and waited for an opportune time to escape. "Where oh where is our splendid fire department with its half dozen stations?" I asked myself. "Is the city in conspiracy with the mob?"'

Several groups of blacks attempted to organize a defence, but they were overwhelmed by the number of armed whites. Many blacks surrendered, others returned fire and were killed. As the fires spread northward through Greenwood, black families continued to flee. Many died when trapped by the flames.

As unrest spread to other parts of the city, many middle-class white families who employed blacks in their homes as live-in cooks and servants were accosted by white rioters. They demanded that families turn over their employees to be taken to detention centres around the city. Many white families complied, and those who refused were subjected to attacks and vandalism. National Guard Adjutant General Charles Barrett arrived with 109 troops from Oklahoma City by special train about 9.15 a.m. He could not legally act until he had contacted all the appropriate local authorities, including mayor T. D. Evans, the sheriff and the police chief. Meanwhile, his troops paused to eat breakfast. Barrett summoned reinforcements from several other Oklahoma cities. By this time, most of the surviving black citizens had either fled the city or were in custody at the various detention centres. The troops declared martial law, and by noon had managed to suppress most of the remaining violence. A 1921 letter from an Officer of the Service Company, Third Infantry, Oklahoma National Guard arriving 31 May 1921, reported taking about thirty to forty African Americans into custody; putting a machine gun on a truck and sending it on patrol; being fired on by black snipers from the 'Church' and returning fire; being fired on by white men; turning the prisoners over to deputies to take them to police headquarters; being fired upon again by blacks and having two NCOs slightly wounded; searching for blacks and firearms; detailing a NCO to take 170 blacks to the civil authorities; and then delivering an additional 150 blacks to the Convention Hall.[10]

The reported number of dead varies widely. On 1 June 1921, the *Tulsa Tribune* reported that nine whites and sixty-eight blacks had died, but shortly afterward changed this to a total of 176 dead. The *New York Times* said that seventy-seven people had been killed, including sixty-eight blacks, but then lowered the total to thirty-three. The *Richmond Times Dispatch* reported that eighty-five people (including twenty-five whites) were killed; it also reported that the police chief had reported to Governor Robertson that the total was seventy-five; and that a police major put the figure at 175. The Oklahoma Department of Vital Statistics count put the number of dead at thirty-six (twenty-six black and ten white), with other estimates in Red Cross documents running as high as 300.[11] Walter Francis White of the NAACP reported that although officials and undertakers reported the numbers of fatalities as ten white and twenty-one coloured, he estimated the numbers to be fifty whites and between 150 and 200 blacks;[12] he also reported that ten white men were killed on Tuesday; six white men drove into the black section and never came out; and that thirteen whites were killed on Wednesday. He reported that the head of the Salvation Army in Tulsa stated that thirty-seven blacks were employed as gravediggers to bury 120 blacks in individual graves without coffins on Friday and Saturday. Maurice Willows, an American Red Cross social worker, reported that up to 300 blacks were killed. He also reported that there was a rush to bury the bodies and that no records were made of many burials.

Of the 800 people admitted to local hospitals for injuries, the majority were white, as both black hospitals had been burned in the rioting. Additionally, even if the white hospitals had admitted blacks because of the riot, against their usual segregation policy, injured blacks had little means to get to these hospitals, which were located across the city from Greenwood. More than 6,000 black Greenwood residents were arrested and detained at three local facilities: Convention Hall, now known as the Brady Theater, the Fairgrounds (then located about a mile north-east of Greenwood), and McNulty Park (a baseball stadium at Tenth Street and Elgin Avenue). Several blacks were known to have died while in the internment centres. While most of the deaths are said to have been accurately recorded, no records have been found as to how many detainees were treated for injuries and survived. These numbers could reasonably have been more than a thousand, perhaps several thousand.

The commercial section of Greenwood was destroyed. This included 191 businesses, a junior high school, several churches and the only hospital in the district. The Red Cross reported that 1,256 houses were burned and another 215 were looted but not burned. The Tulsa Real Estate Exchange estimated property losses amounted to $1.5 million in real estate and $750,000 in personal property ($30 million in 2016). Local citizens had filed more than $1.8 million in riot-related claims against the city by 6 June 1922

A grand jury in Tulsa ruled that Police Chief John Gustafson was responsible for the riot because he neglected his duty, and removed him from office. In a subsequent trial, he was found guilty of failing to take proper precautions for protecting life and property, and for conspiring to free automobile thieves and collect rewards. But the former chief never served time in prison; instead, he returned to his private detective practice. No legal records indicate that any other white official was ever charged of wrongdoing or even negligence. Dick Rowland remained safe in the county jail until the next morning, when the police transported him out of town in secrecy. All charges were dropped. He never returned to Tulsa. No charges were filed against individual white rioters. Other lawsuits against insurance companies for losses were unsuccessful as well.[13]

The division between white and black residents of Tulsa was so deep that the end of the riot did not begin to bring reconciliation. The widespread destruction of Greenwood was not sufficient for those whites who wanted to separate even further from blacks. A week after the riot, W. Tate Brady was appointed to the Tulsa Real Estate Exchange. The Tulsa Chamber of Commerce had created the group to estimate the value of property damaged or destroyed in Greenwood. The Exchange also contrived a scheme to relocate black Tulsans farther north and east of the original Greenwood. In cooperation with the City Commission, the Exchange prepared new building codes for the original Greenwood that would make rebuilding prohibitively expensive for the original owners. The land could then be redeveloped as a commercial and industrial district. The plan was never implemented because the Oklahoma Supreme Court overruled the proposed ordinances as unconstitutional.

In 1996, following increased attention to the riot because of its seventy-fifth anniversary, the state legislature authorised the 1921 Race Riot Commission, to study and prepare a 'historical account' of the riot. The study 'enjoyed strong support from members of both political parties and all political persuasions'. The commission delivered its report on 21 February 2001. In addition to thoroughly documenting the causes of the riot and the damage wrought, the report recommended actions for substantial restitution to the black community; in order of priority: direct payment of reparations to survivors of the 1921 Tulsa race riot; direct payment of reparations to descendants of the survivors of the Tulsa race riot; a scholarship fund available to students affected by the Tulsa race riot; establishment of an economic development enterprise zone in the historic area of the Greenwood district; and a memorial for the reburial of the remains of the victims of the Tulsa race riot.

In June 2001, the Oklahoma state legislature passed the '1921 Tulsa Race Riot Reconciliation Act'. While falling short of the commission's recommendations, it provided for the following: more than 300 college scholarships for descendants of Greenwood residents; creation of a memorial to those who died in the riot, which was dedicated on 27 October 2010; and economic development in Greenwood. The state government has made limited attempts to find suspected mass graves used to bury the unknown numbers of black dead. The commission reported that it was not authorised to undertake the necessary work to verify the claims. Five elderly survivors of the riot filled suit against the city of Tulsa and the state of Oklahoma in February 2003, based on the findings of the 2001 report. Ogletree said the state and city should compensate the victims and their families 'to honor their admitted obligations as detailed in the commission's report'.[14] The federal district and appellate courts dismissed the suit, citing the statute of limitations. The Supreme Court declined to hear the appeal.

Appendix 4

Selected Filmography

THE GANGS OF NEW YORK (2002)

Growing up in New York in the 1950s, Martin Scorsese became fascinated by the older architecture of the city, including tombstones from the beginning of the nineteenth century. He later recalled: 'I gradually realized that the Italian Americans weren't the first ones there, that other people had been there before us. As I began to understand this, it fascinated me. I kept wondering, how did New York look? What were the people like? How did they walk, eat, work, dress?' In 1970, he came across Herbert Asbury's book *The Gangs of New York: An Informal History of the Underworld* (1928) about the city's criminal underworld. He saw in it the potential for an American epic about the battle for the modern American democracy.

After his directorial successes with *Mean Streets* (1973) and *Taxi Driver* (1976), he acquired screen rights to Asbury's book in 1979, but it took another twenty years to start production in partnership with Miramax co-chairman Harvey Weinstein. The result was a sprawling epic starring Leonardo DiCaprio and Daniel Day-Lewis, a lavish production seen by many as a masterpiece, if a flawed one. The screenplay was by Jay Cocks, Steven Zailian and Kenneth Lonnergan.

The film is set in 1862 but conflates about twenty years of gangster history up to the Draft Riots. Day-Lewis plays Bill the Butcher, while DiCaprio is an everyman out to avenge his father, killed in a battle between the Dead Rabbits and a Nativist gang headed by the Butcher. Many real characters are featured, including Tammany Hall's 'Boss' Tweed, Happy Jack Mulraney and Hell-Cat Maggie, but the real-life Bill Poole died a decade before the film's climax. While it plays fast and loose with historical sequence and context, and uses composite characters, the film does accurately reflect the territorial wars fought between Nativists and mainly Irish immigrants, the deep hatreds involved, city hall corruption and the perceived injustices of the draft, and touches briefly on the lynching of blacks during the subsequent riots. Scorsese's recreation of the visual environment of mid-nineteenth-century New York City and the Five Points was impeccable, even though the all the massive sets were built completely on the exterior stages of Cinecittà Studios in Rome.

Scorsese summed up: 'The country was up for grabs, and New York was a powder keg. This was the America not of the West with its wide open spaces, but of claustrophobia, where everyone was crushed together. On one hand, you had the first great wave of immigration, the Irish, who were Catholic, spoke Gaelic, and owed allegiance to the Vatican. On the other hand, there were the Nativists, who felt that they were the ones who had fought and bled, and died for the nation. They looked at the Irish coming off the boats and said: "What are you doing here?" It was chaos, tribal chaos. Gradually, there was a street by street, block by block, working out of democracy as people learned somehow to live together. If democracy didn't work in New York, it wasn't going to happen anywhere.'

The $100 million film was released on 20 December 2002 and grossed $193 million worldwide. The review website Rotten Tomatoes gave the film an approval rating of 75 per cent based on 202 reviews, with an average rating of 7.1/10. The site's critical consensus reads, 'Though flawed, the sprawling, messy *Gangs of New York* is redeemed by impressive production design and Day-Lewis's electrifying performance.'

The *Guardian*'s Peter Bradshaw wrote: 'Scorsese thinks big, acts big, films big. He unfurls a magnificent, painterly canvas, on which 1846 New York is reimagined as a hyperreal wild west of the east, where the rule of law is patchy at best, peopled with brawling villains in bizarre, dreamlike top hats. Scorsese said he wanted the movie to be like a western set on Mars. It's actually like a Kubrick shocker set in a Henry James or Edith Wharton adaptation, where the dirty mob we might glimpse in the background get star status, and the highfalutin ladies and gentlemen get their windows smashed and sofas torched by feral gangsters.'

THE GODFATHER PART II (1974)
Francis Ford Coppola's masterpiece is included because of its substantial flashbacks to New York's Little Italy in the twentieth century.

Robert De Niro plays the young Vito Corleone who, as a child, was smuggled out of Sicily after a local Mafia don killed his father.

A family man, he loses his job due to the nepotism of an extortionist capo, and slips into crime, finally killing him during a neighbourhood fiesta. The murder of a despised petty tyrant makes him a respected figure and, eventually, a Mafia don. He helps a widow facing eviction by pressuring the landlord, while his growing criminal empire is conducted behind the cover of an olive oil business.

The plot and characters are fictitious, but clearly based on the rise of the competing clans inNew York's melting pot. And Coppola's depiction of the hustle and bustle of the packed city streets is superb. It also reflects, as accurately as is possible, the attitudes to crime at the time and the public's mixture of both fear and respect.

Coming after the global success of *The Godfather*, critical reception was mixed, with many disliking the disjointed flow of the story. But it went on to win six Oscars, including ones for De Niro and Coppola, and another for the screenplay for Coppola and Mario Puzo, on whose novel it was based. It was also the first sequel to win best picture. Its reputation now stands as high as that of the original film. Michael Stragow's conclusion in his 2002 essay, selected for the National Film Registry, is that although both films 'depict an American family's moral defeat, as a mammoth, pioneering work of art it remains a national creative triumph'.

In North America it grossed $47.5 million on a $13 million budget.

VENDETTA (1999)

The HBO TV movie depicts the 1891 murder of eleven Italian Americans awaiting trial for the murder of a New Orleans police chief. The screenplay by British writer Timothy Prager is based on Richard Gambino's book *Vendetta: The True Story of the Largest Lynching in U.S. History*.

Directed by Nicholas Meyer and starring Christopher Walken and Luke Askew, it sanitises the lives of the victims, making them all wholly innocent, but nevertheless sticks reasonably close to the actual events. Writing in the *Journal of American History* in 2000, Clive Webb calls the movie a 'compelling portrait of prejudice'.

The lynching is discussed in the 2004 documentary *Linciati: Lynchings of Italians in America*, directed by M. Heather Hartley.

THE MOLLY MAGUIRES (1970)

Based on a 1969 novel by Arthur H. Lewis, the film was directed by Martin Ritt and stars Richard Harris and Sean Connery. The former plays the real-life undercover Pinkerton detective James McParland, sent to a coalmining community to expose the supposed secret society of Irish

Americans headed by Connery. Both are portrayed as working-class immigrants from Ireland with essentially the same aspiration – advancement in the new society to which they have come. McParland coldly betrays the group whose leader he has befriended and, at his execution, the fictitious Connery character tells him that no punishment short of hell can redeem his treachery; McParland retorts: 'See you in hell.'

The tone and look of the film is just right – it was filmed in Eckley, Pennsylvania, a town so unchanged from its 1870s appearance that the only major alterations needed for filming were to remove television antennas. The film is essentially a dialogue between its two stars about the nature of capitalism and how it can place two similar men from similar backgrounds into opposing camps, and in that respect it does reflect the dilemmas of the day.

But there is no evidence that the Mollies dynamited pits and there is little in the film which points to the sordid feuds and vendettas that were perhaps as important to the Mollies as the fight for social justice.

Even though the two stars were at the height of their popularity – with Connery newly escaped from the James Bond franchise – the film flopped at the box office, taking just $2.2 million in North America.

Critic Tom Milne wrote: 'The trouble, as so often with Ritt films, is that the situation remains interesting rather than involving. But at least this detachment means that one has the leisure to savour the textures of Wong Howe's magnificent camerawork.'

MATEWAN (1987)

A dramatisation of events leading up to the Battle of Matewan, the film was written and directed by independent filmmaker John Sayles and starred Chris Cooper, James Earl Jones and Mary McDonnell.

Cooper plays a United Mine Workers union organiser drafted into West Virginia to help striking miners and persuade mainly black workers, brought in by the company, to join the strike. The common cause made between rednecks, blacks and Italian immigrants is believably scripted and the efforts made by the company to crush them is accurate.

The Cooper character is a composite, but David Strathairn plays the real-life Sheriff Sid Hatfield who takes the side of the miners against hired gunmen brought in to kill the ringleaders. The subsequent gunfight is superbly realised, a chaotic, bloody dance of death in which no mercy is asked for or given.

Variety reported: 'Matewan is a heartfelt, straight-ahead tale of labor organizing in the coal mines of West Virginia in 1920 that runs its course like a train coming down the track. Most notable of the black workers is "Few Clothes" Johnson (James Earl Jones), a burly good-natured man with a powerful presence and a quick smile. Jones' performance practically glows in the dark. Also a standout is Sayles veteran David Strathairn as the sheriff with quiet integrity who puts his life on the line.' Critic Desson Howe wrote: 'Cinematographer Haskell Wexler etches the characters in dark charcoal against a misty background. You get the feeling of dirt, sweat and – despite the story's mythic intentions – the grim grey struggle of it all.'

The film was made in West Virginia with the town of Thurmond standing in for Matewan. Other scenes were filmed along the New River Gorge National Park.

The film was a critical success and has gained cult status, but its initial takings were disappointing – less than $2 million in America after a production budget of around $4 million.

JOE HILL (1971)

The Swedish American labour activist and songwriter Joe Hill does not feature in this book because his activities were largely in the West, and he was executed after trumped-up charges in Idaho in 1915. But this biopic by renowned Swedish director Bo Widerberg depicts Hill's arrival as a poor immigrant in New York in 1902, and his involvement with the Industrial Workers of the World.

The cast were mostly unknowns in their first film roles, including Thommy Berggren in the title role. It is the only film that Widerberg made in the US. The soundtrack includes excerpts from Joe Hill's most famous songs, including 'The Preacher and the Slave', 'There is Power in a Union' and 'Casey Jones – the Union Scab', all of which chronicle the harsh life of itinerant workers.

The film is lyrical, romantic and nostalgic, but ambiguous about Hill's culpability. Critic Robert Ebert wrote: 'Widerberg doesn't even tell us whether he thinks Joe was guilty, nor does he give us evidence so we can make up our own minds. What we're left with is a revolutionary seen as moon-struck adolescent. That, and "The Ballad of Joe Hill," written ten years after his death, in which he tells us he never died. He would if he saw this.'

The film won the Jury Prize at the Cannes film festival. *Joe Hill* was mostly unavailable commercially for nearly four decades until a restored and digitally remastered version was produced in 2015 by the National Library of Sweden.

Selected Filmography

BOLSHEVISM ON TRIAL (1919)

America's fledgling film industry exploited every aspect of the public's fascination with and fear of Bolshevism.

Directed by Harley Knoles from a screenplay by Harry Chandlee, it is based on a 1909 novel by Thomas Dixon, the author of another novel that served as the basis for D. W. Griffith's racist epic *The Birth of a Nation*.

It stars Pinna Nesbitt as a wealthy socialite with good intentions is lured into Socialist agitation and buys Paradise Island off the Florida coast to establish a collective colony, a society of 'happiness and plenty.' Her mentor takes charge, establishes a police force, abolishes marriage, and assumes ownership of the women and children. The heroine sees the light and warns: 'The poor deluded people will starve and die as they are in Russia.' The US Navy comes to the rescue and the Red Flag is replaced by the Stars and Stripes, to general acclaim.

The film's advertising called it 'the timeliest picture ever filmed.' *Photoplay* said it was 'Powerful, well-knit with indubitably true and biting satire.' A promotional stunt was devised whereby cinemas would be festooned by red flags to be torn down by actors in uniform. US Secretary of Labor William B. Wilson was appalled by the suggestion, saying: 'This publication proposes by deceptive methods of advertising to stir every community in the United States into riotous demonstrations for the purpose of making profits for the moving picture business ...'

THE PINKERTONS (2014)

The Canadian TV series, officially licensed by the modern-day Pinkertons, is a risibly sanitised police procedural supposedly based on actual cases from the detective agency's 1860s archives. Starring Martha MacIsaac as Kate Warne, the first female detective in US history, and Jacob Blair as William Pinkerton, the founder's son and fellow agent, it mainly concerns cases in a Wild West populated by teen idols in impeccably laundered clothing. In historical terms, it is an embarrassment.

But the Pinkertons have featured in numerous movies and TV shows, most of which dodge the agency's unsavoury history of strike-breaking, from *American Outlaws* (2001) featuring Allan Pinkerton himself and *Titanic* (2007) to Walter Hill's *The Long Riders* (1980) and British TV's *Ripper Street* (2012–2016)

The protagonist of the video game *BioShock Infinite*, Booker DeWitt, is an ex-Pinkerton, known for his violent methods in putting down strikes in a fictional version of the Homestead Massacre.

HATFIELDS & MCCOYS (2012)

The three-part TV mini-series, based on the generations-spanning feud, was produced by The History Channel and boasted a starry cast headed by Kevin Costner, Bill Paxton, Tom Berenger and Powers Booth. Costner directed some scenes himself to help speed the schedule along, having a long-time working relationship with series director Kevin Reynolds.

Although the story is set on the West Virginia–Kentucky border, it was shot in Romania, with the Carpathians standing in for the Appalachians. Anderson 'Devil Anse' Hatfield was twenty-two and Randell McCoy was in his thirties when the war broke out, much younger that Kevin Costner and Bill Paxton, respectively, were when filming. Devil Anse Hatfield's agnosticism of Christianity as depicted in the show is historically accurate. Devil Anse's baptism occurred in 1911, when he was seventy-two years old.

The *Los Angeles Times*'s Mary McNamara wrote: 'Although deftly nailed into its time and place with sets and costumes so vivid you can smell the blue wood smoke and the stink of moonshine sweat, *Hatfields & McCoys* transcends the confines of its age by revealing the feud's posturing, resentments and callous violence that mirror the dynamics of modern urban gangs.'

The show set a cable viewing record as the top-rated entertainment telecast, pulling in up to 14.3 million viewers respectively.

RAGTIME (1981)

Based on E.L. Doctorow's 1975 novel, Milos Forman's film is set in New York, New Rochelle and Atlantic City early in the twentieth century. The film begins with a newsreel montage, depicting real-life celebrities such as Harry Houdini, Theodore Roosevelt and the architect Stanford White, accompanied by ragtime pianist Coalhouse Walker, played by Howard E. Rollins.

The plot, slipping between fact and fiction, involves gangland murder, racial hatred and discrimination, corrupt politicians, businessmen and police, bigoted firemen, child abandonment and the music of the era. Noted black attorney Booker T. Washington is played by Moses Gunn.

The film ends with another newsreel montage involving vaudeville, and Houdini escaping from a straitjacket while dangling several storeys above newsstands declaring America's entry into the First World War. A ten-minute sequence on the Lower East Side featuring real-life social activist Emma Goldman was cut from the final print.

Co-written with Doctorow by Michael Weller, with music by Randy Newman, the film was nominated for eight Oscars. It is also notable for the final film appearances of James Cagney and Pat O'Brien, and for early screen appearances by Samuel L. Jackson and Jeff Daniels.

Critic Roger Ebert wrote: '*Ragtime* is a loving, beautifully mounted, graceful film that creates its characters with great clarity. We understand where everyone stands, and most of the time we even know why. Forman surrounds them with some of the other characters from the Doctorow novel, but in the film they're just atmosphere, window dressing. Forman's decision to stick with the story of Coalhouse is vindicated, because he tells it so well.'

ONCE UPON A TIME IN AMERICA (1984)

Sergio Leone's crime drama, which marked a break from the spaghetti Western genre, has since its release divided the critics into those who regard it as an epic masterpiece and those who dismiss it as a sprawling, incoherent mess.

Most of the action takes place in the 1930s underworld, and is outside the remit of this book. However, numerous flashbacks show Robert de Niro's character Noodles Aaronson as a street kid in the Williamsburg section of Brooklyn in 1920. He and his friends commit petty crime under the guidance of a local crime boss, rob drunks and blackmail a corrupt policeman before setting up their own gang and committing murder.

Based on Harry Grey's novel *The Hoods*, it highlighted the role of Jewish gangs in the growth of New York's organised crime. It was the final film of Leone's career and the first feature film he had directed in thirteen years.

Leone originally envisaged two three-hour films, then a single 269-minute version, but was convinced by distributors to shorten it to 229 minutes. The American distributors further shortened it to 139 minutes. The shortened version was a critical and commercial flop in the United States, and critics who had seen both versions harshly condemned the changes that were made. The original 'European cut' has remained a critical favourite.

Notes

Introduction

1. Guinn, 8
2. Guinn, 13
3. Warren, 187–188
4. Warren, 214
5. Miller, 186–189
6. Wheeler, 79
7. Rezatto, 107
8. *Black Hills Times*, 1 January 1879
9. Athearn, 59–60
10. Holden, 202–203
11. Burns, 33–34
12. Guinn, 6
13. McGrath, 203–205
14. Hollon, 195
15. Webb, 31
16. Hollon, 197
17. Hollon, 195–196
18. McIver, 3–8
19. Streeby, 3
20. Shillingburg, 113–114
21. Roberts, 31
22. Hollon, 203
23. Warren, xiii
24. Thorpe (2015 edition), ix

1 New York: From the Macbeth Riots to the King of Bank Robbers

1. Riis, 1
2. Eric Kaufman, 437–457
3. Burrows and Wallace, 761–766
4. Cliff, 8, 125–129
5. Butsch (2000), 44
6. Butsch, 44
7. Cliff, 260–263
8. Cliff, 120–121
9. *New York Times* obituary, 9 May 1897
10. Cliff, 150–164
11. Cliff, 165–184
12. Burrows and Wallace, 761–766
13. *New York Tribune*, 11 May 1849
14. Anonymous pamphlet, *Account of terrific and fatal riot at New York's Astor Place Theater*, New York 1849
15. Cliff, 234–239
16. Gilge, 1006–1008
17. Burrows and Wallace, 761–766
18. *Ibid.*
19. Cliff, 241, 245
20. Peter Smith, *The Courier-Journal*, Louisville, 30 July 2005
21. Geis (1965), 42
22. Sante (1991), 198
23. Lobo, Flores and Salvo (2002), 703
24. Sante (1991), 197–198
25. Asbury, 170
26. Anbinder, 285–286
27. Maffi, 129
28. Adams (2005), xviii
29. Adams, 1–3
30. O'Kane, 55–57
31. *New York Daily*, 6 July 1857
32. Asbury, 102–103
33. *New York Times*, 6 May 1857
34. Headley, 131–132
35. English, 27–28
36. Asbury, 106
37. Headley, 132

38. English, 28
39. Asbury, 106
40. Asbury, 171–172
41. Asbury, 108–109
42. *New York Times*, 26 December 2010
43. Harris, 279–288
44. *New York Times*, 14 July 1863
45. Martha Derby Parry, republished in *America's Civil War* magazine, May 2000
46. David Barnes, 2–6, 12
47. Asbury, 118–121
48. Asbury, 121–122
49. Asbury, 122–125
50. *New York Times*, 15 July 1863
51. *Ibid.*
52. Harris, 286–288
53. Asbury, 132
54. Iver Bernstein, 24–25
55. Iver Bernstein, 25–26
56. Asbury, 136
57. Martha Derby Parry
58. Asbury, 138
59. *New York Times*, 18 July 1863
60. Rhodes, 320–326
61. *New York Times*, 16 July 1863
62. Martha Derby Parry
63. Asbury, 139–140
64. Col. William F. Berens, 'Report of operations June 3–August 1863', *O.R.*, Series 1 Volume XXVII/2
65. Asbury, 158–159
66. Special orders, Headquarters Department of the East, New York, 13 July 1863
67. 'Reports of Maj. Gen. John Z. Wool, U. S. Army, Commanding Department of the East, with orders, &c. JULY 13–16, 1863.–Draft Riots in New York City, Troy, and Boston' *O.R.*, Series 1 Volume XXVII/2
68. *Ibid.*
69. McPherson, 39
70. Asbury, 154
71. Morison, 451
72. Harris, *passim*
73. Bernstein, 43–44
74. *New York Times*, 26 December 2010
75. Riis, 12
76. Sante (1991), 214
77. Asbury, 210
78. Asbury, 212
79. Sante, 217
80. Asbury, 236
81. Savelli (2001), 1
82. Asbury, 185
83. Asbury, 186
84. *New York Times*, 7 June 1878

2 The Mollie Maguires

1. Boyer and Morais, 63
2. Kenny, 20–21
3. Horan and Swiggett, 129
4. Horan and Swiggett, 151–156
5. Campbell, 122–123
6. Boyer and Morais, 126
7. *Harper's New Monthly Magazine*, November 1877
8. Boyer and Morais, 48
9. Boyer and Morais
10. Boyer and Morais, 51
11. Morns, 94–95
12. Horan and Swiggett, 151
13. Kenny, 117
14. Boyer and Morais, 51
15. Kenny, 199–120
16. Horan and Swiggett, 151
17. Horan and Swiggett, 152
18. Lukas, 183–185
19. Horan and Swiggett, 153
20. Horan and Swiggett, 157
21. Boyer and Morais, 52
22. Boyer and Morais, 53
23. Lukas, 182
24. Horan and Swiggett, 139
25. Lukas, 182–183
26. Boyer and Morais, 54
27. Boyer and Morais, 56
28. Jensen, September 1961
29. Boyer and Morais, 54–55
30. Boyer and Morais, 64–65
31. Matt O'Donnell, Action News Special Report, ABC News, January 2008
32. Kenny, 234–235
33. Boyer and Morais, 133
35. Pennsylvania Historical and Museum Commission website
36. Dailey, 67–109, 159
37. Boyer and Morais, 43

3 The Great Upheaval

1. *Baltimore Sun*, 18 July 1877

2. Irving Bernstein, 217
3. Cozzens, 207
4. Brecher, xxiv
5. *Ibid.*
6. *The Contemporary Review*, September 1877
7. Kleppner, 1556
8. Brecher, 1
9. National Archives, Adjutant General's Office, Letters Received, 1877, No 8035
10. Brecher, 7
11. *Wheeling Intelligencer*, 21 July 1877
12. *Philadelphia Inquirer*, 23 July 1877
13. *Baltimore Sun*, 21 July 1877
14. *Baltimore Star*, 21 July 1877
15. *Baltimore Star*, 21 July 1877
16. Clifton K. Yearley, *Maryland Historical Magazine*, September 1956
17. *Baltimore Sun*, 22 July 2016
18. Scharf, 733–742
19. *Ibid.*
20. *Baltimore Sun*, 21 July 1877
21. Kleppner, 1556
22. Brecher, 11
23. *Report of the Committee Appointed to Investigate the Railroad Riots in July 1877*, read in the Senate and House of Representatives, 23 May 1878
24. *Ibid.*
25. Singer, 47–48
26. *Harper's Weekly*, 11 August 1877
27. Brecher, 13
28. Bruce, 176
29. Report of the Riots Committee
30. *Ibid.*
31. Zinn, 248
32. *Columbus Dispatch*, 25 July 1877
33. Brecher, 14
34. Bruce, 194
35. Schroeder, 56–57
36. Logan, 2–9
37. *Ibid.*
38. *Philadelphia Times*, 3 August 1877
39. Logan, 9
40. Auranch, 8
41. Bratby, 232–233
42. Logan, *passim*
43. Logan, *passim*
44. Bratby, 232–233
45. *New York Times*, 25 July 1877
46. Brecher, 16
47. Bruce, 192
48. Cahan, 33–34
49. Brecher, 17
50. Brecher, 20
51. Bruce, 315
52. Scrabec, 81
53. Brecher, 21–22
54. Ayres, 93
55. Carwardine, 69
56. *Chicago Times*, 13 June 1894
57. Biggott, 39
58. Schneirov, 137
59. Debs, 45
60. Bernstein, 54
61. Wish, 288–312
62. Salvatore, 134–137
63. *Strike Commission Report* 1894, 39
64. *New York Times*, 5 July 1894
65. Brecher, 86
66. Ginger, 170
67. Papke, 35–37
68. Brecher, 93
69. *The Comrade*, April 1903
70. *Time* magazine obituary, November 1926
71. Haywood, 78

4 The Haymarket Affair

1. Art Young, *New Masses*, 2 May 1939
2. Michael Huberman, *The Journal of Economic History*, December 2004
3. David, 21–27
4. Foner, *May Day*, 27–28
5. David, 177–188
6. Green, 162–173
7. *Illinois v. August Spies et al*, trial transcript No. 1, 6 November 1886
8. Avrich, 199–200
9. *New York Times*, 5 May 1886
10. Avrich, 205–206
11. *New York Times*, 14 May 1886
12. Young, *passim*
13. Schaack, 146–148
14. *Chicago Tribune*, 27 June 1886
15. *New York Times*, 4 May 1886
16. Schaack, 155
17. *Chicago Herald*, 5 May 1886
18. Nelson, 188–189

19. Avrich, 221–232
20. Young, *passim*
21. Morn, 99
22. Schaack, 156–182
23. *Ibid.*
24. Messer-Kruse, 18–21
25. Chicago Historical Society Digital Collection, *jury indictments*
26. Avrich, 262–267
27. Avrich, 271–272
28. Avrich, 216
29. Young, *passim*
30. Messer-Kruse, 123–128
31. Young, passim
32. *The Atlantic Monthly*, September 1886
33. *Chicago Tribune*, 11 November 1887
34. Young, *passim*
35. Avrich, 293
36. Young, *passim*
37. Messer-Kruse, 181
38. Morn, 99
39. Messer-Kruse, 8
40. Foner, 40
41. *The Haymarket affair*, illinoislaborhistory.org
42. *Tribune Magazine*, London, 1 May 2015
43. Young, *passim*

5 The Pinkerton Rebellion

1. US Code 3108
2. Haywood, 157–158
3. Krause, 174–192
4. Brody, 52
5. Brody, 54–55
6. Harvey, 177
7. Yellin, 84
8. Brody, 59
9. Krass, 278
10. Brody, 59
11. Wolff, 69
12. Foner, 208
13. Wolff, 90–96
14. Foner, 208–209
15. Krause, 26–28
16. Krause, 15, 271
17. Brody, 59
18. Brecher, 57
19. *New York Times*, 7 July 1892
20. Krause, 26–28
21. Brody, 59

22. Foner, 210
23. Krause, 29–30
24. Krause, 32–36
25. Brecher, 58
26. Krause, 34–36
27. Brecher, 58
28. Krause, 38–39
29. Krause, 337–338
30. Krause, 348
31. Brecher, 60
32. Wolff, 206
33. Wolff, 209
34. Warren, 89
35. Krause, 337–339
36. Krause, 348–350
37. Brecher, 62
38. Brody, 59
39. Henry Clay Frick Foundation archives
40. *New York Times*, 3 December 1919
41. *St Louis Post-Dispatch*, 19 July 1894
42. *Electric Railways Journal*, 1018
43. *New York Times*, 4 November 1913
44. Bodenhamer, 1123
45. *New York Times*, 4 November 1913
46. *Electric Railways Journal*, 1123
47. *Electric Railways Journal*, 1021
48. Bodenhamer, 1122
49. Morn, 186–187, 192

6 Race War

1. Kaufman, 353–579
2. Ware, 23–27
3. Keene, 490–495
4. Winters, 409
5. Winters, 410
6. Arnesen, 824
7. Rodrigues, 826
8. *Nola Arnacha* website
9. *The Weekly Pelican*, New Orleans, 26 November 1887
10. *Ibid.*
11. *Nola Anarcha*
12. *Le Petit Journal* (date obscured)
13. Burns, 141–145
14. Atlanta History Center
15. Burns, 4–5
16. *Atlanta Georgian/Atlanta News*, 22 September 1906

17. Mixon, Kuhn, 2
18. Mixon, Kuhn, 3
19. White, 5–12
20. Mayrick-Harris, 48
21. Mixon, Kuhn, 3–4
22. *New York Times*, 25 September 1906
23. *New York Times*, 28 September 1906
24. Johnson, 151–157
25. Myrick-Harris, 26
26. Archives of the Tuskegee Institute
27. Lemann, 6
28. Tauber, 122
29. Gregory (2005), 12–17
30. US Bureau of Census – Population Division
31. United Press, New York, 5 July 1910
32. Hernon, 183
33. Duster, 184
34. Bay, 67
35. *Guide to the Ida B. Wells Papers, 1884–1976*, University of Chicago Library
36. Wells, *Washington Post*, 9 December 1899
37. Rudwick, 50
38. *New York Times*, 3 July 1917
39. *New York Times*, 4 July 1917
40. *History of the East St. Louis, Illinois, Riot*, Mrs. Ida B. Wells-Barnett, 2
41. Hernon, 195
42. *New York Times*, 2 July 1917
43. Ida B. Wells, *passim*
44. *Chicago Herald*, 2 July 1917
45. *St Louis Post-Dispatch*, 2 July 1917
46. Hernon, 199
47. *New York Times*, 8 September 1917
48. Rudwick, 51
49. Marcus Garvey, speech at Lafayette Hall, Harlem, 8 July 1917
50. Lumpkins, 156
51. *New York Times*, 8 September 1917
52. *Pittsburgh Post-Gazette*, 31 May 2002
53. *New York Times*, 5 October 1919
54. Erickson, 2293–2294
55. Cunningham, 1459–1461
56. McWhirter, 16, 19, 22–24
57. McWhirter, 13
58. McWhirter, 15
59. McWhirter, 14
60. NAACP telegram to President Woodrow Wilson, 29 August 1919
61. Rucker, 92–93
62. *New York Times*, 22 July 1919
63. Barnes, 4
64. Krist, 178
65. *Chicago Daily Tribune*, 28 July 1919
66. *Ibid.*
67. *Ibid.*
68. *New York Times*, 2 August 1919
69. *New York Times*, 3 August 1919
70. *The Electronic Encyclopedia of Chicago*, Chicago Historical Society, 2
71. *New York Times*, 5 August 1919
72. *New York Times*, 1 August 1919
73. *New York Times*, 3 August 1919
74. Whitaker, 53
75. Brown, 289–291
76. *New York Times*, 2 October 1919
77. *New York Times*, 3 October 1919
78. *New York Times*, 4 October 1919
79. Freedman, 68
80. *New York Times*, 13 October 1919
81. *Commercial Appeal*, Memphis, 13 October 1919
82. Stockley, xiv
83. *New York Times*, 5 October 1919
84. *New York Times*, 28 July 1919
85. *New York Times*, 3 August 1919
86. *New York Times*, 5 October 1919
87. McWhirter, 239–241

7 The Early Mafia

1. D. Mack Smith
2. Dash 34
3. Dash 64–65
4. DeLucia, 213–215
5. Dash, 34
6. *Wall Street Journal*, 22 January 2011
7. Jon Black, GangRule.com
8. *Ibid.*
9. Tom Smith, 12
10. Tom Smith, xiii
11. Gambino
12. Newton, 214

13. *Biographical Dictionary of American Mayors 1820–1880*, Greenwood Press 1981
14. Nelli, 66
15. Dash, 83
16. Botein, 264
17. Dash, 84
18. *New York Times*, 20 October 1890
19. Tom Smith, 47–46
20. Dash, 87–88
21. Gambino, 4
22. Dash, 88
23. Tom Smith, 97
24. Botein, 267
25. Botein, 265
26. Maselli and Candeloro, 35
27. Gambino, 150
28. Gambino, 144
29. Tom Smith, 115
30. Gambino, 66
31. Gambino, 15–16
32. Gambino, 41–43
33. Tom Smith, xv
34. Tom Smith, 209
35. Tom Smith, 216
36. Gambino, 105, 154
37. Gambino, 82
38. Dash, 91–92
39. Gambino, 83–84
40. Nelli, 64
41. Gambino, 14
42. *New York Times*, 15 March 1891
43. *New York Times*, 16 March 1891
44. Gambino, 96
45. Botein, 276
46. *Ibid.*
47. Gambino, 126–127
48. Roosevelt, *letter*, 21 March 1891, 1–2, Theodore Roosevelt Collection
49. Tom Smith, xii
50. Dash, 277
51. Jon Black, *The Murder Stables*, GangRule.com
52. Critchley, 37–40
53. *Washington Post* review of Dash, 5 August 2005
54. Stifakis, 312
55. Critchley, 37–40
56. Dash, 110
57. Jon Black, GangRule.com
58. Dash, 169
59. Dash, 3–6
60. Dash, 158
61. *New York Tribune*, 29 November 1917
62. Dash, 161
63. *New York Herald*, 7 January 1917
64. Dash, 248
65. Dash, 257–258
66. Jon Black, GangRule.com
67. *Ibid.*
68. Dash, 295–296
69. Dash, 297
70. Dash, 300
71. Dash, 472
72. Asbury, 254
73. Asbury, 270
74. Asbury, 272–273
75. Capeci, 69–71
76. Puleo, 157
77. Devico, 124–127
78. Gervaise, 9
79. Butts, 110
80. Butts, 109
81. Dash, 348

8 The Red Scare and the Boston Police Strike

1. Foner, Vol. 1, 98
2. Brian Farmer, *The New American*, 15 July 2011
3. *The Nation*, 5 October 1919
4. Brecher, 121–125
5. Murray, 60–63
6. Brecher, 127–128
7. Murray, 65
8. Foner, 75–76
9. Hagedorn, 180
10. Hanson, vii–viii
11. Brecher, 126
12. Brecher, 116–117
13. *The Survey*, 2 August 1919
14. Hagedorn, 54,58
15. *Bolshevick Propaganda 1919*, US Congress paper, 6, 12, 14, 19, 29, 34, 475
16. *Chicago Tribune*, 1 May 1919
17. Avrich, *Anarchist Voices*, 141
18. *New York Times*, 3 and 4 June 1919
19. *Washington Post*, 4 June 1919
20. Avrich, 496
21. Avrich, 153
22. Avrich, 148
23. Avrich, 168–185

24. Hagedorn, 185–186
25. Foner, 91–92
26. Russell, 48
27. Russell, 50–52
28. Russell, 43–46
29. *Munsey's Magazine*, Vol. 15 1896, 487
30. Slater, 245
31. Slater, 243–245
32. *Annual Report of the Commissioner of the City of Boston*, year ending 30 November 1919
33. Foner, 95
34. Murray, 125
35. Murray, 126
36. O'Connor, 192
37. *New York Times*, 10 September 1919
38. *New York Times*, 10 September 1919
39. Slater, 247
40. Brian Farmer, *The New American*, 15 July 2011
41. *New York Times*, 10 September 1919
42. *New York Times*, 10 September 1919
43. Pietrusza, 99
44. Foner, 97
45. Murray, 132
46. Foner, 96
47. Foner, 99–100
48. *New York Times*, 12 September 1919
49. *New York Times*, 14 September 1919
50. Pietrusza, 100
51. Chamberlin, 223
52. Foner, 100
53. Foner, 101
54. *New York Times*, 6 January 1937
55. Hernon, *Riot!* 152–161
56. *Associated Press*, 12 March 1937
57. *New York Times*, 16 July 1974
58. Brody, 233–244
59. Supplementary reports of the Interchurch World Movement commission of inquiry, Harcourt, Brace and Co., New York 1921, 173, 178
60. Foster, 113
61. Joe Rudiak/Peter Gotlieb, *History Matters*, Pennsylvania State Archives
62. Rayback, 287
63. *New York Times*, 25 October 1919
64. Brody, 246
65. *New York Times*, 1 November 1919
66. Coben, 100
67. Pietrusza, 146–147
68. McCormick, 158–163
69. *New York Times*, 21 December 1919
70. Waldman, 2–7
71. *New York Times*, 10 January 1920
72. *New York Times*, 11 January 1920
73. *New York Times*, 13 January 1920
74. *The Public Opinion Quarterly*, Vol. 1, Winter 1946–1947
75. Coben, 234–235
76. *New York Times*, 30 April 1920
77. Coben, 234–235
78. *New York Times*, 4 May 1920
79. *Boston American*, 4 May 1920
80. Gage, 179–180
81. Ackerman, 277–280
82. Coben, 238–239
83. Stone, 226
84. Coben, 145
85. Gage, 184–185
86. *New York Times*, 8 September 1920

9 Matewan and the Battle of Blair Mountain

1. Pearce, 59–60
2. Rice, 26, 70
3. *Sixteen Tons*, Tennessee Ernie Ford, Classic Country/Cowboy Lyrics.com
4. Velke, 26
5. *Roanoke Magazine*, November 1982
6. Lee, 53
7. Mary Jones, autobiography
8. *Journal of the Historical Society*, September 2012
9. Zinn, 280–282
10. Shogan, 18
11. *Richmond Times-Dispatch*, date unconfirmed
12. Bailey, 9–12
13. Savage, 20–22
14. Logan Coal Operators Association, m/s 90, 82, 144
15. *Ibid.*

Notes

16. US Senate Committee on Education and Labor, West Virginia Coal Fields sessions, July 1921
17. *Ibid.*
18. *Ibid.*
19. *Ibid.*
20. *Williamson News*, 20 May 1920
21. Savage, 26–28
22. Savage, 60
23. US Senate Committee, *passim*
24. Shogan, 154–158
25. *Charleston Gazette*, 22 August 1921
26. Shogan, 166–173
27. *Richmond Times-Dispatch*, 25 August 1921
28. Savage, 90–102
29. *Logan Banner*, 26 August 1921
30. Brecher, 136
31. Sylvia Kopald, *Rebellion*, 88
32. Evan Andrews, history.com. 25 August 2016
33. Laurie, 1–24
34. *Associated Press* archives, August–September 1921
35. *Ibid.*
36. *Logan Banner*, 31 August 1921
37. Evan Andrews, *passim*
38. Lee, 103–117
39. Shae Davidson, *The Labor Career of William Blizzard*, Marshall University thesis, 1998
40. Cabell Phillips, American History website/*New York Times*, August 1974
41. West Virginia State archives website (eVW), *Blair Mountain*
42. eVW, David A. Corbin, 7 December 2015

Afterword

1. *Tribune Magazine*, May 2016.
2. Andersen, 427
3. Andersen, 429
4. Andersen, 100–101

5. Hugh Davis Graham and Ted Robert, *The History of Violence in America*, xiv
6. Hollon, 216
7. Brecher, 317
8. *The Times*, 9 December 2017
9. *The Times, Saturday Review*, 28 April 2018
10. *The Times*, 30 December 2017

Appendix 2

1. Original People.org African-American History, 6 February 2014, 2
2. *Ibid.*, 3
3. *Ibid.*, 4

Appendix 3

1. Messer, 59
2. Oklahoma Commission, 28 February 2001
3. Sulzburger, *New York Times*, 19 June 2011
4. Tulsa Preservation Commission website
5. Oklahoma Commission, 37–102
6. Franklin, 195–196
7. Oklahoma Commission, 55–59; Brophy, 654
8. Oklahoma Commission, 60–62
9. Madigan, 131, 132, 144, 159
10. Letter from Captain Frank Van Voorhis to Lieutenant-Colonel L.J. F Rooney, 30 July 1921, pp 1–3
11. Ellsworth, 69
12. Madigan, 224
13. Brophy, 61–96
14. *The Village Voice*, 30 April 2003

Bibliography

Ackerman, Kenneth D., *Young J. Edgar: Hoover, the Red Scare, and the Assault on Civil Liberties* (Carroll & Graf, New York 2007)

Adams, Peter, *The Bowery Boys: Street Corner Radicals and the Politics of Rebellion* (Praeger Publishing, Westport, Connecticut 2005)

Adelman, William J., *Haymarket Revisited* (Illinois Labor History Society, Chicago 1986, 2nd edn)

Anbinder, Tyler, *Five Points: the 19th-century New York City Neighborhood that Invented Tap Dance ...* (2001)

Arlacchi, Pino, *Mafia Business: The Mafia Ethic and the Spirit of Capitalism* (Oxford University Press, 1988)

Arnesen, Eric, *Encyclopedia of U.S. Labor and Working-class History*, Vol. 1

Asbury, Herbert, *The Gangs of New York – An Informal History of the Underworld* (Alfred A. Knopf, New York 1928)

Athearn, Robert, *Westward the Briton* (Scribner's, New York 1953)

Aurand, Harold, *Pennsylvania History*, Vol. 158, No. 4 (1991)

Avrich, Paul, *The Haymarket Tragedy* (Princeton University Press, 1984)

Avrich, Paul, *Sacco and Vanzetti: The Anarchist Background* (Princeton University Press, 1991)

Ayres, Tim, and Susan Eleanor Hirsch, *After the Strike: A Century of Labor Struggle at Pullman* (Labour History, 2003)

Azzarelli, Margo L. and Marnie, *Labor Unrest in Scranton* (Arcadia Publishing, 2016)

Bailey, Rebecca, *Matewan Before the Massacre* (West Virginia University Press, 2008)

Baker, Ray Stannard, *Following the Color Line: an account of Negro citizenship in the American democracy* (Doubleday, Page & Company, New York 1908)

Barnes, David M., *The Draft Riots in New York, July 1863: The Metropolitan Police, Their Services During Riot* (Baker & Godwin, New York 1863)

Barnes, Harper, *Never Been a Time: The 1917 Race Riot That Sparked the Civil Rights Movement* (Walker & Co., New York 2008)

Bauerlein, Mark, *Negrophobia: A Race Riot in Atlanta, 1906* (Encounter Books, San Francisco 2001)

Bay, Mia, *To Tell the Truth Freely: the Life of Ida B. Wells* (Hill & Wang, New York 2009)

Bellesiles, Michael A., *1877: America's Year of Living Violently* (New Press, New York 2010)

Bernstein, Iver, *The New York City Draft Riots* (Oxford University Press, New York 1990)

Bernstein, David E., *Only One Place of Redress* (2001)

Bernstein, Irving, *Turbulent Years* (Houghton Mifflin, Boston 1970)

Bibliography

Bigott, Joseph C., *From Cottage to Bungalow: Houses and the Working Class in Metropolitan Chicago, 1869–1929* (University of Chicago Press, 2001)

Bimba, Anthony, *The Molly Maguires* (International Publishers, New York 1932)

Blatz, Perry K., *Keystone of Democracy: A History of Pennsylvania Workers* (Pennsylvania Historical and Museum Commission, 1999)

Blizzard, William C., *When Miners Marched* (Appalachian Community Press, 2005)

Bodenhamer, David, J., *Encyclopedia of Indianapolis* (Indiana University Press, Bloomington 1994)

Botein, Barbara, *The Hennessy Case: An Episode in Anti-Italian Nativism* (Louisiana Historical Association, 1979)

Boyer, Richard O., and Morais, Herbert M., *Labor's Untold Story: The Adventure Story of the Battles, Betrayals and Victories of American Working Men and Women* (United Electrical, Radio and Machine Workers of America/UE, Pittsburg 1955)

Bratsby, Henry C., *History of Luzerne County*, Vol. 1 (1893)

Brecher, Jeremy, *Strike!* (South End Press, Boston 1972)

Broehl, Jr, Wayne G., *The Molly Maguires* (Harvard University Press, Cambridge, 1964)

Brody, David, *Steelworkers in America: The Nonunion Era* (Harper Torchbooks, New York 1969)

Brophy, Alfred L., *Reconstructing the Dreamland: The Tulsa Race Riot of 1921, Race Reparations, and Reconciliation.* (Oxford University Press, New York 2002)

Bruce, Robert Vance, *1877: The Year of Violence* (Ivan R. Dee Publisher, 1959)

Burns, Rebecca, 'Four Days of Rage', *Atlanta Magazine*, September 2006

Burns, Rebecca, *Rage in the Gate City: The Story of the 1906 Atlanta Race Riot* (Emmis Books, 2006)

Burns, W. N., *Tombstone* (Doubleday & Company Inc., New York 1951)

Burrows, Edwin G., and Wallace, Mike, *Gotham: A History of New York City to 1898* (Oxford University Press, New York 1999)

Butsch, Richard, *The Making of American Audiences: From Stage to Television, 1750–1990* (Cambridge University Press, 2000)

Butts, Edward, *Outlaws of The Lakes – Bootlegging and Smuggling from Colonial Times to Prohibition* (Linx Images Inc., Toronto 2004)

Cahan, Richard, *A Court That Shaped America: Chicago's Federal District Court from Abe Lincoln to Abbie Hoffman* (Northwestern University Press, 2002)

Campbell, Ballard C. (ed.), *American Disasters: 201 Calamities That Shook the Nation* (Facts on File Inc., 2008)

Capeci, Jerry, *The Complete Idiot's Guide to the Mafia* (Alpha Books, Indianapolis 2002)

Carlson, Peter, *Roughneck: The Life and Times of Big Bill Haywood* (W.W. Norton & Co., 1983) Carwardine, William, *The Pullman Strike* (Charles H. Kerr and Co., Chicago 1894)

Chamberlin, Joseph Edgar, *Boston Transcript: A History of its First Hundred Years* (Books for Libraries Press, Freeport 1969)

Cliff, Nigel, *The Shakespeare Riots: Revenge, Drama, and Death in Nineteenth-Century America* (Random House, New York 2007)

Coben, Stanley, *A. Mitchell Palmer: Politician* (Columbia University Press, New York 1963)

Cody, William F., *The Life of Hon. William F. Cody Known as Buffalo Bill the Famous Hunter, Scout and Guide: An Autobiography* (Frank E. Bliss, Hartford, Connecticut 1879)

Conell, Carol, and Kim Voss, 'Formal Organization and the Fate of Social Movements: Craft Association and Class Alliance in the Knights of Labor', *American Sociological Review*, Vol. 55, No. 2 (April 1990)

Cook, Adrian, *The Army of the Streets: The New York Draft Riots of 1863* (University Press of Kentucky, 1974)

Corbin, David Alan (ed.), *Gun Thugs, Rednecks: A Documentary History of the West Virginia Mining Wars* (PM Press, Oakland 2011)

Cozzens, Peter, *The Earth is Weeping – The Epic Story of the Indian Wars for the American West* (Atlantic Books, London 2017)

Critchley, David, *The Origin of Organized Crime: The New York City Mafia, 1891–1931* (Routledge, New York 2008)

Cunningham, George P., 'James Weldon Johnson', *Encyclopedia of African-American Culture and History* (Macmillan, New York 1960)

Dailey, Lucia, *Mine Seed* (Authorhouse, Bloomington 2002)

Dainotto, Roberto M., *The Mafia: A Cultural History* (Princeton University Press, 2015)

Dash, Mike, *The First Family: Terror, Extortion and the Birth of the American Mafia* (Simon & Schuster, London 2009)

David, Henry, *The History of the Haymarket Affair: A Study of the American Social-Revolutionary and Labor Movements* (Collier Books, New York 1963, 3rd edn)

Debs, Eugene V., *Writings and Speeches of Eugene Victor Debs* (Hermitage Press, New York 1948) DeLucia, Christine, *Getting the Story Straight: Press Coverage of Italian-American Lynchings from 1856–1910* (Italian Americana, 2003)

DeVico, Peter J., *The Mafia Made Easy: The Anatomy and Culture of La Cosa Nostra* (Tate Publishing, 2007)

Dray, Philip, *At the Hands of Persons Unknown: The Lynching of Black America* (Random House, New York 2002)

Duster, Alfreda, *Crusade for Justice* (The University of Chicago Press, 1970)

Effinger-Crichlow, Marta, *Staging Migrations Toward an American West: From Ida B. Wells to Rhodessa Jones* (University Press of Colorado, Boulder 2014)

Ellis, Edward Robb, *The Epic of New York City: A Narrative History* (Carroll & Graf Publishers, New York 2005)

Ellsworth, Scott, *Death in a Promised Land: The Tulsa Race Riot of 1921* (Louisiana State University Press, Baton Rouge 1992)

English, T. J., *Paddy Whacked: The Untold Story of the Irish American Gangster* (HarperCollins, New York 2000)

Erickson, Alana J., 'Red Summer', *Encyclopedia of African-American Culture and History* (Macmillan, New York 1960)

Fink, Leon, 'The New Labor History and the Powers of Historical Pessimism: Consensus, Hegemony, and the Case of the Knights of Labor', *Journal of American History*, Vol. 75, No. 1 (June 1988)

Fink, Leon, *Workingmen's Democracy: The Knights of Labor and American Politics* (Urbana: University of Illinois Press, 1983)

Foner, Philip Sheldon, *History of the Labor Movement in the United States* (New World, 1991)

Foner, Philip Sheldon, *The Autobiographies of the Haymarket Martyrs* (Pathfinder Press, New York 1969)

Foner, Philip Sheldon, *May Day: A Short History of the International Workers' Holiday, 1886–1986* (International Publishers, New York 1986)

Foster, William Z., *The Great Steel Strike and Its Lessons* (B.W. Huebsch Inc., New York 1920)

Franklin, Buck Colbert, *My Life and An Era: The Autobiography of Buck Colbert Franklin* (Louisiana State University Press, 2000)

Freedman, Eric M., *Habeas Corpus: Rethinking the Great Writ of Liberty* (New York University Press, 2001)

Fridan, D., and Fridan, J., *Ida B. Wells: Mother of the Civil Rights Movement* (Houghton Mifflin Harcourt, New York 2000)

Friedman, Morris, *The Pinkerton Labor Spy* (Wilshire Book Co., 1907)

Gage, Beverly, *The Day Wall Street Exploded: A Story of America in its First Age of Terror* (Oxford, New York 2009)

Bibliography

Gambino, Richard, *Vendetta: The True Story of the Largest Lynching in U.S. History* (Guernica, 1977)

Geis, G., *Juvenile Gangs: Report to the President's Committee on Juvenile Delinquency and Youth Crime* (U.S. Government Printing Office, Washington DC 1965)

Gervais, C. H., *The Rum Runners – A Prohibition Scrapbook* (Firefly Books, Thornhill 1980)

Gibson, Robert A., *The Negro Holocaust: Lynching and Race Riots in the United States, 1880–1950* (Yale University, New Haven 1979)

Gilge, Paul A., *The Encyclopedia of New York City* (Yale University Press, New Haven 1995)

Ginger, Ray, *The Bending Cross: A Biography of Eugene V. Debs* (Rutgers University Press, New Brunswick 1949)

Goldstein, Robert Justin, *Political Repression in Modern America* (University of Illinois Press, 2001)

Green, James R., *Death in the Haymarket: A Story of Chicago, the First Labor Movement and the Bombing that Divided Gilded Age America* (Pantheon Books, New York 2006)

Gregory, James N., *The Second Great Migration: An Historical Overview, African American Urban History: The Dynamics of Race, Class and Gender since World War II* (University of Chicago Press 2009)

Gregory, James R., *The Southern Diaspora: How the Great Migrations of Black and White Southerners Transformed America* (University of North Carolina Press, Chapel Hill 2005)

Grossman, James R., *Land of Hope: Chicago, Black Southerners, and the Great Migration* (University of Chicago Press, 1991)

Guinn, Jeff, *The Last Gunfight – The Real Story of the Showdown at the O.K. Corral – And How It Changed the American West* (The Robson Press, London 2011)

Hagedorn, Ann, *Savage Peace: Hope and Fear in America, 1919* (Simon & Schuster, New York 2007)

Hallgrimsdottir, Helga, and Benoit, Cecilia, *From Wage Slaves to Wage Workers – Cultural Opportunity Structures and the Evolution of the Wage Demands of the Knights of Labor and the American Federation of Labor, 1880–1900* (2000)

Halliburton, Donald, *Tulsa Race War of 1921* (R and E Publishing, San Jose, 1975)

Hanson, Ole, *Americanism versus Bolshevism* (Doubleday, Page & Co., New York 1920)

Harris, Leslie M., *In the Shadow of Slavery: African-Americans in New York City* (University of Chicago Press, 2003)

Harvey, George, *Henry Clay Frick: The Man* (Beard Books, New York 1928)

Haywood, William D., *The Autobiography of Big Bill Haywood* (New York, 1929)

Headley, J. T., *The Great Riots of New York, 1712 to 1873* (E.B. Treat, New York 1873)

Hernon, Ian, *Crimes That Made The Modern World – From the Tolpuddle Martyrs to Bernie Madoff* (Red Axe Books, London and Charleston 2016)

Hernon, Ian, *Riot! Civil Insurrection from Peterloo to the Present Day* (Pluto Press, London 2006)

Hirsch, James S., *Riot and Remembrance: The Tulsa Race War and Its Legacy* (Houghton Mifflin, Boston 2002)

Hitchcock, Frederick L., *History of Scranton and Its People* (Lewis Historical Publishing Co., New York 1915)

Holden, William C., 'Law and Lawlessness on the Texas Frontier 1875–1890', *Southwestern Historical Quarterly*, V (October 1940)

Holley, Donald, *The Second Great Emancipation: The Mechanical Cotton Picker, Black Migration, and How They Shaped the Modern South* (University of Arkansas Press, 2000)

Hollon, W. Eugene, *Frontier Violence – Another Look* (Oxford University Press, New York 1974)

Horan, James D., and Swiggett, Howard, *The Pinkerton Story* (Putnam, New York 1951)

Howell, James C. and Moore, John P., 'History of Street Gangs in the United States', *National Gang Center Bulletin* (4 May 2010)

Hower, Rob, *1921 Tulsa Race Riot: The American Red Cross – Angels of Mercy* (Homestead Press, Tulsa 1993)

Janken, Kenneth Robert, *Walter White: Mr. NAACP* (University of North Carolina, Chapel Hill 2006)

Jennings, Jay, '12 Innocent Men', *New York Times* (22 June 2008)

Jensen, Richard Rhodes, *Molly Maguires* (University of Illinois, Chicago 2001)

Jeffreys-Jones, Rhodri, *Cloak and Dollar: A History of American Secret Intelligence* (Yale University Press, 2003)

Johnson, Nicholas, *Negroes and The Gun: the Black Tradition of Arms* (Amherst, New York 2014)

Jones, Mary, *The Autobiography of Mother Jones* (Charles H. Kerr, Chicago 1925)

Jordan, Daniel, *The Mingo War: Labor Violence in the Southern West Virginia Coal Fields* (Greenwood Press, Westport, Conneticutt 1977)

Kaufmann, Eric, 'American Exceptionalism Reconsidered: Anglo-Saxon Ethnogenesis in the 'Universal' Nation, 1776–1850', *Journal of American Studies* (1999)

Kaufman, Jason, 'Rise and Fall of a Nation of Joiners: The Knights of Labor Revisited', *Journal of Interdisciplinary History*, Vol. 31, No. 4 (Spring 2001)

Kenny, Kevin, *Making Sense of the Molly Maguires* (Oxford University Press, New York 1998)

Kopald, Sylvia, *Rebellion in Labour Unions* (Boni and Liveright, New York 1924)

Krause, Paul, *The Battle for Homestead, 1890–1892: Politics, Culture, and Steel* (University of Pittsburgh Press, 1992)

Krist, Gary, *City of Scoundrels: The Twelve Days of Disaster That Gave Birth to Modern Chicago* (Crown, New York 2012)

Lee, Howard B., *Bloodletting in Appalachia* (West Virginia University Press, 1969)

Lemann, Nicholas, *The Promised Land: The Great Black Migration and How It Changed America* (Vintage Press, 1991)

Leonard, Mary Delach, 'E. St. Louis Riot', *St. Louis Post-Dispatch* (13 January 2004)

Lloyd, John P., 'The Strike Wave of 1877', *The Encyclopedia of Strikes in American History* (Routledge, 2009)

Logan, Samuel Crothers, *A City's Danger and Defense* (J. B. Rogers Print, Philadelphia 1887)

Lobo, A. P., Flores, R. J. O. and Salvo, J. J., 'The impact of Hispanic growth on the racial/ethnic composition of New York City neighborhoods', *Urban Affairs Review*, Vol. 37 (2002)

Lukas, J. Anthony, *Big Trouble: A Murder in a Small Western Town Sets Off a Struggle for the Soul of America* (Simon & Schuster, 1997)

Lumpkins, Charles L., *American Pogrom: The East St. Louis Race Riot and Black Politics* (Ohio University Press, 2008)

Maffi, Mario, 'Gateway to the Promised Land: Ethnicity and Culture in New York's Lower East Side', *Revealing Antiquity* (NYU Press, 1995)

Madigan, Tim, *The Burning: Massacre, Destruction, and the Tulsa Race Riot of 1921* (Thomas Dunne Books, New York 2001)

Marks, Carole, *Farewell – We're Good and Gone: the Great Black Migration* (Indiana University Press, 1989)

Martin, MaryJo, *The Corpse on Boomerang Road: Telluride's War on Labor 1899–1908* (Western Reflections Publishing Co., 2004)

Maselli, Joseph; Candeloro, Dominic, *New Orleans's 1891 Nightmare: Eleven Italians Lynched* (Arcadia Publishing, 2007)

McCormick, Charles H., *Seeing Reds: Federal Surveillance of Radicals in the Pittsburgh Mill District, 1917–1921* (University of Pittsburgh Press, 1997)

Bibliography

McGrath, Roger D., *Gunfighters, Highwaymen, & Vigilantes: Violence on the Frontier* (University of California Press, 1984)

McIver, Stuart B., '"Hanging Mr Buntline": Dreamers, Schemers and Scalawags', *Florida Chronicles*, Vol. 1 (Pineapple Press, 1998)

McPherson, James M., *Ordeal by Fire* (Alfred A. Knopf, New York 1982)

McWhirter, Cameron, *Red Summer: The Summer of 1919 and the Awakening of Black America* (Henry Holt, New York 2011)

Messer, Chris M., Krystal Beamon, and Patricia A. Bell, 'The Tulsa Riot of 1921: Collective Violence and Racial Frames', *The Western Journal of Black Studies*, Vol. 37, No. 1 (2013)

Messer-Kruse, Timothy, *The Haymarket Conspiracy: Transatlantic Anarchist Networks* (University of Illinois Press, Urbana 2012)

Messer-Kruse, Timothy, *The Trial of the Haymarket Anarchists: Terrorism and Justice in the Gilded Age* (Palgrave Macmillan, New York 2011)

Mixon, Gregory, and Kuhn, Clifford, 'Progressive Era to WWII, 1900–1945', *New Georgia Encyclopedia* (September 2005)

Mooney, Fred, *Struggle in the Coalfields: The Autobiography of Fred Mooney* (West Virginia University Library, 1967)

Morison, Samuel Eliot, *The Oxford History of the American People: Volume Two: 1789 Through Reconstruction* (Signet, 1972)

Morn, Frank, *The Eye That Never Sleeps: A History of the Pinkerton National Detective Agency* (Indiana University Press, Bloomington 1982)

Murray, Robert K., *Red Scare: A Study in National Hysteria, 1919–1920* (University of Minnesota Press, Minneapolis 1955)

Myrick-Harris, Clarissa, *The Origins of the Civil Rights Movement in Atlanta, 1880–1910* (Perspectives, 2006)

Nash, Arthur, and Ferrara, Eric, *Manhattan Mafia Guide: Hits, Homes and Headquarters* (History Press, 2011)

Nash, Jay Robert, *The Great Pictorial History of World Crime, Volume 2* (Scarecrow Press, 2004)

Nelli, Humbert S., *The Business of Crime: Italians and Syndicate Crime in the United States* (University of Chicago Press, 1981)

Nelson, Bruce C., *Beyond the Martyrs: A Social History of Chicago's Anarchists, 1870–1900* (Rutgers University Press, New Brunswick 1988)

Newton, Michael, *Famous Assassinations in World History: An Encyclopedia* (ABC-CLIO, 2014)

O'Connor, Thomas H., *The Boston Irish: A Political History* (Back Bay Books, Boston 1995)

O'Hara, S. Paul, *Inventing the Pinkertons; or, Spies, Sleuths, Mercenaries, and Thugs* (Johns Hopkins University Press, 2016)

O'Kane, James, *The Crooked Ladder: Gangsters, Ethnicity, and the American Dream* (Transaction Publishers, 31 January 2002)

Papke, David Ray, *The Pullman Case: The Clash of Labor and Capital in Industrial America* (University Press of Kansas, 1999)

Parrish, Mary E. Jones, *Race Riot 1921: Events of the Tulsa Disaster* (Out on a Limb Publishing, Tulsa 1998)

Pearce, John Ed, *Days of Darkness: The Feuds of Eastern Kentucky* (University Press of Kentucky, 1994)

Pietrusza, David, *1920: The Year of Six Presidents* (Carroll & Graf, New York 2007)

Rayback, Joseph G., *A History of American Labor* (MacMillan, New York 1966)

Rezatto, Helen, *Mount Moriah – the Story of Deadwood's Boot Hill* (Fenwin Press, Rapid City 1989)

Rhodes, James Ford, *History of the United States from the Compromise of 1850* (Macmillan, 1899)

Rice, Otis K., *The Hatfields and McCoys* (University Press of Kentucky, 1982)

Riis, Jacob, *The Battle with the Slum* (Echo Library, 1902/2009)

Roberts, Gary L., 'The West's Gunmen', *The American West*, Vol. VII (March 1971)

Rodrigue, John C., 'Thibodaux Massacre', *Encyclopedia of U.S. Labor and Working-class History*, Volume 1 (2007)

Rucker, Walter C., and Upton, James N., *Walter Encyclopedia of American Race Riots* (Greenwood Publishing Group, 2007)

Rudwick, Elliott M., *Race Riot at East St. Louis* (Southern Illinois University Press, Carbondale 1964)

Russell, Francis, *A City in Terror: Calvin Coolidge and the 1919 Boston Police Strike* (Beacon Press, Boston, 1930, reprinted 1975)

Salvatore, Nick, *Eugene V. Debs: Citizen and Socialist* (University of Illinois Press, 1984)

Sandburg, Carl, 'The Chicago Race Riots', *The Electronic Encyclopedia of Chicago* (Chicago Historical Society, 2005)

Sandburg, Carl, *The Chicago Race Riots July 1919* (Harcourt, Brace & World, New York 1919)

Sante, L., *Low Life: Lures and Snares of Old New York* (Vintage, New York 1991)

Savage, Lon, *Thunder in the Mountains: The West Virginia Mine Wars 1920–1921* (University of Pittsburgh Press, 1985)

Savelli, L., *National Gang History* (East Coast Gang Investigators Association, 2001)

Schaack, Michael J., *Anarchy and Anarchists, A History of the Red Terror and the Social Revolution in America and Europe, Communism, Socialism and Nihilism in Doctrine and in Deed, The Chicago Haymarket Conspiracy, and the Detection and Trial of the Conspirators* (F. J. Schulte & Co., Chicago 1889)

Scharf, J. Thomas, *History of Maryland From the Earliest Period to the Present Day* (Traditional Press, Hatboro, Penns. 1967 reprint of 1879 edition)

Schecter, Barnet, *The Civil War Draft Riots, North & South*, Volume 10, No 1 (Civil War Society, New York 2007)

Schneirov, Richard, Stromquist, Shelton and Nick Salvatore, *The Pullman Strike and Crisis of 1890s: Essays on Labor and Politics* (University of Illinois Press, 1999)

Schroeder, Stephen Patrick, *The Elementary School of the Army: The Pennsylvania National Guard, 1877–1917* (University of Pittsburgh, 2006)

Seiple, Samantha, *Lincoln's Spymaster – Allan Pinkerton, America's First Private Eye* (Scholastic Press, New York 2015)

Servadio, Gaia, *Mafioso. A history of the Mafia from its origins to the present day* (Secker & Warburg, London 1976)

Shillingberg, William B., 'Wyatt Earp and the Buntline Special Myth', *Kansas Historical Quarterly* (1976)

Shogan, Robert, *The Battle of Blair Mountain: The Story of America's Largest Union Uprising* (Westview Press, Boulder 2004)

Sifakis, Carl, *The Mafia Encyclopedia* (Facts on File, New York 2005, 3rd edn)

Singer, Merrill, *Drugging the Poor* (Waveland Press, 2007)

Skrabec, Quentin, *The 100 Most Significant Events in American Business* (ABC-CLIO, 2012)

Slater, Joseph, 'Labor and the Boston Police Strike of 1919', *The Encyclopedia of Strikes in American History* (M.E. Sharpe, New York 2009)

Smith., D. Mack, *A History of Sicily: Modern Sicily, after 1713*

Smith, Tom, *The Crescent City Lynchings: The Murder of Chief Hennessy, the New Orleans 'Mafia' Trials, and the Parish Prison Mob* (Lyons Press, 2007)

Spear, Allan, *Black Chicago: The Making of a Negro Ghetto 1890–1920.* (University of Chicago Press, 1967)

Stockley, Grif Jr., *Blood in Their Eyes: The Elaine Race Massacre of 1919* (University of Arkansas, Fayetteville 2001)

Bibliography

Stone, Geoffrey R., *Perilous Times: Free Speech in Wartime From the Sedition Act of 1798 to the War on Terrorism* (W.W. Norton, New York 2004)

Streeby, Shelley, *American Sensations: Class, Empire, and the Production of Popular Culture* (University of California Press, Berkeley 2002, 2nd edn)

Sulzberger, A. G., 'As Survivors Dwindle, Tulsa Confronts Past', *New York Times* (19 June 2011)

Taeuber, Karl E., and Alma F., 'The Negro Population in the United States', *The American Negro Reference Book* (Englewood Cliffs, New Jersey 1966)

Thernstrom, Stephan and Abigail, *America in Black and White: One Nation, Indivisible* (Simon and Schuster, New York 1997)

Thorp, Raymond W., and Bunker, Robert, *Crow Killer – The Saga of Liver-Eating Johnson* (Indiana University Press, 1958)

Tuttle Jr, William M., *Race Riot: Chicago in the Red Summer of 1919* (University of Illinois Press, Urbana 1996, originally published 1970)

Valke, John, *The True Story of the Baldwin-Feltz Detective Agency* (2004)

Voss, Kim, *The Making of American Exceptionalism: The Knights of Labor and Class Formation in the Nineteenth Century* (Cornell University Press, New York 1994)

Waldman, Louis, Albany, *The Crisis in Government* (Boni and Liveright, New York 1920)

Warren, Kenenth, *Triumphant Capitalism: Henry Clay Frick and the Industrial Transformation of America* (History/Business History, 2000)

Warren, Louis S., *Buffalo Bill's America – William Cody and the Wild West Show* (Vintage Books, Random House, New York 2005)

Webb, Walter Prescott, 'The American West, Perpetual Mirage', *Harper's* (May 1957)

Weir, Robert E., *Beyond Labor's Veil: The Culture of the Knights of Labor* (Pennsylvania State University Press, 1996)

Weir, Robert E., *Knights Unhorsed: Internal Conflict in Gilded Age Social Movement* (Wayne State University Press, 2000)

Wells, Ida B., *Crusade for Justice: The Autobiography of Ida B. Wells* (Chicago: University of Chicago Press, 1991)

Wheeler, Keith, *The Chroniclers* (Time Life Books, New York 1976)

Whitaker, Whitaker, *On the Laps of Gods: The Red Summer of 1919 and the Struggle for Justice that Remade a Nation* (Random House, New York 2008)

White, Walter Francis, *A Man Called White: The Autobiography of Walter White* (University of Georgia Press, Athens, 1948, reprint Arno Press, New York 1995)

Wilkerson, Isabel, *The Warmth of Other Suns: The Epic Story of America's Great Migration* (Random House, 2010)

Williams, Lee E., *Anatomy of Four Race Riots* (University and College Press of Mississippi, Hattiesburg 1972)

Winters, John D., *The Civil War in Louisiana* (Louisiana State University Press, Baton Rouge 1963)

Wish, Harvey, 'The Pullman Strike: A Study in Industrial Warfare', *Journal of the Illinois State Historical Society* (1939)

Wolensky, Robert P., and Keating, Joseph M., *Tragedy at Avondale* (Canal History and Technology Press, Easton 2008)

Wolff, Leon, *Lockout – The story of the Homestead Strike of 1892* (Harper & Row, New York 1965)

Yellin, Samuel, *American Labor Struggles* (Harcourt, Bruce and Co., New York 1936)

Zinn, Howard, *A People's History of the United States 1492–present* (Harper Collins, New York 1995)

Index

Index

Index